Praise for It's All Speculation

"This collection of papers, spanning from 1950 to 1993, showcases Dr. Tom Hieronymus' influential role in the development of agricultural futures markets in the United States. Addressing the skepticism within the agricultural industry, the papers present a clear argument for how futures markets can be used effectively for commercial purposes. Hieronymus also played a pivotal role in educating both industry professionals and lawmakers, particularly in advocating for the essential role of speculation in ensuring market efficiency. A staunch supporter of free markets, he warns against government intervention in price formation. His writings have had a lasting impact on practitioners, scholars, and extension agents, providing a strong defense of market-based price discovery and risk management. This collection offers invaluable insights into the evolution of agricultural futures markets, capturing the critical debates and shifts in understanding that shaped their development over several decades."

—Teresa Serra, Professor and T.A. Hieronymus Distinguished Chair in Futures Markets, University of Illinois

"Readers will be drawn to Dr. Hieronymus' straight-forward, yet colorful, writing style. In particular, the chapters covering futures trading, speculation, and price analysis are golden. Chapters 30, 31, 33, and 39 all touch on the interaction of speculation and price forecasting in commodity futures markets. Any trader who wants to better understand the game they play must read these chapters (along with Chapter 13 in Hieronymus' *Economics of Futures Trading*). There are thousands of books on speculation and trading, but most of them gloss over the basic realities of trading: "Thus, when the speculator enters the market, he is attempting to take money away from someone else who, in general, is most reluctant to lose." Clearly, Hieronymus gave deep and thoughtful consideration to the "art" of price forecasting, speculation, and trading. The analogies and examples in these chapters are timeless. Perhaps he best sums up the crux of the endeavor in chapter 30: "Let he who is without humility trade oats, and he will learn." Readers will find this book informative, entertaining, and thought-provoking. *It's All Speculation* should be a cornerstone reference for all market regulators, agricultural policymakers, merchandisers, researchers, and traders."

—Dwight Sanders, Professor of Agribusiness, Southern Illinois University

"The post WW II period that extended well into the 1970's was characterized by rapid changes in US agricultural technology, production, and trade that presented new marketing challenges for grain and oilseed producers and merchants. Tom Hieronymus emerged as one of the most recognized and insightful educators of that era. His name became synonymous with agricultural futures markets. This collection of writings produced over a period of four decades illustrates first and foremost Tom's brilliance in understanding agricultural markets and price relationships. Few were more accomplished. In addition, his understanding of agricultural policy, trade, and regulation are on full display. While written in the context of current events, these writings are an absolute treasure for those seeking insight into the world of agricultural markets and policy."

—Darrel Good, Emeritus Professor of Agricultural and Consumer Economics, University of Illinois

"Thank you for re-publishing this book. It is a great read for much more than historical reasons. Crucially, it provides essential and still-relevant information about the various types of cash market participants, as well as their objectives, constraints, and strategies, that finance textbooks either oversimplify or simply ignore. It is the cash market, and the folks and entities behind the physical trades, that make commodity futures markets different from other financial markets. Even today, with commodity markets that have become financialized and where between half and three quarters of the commodity futures trading is automated, this classic work should be required reading for anyone interested in commodity markets and trading."

—Michel Robe, The Patricia A. and George W. Wellde, Jr. Distinguished Chair in Finance, University of Richmond

"Beyond futures and markets, this book is a surprisingly rich resource for those interested in agricultural policy with valuable insights on policy developments in the critical period after World War II and through the 1960s. Dr. Hieronymus' writings provide relevant snapshots of a variety of policy issues during the years in which the New Deal parity system was breaking down, as well as some specific background on the early developments of soybean support policies. This book will be a great resource for additional research into the history and development of agricultural policies."

—Jonathan Coppess, Gardner Professor of Agricultural Policy, University of Illinois

"I was in the second year of my Ph.D. program at the University of Illinois (1996) when the original version of this book was published by the Office for Futures and Options Research. I vividly remember receiving a copy of the book and asking Tom to sign it. On the inside cover Tom wrote "Mark, you may be interested in looking at some of the numbers – prices and quantities in the 50's and 60's." Indeed, a lot has changed since the 50's and 60's but the market wisdom conveyed through Tom's writings has not. *It's All Speculation* is a must read for anyone interested in commodity futures markets and it makes a great companion to Tom's other classic book *Economics of Futures Trading*."

—Mark Manfredo, Professor and Dean's Council Distinguished Scholar, Arizona State University

It's All Speculation

Collected Writings on Markets and Trading

Thomas A. Hieronymus

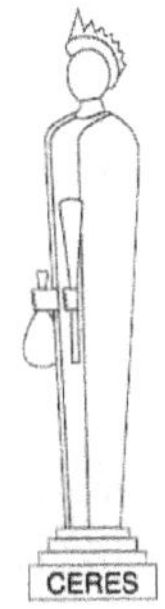

It's All Speculation

Reprinted by permission, 2025

Front cover picture courtesy of CME Group Inc.

Published by Ceres Books LLC

Mahomet, IL 61853

www.scotthirwin.com/books

ISBN 979-8-9912149-6-4

Originally published as **A Revisionist Chronology of Papers by T.A. Hieronymus: A Consistency of Biases**

Office for Futures and Options Research, 314 Mumford Hall, University of Illinois at Urbana-Champaign, Urbana, Illinois 61801

The Office for Futures and Options Research (OFOR) at the University of Illinois at Urbana-Champaign depends on individuals and firms within the futures industry for financial support. If you are interested in learning more about the programs and activities of OFOR and how you can participate, support and make a difference, contact:

Raymond M. Leuthold, Professor and Director, Office for Futures and Options Research, 314 Mumford Hall, 1301 West Gregory Drive, University of Illinois Urbana, Illinois 61801, (217) 333-1811

Contents

Preface

ORIGINAL PREFACE

The Office for Futures and Options Research (OFOR) owes its roots to Professor Thomas A. Hieronymus. OFOR was established with an endowment from Gary and Carlotta Bielfeldt and their family through the Bielfeldt Foundation, Peoria, Illinois. Gary and Carlotta and their three children—Linda, David and Karen—are all graduates of the University of Illinois at Urbana-Champaign (UIUC). While at UIUC, Gary studied under Professor Hieronymus in the late 1950s, earning both B.S. and M.S. degrees. However, the two men remained in contact over the years—Gary the trader, Tom the teacher—sharing common interests, not the least being the price of soybeans and UIUC sports. The Bielfeldt family's leadership toward creating OFOR, and establishing the Thomas A. Hieronymus Professorship in Futures Markets, builds on Professor Hieronymus's many contributions to the development of the futures market industry.

OFOR is honored to present this group of writings by Professor Hieronymus, who served his entire academic career from 1949 to 1981 as a faculty member in the UIUC Department of Agricultural Economics. Careful reading of these papers, dating from 1950 to 1993, will clearly show that Professor Hieronymus has had significant influence not only on the futures industry but also on agricultural policy. The papers show both depth and breadth of expertise about policy, markets, prices, and trade.

Pivotal contributions by Professor Hieronymus were made in the 1950s and 1960s when he explained and demonstrated the use of futures markets to the grain industry. At the time, the markets were languishing, there was little respect for or understanding of futures markets, and the markets were not recognized for their commercial base. Besides some of the papers reproduced here, other important writings were the following bulletins: *Futures Trading and Speculation in Soybeans by Country Elevators,* published in 1951; *When to Sell Corn, Soybeans, Wheat, and Oats,* published in 1961; *Uses of Grain Futures Markets in the Farm Business,* published in 1963; and *Hedging for Country Elevators,* published in 1968. These writings were unique and impacted market practitioners, research scholars, classroom teachers, and extension agents.

His most recognized publication in the futures profession was his textbook, *Economics of Futures Trading,* first published in 1971, with a second edition in 1977. This book became the guide for traders and students in the futures industry during the crucial changes and tremendous market growth of the 1970s and 1980s.

It is the grandparent of futures texts and is footnoted in practically all currently published futures-market textbooks. This book stood for nearly twenty years as the only available textbook on futures theory and practice.

Most readers will not have seen many of the writings reproduced in this publication. Several deal with agricultural policy, especially policy related to soybeans. You will find that Professor Hieronymus began educating Congress about futures markets and speculation as early as 1957 (paper #10), and he repeated that education process with testimonies in 1966 (#24), 1972 (#29), 1973 (#32), 1974 (#34), and 1984 (#41). He did not avoid controversy and even relished it. Examples include a paper at a session on welfare at the annual meeting of the American Farm Economics Association in 1955 (#9). He told the Chicago Board of Trade to get its act together in 1959 (#15) and told Midwest elevators to "get good or get out" in 1964 (#20). He gave speeches on controversial topics in New York in 1962 (#18) and 1970 (#27), advocated cattle futures before a reluctant meat industry in 1964 (#21), led numerous discussions on soybean price and production policy (for example, #7 in 1954), and repeatedly called for the government to stay out of agricultural markets (for example, #17 in 1961 and #18 in 1962). Research ideas run through many papers, often under a common theme, such as calling for research on the role and quality of speculation in 1966 (#23), 1984 (#41), and 1993 (#43). Some papers are basic to futures markets, such as how to hedge (#16 in 1959), futures markets and financial equity (#28 in 1971), definition of hedging (#36 in 1976), designation of delivery points (#37 in 1976), and a definition of manipulation (#38 in 1977).

Professor Hieronymus is clearly a defender of free markets and an outspoken supporter of capitalism and of the futures exchanges. He, perhaps more clearly than anyone else, defines the important role of speculators in directing economic activity. Expression of these beliefs appeared in 1950 (#1) and 1951 (#3), continued through many papers, and are well summarized in 1978 (#39). According to Professor Hieronymus, markets provide the best guide for decision making, and government intervention in price formation is undesirable and counterproductive. The wisdom of the marketplace exceeds that of the government. And, so you know there are no hidden trading secrets, he clearly states that markets work well and that price forecasting and successful speculation are very difficult (#33 in 1973 and #39 in 1978).

You will find these papers challenging, interesting, and even entertaining. They are a unique set and truly vintage Tom Hieronymus.

It is clear that Tom received support from his family over these years, especially from his wife, Jimmie. I wish to thank Tom for making these papers available for an OFOR publication. Special thanks go to Stephanie Spaulding for much of the typing but also for managing these manuscripts as they passed through many hands in the preparation process. Also to be thanked are Nancy Nichols and Francine Weinbaum, who provided valuable editing and proofreading, and Dawn Hachenski, who created the design.

RAYMOND M. LEUTHOLD
DIRECTOR, OFOR
1996

NEW PREFACE

I first heard about the project to publish a book of collected writings by Tom Hieronymus when I was on sabbatical leave at Illinois during the 1993-94 academic year. I was on the faculty at Ohio State at the time. As the original preface (above) highlights, Ray Leuthold thought it was important to preserve a record of Tom's analysis and insights on the wide range of topics that he worked on. A couple of years later, Ray was kind enough to send me a copy of the book when it was printed. I don't know how many copies were originally printed, but probably no more than a few hundred, which Ray mainly sent out to supporters of OFOR and former students. I always thought I was quite fortunate to have been given a copy.

I never had the chance to read the book from cover-to-cover, but I read various chapters over the years as part of my research. I read enough of the book to realize it was a treasury of wisdom about markets. I began to mull over the idea of reissuing the book after I republished Tom's classic book *Economics of Futures Trading* in 2022 as the first release of my new imprint Ceres Books. Since the University of Illinois owns the copyright on the OFOR volume, I first needed to obtain permission to reprint it from the University, which I did. Fortunately, I had digitized my original physical copy several years earlier, and therefore, had a pdf file to start the production process. With some terrific help from Hongxia Jiao, I was able to convert the pdf version of the book to a Word file. I then used the Word file and the book editing software Atticus to generate the newly published version of the book.

Tom's original title for the book was *A Revisionist Chronology of Papers by T.A. Hieronymus: A Consistency of Biases*. An eclectic title like that is not surprising if you knew Tom. While the title may have fit Tom's personality, I did not think it did justice to the content of the book. I thought the book needed a new title that would better describe what the book was really about, and of course, attract the interest of readers today. I struggled for a long time to think of what a better title would be. After reading and editing the first half of the book for typos, a significant theme emerged. Tom consistently emphasized the central role of speculation in markets during his professional career. In the realm of commodity futures markets, he turned conventional wisdom on its head, arguing that speculation, properly understood, was the main driver of the markets rather than hedging. After reading Tom's argument numerous times, I remember thinking to myself, "It's all speculation to Tom." Instantly, I knew I had the perfect title: *It's All Speculation*. Not only is this the main theme running through Tom's writings, but it also has a humorous double meaning that I am sure Tom would appreciate. I added the sub-title "Collected Writings on Markets and Trading" to complete the full title of the reissued book.

After reading the book cover-to-cover, I am more than ever convinced about the brilliance of Tom's market analysis and insights. Some parts of the book are truly jaw-dropping. My favorite example is Chapter 30, unceremoniously titled "Note on the Soybean Price and Speculation." In the spring and early summer of 1973, soybean prices skyrocketed to incredible levels. On June 5th of that year, nearby soybean futures prices reached a new all-time high of $12.90 per bushel. On that very day, Tom sat down and wrote out his thoughts on what was driving the surge in prices, and of course, the role of speculation. Who does that on the exact day that soybean prices hit an all-time high that would not be surpassed for over 30 years?

I could not be more excited and honored to share this book with a new generation of readers. Whatever you do, don't miss the author's notes that Tom wrote to introduce each chapter. More than anything, they reflect the wit and wisdom of the man.

SCOTT H. IRWIN
PUBLISHER, CERES BOOKS
2025

Foreword

One solid rule of life is that people who live a long time tend to collect a lot of stuff. Stuff takes a variety of forms: pictures, recipes, quilts, autographs, books, beer cans, etc. Some professors are particularly avid collectors with a tendency toward diplomas, citations of merit, awards, and in a context of "publish or perish," literature that they have written. There is nothing quite as deathless as one's own prose. But collections of stuff eventually present a problem: how to dispose of it if one runs out of space or how to preserve it for eternal use and appreciation.

In my own case I found myself moderately at peace in that my great-grandfather's gold watch was in good repair and with instructions that my sons share it year-about, and the books, monographs, bulletins, circulars, and journal articles that I had written had been properly catalogued and libraried. But a problem remained. There were about twenty notebooks filled with manuscripts of speeches, papers, testimony, seminar presentations, etc. I knew that eventually something had to be done. The thought of wholesale dumping into the garbage receptacle was too horrible. I decided to sort and select.

The first run-through took out about three-quarters as repetitive or embarrassing. Over the years I had received a lot of attention for price outlook particularly that of soybeans; being conversant about the current situation was useful in opening a lot of doors. But outlook statements are loaded with numerical detail and are timely rather than timeless. So, they went without being graded right or wrong. My best guess is that it was about 50-50, which is par for the course. As for the rest, there was a lot of repetition; the audiences were diverse, from fellow academicians, to government, to legislators, to courts, but mainly to commodity tradespeople. The geography of presentation was widespread-as far north as Dawson Creek, British Columbia, as far south as Lima, Peru, as far west as Zheng Zhou, China, and as far east as Bucharest, Romania. Most were within the United States with a heavy emphasis on the Midwest.

A second run took out about half of the remaining material, primarily on the basis of redundancy. What remains? For the most part, they are papers that were fun to write and the occasions of presentation that were particularly interesting. They have not been edited or corrected (I tried to be at least reasonably honest), but substantial sections have been purged from many to reduce bulk and increase readability. They are arranged chronologically, so, in a sense, it is a career history. The time span from first to last is forty-three years. The activities that this collection represents were an interesting part of my career.

I have no illusion that anyone will read an appreciable amount of this stuff, but I rest in peace knowing that it is now part of other people's stuff.

TAH
Champaign, Illinois
July 1995

Chapter One

Futures Trading and Speculation in Soybeans

1950

AUTHOR'S NOTE: The first venture out with research results to an operational group seems to have been a talk at a grain elevator managers' school in Decatur, Illinois, on December 4, 1950. It was based on research, particularly field studies, at country elevators, soybean processors, grain merchants, and feed manufacturers. It set a pattern of generalizing from specific, descriptive information that seems to have persisted.

My topic is a very broad one. To narrow it down somewhat, it should probably be called "Speculation in Cash Soybeans." There are four subtopics under the general title that I want to talk about: (1) some basic aspects of futures trading and speculation; (2) risk in soybean marketing; (3) country elevator operations in soybeans; and (4) country elevator policy regarding soybean speculation.

SOME BASIC ASPECTS OF FUTURES TRADING AND SPECULATION

A speculator is one who buys something, expecting to sell it later at a higher price; or one who buys something to use at a later time, expecting the price to increase; or one who holds something that is ready for sale, expecting the price to go up; or one who sells something for deferred delivery, expecting the price to decrease. This makes us all speculators in one sense or another.

Grain marketing is basically a speculative business. The prices of grains fluctuate through wide ranges. Grains, including soybeans, are harvested during a period of a few weeks and are consumed at a fairly even rate throughout the year. Some of the soybeans harvested last October will be crushed into oil and meal next September. Someone must own them from the time they are harvested until they are consumed, and that is a speculative proposition. At the outset, let us understand that speculation is an essential part of grain marketing.

ORIGIN OF FUTURES TRADING

Organized trading in futures contracts was preceded by the use of "time contracts" and purchases "to arrive" at substantially deferred times. The first pressure for futures trading seems to date from the opening of the Illinois and Michigan Canal in 1848. By 1850 many corn cribs had been built on the banks of the Illinois River. Corn was hauled from farms to these cribs during the winter months when country roads were frozen and passable.

The corn was held in the cribs until spring, when navigation on the waterways and Great Lakes opened and the corn had dried sufficiently to be storable as shelled corn. These river corn dealers were therefore forced to retain possession for several months. They thus faced two problems: they had to finance the corn while it was in storage, and they had to take the risks of unfavorable price changes between winter and spring. They quickly developed the practice of going to Chicago and hunting for someone to buy corn for spring delivery. The first record of a time contract was found in the *Chicago Journal* of March 13, 1851. It called for delivery of 3,000 bushels of corn in June at a price one cent under the quotation of March 13 for spot corn. The use of time contracts grew rapidly, and the contracts became comparatively standard in their provisions. As early as 1855, it was estimated that all of the corn passing through Chicago changed hands at least one or twice before it was shipped.

While little is known about the identity of the contracting parties, the rather large amount of trading suggests that all of the contracts were not made with grain receivers but that professional speculators were active in the market. The practice of short selling developed early. In March 1863, the Chicago Board of Trade recognized time contracts by providing that any member who entered into such a contract must honor it or be suspended. Rules for trading in time contracts were established in 1865. Interestingly enough, futures trading was forced on the Chicago Board of Trade. The board apparently disapproved of time contracts and stalled formal trading in them for fourteen years. Futures trading started seventeen years after the Board of Trade was organized (1848).

My second point, then, is that futures markets grew out of a need for shifting risks and that risk-shifting systems preceded futures trading and are bound to exist, whether they are formal, as in such markets as the one at Chicago, or whether they are disorganized and informal. It is possible to separate risk bearing from other grain marketing jobs, and systems for doing so evolved naturally.

RISK PREMIUMS

I have talked to a considerable number of feed manufacturers about their inventory policies and find that they build up inventories only when they can buy for less than they expect to have to pay later. People undertake speculation only when they expect to sell or buy later for a profit. It is necessary to pay a risk premium to get people to speculate voluntarily.

Different people or firms require different risk premiums. They vary in their willingness and ability to carry risks. A few people enjoy speculating and will do so without expecting a profit; others will not speculate at all. Some people have a large capacity to absorb losses, and others have little or none; that is, some people can afford to speculate and others cannot. Banks typically disapprove of speculating in grain with borrowed funds.

Generally speaking, firms engaged in doing the ordinary grain marketing jobs of buying, selling, storing, shipping, processing, etc., are not logical risk bearers. They operate on rather narrow margins and so do not have large earnings with which to speculate.

My third basic point about futures trading and speculation is that premiums must be paid to get people to assume risks and that people differ in their willingness and ability to carry risks and, accordingly, in the size of risk premiums that they require.

FUNCTION OF FUTURES MARKETS

The job of futures markets is to provide a system for marketing risks. That system must provide a continuous and ready outlet for the risks that grain firms want to shift by hedging. And it must shift the risks to those people who will carry them the most cheaply. For grains, the futures markets do a good job of performing this function. Good hedging facilities are readily available, and they get the job of speculation done so cheaply that not everyone agrees with me that risk premiums are paid.

RISKS IN SOYBEAN MARKETING

During the past two years or so, I have rather carefully examined risk bearing and risk shifting in marketing soybeans. I studied two crop years in particular, 1947-1948 and 1948-1949. Before discussing country elevator operations in soybeans, I think it may be desirable to look at these general results.

FARMER SALES

In the past, farmers typically sold the bulk of their crop of soybeans at harvest. On January 1, 1948, they held 19 percent of their crop; on January 1, 1949, 34 percent of the 1948 crop; and on January 1, 1950, 28 percent of the 1949 crop. Of these amounts they had to retain 7 to 8 percent for seed and some feed. I estimate that farmers had sold 76 percent of their salable soybeans by the end of the 1947 harvest and 69 percent of their crop by the end of the 1948 harvest. Prior to the 1950 crop year, farmers did not assume the bulk of the soybean risk.

COUNTRY ELEVATORS

Country elevators bought most (95+ percent) of farmers' soybeans. They held a few of them open but sold most of them to processors-some direct, some throughout interior carlot dealers or track buyers, and some through commission firms. Part of the sales to processors were shipped immediately, and part were put into storage for processor accounts. The elevator assumed a relatively small percent of the total soybean risk.

PROCESSORS

Prior to this year, processing capacity exceeded the supply of soybeans. To get enough soybeans to crush, processors had to buy when farmers wanted to sell, and thus they accumulated large inventories of cash soybeans. They owned an average of about 65 percent of the soybeans during the 1947-48 season and about 58 percent during 1948-49. During 1947-48 they carried only 9.5 percent of these inventories open, and in 1948-49, 15.5 percent. Their open positions were greatest, in terms of both bushels and percent of gross position, before and during harvest.

During 1947-48 they shifted 5 to 6 percent of their risks by hedging in futures markets, mainly at Chicago; during 1948-49 they hedged 14 to 15 percent. The rest of the risks that they shifted were handled through forward sales of oil and meal. Processors had large inventories of soybeans, but they carried relatively small risks.

FORWARD SALES

A relatively small amount of soybean oil and meal is sold for spot or current month delivery. Eighty-eight percent of the oil produced was sold forward in 1947-48 and 71 percent in 1948-49. In 1947-48, 82 percent of the meal was sold forward; and in 1948-49, 58 percent.

These forward contracts are private treaties just like cash sales except that they are made for substantially deferred times. Currently, soybeans are being sold for delivery this week in December, December-May, and January-March.[1] Around-the-clock sales of meal are standard practice during harvest. In an around-the-clock sale, equal amounts are sold for delivery in each month of the

---

1. See commodity page, fats and oils, and feedstuffs columns, *Chicago Journal of Commerce.*

crush year at one price. The December through May position means that equal amounts are to be delivered in each of the six months at one price. This position was selling for $59 to $61. Currently, oil is selling for delivery this week, first half of December, December, January, and February through March. All of these positions reflect different prices.

Forward sales of meal are made mainly to two groups of firms: (1) resellers or dealers and (2) feed manufacturers. Almost all of the oil forward contracts are made with oil refiners and users. I think that over 75 percent of the forward contracts were bought by fewer than 10 firms.

RISK BEARING

The final evidence of soybean risks in the two years was as follows:

	1947-48 *(percent)*	**1948-49** *(percent)*
Farmers	29.22	41.63
Oil users	25.97	15.26
Feed manufactures	21.66	16.29
Processors	6.16	8.40
Country elevators	4.39	3.15
Meal resellers	3.50	2.67
Hedged in oil futures	3.57	2.44
Hedged in soybean futures	2.87	8.25
Oil speculators	1.55	0.90
Meal retailers	0.82	0.61
Hedged in meal futures	0.34	0.33
Intermediaries	0.16	0.10
	100.00	100.00

The principal speculators in soybeans were farmers, oil users, and feed manufacturers. The main method of shifting risks was forward sales.

DISCOUNTS

Forward positions typically sell for less than spot delivery. In 1947-48 the average discount per month per pound of oil was .493 cents; and in 1948-49, .248 cents. In 1947-48 the meal discount was 79.4 cents per ton per month, and in 1948-49, $1.01. The weighted average price of soybeans was 27.5 cents less in 1947-48 and 21 cents less in 1948-49 than it would have been had forward sales been made at spot prices. On November 25, 1950, spot oil sold for 18 cents; December oil, 16 to 16.50; January oil, 15.75; and February-March oil, 15.25. The discount from spot to March first was 2.75 cents. That amounts to 27.5 cents per bushel of soybeans. The meal price was about the same in all positions.

FORWARD SALES AS A RISK-SHIFTING SYSTEM

This development of forward sales to shift risks illustrates perfectly my earlier point that futures markets evolve naturally and are basically a risk-shifting system. When you start a futures market, you do nothing but establish a set of rules and formalize already existing practices.

How good a risk-shifting system are forward sales? I think they are poor. As we saw, they are expensive. Earlier, I said that a risk-shifting system must be readily available, and it must reach those speculators who will carry risks most cheaply. Only a few people are eligible to buy forward positions, or even know about them. In oil, as I mentioned, there are only a handful. In meal, it is doubtful whether the number exceeds 5,000, and not over 200 of those are really important. They may or may not want to buy when processors want to sell. They are ordinary businessmen, operating for a profit from their manufacturing activities. Logically, they are risk bearers similar to processors and country elevators. They must be paid well to get them to take risks.

I think it is the large discounts on forward positions—the reluctance to assume risks—that have accounted for the large average seasonal increase in soybean prices. The absence of a broad speculative market in soybeans and soybean products has made soybeans a very profitable speculation in recent years.

I think that traders on futures markets carry risks much more cheaply than will forward purchasers. This has accounted for the rapid growth of the soybean futures markets. From July 1947 to June 1948, total trading in soybean futures amounted to 40.2 million bushels. In 1948-49 it was 1,508 million bushels. There are not more recent summary figures available, but last Monday 16.5 million bushels were traded. The open interest was 57 million bushels. A good speculation will attract speculators. A crude soybean oil futures market was opened in Chicago during the past year and is attracting attention. Last Monday [November 27, 1950], 656 contracts of 60,000 pounds were traded. The open interest was 2,377 contracts. These figures are the oil equivalent of 3,936,000 and 14,262,000 bushels of soybeans, respectively.

COUNTRY ELEVATOR OPERATIONS IN SOYBEANS

Positions taken by country elevators were small in relation to both total volume of soybeans handled and stocks on hand at the elevators. A large proportion of the stocks on hand were in store for processors and farmers. Most of the rest of the stocks had been sold and were awaiting shipment. During October, November, and December 1947, country elevators bought 48 million bushels and owned unhedged only 2.8 million. During the same period the next year they bought 55.7 million bushels and carried open only 2.4 million. The average position was 1.3 million the first year compared with 1.1 million the second year. These averages have been blown up to a state-wide basis. The average annual position per elevator was 2,500 bushels the first year and 2,200 bushels the second. Peak positions were about 6,500 bushels per elevator in 1947-48 and 5,600 bushels in 1948-49.

The variation in the size of positions taken was great. Some elevators were never more than 100 bushels long or short. They did not speculate at all. At the other extreme, some elevators did not sell a single soybean during harvest. They were long all they purchased. These latter cases were rare. Generally speaking, not very many elevators ever had positions larger than 10 to 15 percent of their total yearly purchases. During 1947-48 four elevators did not take positions at any time larger than 1,000 bushels. In 1948-49 fourteen elevators fell in this group.

There was a wide range in speculative profit per bushel. The profit depended largely upon the size of positions taken. Those firms that did not speculate, of course, did not make or lose money on speculation. Of those elevators that did speculate, two lost money the first year. Both losses were small, one less than $800 and the other less than $200. None lost money speculating the second year. No doubt there are elevators in Illinois that have lost money speculating in recent years. Speculative profits ranged up to $1.00 per bushel; 25 cents per bushel was not rare.

NATURE OF THE SPECULATION

The exact position of an elevator is not easy to keep track of; you know that better than I do. It is the nature of the business to be a little bit long, especially at harvest. Some speculation is unavoidable, though I think nearly all that I encountered—at least 85 percent—was deliberate.

Possible gains and losses from soybean speculation are great. Had the average elevator in the main soybean belt carried open all of its purchases from the fall of 1947 to the spring of 1948, it would have doubled its net worth. Had it carried them open and had the market gone the other way, the results would have been catastrophic. A small position can eat up or double the handling margin.

COUNTRY ELEVATOR POLICY REGARDING SOYBEAN SPECULATION

All I have said thus far is designed to serve as a basis for determining the policies that country elevators should follow with regard to soybean speculation. Should a country elevator speculate in soybeans? I am not going to answer that question directly, as I do not think there is any one single answer for all situations. The answer depends upon the individual situation of the elevator.

On the positive side, we can list three main factors: First, someone must carry soybean risks, and whoever carries them will likely be paid for it. Second, the existing risk-shifting system is not particularly good. Large risk premiums are required, which make soybean speculation profitable. Third, for five years in a row extraordinarily large profits have been made by speculating in cash soybeans and soybean products. The record is five for five since the end of price ceilings. One of the hardest things I know how to do is to argue with success.

As more people try to take advantage of soybean seasonals, the seasonal will tend to disappear. Buying in the fall and selling in the spring increases the harvest price and decreases the spring price. If enough people did this, the thing could be tipped the other way. We may be approaching the time when the soybean seasonal will be small.

Finally, the outstanding single cause of country elevator failures has been speculation, and many of the most successful grain businesses have a strict policy of not speculating. Again, I say it is hard to argue with success.

Chapter Two

Soybean and Soybean Product Ceilings

1951

AUTHOR'S NOTE: A first review of governmental policy was in a paper written on March 5, 1951. With the onset of the Korean War, the Office of Price Stabilization was established, and wage and price controls were imposed. Disapproving of the whole concept, I decided to attack in a small area in which I had a high level of expertise: the soybean complex. The paper was distributed to the media with particular attention to publications reaching soybean producers. The thought was that farmers were being had by ceilings. It got quite a lot of attention and response from farmers and farm organizations and brought down the wrath of soybean processors.

In reciting the effects, I missed the one that was most interesting. Jasper Giovana of Decatur Soy Products discovered that while there were price ceilings on soybean meal, there were no ceilings on mixed feed. He put out a mixed feed that was 80 percent soybean meal and 20 percent various minerals such as limestone. Other processors followed so that there was eventually mixed feed guaranteed to be 99 percent soybean meal. The final absurdity was daily quotations in the Chicago Journal of Commerce showing soybean meal at a nominal $74 and soybean meal mixed feed at a variety of prices some $24 to $40 over soybean meal. I was increasingly aware of the inevitability of market prices.

On Tuesday, February 13, 1951, the Office of Price Stabilization issued an order establishing maximum prices on soybeans and soybean products. Basic prices were as follows: soybeans at Chicago, $3.33; loaded on track at country stations Illinois points, $3.23, or Chicago minus freight, whichever is greater. The effective price in the main Illinois bean areas is $3.23. Price to interior dealers is $3.25; price to farmers in Illinois, $3.16; crude soybean oil 20.50 cents per pound bulk Decatur, Illinois; and soybean meal $74 per ton bulk Decatur. Margins allowed under these prices will bear examination.

METHOD OF APPRAISAL AND PERIODS

The method employed was to calculate the margins actually obtained during certain historical periods and compare them with margins allowed if soybeans and soybean products reach and stay at the ceilings. The detail of the selection of periods, prices, and yields, and the calculation of margins is explained below.

The historical periods used together with the reasons for the selection of each were as follows:

1. February 8, 1951; the weekend just prior to the imposition of controls.
2. December 19, 1950, to January 25, 1951; the period used in establishing general controls.
3. October 16 to November 10, 1950; the peak of the 1950 harvest and hence the period of the heaviest soybean and soybean product marketing.
4. May 25 to June 25, 1950; the period mentioned by the Defense Production Act of 1950.
5. December 19, 1949, to January 25, 1950; the period just one year before the general control period.
6. October 17 to November 12, 1949; the peak marketing period for the 1949 crop.

(There followed lengthy and complex calculations of processing margins during each of the six time periods with results as follows: ceilings 64.4 cents; February 8, 1951, 50.6 cents; December 1950 to January 25, 1951, 44.2 cents; October 16 to November 10, 1950, 41.9 cents; May 25 to June 25, 1950, 9.9 cents; December 19, 1949 to January 25, 1950, 23.3 cents; and October 17 to November 12, 1949, 30.7 cents.)

RESULTS

The actual margins by periods (10 and 47 yield) ranged from 5.1 cents to 55.9 cents. Margins during the current crop year have averaged 36 cents and have rarely been below 30 or over 40 cents. During this period of 36-cent margins, soybeans have been crushed at a rate of 23 million bushels per month—both a record rate and a sufficient rate that there will be little if any carryover next October first. Production was in excess of 280 million bushels as compared to 225 million bushels last year. Many marginal crushing units were brought into use. Crushing-margins were about 10 to 15 cents per bushel more than during the preceding year. This presumably reflected the larger crop and the use of marginal crushing units. It seems that a 25-cent margin will get a 225 million bushel crop crushed and a 35-cent margin a 280 million bushel crop crushed. It appears that the margin allowed in Illinois under soybean ceilings is 20 cents higher than necessary. There is no historical basis for a 64-cent margin.

In discussing the effect of ceiling prices, we can only assume that they will not be violated. They are especially vulnerable to violations because of the very large number of soybean producers and handlers and users of soybean meal. It seems doubtful that these two prices can be effectively held under their market value.

Under ceilings all processors will attempt to buy all of the soybeans possible. The efficient processors will have no buying advantage over the inefficient ones, with the result that supplies will be shared on the basis of buying persuasion rather than operating efficiency. Efficient capacity may stand idle while inefficient capacity is used.

The large price increase in soybeans as compared to last year has been, for the most part, the result of the increased oil prices. Oil is the really scarce product at the present time. Sharing of soybeans among all processors will result in lower average oil production per bushel of soybeans.

In attempting to buy as many soybeans as possible, processors will increase their buying radius with a resultant crisscrossing of soybean shipments and transportation inefficiency. For example, soybeans in west-central Iowa are worth 12 to 15 cents less to Decatur, Illinois, processors when transportation and oil yields are taken into account than are east-central Illinois soybeans. Under ceilings Illinois processors can buy Iowa soybeans.

Not all of the increase in margins was given to processors. The margin of interior grain dealers during the current crop year has been 1 cent per bushel and under ceilings is 2 cents. Terminal merchandisers are allowed 3 cents per bushel. At that figure they are likely anxious buyers of soybeans.

The bulk of the margin increase normally goes to processors. They will likely get flimflammed out of a lot of it. A first development will be to offer storage to country elevators. The season storage rate is 7.5 cents. Some soybeans that processors have room for in their own bins may be stored in the country for some very short periods.

A second development will be to route soybeans through the maximum length marketing channel. For example, $3.23 soybeans located on an 8-cent freight rate from Chicago can be sold to an interior dealer who can charge $3.25 to a terminal merchandiser, who in turn can charge 3 cents plus 1.5 cents to 2.25 cents elevation of a processor on a 13-cent rate. Cost laid down in Decatur is $3.64 as compared to a normal movement cost of about $3.55, and the processor can afford to allow up to 20 cents of this.

A third development will be traffic in soybean meal. At $74 meal will likely be in short supply by May. Processors will offer purchase rights to meal in exchange for purchase rights to soybeans. The resultant distribution of meal will likely not take full advantage of milling-in-transit privilege with an accompanying economic waste. Under such a system it is doubtful that meal will get into the hands of those people who can use it most effectively. The concentrations of soybeans and livestock production are not in the same areas. Is there anything in the law that prohibits processors from giving meal to farmers in exchange for purchase rights to soybeans?

When we will get into absurdities of women's underwear and corn syrup is conjectural. With the large sums involved the list of evasions will likely get much larger than the above. Because of the extent to which processors will lose a part of the margins permitted and because only partial capacity may be used, the regulation, in spite of its generosity, may prove disadvantageous to efficient processors. It eliminates effective price competition in the industry.

THE PROBLEM OF PRICE RELATIONSHIPS

The establishment of arbitrary maximum prices necessitates consideration of price relationships. The first of these is the corn-soybean ratio. A normal figure is 1.8, which is that of $1.7 corn and $3.16 soybeans. But the inflation is in oil. Presumably we need more oil, and so it appears that the logical thing to do is to widen the ratio by increasing the price of soybeans. With increased cotton and corn acreages it is doubtful that the USDA goal of 14.3 million acres of soybeans will be realized with a 1.8 ratio.

With $1.70 corn and $74 meal the corn-soybean meal ratio is 1 to 1.23, which is a normal one. It appears that with a high price for oil (as it is), normal com-soybeans, corn-soybean meal, and soybeans-soybean product ratios are not possible.

The prevailing price relationships of soybeans located in the different states were rather thoroughly shaken up. With ceilings, the Illinois price was decreased about 5 cents. The Iowa price went up about 12 cents. Prices in the southern states went up possibly as much as 20 cents. The Indiana price is now closer than usual to the Illinois price.

RECOMMENDATIONS

Recommendations vary by the extent to which it seems necessary to impose ceilings on the soybean price structure. Accordingly, several alternative suggestions are listed:

1. Dispose of price controls of soybeans and soybean products. No system of arbitrary controls can be as efficient or as fair as free market prices.

2. Place ceilings on oil and meal in line with historical relationships, and let

the price of soybeans work out its own level. There is nothing inflationary in this because soybean prices cannot get out of line with product prices.

3. If we must place ceilings on soybeans, the price at Illinois country points should be increased by 20 cents for the remainder of this crop year, with a complete revision announced for next September 15.

4. If ceilings are retained, a substitute for the pricing system must be worked out. A requisition and allocation system for soybeans, soybean oil, and soybean meal will be necessary by May 1, 1951. If prices are arbitrarily fixed, each producer and handler of soybeans and soybean products must be told to whom, where, and when he will sell his product. That is the central hard fact of price controls.

Chapter Three

A Comment on Margin Requirements in Futures Trading

1951

AUTHOR'S NOTE: The report of the Administrator of the Commodity Exchange Authority of the USDA occasioned the next venture into the governmental policy area. The comment was published in the New York Commercial and Financial Chronicle on April 19, 1951. It had a fairly long life because the issue of control of margin requirements kept coming to the surface for the next twenty or more years. Each time that I was asked for an opinion by members of Congress, exchanges, and farm organizations, I responded with a copy of the paper. It says two things: that speculation is a positive force in directing economic activity and that governmental intervention in price formation is undesirable.

For some time the Commodity Exchange Authority of the U.S. Department of Agriculture has been promoting legislation to give it authority to regulate margin requirements on speculative transactions in commodity futures markets. The most recent attempt was with the Defense Production Act of 1950, which provided for the regulation of margins, among other things. The margin control provisions of the act were defeated. The 1950 "Report of the Administrator of the CEA" continues the campaign.

The Commodity Exchange Authority takes the position that the low speculative margins required by the exchanges encourage excessive speculation and speculation with insufficient capital. They note that upsurges of speculative activity are accompanied by rising prices, and cite the January 1948 price increases and rapid increase of soybean prices following the outbreak of the Korean War.[1] They suggest that higher margin requirements would curb such speculative booms.

Because of the importance of commodity markets and the significance attached to the margin question by both the CEA and the exchanges, a review of margin requirements seems desirable.

NATURE OF THE MARGIN REQUIREMENT

Commodity exchange clearinghouses require that clearing members post margins to guarantee contract fulfillment. Trading members in turn must require their clients to post certain minimum margins. Commission houses may require larger than minimum margins. The historical purpose of the margin has been the prevention of contract default.

FUNCTIONS OF FUTURES MARKETS

Futures markets have two basic functions: (1) the registering of grain prices and (2) the shifting of risks. Grain prices should reflect both current and anticipated values. Buyers and sellers must make estimates of total supplies and the demand for them, and form expectations of the average prices that will prevail at future times. If current prices are above the average expected, the quantities offered for sale are increased; if they are below, quantities are decreased. This is a process of discounting the total supply-demand conditions into current prices. It is essential in regulating the flow of grains onto the market at a rate that will make supplies last the full year but at the same time have them all consumed. Current prices are functions of expectations of futures prices. If the supply-demand conditions change so that expectations are changed, these changes should be immediately registered in current prices. The extent to which they are so registered depends upon the effectiveness of the discounting system, which in turn depends upon the level of speculative activity. The discounting process requires speculation.

---

1. See "Reports of the Administrator of the CEA," 1948, 1949, and 1950.

Futures markets with an extensive speculative interest are singularly good discounting markets and especially useful in rationing supplies over time.

Price risks in grain marketing are extensive. Crops are harvested during a few weeks of each year and are consumed at a fairly even rate. Part of the stocks must be owned for as long as twelve months. Speculators in futures markets assume much of the risk in marketing grain. Risk premiums must be paid to get risks assumed; anyone purchasing for deferred delivery must be able to buy more cheaply than he expects to be able to sell later.

A good risk-shifting (hedging) market must (1) provide a liquid market so that hedges can be placed and removed instantaneously without price penalty and (2) get risks into the hands of those persons who require the smallest risk premiums.

NECESSARY VOLUME OF TRADING

The volume of trading necessary for a good hedging market is not known. We only know that the volume in some markets is at least large enough and in other markets not large enough. From a hedging point of view, too large a volume of trading is impossible. There seems to be no objective evidence that a given amount of trading is the minimum necessary. Whether the minimum is just equal to the size of the crop or five, ten, or fifteen times the size of the crop is not known. Neither is it known that ten, fifteen, or twenty times the size of the crop is more than necessary. *Volume in relation to the size of the crop may or may not be the appropriate measure.*

A large volume of trading is essential to uncontrolled and sensitive price adjustment. A small volume of trading by a few people results in prices that are *infrequently* adjusted by relatively large amounts, while a broad market with many traders results in prices that change more often and by smaller amounts. A broad market is less susceptible to influence by one or a few traders than a narrow market. How large a volume of trading is necessary to assure uncontrolled prices is not known. Volume cannot be too large for this purpose. Much speculation helps assure free prices.

VOLUME OF TRADING AND PRICES

Increases in the volume of trading and erratic price changes seem to occur at the same time. This does not mean that erratic price changes are caused by a large amount of speculative activity. A more logical line of reason is that erratic price changes cause a large volume of trading. There is no logic in speculating in prices that do not change.

Speculators buy when they think that prices are too low and sell when they think prices are too high. They differ in their opinions about what is too high and what is too low. The actions of individual speculators in buying and selling tend to force prices to the average expected by the market participants. Speculation tends to eliminate the reason for speculation. If the judgment of speculators were perfect, prices would change only when the underlying economic conditions changed.

Speculation cannot affect prices very much in a liquid market. Cash and futures prices are tied together by the delivery feature. Grains must move on the market for what the market can afford to pay. They cannot be held above or below that level.

A large volume of trading does not mean futures prices are above real commercial values. In December 1950 the volume of trading in soybean futures was about 10 to 12 million bushels per day, an annual rate of eight to ten times the size of the crop. Oil and meal values reflected an unusually wide processing margin. East central Illinois cash prices were not as much below Chicago prices as the freight cost to Chicago. If anything, Chicago prices were deflated in terms of cash soybean, oil, and meal prices.

In the summer and fall of 1950, profits from long positions in soybeans were much greater than the margins required. The Commodity Exchange Authority states that the summer market was 67 to 75 percent speculative. For every purchase there is a sale, for every long a short. Losses from short positions must equal profits from long positions and vice versa. Was trading itself inflationary, or did price increases stem from underlying economic conditions?

MARGINS AND THE COST OF SPECULATION

The principle of buying at the lowest price is to shop in the broadest market possible. The principle of shifting risks is to get them into the hands of those people who will carry them for the smallest premiums. Low margin requirements broaden the market for risk and reduce its costs; efficiency of marketing is increased. Such savings result in higher farm prices and lower consumer prices.

Speculators perform an essential marketing function. Successful speculators must operate on the basis of a rather modest return. If a speculator were willing to take market risks for a 10 percent return on his risked capital and margins were doubled, he would be getting only 5 percent. Fewer people would be willing to speculate, and the market for risk would be narrowed. Further, if a 10 percent return on risked capital is the reservation price for risk bearing, an increase in margin requirements would result in a corresponding increase in the cost of getting risks assumed.

CONTROL OF PRICES

The argument for federal control of margin requirements is that excessive price changes are caused by excessive speculation and that the volume of speculation can be controlled by adjusting margin requirements. Principal criticisms have been leveled against price increases and the low margins required by the exchanges. The implication is that if margins and the volume of trading can be controlled, excessive price changes can be prevented. As it would be judged that prices were too high, margins would be increased; and as prices were too low, margins would be decreased; that is, to control margins is to control prices. Some of the statements above cast considerable doubt on the practicability of such control. Whether or not it would work is beside the issue. The use of margins for any purpose other than the guarantee of contracts is a violation of the principle of competitive pricing of commodities and would tend to take pricing out of the hands of economic forces and submit it to administrative decision.

Chapter Four

Principles of Inventory and Risk Management

1951

AUTHOR'S NOTE: In 1950 I participated in a national survey of the ingredient hedging activities of feed manufacturers. I was assigned to survey the Midwest. The survey included all of the large firms and numerous small firms. They were on-site, in-depth interviews with repeat visits over a time span of several months. The focus was on the use of futures by feed manufacturers, but the study evolved into a review of total risk management activities of feed manufacturers. Exposure to the complexities of managing ingredient price risks was extremely useful in subsequent research and teaching in matters having to do with the use of futures by commercial firms. I learned about hedging from the ground up. The paper was widely circulated in the industry and resulted in the exchange of information and views with people in the industry for many years.

In considering the accumulation of inventories and disposition of risks, certain basic principles must be taken into account.[1]

First, futures trading is not a standardized, foolproof method of operating with complete immunity to price changes. Hedging is not the direct transfer

1. T. A. Hieronymus is assistant professor of marketing, University of Illinois. Talk given at meeting of American Feed Manufacturers Association and USDA Extension Service, Buffalo, New York, October 16, 1951.

of risks but, rather, the assumption of additional risks, presumably opposite to the hedged position in the expectation of gain or loss. For example, if a feed manufacturer has an inventory of corn and sells corn in a futures market, he has taken on an additional speculation. It is the similarity of movement of the prices of cash corn and corn futures that reduces his total risk. In effect, he has substituted a basis speculation for his original inventory speculation.

This basis does not, however, remain constant. It may change to the advantage or disadvantage of the hedger. At times the basis is a good one for hedging, and at other times it is not. Hedgers must understand the basis and watch it carefully. It is not possible to hedge successfully by buying cash commodities and automatically selling against them without regard for relationships between cash and future prices.

Second, futures trading does not meet all of the direct hedging needs of feed manufacturers. There is no futures trading in many of the important feed ingredients, and the volume of trading in some contract markets is not large enough to provide the liquidity essential to hedging. However, with new contract markets in soybean meal and grain sorghums and increased volume in others, the markets seem to be improving in this respect.

Third, feed manufacturers as a group do not hold inventory risks to the minimum consistent with adequate supplies of satisfactory quality. They accumulate much larger than minimum inventories when price increases are expected, and reduce inventories to very low levels when declines are expected. The amount of ingredient speculation varies among firms, both in absolute size of inventories and in relation to the length of time that inventories are expected to last. Whether the maximum inventories are expected to last three weeks or twelve months, they are varied on the basis of price expectations. In the Midwest the proportion of firms that held inventories to a minimum was not large. Because mixed feed is priced on the basis of replacement cost of ingredients, manufacturers must take inventory profits and losses. It is not possible to hedge and speculate at the same time. No system can possibly guarantee against speculative losses and at the same time retain the potential of speculative profits.

Fourth, individual feed manufacturers vary in many respects: in size, location, kinds of feed manufactured, capital structure, capacity to withstand losses, and inclination to speculate. These differences affect inventory and hedging programs in such a way that it is not possible to apply one inventory and hedging program to all firms. Inventory and hedging programs must be individually tailored.

Fifth, in view of these four things—basis risk, inadequacy of existing futures markets for the direct hedging of feed ingredient inventories, the desire of the industry to speculate in ingredient prices, and the individual nature of inventory problems—we need to consider the total inventory management problem of firms rather than the hedging of ingredient inventories in futures markets. The problem is how to manage inventories so that inventory profits can be maximized and losses held to a minimum. The first phase of the problem is how to avoid being forced into unwanted speculative positions, and the second is how to stack the cards in favor of gaining as compared to losing. Trading in futures markets is *one* part of an inventory management problem.

ELEMENTS OF AN INVENTORY MANAGEMENT PROGRAM

An inventory management program must include the entire inventory problem of the firm. An inventory program includes several separate elements. It must insure that sufficient supplies of ingredients will be on hand to meet the physical requirements of mixing plants. No plant can afford to run out of any single feed ingredient or fall behind in its delivery schedule, nor can it afford to overcrowd its working space with supplies of some ingredients at the expense of others.

The procurement program must assure supplies of satisfactory quality, advantageously located with regard to freight rates. Because considerable time is required to get supplies of some ingredients into mixing plants after they are purchased, inventories of such supplies must be larger than the quantity actually on hand at the plant. This inbound flow of raw materials must be maintained. It is particularly important for large companies to keep supply large enough to insure operation. Sometimes market supplies of some ingredients disappear, or so nearly disappear that they cannot be obtained in sufficient quantity on a hand-to-mouth basis. Frequently, the desired qualities of ingredients can be obtained only if they are procured well in advance. Such situations must be anticipated. When ceiling prices are in force, the problem becomes more acute, and it is necessary to reach out farther for supplies. The tight soybean meal situation during the last two weeks of September of this year is an excellent example.

Transportation costs are also important, and ingredients from some locations carry better freight billings than others. If supplies are out of position, freight costs are increased.

The sales and pricing policy is another important element of an inventory program. Although most mixed feed is priced on the basis of replacement cost of ingredients and forward bookings are usually limited, there are exceptions. Some firms price on an average-cost basis and others on actual cost. Some firms make rather extensive forward sales of feed, and others contract at firm prices for bulk tonnages. These sales represent inventory positions quite as much as ingredient purchases.

Many firms tend to eliminate the extreme highs and lows of ingredient prices in calculating price lists. Tight spot markets on certain ingredients are usually not reflected in feed prices. For example, we have rarely seen $100 soybean meal figured into feed prices, although the spot market has sometimes reached that figure in recent years. An important aspect of inventory management seems to be the avoidance of tight spot markets.

Another very important element is risk policy. There is no industry risk policy. It would be difficult to find two firms whose risk policies were identical-and rightly so, because firms vary in their need for speculative profits, inclination to speculate, capacity to withstand losses, skill in forecasting price changes, and amount of attention they can afford to give to their inventory positions. The important aspects of a risk policy are (1) that it be definite, (2) that it fit the individual situation of the firm, and (3) that it be consistent and continuing.

Every firm should have a carefully-worked-out risk policy and should adhere strictly to it. First, the policy should clearly recognize the fact that inventory positions are basically speculative. The fact that inventories are accumulated for later consumption makes them no less speculative than those purchased for resale. Second, the firm should know how much it can and is willing to take and should establish the policy of never exceeding this maximum. Third, it must establish a policy regarding its unavoidable inventories of ingredients-those accumulated to assure supplies, quality, etc. This policy may be (1) to hold inventories to a minimum and carry them open, expecting gains and losses to average out, (2) to try to hedge them all with sales of some kind or other, and (3) to selectively hedge them; or (4) to use a combination of the three plans. Fourth, a firm should know under what conditions it wishes to speculate. Few firms will speculate unless the chances of gaining seem greater than those of losing. Some firms will speculate if the odds seem only a little in their favor. Others require that the speculation seem nearly a sure thing. There are all gradations between. There is no articulate way to express this certainty level, but each firm must form an idea of it and consistently apply it.

Out of these several elements each firm must build its procurement and hedging programs; these two programs are intermixed and mutually dependent. Hedging programs for inventories and requirements depend, of course, on the procurement of supplies. That hedges depend on inventory position is obvious. A more important point is that in general procurement programs depend on opportunities to hedge or speculate on a satisfactory basis.

HEDGING

Hedging is a term hard to define. It means different things to different people. For our purpose, hedging may be defined as any market operation that is expected to offset an existing market position. A hedge is therefore an opposite or offsetting position, although not necessarily in the same commodity.

As was noted earlier, a hedge involves the assumption of additional risk, the changing of a market speculation to a basis speculation. It follows, then, that successful hedging depends upon a thorough knowledge of price relationships.

There are several different kinds of hedging problems. The first and simplest is disposition of the risks that accompany minimum inventories. If the overall inventory program of the firm indicates that these minimums should be hedged, the problem is to find the appropriate short positions.

The second kind of hedging problem is the selection of ingredients for accumulation that can be hedged advantageously. This is the principal hedging problem of terminal grain merchants. They buy grains when they expect the basis to hold steady or narrow, and sell when a wider basis is indicated. It is through this basis change that they earn carrying charges.

The third hedging problem is that of limiting speculation. One such problem is the fixing of speculative profits. Suppose that a feed manufacturer accumulates a long line of alfalfa meal for scattered shipment in the fall, and the price goes up by December to a level that offers a nice profit and that seems vulnerable to decline. His problem is to fix the profit while retaining control of the meal. Or suppose that he has accumulated a line of soybean meal in some period as February 1951, at the $70-$72 level and by April has taken all of the loss that he can afford. His problem is how to stop his losses. Or suppose that feed grains get out of line with vegetable meals but that it is uncertain whether feed grains will decline or meals will increase. The problem is to limit the speculation to the difference between the two sets of prices.

HEDGING PROGRAMS

There are three rather distinct kinds of hedging programs that will meet the different hedging problems of feed manufacturers. These we may call direct hedging, cross hedging, and selective hedging.

DIRECT HEDGING

Direct hedging is the maintenance of an even market position by taking opposite positions in the futures markets in the same commodity as the inventory position. For example, an inventory of 100,000 bushels of corn is hedged by selling the same amount in corn futures. In this program each inventory is considered separately-corn is hedged without regard to positions in soybean meal, etc. This is the traditional hedging method and is the one used by grain merchandising firms. It is not the answer to feed manufacturers' needs, however, because the ingredients that can be so hedged are usually obtainable on spot markets at no disadvantage and because so few ingredient inventories can be covered in this way.

Direct hedging is used principally by feed manufacturers to earn carrying charges. This is particularly true in areas where grains are produced, but not in sufficient volume to serve all the needs of the area. For example, corn is usually worth substantially more in the eastern states than at Chicago; but at certain times-harvest in particular-the price in the East may be no more or even lower than the price at Chicago. At such times corn can be hedged in Chicago futures with the nearly certain expectation of a remarkable basis gain. This carrying charge may be realized whether corn goes up or down in price. This example illustrates not only an important use of futures markets but also the need for selecting inventories on the basis of their hedgeability.

The basis, or difference between cash and futures, behaves in patterns that repeat themselves over and over. But they do not repeat themselves because of habit. They repeat themselves because the factors affecting the basis recur regularly. If these factors change, the behavior of the basis will change. A hedger must look at the factors that affect the basis in each individual hedging. For example, the price of millfeeds is usually higher in Buffalo than in Kansas City. But this relationship varies. Floods in Kansas City or heavy importations of millfeeds from Canada reverse the usual relationship.

If millfeed inventories are hedged in the Kansas City market on a normal basis, and the relationship is reversed, losses may be greater than they would have been had the inventory been carried open. The effects of the Kansas City floods were anticipated as soon as they started, and the hedges were lifted by hedgers who were alert. The importation of Canadian millfeeds was less easy to foresee, and the only way to defend against it was to hold inventories at an absolute minimum. The essential points are that automatic hedging can lead to difficulties and that the hedger must be continually alert.

CROSS HEDGING

Cross hedging is the hedging of a cash position in futures markets for different commodities, that is, short sales of corn against soybean meal, oats against millfeeds, corn against grain sorghums, etc. It involves generally balanced positions and logically considers each inventory separately in the hedging program.

Cross hedging has several purposes: First, it is used to cover commodities for which there are no futures markets. Second, it is used to cover commodities which the existing futures markets are not liquid enough to hedge effectively. Many feed manufacturers who do not feel that they can hedge effectively in certain futures markets prefer cross hedging.

Third, cross hedging is used when the direct hedging basis is not satisfactory. There are situations in which cross hedges work better than direct hedges. For example, it is thought that Iowa may import some oats this year because of the short domestic crop. But because of the Canadian imports, total oat supplies seem adequate. Oats could have been bought in Iowa at freight off Chicago at harvest. At that time the logical hedge was in oats. If the price of oats in Iowa increases to the Chicago price or above, this hedge will be very risky; and a logical hedge for oats might well be in Chicago corn, which can be expected to maintain a carrying charge. In other words, in placing a hedge, the hedger should sell the highest things, which in this case *may* be Chicago corn.

A fourth use of cross hedging is to take advantage of seasonal tendencies in price relationships. During some seasons of the year some commodities gain on others, and at other seasons they lose. There are certain normal relationships that guide hedging programs. Soybean meal seems to gain on corn from fall to early winter, lose into the January-March period, and gain into summer. The ratio depends on the relative supplies of each, both for the year as a whole and for the different seasons of the year. A careful watch of this relationship and the factors affecting it may make it possible to develop a pretty good hedging program for soybean meal. Other rather regular relationships exist.

There is considerable difference of opinion about the advisability of cross hedging. Some firms do quite a lot of successful cross hedging, while others prefer to carry inventories unhedged. A thorough knowledge of price relationships is essential to effective cross hedging. There are severe problems in cross hedging in addition to the one of price relationships. One is the quantity to sell against an inventory. Whether to sell pound for pound, value for value, or in some other combination requires a careful study of historical price behavior. Another problem is locational differences. Relative values at different points seem to be much more erratic in feed ingredients than in grains, and this erratic behavior must be recognized in placing cross hedges. It does, however, have the offsetting advantage of offering basis profits for those hedgers who understand it.

SELECTIVE HEDGING

The third kind of program, selective hedging, might better be called selective speculation. It is fundamentally a speculative program. It is, however, less speculative than carrying open inventory positions. Selective hedging is the careful selection of inventory positions and hedging plans in order to take maximum advantage of market changes with a minimum of price risk. It involves both direct and cross hedging, as well as generally unbalanced market positions, which are taken on the basis of expected price and price relationship changes. A selective hedging program is a blending of the entire inventory management program with all of its separate prices into one coordinated balance of market positions. This seems to be the single hedging program that fits both the problems and the desires of mixed feed manufacturers.

A selective hedging program should be designed to accomplish several different goals: First, it must limit the total risk of the firm to the amount of loss that it is willing to take. If this involves the hedging of part or all of the minimum inventories, then it must provide for these hedges.

Second, the program must assure liquidity of operations. Every purchasing agent must be able to make independent decisions. But the outlook for supplies, prices, and requirements changes very rapidly, and he must be nimble enough in his thinking and trading to adjust to the changes. The inventory program must also be liquid enough to make it possible to adjust to changes. Taking a position and holding it for a long period without the possibility of making adjustments is dangerous.

Suppose that a feed mixer buys soybean meal in October for delivery from January through March at $60 a ton. He believes that it is priced below the average for the year and that the meal will cost more than that in January, February, and March. By December the price goes up to $70, which the mixer considers too high. He thinks that the price will decline to $63. Suppose that he is exactly right in his appraisal. If he carries the original speculation through to its conclusion without deviation, he will make net $3 a ton. Actually he will have made $10 and lost $7. The inventory value of the meal in December is $70, not $60. With a flexible inventory program, he could have gotten off a sale against the meal contract and cashed the $10.

A good military commander always plans his retreat before he launches an offensive. All feed manufacturers who take inventory positions get into situations that go against them. This cannot be helped. The thing to do then is to stop the losses before they get too large. Again you can see the importance of being able to even up quickly. One of the most important uses of futures markets is to provide liquidity. Cash positions are relatively inflexible. They are tied to considerations of adequate supply, proper quality, and transportation costs. You tend to get married to cash positions.

One serious inventory problem is the changing volume of feed sales. A decline in mixed feed prices is usually accompanied by a decrease in volume of sales, and an increase in prices by an increase in sales. Accordingly, an inventory of a given size lasts longer on a declining market than on a rising market. It is difficult to maintain an inventory of constant size in terms of consumption. This is another reason liquidity is important. In a declining market, something in addition to feed sales is needed to get inventories down fast enough.

Third, a selective hedging program is designed to make profits from long positions. This is the *selective* part rather than the hedging part of selective hedging. The program calls for deliberate speculations after the potential gains and losses have been appraised and the gains outweigh the losses at the level at which the individual firm is willing to speculate.

Fourth, the program should fix profits from speculations when the balance of potential gains and losses is unfavorable. This is the hedging part.

Fifth, the program is designed to take maximum advantage of carrying charges and price relationship changes and to integrate them into the overall storage and risk program. The overall storage capacity for some ingredients —soybean meal and alfalfa meal in particular—does not seem to be adequate. Erratic price changes indicate this fact. Carrying-charge potential is usually great when commodities are subject to short-run market gluts and shortages. It is possible to take advantage of these temporary market conditions without accepting the risk of changes in the price level.

IMPLEMENTING A SELECTIVE HEDGING PROGRAM

For the sake of presenting a program, we will think in terms of certain steps, but they should not be accepted by and applied to individual firms. Each firm must work out its own checklist.

The first step is to define the risk policy—to establish the maximum load of the firm and determine the level of uncertainty at which the firm will speculate. This latter is a question of how good the odds must be to get into the market.

The second step is to establish the level of minimum inventories that must be maintained. If this minimum level exceeds the maximum risk load, the problem becomes one of how to hedge some of the risks. Even in such a situation the firm may not want to limit its speculations to the minimum-inventory group. The best policy may be to cover them all and take the speculations in other ingredients.

Third, the firm should appraise the speculative potential of the entire list of ingredients. This appraisal should be in terms of prospective gains and losses and the degree of certainty that is felt about the forecasts.

Fourth, the hedging potential should be appraised in terms of basis change. Both direct and cross hedges should be considered.

Fifth, those inventory positions, hedged or unhedged, should be selected that offer the greatest potential profits in relation to potential losses. These should be selected in the order of their favorability up to the desired risk load of the firm.

Sixth, a liquidity program should be worked out. Lines of retreat should be chosen in such a way that, as the situation develops, the inventory program can be kept within the limits of the risk policy of the firm.

This inventory program is a continuous operation. It is not like the plans for a new feed plant because it can never be considered finished and put aside. It does, however, resemble the plans for a new plant in the careful planning and engineering that go into it. It involves a great deal of knowledge and careful and continuous attention.

In the final analysis, all that I have said can be reduced to three main points: (1) decide how much and under what circumstances you want to speculate; (2) plan your speculations carefully with your eyes wide open and take no speculations in which you do not have faith; and (3) integrate your inventory operations into a well-coordinated program.

Chapter Five

Price Supports Should Be Lower!

1953

AUTHOR'S NOTE: Working with and observing people in the soybean industry during the late 1940s and early 1950s resulted in a major interest on my part in soybean market growth and soybean and product prices. Prices became a focal point in conversations with farmers and tradespeople, and some forecasts were made and published. An audience had been developed by 1953. The Soybean Digest seemed a good forum for discussion of the relationship of market development and price. There followed more than fifteen years of discussion of the price support subject.

For the past several years soybean prices have been supported at 90 percent of parity on December 1 of the preceding year.[1] Announcement of supports has been made in the fall. Soybean supports are not mandatory; the level of support is at the discretion of the Secretary of Agriculture. There are indications that a support level of 90 percent of parity for 1954-crop beans would be unwise.

If restrictions on production of soybeans for crops following 1954 are to be avoided, they must be priced at levels that will keep them from being tied up in a loan program. This will likely require prices lower than 90 percent of parity. The support level for the 1954 crop should recognize the likelihood of a sharp increase in soybean production in 1954 as a result of the support programs for wheat, cotton, and corn.

---

1. Reprinted from *Soybean Digest,* October 1953.

1954 SOYBEAN ACREAGE

How large an acreage of soybeans will be planted in 1954? It is much too early to make an accurate estimate. For seven years, 1943-1949, an average of 10,555,000 acres was harvested for beans. There was no major trend in acreage during the period. In 1950 the acreage harvested for beans increased 3,332,000 acres to 12,545,000 acres harvested for beans; in 1952, 14,075,000 acres; and 14,335,000 acres are indicated for 1953.

Acreage allotments and marketing quotas for cotton, peanuts, and tobacco were in effect for the 1950 crops. There were acreage allotments for com, wheat, and rice. Farmers have approved acreage allotments and marketing quotas for the 1954 wheat crop.

SHARP INCREASE IN 1950

The acreage allotments for 1950 indicated reductions of 6,359,000 acres of cotton, 15,987,000 acres of wheat, and 11,333,000 acres of com. These allotments apparently caused the sharp increase in the 1950 soybean crop. Similar allotments for 1954 will likely have similar results. Since 1950 the soybean belt has spread out and become less concentrated. Such states as Minnesota, Kansas, Missouri, Arkansas, and Mississippi have increased soybean acreage. It appears likely that a higher proportion of the land taken out of wheat and cotton will be planted to soybeans than was the case in 1950.

Soybean acreage increased 32 percent from 1949 to 1950. If we assume a 32 percent increase from 1953 to 1954, apply the yields of the past five years, and make allowance for seed, farm usage, and export, we find that soybean oil and meal production from the 1954 crop will be about 40 percent more than from the 1953 crop.

Current indications are that we will be able to use up the 1953 crop of soybeans at prices that will reflect 90 percent of parity. It does not seem reasonable to expect that the market will absorb 40 percent more oil and meal without a reduction in price. The reduction in price will not need to be as great, percentagewise, as the increase in production. Soybean meal makes up about 60 percent of vegetable meal supplies and about 45 percent of high-protein feeds. There will be some compensating decrease in cottonseed meal supplies. We have an expanding market for high-protein feeds. Our vegetable meal supplies are about three times as large as they were in 1935. The market has absorbed this tremendous increase without any reduction in soybean oil meal prices in relation to feed grain prices. We are a long way from a surplus of soybean meal in any fundamental sense.

Soybean oil makes up about 40 percent of our domestic edible fat and oil supply. It makes up about 5 percent of the world supply of fats and oils. After reaching a peak in 1951, world fat and oil supplies per capita appear to be declining.

It is not possible to accurately forecast the price effects, both short and long run, that an increase of 100 million bushels of soybeans would have. If we take the several factors into account and assume a constant to growing livestock population and a constant level of consumer income, it appears that a decline of about 15 percent in the price would keep a large stock of soybeans from developing-that is to say that a support price of 75 percent parity would likely preserve an essentially free market for soybeans and would allow farmers to avoid acreage restrictions on soybeans. Seventy-five percent of parity is currently $2.10 at Illinois farms. Ninety percent of parity is $2.51. Cottonseed is now supported at 75 percent.

CHOICE IS CLEAR

The choice to be made is fairly clear. If soybeans are supported at 90 percent of parity, there will likely be a sharp increase in acreage. Farmers with storage will receive a high price for a big crop. But the following year it will be necessary to restrict acreage, and there will be a price-depressing surplus overhanging the market. When corn, wheat, and cotton farmers lose soybeans as a crop to substitute on acres taken out of production in compliance with other support programs, they will not have another high-profit crop to which to turn. Land will have to be taken out of high-profit crops and put into low-profit crops.

If soybeans are supported at 75 percent of parity, the increase in acres planted will likely be less. Returns from soybeans will likely be less the first year. Farmers will be able to keep productive land in high-value crops.

Chapter Six

Prospects for Further Increase in Soybean Production

1954

AUTHOR'S NOTE: Through 1954 there had been a rapid increase in soybean acreage and production. Questions were raised about the future, particularly in the context of price and income support programs for U.S. agricultural crops; that is, market growth was a policy issue. This article was replete with tables and charts, here deleted, to support the factual statements.

Soybean production has increased rapidly during the past twenty years.[1] It is desirable to occasionally pause to look at possibilities for the future. Are we overexpanded now? Is there room for further expansion?

New varieties of soybeans have been continually developed so that the crop is now adapted to a wide geographic area. From an agronomic point of view, it appears that soybeans can continue to expand so long as they can displace crops that compete with them for the use of land.

Soybeans compete primarily with corn, cotton, and wheat. In the original soybean belt of Iowa, Illinois, Indiana, and Ohio, competition is mainly with corn. Acreage in this area appears to have reached a plateau. Both north and south of this core area in the corn belt, soybean acreage is still expanding. Southern

---

1. T. A. Hieronymus is associate professor of marketing, University of Illinois. Article dated October 20, 1954.

Illinois, Minnesota, northern Iowa, and Missouri are the corn belt areas of most rapid expansion. Other areas of rapid expansion are Arkansas, Kansas, Kentucky, and the Mississippi delta. In these latter regions, contraction of cotton and wheat acreages are an important factor.

To get land space, soybeans must sell for enough to hold a comparative advantage over competing crops, all cost differences taken into account. So long as they continue to hold an advantage, they will continue to expand.

Comparative advantage is mainly a function of relative prices, and prices in turn are a function of the strength of markets. Accordingly, any further expansion of the soybean crops depends mainly upon the capacity of the markets for soybean oil and soybean meal to absorb additional products at prices that will enable soybeans to compete successfully with other crops.

THE MARKET FOR MEAL

Soybean meal is a high-protein concentrate of excellent quality. Most of it is used as livestock feed.

For the past twenty years, soybean meal has had a rapidly expanding market. We now use nearly twice as much high-protein concentrate[2] per grain-consuming annual unit as we did in the crop year 1935-36.

Most of the increase in the production of high-protein concentrates has been the result of expansion of soybean meal production. Increases in production of high-protein concentrates other than soybean meal have been small, and production per grain-consuming unit has declined slightly.

With the exception of soybean meal, our high-protein concentrates are by-products of the production of other crops: cotton, coconut oil, meats, etc. It is not feasible to expand these crops to get livestock feed. Accordingly, the expansion of the use of high protein that we have had has been possible only through expansion of soybean production.

---

2. The high proteins included in this tabulation are cottonseed, soybean, peanut, linseed, copra meals, tankage, meat scrap, and fishmeal.

Through the years of rapid expansion in the use of soybean meal, its price has not changed appreciably in relation to feed grain prices-that is, the livestock industry has absorbed rapidly increasing amounts of high protein without any offsetting decrease in price. This can have only been the result of a rapidly increasing evaluation of high proteins as livestock feed. It indicates that there has been a basic need for more high protein and a growing awareness of this need.

Have the requirements for high-protein concentrates per grain-consuming annual unit been satisfied? Apparently not. R. D. Jennings concluded that the protein shortage for the years 1942-49 was the equivalent of about 6 million tons of soybean meal. [3] This is slightly more meal than we now produce-that is, on the basis of current livestock numbers there is a basic market for about twice as much soybean meal production.

It is not likely that the market would immediately increase an additional 6 million tons of soybean meal without severe price declines, but there appears to be good reason to expect that the demand for high protein will continue to expand.

Recently, urea has been introduced into the feeding picture on a commercial scale. Urea is a synthetic chemical product that is converted into protein by combination with starch and bacteria in the digestive tract of ruminants. One pound of urea plus 7 pounds of grain will replace about 7 pounds of soybean meal.

Recent experiments indicate that a very high proportion of nitrogen can be supplied with urea.

The use of urea does not appear to be a very serious detriment to further expansion of the market for soybean meal. The use of urea is as yet limited to ruminants, while the bulk of soybean meal is consumed by hogs and poultry. It has been mainly the rapid expansion of poultry and hog protein consumption that has been responsible for the increase in soymeal use. Further, the greatest protein deficiency appears to be in hogs. Second, soymeal has certain characteristics, as yet not fully explained, that make it a highly desirable supplement beyond its use as a protein.

---

3. R. D. Jennings, "A Look at the Protein Situation for Livestock," USDA, processed report, March 1950.

Third, the main effect of urea will be to put a price ceiling on the premium that soybean meal can carry over feed grains. Obviously with corn and soybean meal at the same price, users cannot buy urea to convert corn to soymeal equivalent. At some differential, the substitution can be made, putting an effective ceiling on the differential.

ADDITIONAL LIVESTOCK POPULATION

We have an erratically increasing livestock production, while the U.S. population is growing at an increasing rate.

Livestock production per capita is below the 1926-32 level. If we even out the low production of 1933-38 and the high production of 1941-46, we find that for the twenty-seven year period, there is no discernible trend in livestock production per capita.

Three conclusions are warranted: one, our livestock production is not now keeping pace with our population growth; two, we have at times in the past, other than war years, absorbed more livestock production per capita than we are now absorbing; three, our population is expanding at an increasing rate, and accordingly we must expand livestock production at an increasing rate to maintain our dietary standard.

CONCLUSIONS

The foregoing discussion indicates that the growth trends of soybean meal utilization have not stopped, that from a nutritional standpoint soybean meal is in short supply, and that increasing amounts of soybean meal will be required to maintain existing livestock nutritional standards. The market for soybean meal will not become saturated short of a vastly larger production than we now have.

THE MARKET FOR SOYBEAN OIL

Our domestic situation in food fats and oils is in sharp contrast to our protein situation. We produce about 20 percent more edible fat than we need. The key market for soybean oil is exports.

Our production of food fats has increased about 4 billion pounds, or 75 to 80 percent, since the middle 1930s. Some 60 percent of the increase has resulted from increases in soybean oil production.

Fat is a basic dietary requirement and is low in price. Accordingly, the demand is extremely inelastic. Consumption is not responsive to the changes in supply and price. We cannot push our surplus production into domestic edible use.

Since 1935 we have shifted from a deficit to a surplus situation. In 1935, 1936, and 1937, production was less than domestic disappearance. Currently, production is about 1.5 billion pounds over domestic appearance. The shift from deficit to surplus generally parallels the increase in soybean oil production. However, the increase in domestic surplus is not as great as the increase in soybean oil production. Without the increase our deficit would be about one billion pounds. The production of food fats and oils other than soybean oil has not kept pace with population growth.

We have shifted from an import to an export nation. In 1952 and 1953, our exports were below the level required to dispose of our surplus production, and huge stocks were built up in the United States.

It is clear that we must either export substantial quantities of edible fats and oils or curtail production. Soybean oil is the only edible fat of which the supply is readily adjustable, and we need the meal.

By 1951, world fats and oil production per capita had regained its 1938 level. Increases since 1951 have been at about the same rate as population increases.

Is the export market large enough to absorb current or a larger quantity of American fats and oils? Likely so. There are several reasons for being optimistic about fat exports over the next decade.

First, fat production outside the United States is not increasing as rapidly as is the population outside the United States. It can be made to increase more rapidly. The supply of fats and oils in the United States is largely from by-products, such as cottonseed oil and lard, and is therefore inelastic. The supply of much of the world's fats and oils is elastic. Peanut oil, palm oil, copra, and whale oil have considerable elasticity of supply.

Second, the world's population is increasing at a rapid rate. Because fats are basic dietary requirements, an increasing population means a higher level of demand.

Third, the level of productivity is increasing in many parts of the world. Through the production of more goods and services, the fat-short areas gain purchasing power with which to buy. There are many areas of the world in which fat intake is below levels desired by consumers. With increasing productivity, they will buy increasing quantities of fat per person.

Fourth, large areas of the world are basically undersupplied with fats, and the peoples of these areas are bringing great pressure to get a higher dietary standard. Fats have a very high priority. In this connection East Europe, Russia, China, India, and likely most of Africa are particularly worthy of mention.

Pre-war U.S. exports were very small. U.S. exports are now nearly one-fourth of the world's total. About one-third of U.S. exports are inedible tallow. Some of this tallow finds its way into edible uses, but in the main it is used for soap.

Other American countries except Argentina and Uruguay ship less than they did pre-war. The bulk of the decline is in Mexican cottonseed oil. The Philippine copra industry has expanded by about 35 percent from pre-World War II. Exports from Africa have expanded sharply. This is primarily peanut oil from a belt across Central Africa. Argentina and Uruguay exports have declined sharply. This is mainly the result of a decrease in flaxseed production. Indian exports have dropped very sharply from their pre-war level. This represents decreases in cottonseed, rapeseed, and peanut oils. Indonesian exports are down by 30 percent. Australian exports are down.

The biggest decrease in fats and oils exports has been from China and Indo-China. This is a decline in soybeans, cottonseed oil, and peanut oil. It appears that Chinese production is about the same size as it was pre-war. What has happened to the oil formerly shipped to Europe and Japan is not clear. Some of it likely goes to Russia. But it is thought that the bulk of it moves from sparsely settled North China and Indochina into the more heavily populated regions to the south.

Other countries fall into the same pattern of decline.

Whale oil is about the pre-war volume.

Before World War II, Africa, India, China, and Manchuria were the great suppliers of fats and oils other than copra. The main movement was to Europe with a secondary movement to Japan. India, China, and Manchuria have been replaced by the United States. African importance has increased.

Reduced to its bare essentials, the great shift in edible fats has been from Manchurian soybeans and Indian and Chinese cottonseed and peanut oil to American soybeans and soybean oil. (As a result of U.S. price support systems, soybean oil has been replaced by cottonseed oil since March 1954.)

The major shift in export pattern is the result of two big changes: it has been made possible by increased U.S. production, and it is the result of increased pressure to consume in Asia. This pressure will likely continue. It is difficult to foresee the return of China and India to the ranks of major exporters. It is reasonable to expect that our large Japanese market for soybeans will go back to Manchuria in the not-too-distant future.

The substitution of U.S. for Asiatic fat in world trade is partly the substitution of inedible tallow for edible fats. The total world exports of edible fats are down from pre-war exports.

The two big competitors for our exportable surplus are copra from the Philippines and Indonesia and peanut oil from Africa. These are both primary oils with an adjustable production and so can be priced out of the market.

The future of African exports is questionable. So long as Africa remains essentially colonial, it is likely that the exportable surplus of peanuts can be increased. However, once Africa starts to increase its overall productivity, all possible increases in fats and oils production will be needed for dietary improvement. If Africa follows the trend of Asia, this will be the case.

Importing countries have increased fats and oils production. This was first a wartime measure and has been continued to make up deficits and in the interests of self-sufficiency. Likely a lot of this production costs more than imports would cost. In the long run, assuming a more peaceful world and freer trade, some of this production will be discontinued.

SUMMARY

These several things point to an increasing market for surplus fats from the United States. We should recognize and remember that we are the sellers, that we must service our export market.

The first requirement of a broad export market is a proper price policy. We must sell at prices that are low enough so that people can buy, and that are low enough so that they will not encourage competing production of copra and peanuts.

The second requirement is that we sell the products that the market wants. We are currently selling refined cottonseed oil. We sell our lowest quality soybeans for export and without a reliable grading system.

The third requirement is that we trade. We require payment for most of our fats in dollars. We need to take what we can get-what customers have to offer. This means accepting payment in other currencies and in goods.

The burden of trading rests on the seller. We need to recognize this principle much more than we have in the past.

There is an adequate market for more soybean oil than we now produce. To a large degree, the future of the soybean industry rests on our success in properly servicing the export market for oil.

Chapter Seven

A Comment on Mr. Blake's Paper

1954

AUTHOR'S NOTE: An article by Mr. Blake in the September 1954 Soybean Digest made the case for bringing the soybean price and acreage into line with those for other crops-cotton and cottonseed in particular. The soybean crop then was approaching 300 million bushels compared to 2,000 million in 1994. It is interesting to reflect in the 1990s how much discussion of agricultural commodity price and use was in the context of government programs during the 1950s and 1960s. We have traveled a long and rocky road. This article was published in the November 1954 Soybean Digest.

In his paper delivered at Memphis, Mr. Blake said, "If there are those who still persist in kidding themselves into thinking that soybeans are not in surplus now, I don't believe even they would contend that soybeans will not become surplus if their exports are retarded."[1] I do not think that soybeans are in surplus now nor do I think they become surplus so long as the soybean industry does not make the suicidal error that the cottonseed industry made when it got its primary product oil supported at too high a level. I do not think that oil and soybean exports will be retarded if we follow a realistic price and trade program.

---

1. William Rhea Blake, "Interdependence of the Cotton and Soybean Industries," *Soybean Digest*, September 1954.

The "intolerable situation" that Mr. Blake seeks to correct has arisen because soybeans have been supported at comparatively low levels. Parity for soybeans seriously undervalues them. Soybeans were wired into the parity system in the middle 1930s when their products had not yet found their markets. Soybean oil was inferior compared to cottonseed oil, and soybean meal had not gained farmer acceptance. With the disruption of international trade in fats and oils during World War II and technological improvements in the quality, the oil fraction of the soybeans rapidly improved its competitive position. With improved feeding practices, the rapid growth of the mixed feed industry, and consumer acceptance, soybean meal quickly increased its competitive value as a feed. As a result of this growth of markets, parity for soybeans is much too low when compared to parity prices for corn, wheat, cotton, etc.

Unfortunately, this happy situation is in the process of correction. The new system of calculating makes the parity price of a commodity depend upon its average free market price for the most recent ten years. We shall now proceed to watch a wartime scarcity of fats and oils with its accompanying high prices translated into parity for soybeans in a period of relative abundance of fats and oils.

The real irony of the situation that Mr. Blake so capably explains is that the cottonseed industry, favored by a high support price and a system of supporting the price that works, has been hurt; while the soybean industry, treated like an ugly stepchild with a low level of support, has prospered.

We can only conjecture about what would have happened to the soybean industry had there been support prices through the years as high in comparison to commercial value as those for com, wheat, and cotton. To gain their markets, products have to make sacrifices. They have to move in and demonstrate their merit. Soybeans were fortunate in the timing of their expansion. They grew up when competition was not great. However, it is not unreasonable to think that the growth of the industry would have stopped with the 1948 or 1949 crops had we had a price policy that would have retarded consumption and developed a "surplus." Would we have been able to develop our markets had the parity price been realistically high? There is room for considerable doubt.

I think that soybeans are not now in surplus nor likely to become surplus in the foreseeable future because the markets for products—meal and oil—are adequate and increasing. The only thing that we need to do to avoid surpluses is to price soybeans realistically.

We are now using over one and one-half times as much high-protein concentrate per animal unit as we did in the late 1930s. The livestock industry has absorbed these huge increases without any price concessions. Soybean meal now sells higher in relation to the index of feed grain prices than it did in the late 1930s.

It is generally agreed that present levels of protein intake by livestock are inadequate. Estimates of the deficiency indicate that we need a 50 percent increase in total high protein. We would have to double our soybean meal production to attain this level.

Our population is increasing, and our dietary level is improving. A larger livestock population is indicated. It is clear that we have not saturated the market for high proteins.

When the soybean crop was in its infancy—the mid-1930s—we did not produce enough edible fats and oils for our domestic requirements. We were net importers. We now produce very much more edible fat that we have domestic need for. We either export or stockpile this domestic surplus. The amount of the change from net importer to net exporter from 1935 to 1951 was about the amount of oil produced by a 300-million-bushel soybean crop. Our domestic market for total fat will increase no more rapidly than our population.

I think that the world market will readily absorb our exportable surplus, that the world market has a basic need for more fats. I will cite three principal reasons.

First, the world population appears to be increasing at a more rapid rate than production of fats and oils. This is certainly true for ex-U.S. production. Because fat is a basic dietary need, requirements are a function of population.

Second, the production of goods and services is increasing throughout the world. Out of this increased productivity will come the ability to pay for American fats and oils. The level of fat intake in much of the world is below levels that consumers want; that is, while the U.S. per-capita market will not grow as people are able to pay, the world market will expand.

Third, and I think most important, the populations of much of the world are strongly demanding a higher dietary level. Fat is one of the first things which they want to expand consumption. India has changed from a major exporter to an importer of fats and oils. China has not regained its prewar position as an exporter. There appear to be pressures for more fat in Russia and eastern Europe. As Africa develops, her domestic food requirements will increase rapidly. Again fats will have a high priority.

The immediate outlook for fats and oils exports is favorable. In 1951 and 1952, large stocks of fats and oils were built up in Europe as a war measure. Our exports were large. In 1953 and early 1954, these stocks were largely liquidated. It was during this period of European destocking that our exports fell off sharply. They are now back up. Our exports of principal fats, oils, and oil seeds, October 1953 through June 1954, were a record for that nine-month period. It appears to me that they will be very large in the year ahead.

Our stocks of soybean oil, cottonseed oil, and lard are now smaller than they were a year ago. A further decline will likely occur in the year ahead.

Our problem is not how to achieve a balance of burden among our various fats and oils but how best to service our export market. There are certain steps:

First, our price policy must be right. As Mr. Blake points out, the cottonseed support program has held an umbrella over soybean growers. It has also held an umbrella over the copra producers of Indonesia, the peanut growers of Africa, and the Antarctic whale ships, to mention only a few. We backed the world's inventory into the hands of CCC. We lost export volume.

Second, we must sell our customers the products they want. The support program has worked so that we are trying to sell refined cottonseed oil to people who want soybean oil, soybeans, lard, and crude cottonseed oil.

Third, we must trade. We must stand ready to take anything of value or any kind of money in exchange for our surplus products.

These things are not consistent with the existing cottonseed support program. Nor would the situation be helped by a higher parity price for soybeans.

The best long-run interests of the soybean and cottonseed industries will be served by doing away with support programs that distort competitive prices. We need look no further than the current cottonseed and soybean situations to realize this.

The cottonseed growers have taken a severe competitive drubbing from soybeans. This is unfortunate. But it is a part of the ruthless competitive process that has led to such remarkable economic progress in the United States. I do not want to see the promotion of economic stagnation in the name of social justice.

Chapter Eight

Should CCC Initiate a Buying Program for Cottonseed and Soybean Oils?

1955

*AUTHOR'S NOTE: In early 1955 it looked as if a substantial inventory of cottonseed and soybeans might develop from price support programs. The cottonseed and soybean processors proposed a program for CCC purchases of soybean and cottonseed oils. That would help hold oil prices at levels that would permit soybean meal and cottonseed meal to sell at market prices and that would keep soybeans and cottonseed out of the loan structure. It would have been the best of all possible worlds for processors. It did not seem to me to be in the best long-run interest of the soybean industry. This article was prepared for the Commodity Credit Corporation of the U.S. Department of Agricul*ture.

A request by cottonseed and soybean crushers for a CCC oil-buying program is being studied by the USDA. I think this request should be denied.[1]

First, an oil-buying program would retard the movement of oil into consumption. We are just now concluding one experience with an oil support program that has been expensive, both in terms of CCC losses and of the loss of markets for U.S. fats.

---

1. T. A. Hieronymus is associate professor of marketing, University of Illinois. Article dated July 14, 1955.

Second, existing price support programs have not harmed soybean crushers, nor are they likely to harm soybean or cottonseed crushers in the future.

BASIC FACTS

Certain basic facts about U.S. production and use of edible fats and oils dominate the marketing problem. Production of edible fats is larger than domestic requirements. Four fats comprise some 90 percent of U.S. production of edible fats. The average amounts of these produced in the five crop years beginning October 1, 1949, are as follows: butter, 1,581 million pounds; lard, 2,334 million pounds; cottonseed oil, 1,729 million pounds; and soybean oil, 2,614 million pounds; an average total of 8,258 million pounds. The average total edible fats and oils produced in these five years was 9,086 million pounds.

Average domestic disappearance of the four major fats for the above period was about 6,858 million pounds.

The average difference between production and disappearance was 1,400 million pounds. Domestic disappearance was 83 percent of production; production was 20 percent greater than domestic disappearance. Production and disappearance are increasing at about the same rate.

1. Production of edible fats cannot be readily adjusted to market conditions.

2. Butter production appears to be very slowly declining. Because of the great difference between butter and the other edible fats, its production does not respond to the overall fat supply situation.

3. Cottonseed oil is a by-product of cotton production. Its volume depends upon cotton production, which, in turn, is not related to fat and oil supplies.

4. Lard is a by-product of hog production. The price of lard has very little effect on hog production.

5. Soybean oil is a joint product with soybean meal. We have a rapidly expanding market for soybean meal in the United States. We apparently

> need more high-protein concentrates than we now have. So soybean oil production is affected by soybean meal requirements. More recently, it has been affected by price support programs for cotton, wheat, and corn. This is likely a passing influence.

Domestic demand for edible fats is inelastic; that is, consumption changes very little in response to changes in price. We require a minimum quantity of fats in our diets and want this minimum very badly. Any more is objectionable. Food use of all fats and oils per capita has remained stable at about 43 pounds for the past 20 years. We can expect that the domestic use of fats and oils for food will increase at about the same rate as the population.

These three facts lead to an inescapable conclusion: we must either export our surplus fats or move them into nonfood uses. It is not at all clear that nonfood uses could absorb them. Certainly, it would take a drastic price reduction to move them.

The key market for U.S. edible fats and oils is the world market. U.S. production is an integral part of world production, and the world production requirement balance is as important to soybean producers as is U.S. production and requirement. We are a part of the world fats and oils market.

WORLD EXPORTS

Total world exports of fats and oils are now approximately the same size as they were before World War II. They were then and are now 6,500 thousand short tons annually. This is now about 35 percent of world production. Prewar about 73 percent of exports were food fats, but in 1954 only 65 percent of total exports were food fats.

There have been major changes within the total world exports. U.S. exports have increased from 111,000 prewar to 1,579,000 short tons in 1954. Exports from the Philippines have increased from 387,000 to 533,000 tons. Exports from Africa, the most important exporter with 1,628,000 short tons, are 380,000 tons higher than prewar. Exports from all other areas of the world have decreased. The largest decreases have been 450,000 tons from India and Ceylon, 171,000 tons from Indonesia, 644,000 tons from China and Manchuria, and 309,000 tons from ex-U.S. countries.

The increase in Africa is mainly in palm, palm kernel, and peanut oils. Africa has increased in importance as a supplier of European edible oils. The decrease in "other America" is mainly in flax and linseed oil from the Argentine and Uruguay.

The great shift in supplying Europe with food fats and oils has been from Asia to the United States. The decrease in India and Ceylon was mainly in peanut oil and flaxseed. The decrease in China and Manchuria was mainly in soybeans and cottonseed oil. The bulk of the increase in U.S. exports was in soybeans and cottonseed oil. The export of cottonseed oil was unusual, as normally little is exported. The cottonseed oil that was exported in 1954 replaced soybean oil that would have been shipped.

During 1935-39 the United States was a net importer of edible fats and oils. We are now the world's most important supplier. The change in our position, excluding inedible fats and oils, is about as large as the oil produced from 250 million soybeans. *The U.S. soybean crop has replaced Manchurian soybeans and Indian peanuts in world trade.*

POTENTIAL EXPORTS

What is the future of our export market? Several things indicate a large and growing export market.

1. World production of edible fats per capita is still below prewar levels.

2. World population appears to be increasing faster than production of edible fats outside the United States.

3. There is a great pressure by many people for better diets.

Two things seem clear: we must export, and the world needs our surplus production. In order to export our surplus fats and oils, four conditions must be met: (1) There must be a need; (2) The importing countries must be able to pay; (3) We must export the kinds of fat the importing countries want; and (4) The price must be right. The first two of these conditions exist. The third does not. We are now exporting refined cottonseed oil, whereas our customers want soybean oil, soybeans, and lard. Germany has been unable to participate in our refined cottonseed oil sales. South Europe appears to prefer soybean oil to cottonseed oil.

We are currently pricing our export fats at the world level. We are approaching the time when our soybean-cottonseed oil price relationships will be such that we can again export soybean oil in volume. Current prices suggest that soybean oil need decline less than a cent a pound to be competitive.

The relationship of our oil price policy and our exports is clear. The surplus of edible fat (lard, soybean oil, and cottonseed oil) over domestic disappearance, exports, and changes in carryover in millions of pounds in recent crop years (October 1-September 30) was as follows:

Year	Domestic Surplus	Exports	Change in Stocks
1948-49	1,166	1,162	4
1949-50	1,080	1,085	-5
1950-51	1,487	1,400	87
1951-52	1,545	1,235	310
1952-53	1,453	944	509
1953-54	1,138	1,304	-166

There will be a stock reduction of about 500 million pounds in 1954-55. There is a close relationship between our price policy and changes in stocks. The package program (basically oil buying) was started in 1951-52. Under it we accumulated fat until our cottonseed oil prices were reduced to world levels in February 1954. CCC got into the oil business with a high-price policy and out of it with a world price policy.

The original theory behind the package program was that the demand for cottonseed oil was extremely inelastic; and accordingly, any reasonable price could be charged for it. This theory did not work out in practice because it failed to recognize that edible fats and oils are readily substitutable.

The world demand for fats and oils is not so inelastic as the U.S. demand. First, world fats and oils consumption is below saturation levels. As prices are lower or incomes higher, people will use more oil if it is available. Second, world supply is relatively elastic. African peanuts have some growth potential. Palm and palm kernel oil production can be increased rapidly when prices are high enough to cover costs which are mainly for harvest and transportation. The same is true of coconut oil production. The time that whaling ships stay out is a function of the prices of fats.

To hold our export market, we must not interfere with market prices of fats and oils. We must either hold this market or reduce soybean production.

OIL-PURCHASE PROGRAM

This is the factual background against which we must consider an oil-purchase program. What would be the effects of an oil-buying program?

1. If it were effective, we would either build up stocks of oil or take sharp losses on foreign resale. In either event, we would create a situation that would require correction. We have not yet progressed to the point with our price support programs where we are willing to recognize that they are chronic money losers. The way to correct oversupply of oil if we are not willing to lower prices is to reduce soybean production. This seems to be impossible in view of the acreage reduction programs for other crops.

2. An oil-buying program would disrupt normal trade channels. How can a CCC inventory operation, no matter how skillfully accomplished, do as effective a job as free market prices in getting the right oil to the right place at the right time? To have a workable program, CCC would need to accumulate a stock of refined oils. This involves refining, storage, and administrative costs. No government can be as successful as the forces of competition in getting these jobs done cheaply.

3. An oil-buying program would place the full burden of supporting prices of the seeds on the oils. The three components in the making of soybean prices are the price of oil, the price of meal, and the processing margins. For cotton seed, prices of linters and hulls must be added, making a total of five variables. If the problem is to support the raw material price and the price of oil is put at the level needed to accomplish this, then prices of the other products and services lose their effectiveness in regulating

the flow of products onto the market and in forcing maximum prices of the other products.

OIL-SUPPORT PROGRAM

How would an oil support program work? The simplest way to establish the CCC buying price for oils would be to buy soybean oil whenever soybean prices got below the support price and cottonseed oil whenever cottonseed got below the support price. The buying price for oil would need to be changed as the market prices of the other products and marketing margins changed.

The question of what soybean price to support would be left open. Loan differentials by location are not the same as market differentials. In 1955 soybeans were taken over in Minnesota while the market price was still above the loan price in Illinois. If prices were forced up to the support price in Minnesota, they would be above it in Illinois, etc. The price of soybeans would be supported at more than 70 percent of parity at some points or less than 70 percent at others.

The USDA is not obligated to fix the minimum price of any commodity. It is only obligated to see that farmers have an opportunity to obtain the support price if they meet certain conditions, generally including storage. The prices of wheat and corn in many areas are substantially below support levels, but farmers who are willing to store can get support prices less costs.

The loan rate for 1953 soybeans was $2.60 in east-central Illinois. In October 1953 the Track Country Station Illinois points price averaged $2.57, which meant farmers received about $2.51. Had there been an oil-buying program, it would have become effective. In April of 1954 the average Track Country Station price was $3.80. The seasons average price was $3.26.

Such a program would result in a badly confused oil price structure. Buyers of edible oils have sufficiently complicated problems now without adding meal, linters, and hulls.

A second method of establishing a CCC buying price for oils would be to establish a "package" value and buy and sell oil to maintain this value. The key problem here would be the choice of the processing margins. The USDA has published studies of the cost of processing. But for soybeans, margins have been much below these published costs in recent years. Inasmuch as this is an *agri-*

cultural price support program, an average of margins for the last three years would be a reasonable way to establish the margins allowed under a package program. The operation of the package program for cottonseed would make the establishment of cottonseed crushers' margins even more difficult.

A third method would be to forecast the minimum price of oil that would be required to hold soybeans and cottonseed at about support levels and use this as the buying price. The relation of the actual support price to the desired support would depend on the accuracy of the forecast. In considering a vegetable oil buying price, it must be kept in mind that this is a soybean and cottonseed support program, not an oil support program.

LOAN PROGRAMS

What will be the effects of existing loan programs? They will not have any effects except that they may or may not cost CCC some inventory losses. The machinery for loan programs is in existence. No new handling programs need be undertaken.

CCC stands a better chance of recovering cost from soybeans and cottonseed than from the respective oils alone. By owning the seeds, it can make use of strength in meal, oil, or both, in getting rid of any inventories that it might acquire. Losses will be smaller under a loan program than if an oil purchase program were substituted.

I do not think CCC will build up an appreciable inventory of soybeans under the loan program. Our export markets for oil are strong. We have a basic shortage of high proteins in the United States. Soybean meal usage per animal is increasing. There is room for further expansion in per-head use by hogs and cattle. We have very large supplies of feed that will be fed to livestock. We can look forward to increasing livestock numbers.

Soybean growers have initiated reductions in the support prices for soybeans as it has looked as if soybeans might be tied up in the loan program. It is significant that producers have not waited until the crop got into trouble. The alternative to growing soybeans in the Corn Belt is to grow grass. Many Corn Belt producers can afford to take lower soybean prices rather than switch to grass, and they seem to be perfectly aware of this. Thus far the soybean loan has been mainly a financing device and will remain one.

CCC has offered the soybeans taken over from the 1954 crop at prices lower than existing TCS Illinois points prices. There is no indication that CCC will allow an artificial scarcity to develop.

If the 1955 crop develops, as now looks likely, the 1955-56 crush will be of record size. The large prospective crush is partially the result of cotton, wheat, rice, and corn support programs. Agricultural price support programs have acted to increase rather than decrease soybean-crushing operations.

There is no reason to expect the loan program to decrease processing margins below the level that would otherwise exist. We will have a large supply of soybeans, and it will be crushed. Processing margins depend upon the quantities of soybeans to be crushed and the amount of facilities available to crush them. Except for the small quantities that are consumed as soybeans in the Far East, the only thing that can be done with soybeans is to crush them into oil and meal—either in the United States, in Europe, or the Orient. The factor that establishes the size of margin of any one processor is the price he must pay to get soybeans away from other processors. If agricultural price support programs have any effect on processing margins, it is to increase them by inducing a larger production. The only real complaint that processors can have against loan programs will come if they result in reduced production.

The main reason the package program was developed was that cottonseed was not storable. So the total cottonseed production will be available for crushing each year. CCC cannot sell cottonseed at prices higher than crushers are willing, and therefore presumably able, to pay.

If cottonseed crushing margins are reduced, it will be because (1) there is lower cottonseed production; and (2) the loan program cuts them loose from any build-in margins there may have been in the package program.

In view of the reduced production of cottonseed and the lower support price, the market price of cottonseed will likely be above the support price in 1955-56.

Chapter Nine

Welfare Implications of Market Prices

1955

AUTHOR'S NOTE: This paper is a switch from writings describing operations, processes, and current problems to a generalized theoretical discussion. It was one of the several presentations in a general program, "Welfare Implications in Marketing Research and Extension," at the 1995 annual meeting of the American Farm Economics Association. That I was invited was a fluke. The bias of the program was in the direction of governmental responsibility in the welfare of family farms and rural America and the role of research and extension in developing, evaluating, and directing welfare programs. My biases and those of the audience were substantially incompatible. Needless to say, a vigorous discussion ensued. I do not know to this day why I was chosen for the topic. This paper was published in the Journal of Farm Economics, 37(1955): 904-11.

DEFINITIONS, LIMITATIONS, AND HYPOTHESIS

To describe the area of discussion under this broad title, a definition of terms, limitations of the area considered, and statement of a hypothesis are in order.[1]

---

1. Presented by T. A. Hieronymus at a session entitled "Welfare Implications in Marketing Research and Extension," chaired by G. W. Hedlund, Cornell University, at the 1955 meetings of the American Farm Economics Association.

DEFINITIONS

In this context, welfare may be defined as a level of prosperity. The title of this paper can be stated as a question: What is the relative level of prosperity resulting from an economic system in which there are market prices?

Market prices are prices established by a free interplay of economic forces. Market prices are established by various kinds of pricing mechanisms. The term market prices does not imply a particular institutional structure. Specifically, it is possible to develop a system of pricing in which government plays a role and still have market prices.

In contrast, administered prices are prices established by something other than the free interplay of economic forces. Prices may be administered by governments or by individuals or firms. The establishment of prices by governments is usually undertaken in the interest of social justice, i.e., income distribution. The administration of prices by individuals or firms is undertaken to obtain monopoly revenue. The administration of prices involves (1) the control of supplies and (2) product differentiation, which is based on buyer ignorance of quality or on control of the marketing mechanism.

LIMITATIONS

This paper is limited to the welfare of farmers and to prices of agricultural products. It is also limited to publicly administered prices.

HYPOTHESIS

The aggregate welfare of agriculture and of individual farmers is maximized by pricing agricultural products at their market values. Conversely, systems of pricing agricultural products that seek some goal of income distribution that is determined by nonmarket considerations are detrimental to agricultural welfare.

FUNCTIONS OF PRICES

GUIDING PRODUCTION

Prices have certain functions to perform in the production of goods and services. Presumably this is known and understood by agricultural economists. It appears to be amazingly little understood by nonprofessionals and amazingly ignored by agricultural economists when matters of agricultural price policy are discussed. By way of quick review, I list three such functions.

1. Allocate productive resources. The pricing system should allocate productive resources in such a way as to maximize the marginal returns from each unit. This applies to both the allocation of resources between agricultural and nonagricultural production and the guiding of production within agriculture. Relative prices are the means by which the market tells producers what kinds, qualities, and quantities of products to produce.

2. Move products into consumption. The pricing system should operate in such a way that products move into consumption at the highest net returns. Each different combination of uses of a product will yield a different return, and only one combination will yield the highest return.

Obviously, it is impossible to consume more of a product than is produced. But it is possible to consume less by building up stocks. A function of the pricing system is to eventually move all of every product into consumption. If prices are to serve as an adequate guide to production, they must find the level at which all of the supply can be used.

The pricing system must guide products through the market processes. They must establish the uses, users, places, and amounts of marketing services.

3. Regulate the rate of consumption. Agricultural commodities are produced at varying rates during the different seasons of the year and in different amounts in different years.

Supplies must be made to last until the next harvest or flush production season. At the same time they must be used up. Prices must be such that this is accomplished. Reserves of farm products must be carried from year to year to provide against short crops and to allow livestock numbers to adjust to changing feed supplies. Establishing the size of reserves is a function of prices.

DIVISION OF THE ECONOMIC PRODUCT

Prices determine who gets what. How much farmers get to consume and save depends upon the prices they receive for the products they sell and the prices they pay for the things they buy. The wages paid for labor in relation to the cost of living establish the level of consumption of workers, etc.

This is the function of prices that people clearly understand. From the point of view of an individual, the division of product is the single important thing that prices do.

In the thinking of individuals and in discussion of public policy, judgments are made of the "fairness" or "unfairness" of prices. Market prices, i.e., prices obtained in competitive markets, are said to be too high or too low. Accordingly, attempts are made to modify them. Minimum wage laws are one such attempt. Our system of agricultural price supports is another; it is built upon a "fair" price concept.

Obviously, the guiding functions of prices do not get done or get done differently under a system of administered prices than would be the case under market prices. This leads to the difficulties with which we are all so familiar from our observations of existing price-support programs. It seems to be extremely difficult to devise substitutes for market prices in performing the production functions of prices if at the same time we are to have '"justice" in our economic system. It does not appear necessary to enlarge upon the difficulties that have been encountered in attempting to support agricultural prices above market levels. Current literature in the field of agricultural price policy is primarily concerned with methods of resolving the conflict resulting from (1) the necessity to perform the functions of guiding production and (2) the alleged injustice of market prices.

This conflict is resolved in classical economic theory by stating that market prices reward each in the amount of his production and that this is a just amount except insofar as incomes are affected by charity. It further states that the welfare of individuals and the aggregate welfare are compatible and that the incomes of both are maximized when productivity is maximized.

WELFARE EFFECTIVENESS OF SUPPORT PROGRAMS

UNDERLYING ASSUMPTIONS

The basic assumption on which price-support programs are based is an inelastic demand for farm products. These programs are of three kinds: (1) storage programs designed to stabilize year-to-year variations in prices and incomes; (2) production control programs designed to limit supplies to amounts for which satisfactory prices can be obtained and which presumably result in greater total revenue; and (3) surplus disposal programs.

Storage programs can be income-stabilizing only if variations in market prices are greater than variation in market supplies. Otherwise changes in the quantity factor in the income equation will more than offset the price factor. There appears to be sufficient empirical evidence of the inelasticity of demand when annual average prices and quantities are related to justify the contention that storage programs are income-stabilizing.

To be effective, public storage programs must not be tied to an arbitrary price or prices. The prices must be equal to market prices averaged over a period long enough for random production variations to work themselves out. Our storage programs have never met this requirement.

Why do public storage programs result in greater price stability than market storage operations? First, the cost of storage is not taken into account in the price, and second, the storer, being motivated by things other than profit, does not take risk into account.

Although it appears that storage programs stabilize prices and incomes, their effects on average income are obscure. Is there a loss of revenue if scarcities are not allowed to develop? The answers depend upon which segments of demand schedules are relatively least elastic. Empirical evidence on this point is limited, but most theoretical demand schedules are drawn with the most inelastic segments to the left. Commodity people discuss this as the chronically depressing influence of overhanging supplies. Farmers are fully aware of the short-run merit of scarcity. It may well be that storage programs result in more stable income from individual commodities but at a lower level of total income.

Production control programs for individual products involve protracted time spans. Presumably they are a permanent part of production. An inelastic demand *after short-run effects of changing supplies are worked out* is essential to their success in increasing income. Most studies of the elasticity of demand use annual average prices and quantities. The coefficients thus determined do not necessarily hold true when periods of several years are taken into account. Likely, the greater the time span, the relatively more elastic the demand schedule. The important point here is that programs have been undertaken without any clear knowledge of the possibilities of their success.

However, it is likely that control programs can be made to increase total revenue from an individual product if certain conditions are met. First, the demand for the product in its domestic uses must be inelastic-that is, in the long run synthetic fibers will not replace cotton, etc.

Second, if exports are an important segment of the market, provision must be made for realistic pricing of the export fraction. This includes a multiple price system or direct public subsidy.

Third, some provision must be made for use of resources diverted from production of the supported commodity. Currently, such diversion is made to other agricultural commodities. The big increases in soybean acreage in 1950, 1954, and 1955 are illustrative of the effects of production controls for selected commodities. Although measurement is difficult, losses to producers of substitute commodities may be as great as gains to producers of restricted commodities; specifically, wheat and cotton production limitation programs may or may not have increased revenue from these crops, but they have clearly reduced incomes of farmers who are not wheat or cotton producers. Lands taken out of wheat and cotton have been diverted in the main to feed grains and soybeans. Obviously, producers of feed grains who are not also producers of wheat or cotton have a smaller revenue as a result of the limitation programs. The question, as far as aggregate agricultural welfare is concerned, is whether the losses to feed grain producers are smaller, the same, or greater than the gains to wheat and cotton producers.

Control programs for total agricultural production can succeed in increasing total revenue only if the demand for the aggregate of agricultural production is inelastic. This demand must be long-run inelastic. It must be inelastic after adjustments are made for kinds, quantities, and qualities of products demanded in consumption. Our price-support programs are not short-run emergency operations. It is difficult to demonstrate that any agricultural emergency has existed since 1940. Price-support operations have been designed to gain a "fair" share of the national income for farmers. They must be considered in their long-run aspects.

So far as I know there are no conclusive studies of the long-run demand for agricultural products. One fragment of evidence is the rate of consumer expenditure for food. Agricultural production has increased much more since 1939 than has population. At the same time, the proportion of consumer incomes spent for food has increased. A much smaller proportion of consumer income would be required to support the 1939 dietary level than is now spent. Changes in the demand for food have been positively associated with changes in real income. Whether or not there is a causal relation is not clear.

American agriculture is an advanced livestock economy. We use much of our crop lands in the production of food grains as are needed and use the balance for feed grains, which, in turn, go into the making of livestock products. These are the marginal products of agriculture. It is at this margin that the long-run elasticity of demand must be measured.

If we can use meat as typical of these products, then some light can be shed on elasticity. E. J. Working says, "From the standpoint of national policy concerning livestock production, the most significant result of the study is the evidence developed to show that there is a difference between the short-run and the long-run elasticity of the demand for meat. Year-to-year changes of meat supplies result in somewhat larger percentage changes of retail prices in the opposite direction. In other words, in the short run the demand for meat at retail is somewhat inelastic. However, if the supply of meat is decreased and the supply is maintained at that lower level over a period of years, the price will, after its initial rise, gradually fall until it stabilizes at a point where the increase in price is less than proportional to the decrease in supplies. In other words, the long-run demand for meat at retail is elastic, and a decrease in supplies will result in a smaller aggregate retail value than will the larger supply."[2]

These retail prices must be translated into farm prices and production adjustments made. In the long run under a system of market prices, production will adjust to consumer demand and the demand for agricultural products will be the same at the farm level as at the retail level. The observed difference in elasticity at the two levels, when annual average prices and quantities are compared, is the result of the slow rate of change of marketing margins. In the long run, marketing margins are, of course, perfectly flexible. It appears reasonable to conclude that the long-run elasticity of demand for farm products may be greater than one.

Surplus disposal programs, both domestic and foreign, are systems for taking inventory losses on commodities that have been purchased at higher than market prices. They can increase farm income only by the amount of the subsidy. They reduce farm income insofar as they result in misallocations of productive resources that decrease the size of the nonsubsidized market.

WELFARE EFFECTIVENESS

If we conclude that the demand for farm products is elastic, the only way that publicly administered price-support programs can increase the level of prosperity of agriculture is through subsidies.

WELFARE EFFECTIVENESS OF MARKET PRICES

If, on the other hand, we conclude that the demand for farm products is elastic and that there is an expanding demand for livestock products, then we must conclude that the aggregate agricultural welfare is maximized by a system of market prices. Under this condition the problem becomes one of developing markets and producing for them. In the main this is a problem of improving quality and expanding high-value uses. Farmers are in the business of producing luxury products for luxury markets. The population of the United States may be

2. E. J. Working, Demand for Meat, University of Chicago Press, 1954, p. xi.

malnourished, but it is not undernourished. It is necessary to select the pricing system that will most effectively guide production and marketing.

It takes but a cursory comparison of market and administered prices to reach a conclusion about their relative effectiveness in this regard. A case in point is the most recent milk-support program. As soon as purchases were commenced, the proportion of milk going into fluid use declined, and the amounts of dried milk consumed in all uses but one decreased.

Two of the most rapidly expanding segments of agriculture have been broilers and soybeans. The broiler industry has expanded because of a rapidly improving technology that reduced costs and because of improvements in quality. Broiler production is a notably risky business. How large would this industry be now if the first time it took losses a support program had been initiated?

The soybean industry has grown because of rapid improvements in the quality of oil, an expanding foreign market for oil, and an increasing real demand for soybean meal. Both products have had to buy their way into their respective markets with low prices. How large would be current soybean production had support prices not been relatively low? The outlook for peanuts in 1945 was quite as promising as that for soybeans. This industry became involved in an administered price program and has declined. There have also been other factors in the decline of peanuts.

The aggregate welfare of agriculture will be maximized if production of the kinds and qualities of products that the market wants is maximized. Administered price programs have resulted in the misallocation of productive resources. Sufficient correction of them to prevent further waste appears unlikely. Waste of resources cannot possibly maximize the long-run agricultural welfare.

ALLOCATION OF AGRICULTURAL INCOME

Granted that market prices maximize aggregate agricultural welfare, we must yet treat the problem of allocation of income within agriculture. There is great disparity of incomes within agriculture. There is said to be a problem of poverty in agriculture.

One criticism of existing price-support programs is that they do not alleviate and in some cases actually aggravate existing disparity.

It is clear that producers are paid in proportion to their productivity under a system of market prices. Is the resultant disparity socially desirable? What pattern of income distribution is the optimum one? These are questions that I do not presume to answer. They are beside the point in issues of market prices.

In considering income distribution in agriculture, the deceptiveness of existing statistics should be kept in mind. Not all rural residents who are counted as farmers are farmers in any real sense. Nor is income of people who reside on farms limited to income from agricultural production. There is much part-time farming in the United States.

There is a decreasing agricultural population. It is decreasing because relative opportunities are greater off farms than on farms. A system of market prices for productive resources is allocating them between agricultural and nonagricultural segments of the economy. To hamper this process by income reallocation programs would be to reduce total productivity. The problem of disparity of incomes among farmers is a problem in poor relief; of underproductivity of individuals. Its treatment should not interfere with the workability of a system of market prices.

SUMMARY

The success of price-support programs in increasing agricultural income rests upon the assumption of an inelastic demand for farm products. Such evidence as is available indicates that this assumption is not valid.

A system of market prices is more effective in performing the functions of prices in guiding production than is a system of administered prices. Market prices are especially more effective in increasing quality, and quality in turn is important in stimulating higher levels of consumer expenditures for food.

Chapter Ten

Futures Trading in Onions

1957

AUTHOR'S NOTE: The statement on Futures Trading in Onions was an exercise in frustration. There was a bill before Congress to prohibit futures trading in onions. I was asked by the Chicago Mercantile Exchange to prepare and make a statement evaluating onion futures trading. I spent spring break 1957 putting together a fairly detailed and somewhat lengthy statement, assuming that the subcommittee was knowledgeable and sophisticated in matters regarding futures trading and its regulation. At one point my presentation was interrupted by a committee member asking, "Pardon me, professor, but what do you mean by open interest?" I was startled but proceeded with a definition. A short while later another committee member came late into the room and soon interrupted to ask what open interest meant. The chairman said that we had just had a lecture on the subject and that late arrivers should read the record. The bill had been initiated by a group of growers and had strong political support. It was my fairly well-founded judgment that the growers were speculators who had sold cash onions at strong prices and replaced them, and more, with long futures positions in what turned out to be a drastically falling market. The bill passed, and onions achieved the distinction of being the only commodity for which futures trading was prohibited by law.

It is my opinion that it would be a grave mistake to abolish futures trading in onions through legislative action.[1] In support of this point of view, I wish briefly to discuss four phases of this matter and attempt to appraise the effect that abolishing futures trading in onions might have. The four topics are

1. Inherent variation in onion prices

2. The evolution and functions of futures markets in general

3. Onion futures as a hedging medium

4. Criticism of the onion futures markets.

INHERENT VARIATION IN PRICES

The basic price-making facts about onions are very well summarized in a mimeo-graphed publication of the Commodity Exchange Authority entitled *Futures Trading in Onions*, released in December 1956.

From a consumer's point of view, onions are a condiment. We eat them because we like them rather than because of their nutritional value in our diets, although they do have a definite nutritive value. They lend variety and spice. They are consumed as special onion dishes, in soup, on hamburgers, etc. They are not very important in consumer budgets and, at the consumer level, are not regarded as expensive. When we want onions, price is not a major factor. A low price, on the other hand, does very little to stimulate consumption. The demand for onions then is relatively inelastic. It takes a very big change in price to affect consumption.

Onions are perishable. There are early, mid-season, and late onions. The earliest crop is harvested in Texas in March, and the latest crop is harvested in the northern states in September. If we are to have onions in the winter, they must be stored from September until the early harvest.

---

1. Statement by T. A. Hieronymus, associate professor of agricultural marketing at the University of Illinois, before the House Agriculture Domestic Marketing Subcommittee, May 3, 1957.

When early onions become available, the old-crop onions have little value. They degenerate rapidly in the spring. They are not as savory, and they cannot be carried over. The whole of the crop must be used up or thrown away.

These two factors, an inelastic demand and perishability, together with unstable production, confront the onion industry with a very difficult pricing problem. The supply must be made to last, and yet the whole of it must be used up. The supply is not precisely known. The National Onion Association and the USDA make estimates of supplies, and these estimates may differ sharply. And a small difference in supplies makes a big difference in onion prices.

The problem comes closest into focus late in the season. The greatest price changes usually occur late in the crop year. This is why the excitement about onion futures typically occurs in February. The following table showing average monthly prices received by farmers from January 1928 through December 1956 depicts this characteristic of onion prices.

Extreme swings in onion prices were not unusual before futures trading, and they have not been unusual since. They are inherent in the production of onions. We can hope to reduce them through improvements in the pricing system; and the futures market, as a pricing system, affords the best means of improvement.

EVOLUTION AND FUNCTIONS OF FUTURES MARKETS

My second topic is the evolution and functions of futures markets. You gentlemen are familiar with futures markets, and I certainly do not wish to impose a lecture about theory upon you. But certain fundamentals need to be reemphasized to bring the problem into perspective. Futures markets are systems of transferring the risks of ownership of commodities to people who are best able to carry them and who wish to assume the risks. They are systems of appraising and bringing into focus all of the factors that affect prices so that a price is established. They do not determine prices; rather, they help determine the prices which will move supplies.

COMMERCIAL ONIONS FOR FRESH MARKET

Average monthly prices received by growers.[1] United States, January 1928-December 1956

Dollars per cwt.

YEAR	JAN.	FEB.	MAR.	APRIL	MAY	JUNE	JULY	AUG.	SEPT.	OCT.	NOV.	DEC.
1928	1.80	1.90	2.90	3.00	1.60	1.20	1.40	1.70	2.20	2.30	2.70	3.10
1929	3.50	3.80	3.50	2.10	2.20	1.80	1.50	1.60	1.30	1.10	1.10	1.20
1930	1.20	1.40	1.20	1.50	1.40	0.60	1.30	1.10	0.86	0.74	0.66	0.86
1931	0.78	0.72	0.72	1.40	1.40	1.40	1.30	1.50	1.70	1.70	1.60	2.40
1932	3.10	3.40	4.70	4.10	1.00	1.10	0.94	0.60	0.52	0.50	0.40	0.56
1933	0.56	0.60	0.66	1.00	1.10	1.70	1.30	1.30	1.20	0.96	1.00	1.40
1934	1.70	1.60	1.40	1.30	1.00	1.50	1.40	1.20	0.94	1.00	1.30	1.40
1935	1.30	2.20	3.30	3.30	2.40	1.70	1.00	0.94	1.10	1.10	1.40	1.30
1936	1.40	1.40	0.98	0.88	0.62	0.80	0.98	1.00	0.74	0.62	0.60	0.74
1937	0.66	1.30	1.60	1.70	1.40	0.86	1.10	1.10	0.98	1.20	1.30	1.40
1938	1.90	1.90	1.30	1.50	1.10	1.50	1.10	0.82	0.84	0.98	1.00	1.20
1939	1.20	1.10	1.50	1.40	0.94	0.74	1.10	0.84	0.74	0.68	0.72	0.74
1940	0.84	1.10	1.20	2.70	3.40	2.00	1.90	1.10	0.98	0.86	0.92	1.00
1941	1.20	1.20	1.30	2.20	2.90	3.10	1.90	1.50	1.30	1.50	1.90	2.30
1942	3.30	3.70	4.20	3.30	1.40	1.50	1.70	1.70	1.60	1.80	2.00	2.20
1943	2.60	3.00	3.60	4.70	3.60	3.50	3.60	3.40	2.60	2.70	3.10	3.50
1944	4.00	4.20	6.20	5.20	3.00	2.70	2.80	2.40	1.90	1.70	1.70	2.00
1945	2.40	2.60	2.00	3.00	3.30	4.70	3.80	3.50	2.70	2.80	3.30	3.50
1946	4.20	5.10	5.30	3.90	3.00	2.60	1.70	1.40	1.10	1.20	1.30	1.40
1947	1.50	1.50	2.30	2.80	2.50	2.60	3.20	3.10	2.90	3.60	4.90	5.50
1948	6.70	9.10	10.20	6.80	4.90	4.20	3.40	2.10	1.90	2.00	2.10	2.00
1949	1.80	1.80	1.70	2.40	3.10	3.10	2.30	2.50	3.10	3.20	3.70	4.00
1950	3.10	1.90	1.40	1.90	2.30	2.10	2.40	2.20	1.40	1.10	1.00	1.30
1951	1.40	2.40	1.90	3.20	4.80	3.20	2.50	2.10	1.90	2.30	3.00	3.40
1952	4.60	4.90	7.20	7.80	5.80	4.30	4.10	3.80	3.10	4.20	4.70	4.40
1953	5.30	6.00	5.20	2.00	2.00	2.20	1.90	1.30	1.20	1.10	1.20	1.20
1954	1.00	0.82	0.98	2.00	2.70	2.80	3.00	2.30	1.80	1.80	2.20	2.00
1955	2.10	1.80	2.10	2.80	2.80	2.70	2.50	2.10	2.30	2.50	2.60	2.40
1956	2.20	1.80	1.50	2.20	3.90	6.90	7.40	3.60	1.90	1.70	1.70	1.90

These figures are taken from *Agricultural Prices*, February 1957, of the Crop Reporting Board, U.S. Department of Agriculture.

[1]Monthly prices are weighted average for the United States and are counted from estimated prices and quantities sold in major commercial states in the months indicated. Data for 1956 are preliminary.

Most crops are harvested seasonally. In the majority of instances, the supply must be made to last the whole of the year. Someone must own commodities, and, generally speaking, whoever does is taking a chance on prices. Whether it is the onion grower, the onion dealer, the wholesale grocer, or the speculator in a futures market, someone must carry the risk.

Farming is the most risky business there is; and farmers are our most important commodity speculators, not in futures, but in cash commodities. At any one time they own most of the crop in our major commodities: wheat, cotton, corn, etc.

These commodity owners are important in establishing short-run prices. Whether they hold or sell today is a factor in today's price. This is true whether they represent ownership in cash commodities or in futures contracts.

Futures markets are used to hedge commodities. Hedging is a process of shifting risks from an owner of cash commodities to a speculator in futures contracts. After hedging, the owner of cash commodities is no longer affected by changes in price; the speculator is affected.

The amount of hedging in futures markets can be measured by the number of open contracts. Generally, hedgers are short futures contracts, and, on balance, futures market speculators are long futures contracts. The number of open contracts is usually larger than the amount of the commodity hedged; that is, there is a speculative long and short position in addition to the speculative long that is opposite the net short position of hedgers.

The open interest builds up as the crop is grown and harvested and hedges are placed. It declines as the crop is taken out of storage.

The open interest is the appropriate measure of the amount of speculation in a market. It measures the amount of risks that are taken and carried by futures market speculators. The volume of trading is not a measure of the amount of speculation. It only indicates the rapidity of turnover of contracts. Generally the volume goes up as prices change rapidly and goes down when prices remain relatively stable. The number of open contracts and the volume of trading are not closely related.

ONION FUTURES AS A HEDGING MEDIUM

Against this background we can evaluate futures trading in onions as a hedging medium.

Chart I of the CEA publication, *Speculation in Onion Futures*, January-March 1957, shows the orderly buildup of open contracts as the growing and harvesting season progressed and the decline in open contracts at the end of the season. It should be particularly noted that the volume of trading is not directly related to the open interest. The number of open contracts declined as the season progressed, even though the volume of trading went up sharply.

On page 10 of the publication I just mentioned are analyses of the market position on January 31 and February 15, 1957. On both days over half of the open contracts were classified as hedging. Speculators were about two-thirds long and one-third short. Hedgers were almost entirely short; that is, speculators were carrying the inventory risks of the hedgers.

The total of open contracts that were hedges was smaller than is typical of the market. For example, on November 1, 1955, the reporting hedgers were long 2.2 percent of the total open contracts and short 43.9 percent. Reporting speculators were long 40.5 percent of the open contracts and short six percent. The other open contracts were straddling (both long and short) or not known. Hedgers' positions were 93 percent short and 7 percent long, whereas speculators' positions were 87 percent long and 13 percent short. The aggregate positions of reporting speculators and hedgers were about equal, so that it is clear that hedgers stood opposite speculators.

Near the end of the 1956-57 season, the proportion of the total open contracts that were short hedges declined. On page 15 of the report mentioned above, the following statement is made:

During the important marketing period (November to March) short hedging commitments showed a steady decline and were being replaced by a large proportion of speculative positions. In other words, during this critical period when onion futures contracts were maturing, the market became increasingly speculative.

Offhand, this might give one the impression that there was something sinister in this increase in speculative activity in the onion market. In the case of onions, the hedges are placed early in the marketing period and lifted as time goes on; and, quite naturally, the number of speculators in proportion to hedgers increases. The process is reversed at the end of the season. It is all quite normal and typical.

On October 31, 1956, 64 percent of the open contracts were short hedges of reporting traders, compared to only 35 percent by the same group on February 15, 1957. How does this compare with older, more stable futures markets? I chose the most recent available data for wheat and found that on October 31, 1955 (soon after the end of harvest), 42 percent of the open contracts were short hedges by reporting traders; while on April 15, 1956 (which compares with February 15 for onions), only 20 percent of the open contracts were short hedges by reporting traders. The decline in the proportion of hedges in onions as the season neared its end was less than in wheat.

The decline in the proportion of open contracts that one hedges as the season's end approaches is typical of a futures market. The total amount of speculation declines. The proportion of the open interests that is speculative increases.

The proportion of the onion crop that is hedged is large when compared to other commodities. On January 1, 1957, the total stock of onions was estimated at 15,760 car-lots. Open contracts on that day were 4,810 car-lots, about one-third of the total. On April 1 of this year, there were about 235 million bushels of soybeans; and open contracts in soybean futures were about 75 million, a ratio of about the same as onions. For corn the ratio is about 30 to 1 instead of 2 to 1; wheat, fairly typically, is about 12 to 1.

This comparison indicates to me that the onion futures market is used very extensively as a hedging medium.

In grains and cotton, farmers make little direct use of futures markets. The markets are indirectly beneficial. Farmers sell to merchants, who in turn hedge. The merchants could not buy at as high prices as they do if they could not hedge. There are no comparable processor interests in onions, but indications are that many onion producers hedge.

There are two CEA publications that include data directly bearing on the question of hedging, grower hedging in particular. One is a survey of open contracts on September 30, 1955, and the other is a survey of open contracts on December 31, 1956. Table 4 is the pertinent table in each publication.

On September 30, 1955, there were 813 traders in the market, and of these 125 were hedgers. There were 70 grower hedgers who were long 359 car-lots and short 577 car-lots. There were 53 onion dealers of various kinds classified as hedgers. They were long 320 car-lots and short 3,073 car-lots. These positions indicate that growers made extensive use of the futures market to reduce their price risks, both directly and indirectly. The short positions of the various onion dealers most probably were hedges against purchases of cash onions from growers.

What price could these dealers have paid for onions had they not been able to hedge their positions in onion futures and if they were forced to assume the risks themselves? They sold to the highest bidders, to people who would pay more than onion users and to people who would pay higher prices than those at which the onion dealers would assume the risks of ownership themselves. The futures market offered the best possible outlet for onion growers who wished to sell on September 30, 1955.

On December 31, 1956, there were 765 traders in onion futures, of whom 53 were hedgers. There were 19 grower hedgers who were long 49 car-lots and short 887 car-lots. The 33 onion dealers were long 167 car-lots and short 1,591 car-lots. Here again is evidence of extensive use of futures markets for hedging grower positions and sales.

What would have been the price of onions had the futures market not been available as an outlet? On December 31, 1956, grocer organizations and processors and manufacturers of onion products (both hedgers and speculators) were long 106 car-lots and short 24 car-lots for a net long position of 82. The net short position of hedgers was 2,200 car-lots. Obviously, users were not as willing buyers as were futures market speculators. Without futures markets available to bring in the speculating public, onion dealers and users would have been the primary outlet for growers, and, in my opinion, prices definitely would have been lower.

Additional statistical evidence of the direct use of futures markets by onion growers in hedging their crops is found in the position reports of the CEA. Small-scale traders are not required to report their positions to CEA. In markets generally, small-scale traders are speculators, and they are typically long. The small-scale traders who are short include the grower hedgers. Thus, the ratio of small traders who are long to small traders who are short is some indication of the grower hedges.

During the soybean harvest in 1955, small-scale traders were long in a ratio of 1.5 to 1, indicating, to a degree, that a moderate number of farmers were hedging.

At the end of September 1955, nonreporting onion traders were long in a ratio of 1.3 to 1, indicating a slightly higher proportion of grower hedgers in onions than in soybeans.

By January 1956, the ratio of nonreporting onion traders had increased to long 3 to 1. To me, this tends to indicate rather extensive grower hedging at harvest.

All of the statistics of onion futures trading indicate a quite extensive use of the market for hedging. In a market in which the price is so inherently variable as onions, a hedging medium is especially important. It appears that onion growers can gain price protection from the onion futures market. It is eminently clear from the price variations that they need price protection.

CRITICISM OF FUTURES TRADING IN ONIONS

Judged by past performance, the onion pricing system has needed improvements, which appear to have been made by the Exchange and CEA. In general, stability in prices is desirable.

The price of onions depends upon the underlying conditions of supply and demand. Stability of prices depends upon how accurately the basic economic considerations are foreseen and bid into current market prices. Two things are involved: complete and accurate information, and accurate interpretation of the meaning of the facts. In addition, a third thing is required for price stability, and that is the absence of control or undue influence by individuals or groups.

Only after markets develop large volume and broad public participation do they become impossible to manipulate or influence with rumors.

In the past years, before CEA regulation, it appears that onion futures were subjected to short selling by a few commercial interests. The best cure for this condition is a large group of well-informed speculators who stand ready to absorb this kind of selling. The public behaves irrationally at times in its market trading, but it offers the best available protection against control of a market, and I know of no one better qualified to establish price than the public.

The increase in the volume of futures trading in onions in recent years is encouraging. Stability will be increased as the quality of speculation improves.

EFFECT OF ABOLISHING FUTURES TRADING IN ONIONS

What effect would abolishing futures trading in onions have? Would it stabilize prices and enable the producers to get more for their crops? I do not think so. The onion market would be in a state of flux for a short time, but very quickly there would be devised a system for shifting risks and establishing prices that would closely parallel the futures market.

If we look back at our four evolutionary steps, we see that futures trading is nothing more than the codification of existing trade practices. It is refined and supervised, but there is no basic economic difference between futures trading and the systems of forward trading that have developed, commodity by commodity.

If futures trading in onions is abolished, I have already stated that a parallel forward pricing system will evolve. Such a system, if it comes to pass, will have some disadvantages in relation to the present pricing system. First, there will be much less information about trading, prices, and market conditions. Second, there will not be as much financial responsibility toward contracts as is possible through an exchange system. Third, there will be less public participation and a less effective system of hedging. Buyers will be able to sit back and buy at lower prices when they do not have to compete with the speculating public. Furthermore and finally, the market will not be supervised or regulated. It will be much more subject to manipulation and undue influence by a few people.

There is now an open, competitive, public, supervised market that appears to be growing and improving. I do not think it wise to take legislative action that will rob it of its broadening base resulting from the presence of speculators and of governmental supervision.

One must not lose sight of the fact that the buyers who would be in the market after the abolition of futures trading would purchase as cheaply as possible in view of the risks they would have to take. Furthermore, there would be no uniformity of price, since each buyer would strive for an individual bargain, and the government does not furnish enough price information to make up for the loss of price data which would follow destruction of the futures market.

Summed up, I think abolishing the futures market would be a backward step which would injure the producers and the entire onion industry. That concludes my statement. I appreciate very much the opportunity to have been heard.

Chapter Eleven

The Feed Grain Problem

1957

AUTHOR'S NOTE: A major focus of agricultural economics throughout my career was on price, production, and income programs of the federal government. Program focus was on some concept of social justice generally tied to the family farm. There were continuous attempts to adjust agricultural production and prices in ways that were "fair" to agricultural producers. These inevitably flew in the face of market forces and the dynamics of farm organization, technology, and markets. They were attempts to deny the realities of the market forces. An invitation to speak at an American Farm Bureau Convention provided an opportunity to describe the real world within which social problems had to be addressed. The statement is long, tedious, and saturated with numbers. It was a statement about the inevitability of markets. It may or may not have had an impact.

This paper is an attempt to review the feed grain problem as it currently exists in American agriculture.[1] Four questions appear to be pertinent:

1. What is the nature of the problem?

2. How did it develop?

---

1. T. A. Hieronymus is associate professor of agricultural marketing, University of Illinois. Paper delivered at the American Farm Bureau Convention, Chicago, December 9, 1957.

3. How does it relate to the total agricultural problem?

4. What are the guideposts to solution?

THE NATURE OF THE PROBLEM

The current problem has two principal parts: There are substantial carryover stocks of feed grains, largely owned by the Commodity Credit Corporation, and current rates of production of feed grains are greater than current use. The second of these two parts is more significant than the first. Not only is there a large stock with which we must deal, but this stock appears to be getting larger each year. If the inventory buildup can be stopped, the problem of liquidation can be undertaken. The urgency of the situation is imparted by the chronic buildup. Liquidation of stocks is less urgent. The price effects of a large inventory that is static are not known. But the downward effects of a chronically increasing inventory are undoubtedly more serious than those of a static inventory.

The carryover of feed grains at the beginning of the current crop year was estimated at 47.1 million tons. It consisted of 1,356,652,000 bushels of corn, 238,542,000 bushels of oats, 126,710,000 bushels of barley, and 45,158,000 hundredweight of grain sorghums. Percentagewise, these are corn, 81; oats, 8; barley, 6; and grain sorghums, 5. As is usual, the bulk of the accumulation is com.

It is difficult to say what a normal carryover of feed grains is. As production and utilization both increase, the carryover is also expected to increase. Starting with 1926 and eliminating the years in which price-support programs appear to have been a factor in the carryover, the carryover has averaged 10.2 percent of production. Production in the past three years has averaged 133.1 million tons, and 10.2 percent of this amount is 13.6 million tons, the indicated normal carryover. Eighty percent of this normal carryover is 388 million bushels as a normal carryover of corn. On this basis, the indicated normal carryovers. of the other feed grains are oats, 136 million bushels; barley, 41 million bushels; and grain sorghums, 18 million hundredweight.

Comparing these normal carryovers with current ones, we find that the surplus amounts to 969 million bushels of corn, 102 million bushels of oats, 85 million bushels of barley, and 27 million hundredweight of grain sorghums, which is a total of 33.5 million tons. This amount of grain is equal to 25 percent of the average production in the past three years.

Because of the 1947 drought, inventories at the start of the 1948 crop year were unusually small. Starting with the 1948 crop, accumulation by years, in millions of tons, has been as follows:

1948	22.6	1949	0.1	1950	-1.9
1951	-8.5	1952	6.9	1953	4.7
1954	7.4	1955	4.2	1956	3.8

The algebraic sum of these figures is 39.3 million. This is 5.8 million tons greater than the 33.5-million-ton surplus indicated above, which is the amount allocated to bring the carryover at the start of the 1948 season up to normal. The average accumulation, 1948 to 1952, was 1.6 million tons a year, or 1.3 percent of production. Beginning with 1952, the accumulation has amounted to an average of 5.4 million tons a year, which is 4.4 percent of production.

These data indicate that the feed grain surplus problem is most properly dated from the fall of 1952. No single accumulation is alarming in proportion. It is the regularity of the accumulation that has given rise to what is now a troublesome carryover, and that indicates the need for corrective action. USDA estimates indicate an increase in carryover during the current crop year, of 9.9 million tons.[2] The problem appears to have become chronic and is not becoming any less severe. In looking at these data, the one encouraging thing we find is that the annual accumulation rate is not great. Accordingly, corrective action need not be especially violent.

DEVELOPMENT OF THE PROBLEM

What caused the development of this problem of chronically accumulating inventory of feed grains? Obviously, production is greater than use—which is precisely the same as saying that use is smaller than production.

2. U.S. Department of Agriculture, Feed Situation, October 1957.

Examination of annual totals of feed grain production for the past 32 years reveals an interesting pattern. Production in the past four years has averaged 131 million tons compared with a 1926-30 average of 97 million tons. This is an increase of 35 percent, or about 1.23 million tons a year. But the rate of increase has not been regular. Production was essentially stable from 1926 to 1940, not counting the drought years of 1934 and 1936. The average in 1926-30 was 96.7 million tons, compared with 97.8 million tons in 1937-40. The 1941-45 production was 113.7 million tons, 16 percent above the prewar level, and was rather stable at this figure. From 1946 through 1953, production was relatively stable at an average of 118.l million tons; the 1947 total was quite low and the 1948 total quite large. Production totaled 123 million tons in 1946 and 118 million tons in 1953. Since 1953 it has averaged 131 million tons, but this average is not significant because production has been increasing rapidly.

Thus, there have been two periods of major increase in feed grain production: from the prewar to the postwar period and during the past four years. The prewar to postwar increase amounted to 20 million tons, or 20 percent. The increase from 1953 to 1957 was 21 million tons greater and that of the past four years-13 million tons greater than the average of the first eight postwar years.

The accumulation of inventory noted on the preceding page, which is causing the feed grain problem, is associated primarily with the increases in production of the past four years.

Increases in production of the different feed grains have not been uniform. Production of each of the four feed grains was essentially stable during the 15 prewar years. Seventy-three percent of the total was corn, 19 percent was oats, 6 percent was barley, and 2 percent was grain sorghums. Prewar to postwar changes in the relative importance of the different feed grains were not large. Corn went up 1.4 percent, and oats went down 1.3. Barley and grain sorghum changes also offset each other, with barley down 1 percent and grain sorghums up 1 percent. What this means is that increases in production were not concentrated in any one feed grain. Grain sorghum production about doubled from prewar to postwar; but because it was small in comparison with other grains, the share held by each feed grain was not importantly affected.

Changes in the relative importance of the different feed grains have been substantial during the past four years. The share of the total represented by corn decreased from 74.4 percent during the first eight postwar years to an average of 69.8 percent the past four years. During this same period the relative importance of oats decreased from 17.4 to 16.6 percent, barley increased from 5.3 to 7.3 percent, and grain sorghums increased from 3.1 to 6.4 percent.

From 1953 to 1957, feed grain production increased by 21.1 million tons. Of this increase, 2.6 million tons was corn; 2.9 million tons, oats; 4.4 million tons, barley; and 11.2 million tons, grain sorghums. Corn, which normally makes up about three-quarters of the total production, contributed 12 percent of the increase; barley, with a normal share of 6 percent, contributed 21 percent; and grain sorghums, with a normal 3 percent, contributed 53 percent.

We can now further tie the increase in feed grain carryover down to increases in barley and grain sorghum production during the past four years.

Part of this change in production is the result of increased yield, and part is the result of changes in acreage. Corn acreage in 1957, currently estimated at 72.3 million, is the lowest of any time since the last century. Acres in corn gradually increased from 1900 to a peak of 111 million in 1932. They then declined to 85 million in 1941. The wartime peak was 94 million acres in 1944. Prior to acreage allotments in 1950, about 85 million acres were planted in corn. The 1950-53 acreage was about 81 million. There have been acreage reductions in each of the past four years.

Corn yields have increased gradually since the beginning of the use of hybrid corn in the 1930s. Recent increases have been associated with the advancement in fertilizer use and selection of the best land for corn. Increases in yield have slightly more than offset acreage decreases.

Acres planted in oats reached their highest level, 45.5 million, in 1921 and gradually declined to 33 million in 1939. From a peak of 43 million in 1946, acreage has again declined to about 34 million at the present time. There appears to be substantial substitution of soybeans for oats, particularly in northern Iowa and Minnesota.

Oat yields are now higher than before World War II but have shown no discernible trend during the past 10 to 15 years.

Barley acreage is now at about the same level as the World War II peak. From a wartime peak of 17 million acres, barley acreage declined to a low of 8 million in 1952 and subsequently increased to 15 million acres in 1957. Years of sharpest increase were 1950 and 1954 through 1957.

There has been a trend for barley yields to increase about 15 percent during the past 10 to 15 years.

Before the war about 4 million acres of grain sorghums were harvested. The wartime peak was 9 million acres in 1944. The 1949 acreage totaled 6.6 million and the 1950 acreage 10.3 million. The 1951-53 average was 6.7 million. Since 1953, annual acreages have been successively 11.7 million, 12.9 million, 9.3 million, and 18 million.

Grain sorghum yields are sharply higher now than the prewar level. It is difficult to detect any important trends at the present time, although 1957 yields are unusually large.

The expansion in feed grain acreage and feed grain production is due to a considerable extent to the expansion in barley and grain sorghum acreage and production during the past four years. Without these increases in grain sorghums and barley production, the accumulation of feed grains would have totaled 8 million tons instead of the 25 million tons currently estimated. About two-thirds of the accumulation of feed grains is associated with increases in barley and grain sorghum production.

Increased acreage of feed grains has been closely associated with production controls imposed on other crops. Since World War II, marketing quotas and acreage allotments have been in effect in 1950 and 1954 through 1957. Since 1953, harvested acres of wheat, cotton, and rice have decreased by 36 million. Corn acreage harvested has decreased by 8 million. During the same period, barley acreage has increased by 6 million, grain sorghums by 12 million, and soybeans by 7 million. Land has been taken out of allotment crops and put into feed grains and soybeans.

Cotton and wheat production and disappearance have been about brought into balance during the past two years. But the problem has popped out elsewhere. From this, one important lesson should finally have been learned; that is, if controls are imposed, they must be imposed on an across-the-board basis.

Production is greater than use. But also, use is smaller than production. Is the current difficulty the result of overproduction or underconsumption?

Feed grains are used for feed. For the crop years 1952 through 1957, feed grain disappearance will have averaged (if all goes as forecast) 122 million tons. Of this total, 103 million tons (84.5 percent) is for feed; 12.4 million tons (10.2 percent) for seed, human food, and industrial use; and 6.5 million tons (5.3 percent) for export.

Domestic use of feed grains for nonfeed uses not only is rather small but is also quite stable. There is a tendency for it to increase by a small amount each year. Nonfeed uses of feed grains have extremely limited expansion possibilities. They are expanding with population and increases in acreage of barley and grain sorghums. If seed requirements are subtracted to obtain a net production, the most important use of feed grains for nonfeed purposes is the wet milling of com, which takes about 4 million tons. The requirements for com oil, com starch, and com syrup are not appreciably expansible per capita. The same is true of breakfast food and hominy grits. Feed grains are used for alcohol for liquor. This use takes about 1 percent of corn production.

There is no nonseed, nonfeed, domestic use of feed grains except wet milling of com that takes a significant amount, nor is there any such industrial use that holds promise of requiring a significant quantity in the future.

Exports of feed grains have been pushed vigorously in recent years. There is a long list of programs that foster exports. In the crop year beginning October 1, 1952, feed grain exports totaled 5.1 million tons. In the year beginning October 1, 1956, they were 7.3 million. Not much is known about the amount of feed grains consumed by the various kinds of livestock. From the 1949 crop the percentages of feed grains consumed by the various classes of livestock were dairy cattle, 16; beef cattle, 9; hogs, 46; poultry, 20; and other (mostly horses), 9.

Year-to-year comparisons of livestock numbers and feed grain supplies show very little relation except for hogs. The numbers of poultry, dairy cattle, and beef cattle appear to be unaffected on a year-to-year basis by the amount of feed grains available. These kinds of livestock are fed sparingly when feed is scarce and liberally when feed is abundant.

There is, however, a close relation between the available supply of feed grains and the number of hogs raised when prices of feed grains are allowed to fluctuate freely. Historically, feed grain production and use have been kept in balance in the short run by adjusting hog numbers.

Long-run and short-run effects of changes in feed grain supplies on livestock numbers are different. The initial impact of a feed grain supply increase is on the hog population, but as the increase persists it becomes distributed over the entire livestock population through the interworking of the various livestock-feed price ratios; that is, increases in hog numbers result in less favorable hog-feed ratios than egg-feed ratios, milk-feed ratios, etc. This in turn results in shifts from hogs to poultry, dairy, etc., and brings the livestock population into balance at the higher level.

Disappearance of feed grains for livestock feed has not increased so rapidly as production. During the period 1946-51, feed grain production and use were essentially in balance. The very large 1948 corn crop had not been completely liquidated by the close of the 1951 feeding season (October 1, 1952), but the carryover was not large and it was declining. As noted above, the surplus problem is most properly dated from the fall of 1952. Feed grain use by livestock has increased gradually since the 1952-53 feeding year. The 1946-51 average used was 99.2 million tons. In the 1952-53 season it was 96.7 million tons, and it has increased every year since then to an estimated 108.7 million tons in the year ending next October 1.

From the 1946-51 average to the 1956 amount, feed grain production increased by 12.2 million tons a year. Use of feed grains for livestock feeds increased by 7.8 million tons during the same period. Use of feed by livestock has increased significantly, but at a slower rate than production.

Production of feed grains increased 6.0 million tons from 1951 to 1952. Use of feed grains for livestock feed decreased by 9.5 million tons during the corresponding feeding seasons. Beginning with the 1953 crops and extending through the 1956 crops, production increased at the rate of 2.5 million tons a year, and use by livestock at the rate of 2.25 million tons a year. Accordingly, had the use of feed grains by livestock expanded in the 1952-53 feeding season in line with production, and had the rate of increase in feed use held at the rate that has actually existed during the past four years, there would not be any appreciable surplus of feed grains. In fact, the result would have been a carryover of minus 3 million tons in the fall of 1957. The expansion in rate of use that has existed in the past four years could not have been sustained had a substantial imbalance not developed in the 1952-53 feeding season.

What caused this imbalance? Decreased use in a year of increased production? In the year beginning October 1, 1951, a total of 167.3 million units of grain-consuming livestock was fed. In the next crop year, that of the 1952 crops, 158.8 million units were fed. Dairy and beef cattle units were up moderately. Hog units were down 14 percent. In spite of an increase in feed grain supplies, there was a sharp reduction in number of pigs farrowed in the spring of 1953.

The hog-corn ratio (Chicago basis) in November and December 1952 was 10.6. With this ratio in the breeding season, pig farrowings can be expected to decline—and they did. A ratio of 12.5 would probably have called out the needed increase. The price of hogs (barrows and gilts, Chicago) was $16.97 in November-December. With corn at $1.36 at Chicago, hog numbers would have increased. With corn at $1.48 to farmers and $1.60 at Chicago, hog numbers decreased. The loan rate that year was $1.60.

And so this is how the surplus feed grain problem started and has since developed. From all of this, one lesson stands out with absolute clarity: if feed grains are to be used, they must be priced at levels that will return profits to feeders.

RELATION TO THE TOTAL AGRICULTURAL PROBLEM

The problem of agricultural surplus production has by now quite logically backed into the area of feed grains. A relative increase in the production of feed concentrates and livestock has long characterized American agriculture. It is characteristic of any agriculturally wealthy nation. Every nation or area harvests its lands that are fit only for grazing with animals cattle, sheep, goats, and reindeer. It puts its croppable lands into food crops, such as wheat, rice, rye, oilseeds, vegetables, etc. As production from these crop lands increases past minimum caloric requirements, crop land is diverted to the production of feed, particularly feed grains. Feeding livestock from the products of croppable lands reduces the total volume of production to requirements on a caloric basis. Only a few areas of the world can afford this relatively expensive type of feed production. Approximately three fourths of the products of U.S. crop land are used for feeding livestock.

For some time agricultural production has been expanding faster than population. Diversion of land from food to feed is to be expected in this circumstance. How much of the diversion described above, which has caused feed grain production to increase rapidly in the past four years, would have occurred without the impetus of price programs for cotton, wheat, and rice is impossible to say. Probably the rate of diversion would have been slower. The diversion to soybeans would probably have had the same effects but would have occurred more slowly.

The diversion of acreage by price programs has regional repercussions. Production of feed grains and soybeans, outside the Corn Belt, on land diverted from cotton, wheat, and rice aggravates the problem in the Corn Belt states. For example, in 1957 almost as many acres of grain sorghums were planted in Kansas as acres of corn in Iowa, and nearly as many acres of grain sorghums in Texas as corn in Illinois. Even allowing for the normal shifting of land from food to feed, one cannot but wonder whether the Corn Belt has not been forced to carry a disproportionate share of the load.

A more subtle repercussion is being felt within the Corn Belt. A substantially larger share of corn (including corn forfeited under the loan) has been sold off farms in the years since price supports have become operative. This increase in sales has been quite large in the western part of the Belt and quite small in the eastern part. Corn taken over by CCC is subsequently sold, primarily into commercial channels. These sales compete for markets with the normal sales by cash-grain farmers east of the Mississippi river. During the past two or three years, these cash-grain farmers have found their markets flooded with CCC corn—a lot of it from the West—and soybeans from an expanded production area.

GUIDEPOSTS TO SOLUTION

As we contemplate the problem, the first question that occurs to us is what would have happened had there been no price programs since the Korean War. The question has two parts: what would have happened to production, and what would have happened to use? While we cannot turn back events, an answer to this question would be helpful in correcting mistakes and guiding future programs. Unfortunately, we can only conjecture.

Less feed grain would likely have been produced. Land would have been diverted from wheat, cotton, and rice at a slower rate, although probably not much slower because wheat, cotton, and rice have limited markets that are difficult to expand. More likely, about the same amounts of each of these allotment crops would have been produced on more acres with less intensive cultivation.

It is doubtful that price programs for feed grains have had much direct effect on production. Possibly some land in grain sorghums and barley would have reverted to grass. Compliance with corn acreage allotments has not been great. Some land has been diverted from corn to soybeans, but soybeans are 80 percent (by weight) feed. Corn production practices have been intensified.

The fact is that it is difficult to find any very productive land that has been taken out of production in recent years. When food and fiber needs are met, land produces feed.

The real difference that the absence of programs would have made is in the utilization of feed. One thing is certain: *feed production and utilization would have been in balance*. Feed would have sold at prices that would have made possible an increase in livestock production. No one but the U.S. government would have accumulated the inventory that now exists.

Unanswered is the question about the prices that would have prevailed. To answer this question we need to make certain assumptions: first, that production would have been the same as it has been; and, second, that all of the adjustment would have been made in hog production.

Feed grain disappearance for feed the five crop years 1952-56 totaled 102 million tons. The best guess is that 47 million tons went to hogs. The average accumulation was 5.4 million tons a year. Accordingly, feed for hogs should have totaled 52.4 million tons a year, or 11.5 percent more than actual use.

During the five years 1952-1956, pork consumption averaged 66.4 pounds per capita; 11.5 percent more is 74.0 pounds. Total meat consumption averaged 157.1 pounds per capita. Adding the increase in pork to this total makes 164.7 pounds, or a 4.8 percent overall increase. This is not more meat than we could have used. Per-capita use in 1956 was 166.8 pounds, or 2.1 pounds larger than the figure postulated here.

The price effects of additional meat production are uncertain. The general thought is that a small increase in hog production has a decidedly depressing effect on price. In the short run this is true. As hog marketings increase from summer lows to winter highs, prices decrease much more than proportionately. Similarly, year-to-year changes in hog prices are proportionately greater than year-to-year changes in supply. But these two facts are not closely related to the question at hand. They have to do with the short run, and this with the long run. They have to do with live animals, and this with meat consumption. Given the long run, in which consumers have an opportunity to adjust to the larger supplies and the effects of consumer reaction work themselves through the marketing system, the relation of quantity and price becomes quite different.

E.J. Working, after a very thorough study of the question, concluded, "In the short-run the demand for meat at retail is somewhat inelastic. However, if the supply of meat is decreased and the supply is maintained at that lower level over a period of years, the price will, after its initial rise, gradually fall until it stabilizes at a point where the increase is less than proportional to the decrease in supplies. In other words, in the long run demand for meat at retail is elastic, and a decrease in supplies will result in a smaller aggregate retail value than will the larger supply." From this result, and given time for adjustments between retail meat prices and live animal prices, we can logically argue that hog prices would have averaged 4.8 percent lower than they actually did during the five years in question. During these five years the average price was $18.46 per hundredweight for barrows and gilts at Chicago. Correction for a 4.8 percent increase in meat supply would give $17.61 as the average at the higher production rate.

A hog-corn ratio of about 12 to 1 is approximately equilibrium-the amount that will keep production and use of feed in balance. A per-hundredweight price of $17.61 divided by 12 is $1.47, the indicated five-year average price of No. 3 corn at Chicago. The price of No. 3 yellow corn over the past five seasons has averaged $1.47 a bushel. This is not a provable figure, but the method is logical and the figure reasonable. The size of the accumulation has not been great in individual years. One would therefore expect that the effects of not accumulating would not have been great.

The pattern of prices during the five-year period would have been different. Prices would have been lower at the beginning and higher at the end. There can be little doubt that without price programs, the price of corn would now be higher than it is and there would be a normal carryover of feed grains.

As we look at the feed grain problem, several things appear to be reasonably clear.

First, the present program is untenable. Inventory increases are being accumulated each year. At some point this buildup must be stopped.

Too much money is going into costs of programs and handling of inventories. We can reasonably calculate that some of the corn now being sold by CCC below the current market has cost $2.60 or more a bushel. Part of this cost is for administering the programs, part for interest, and a large share for storage. These are monies that do not get back to farmers.

Second, it is doubtful that the answer to the problem lies in the direction of production controls. There is nothing in the record to indicate that they have worked in the past. Reaction to the soil bank seems to indicate that the cost of getting productive land out of production of feed grains in sufficient volume to importantly affect the balance of production and use would be prohibitive.

Third, the answer also does not lie in the direction of increased nonfeed use. There are no new industrial uses with expansible markets. The logical destination for exports of feed grains is North Europe, where livestock populations are large. But throughout this area there is a problem of lower-than-desired farm prices. Most of these countries have schemes for protecting domestic prices. As the United States lowers export prices, this protection is increased. The most prosperous consumer market, and hence the best market for feedstuffs, is in the United States.

Fourth, in designing price programs, interregional effects must be taken into account. If areas that specialize in particular commodities elect to build programs on production controls, they must go the whole control route and actually reduce overall agricultural production.

Fifth, there appears to be no method of bringing feed grain production and use into balance except by pricing feed grains so that they can be profitably fed to livestock. This is the scheme that will inevitably be followed, whether now or later. The longer this solution is postponed, the more serious the problem will become.

Sixth, the principal feed grain producers of the United States would have been very much better off had prices been reduced five years ago. Very little has been gained and a great deal has been lost. Consumption potential has been forgone. The money consumers would have paid for meat is lost and cannot be recovered. A mistake was made in 1952 when production and consumption were allowed to get out of balance. The consequences of this mistake are now apparent. Because of the size of the carryover inventory, these consequences will be with us for some time to come.

Seventh, the imbalance between feed grain production and use is not great. Accordingly, the effects of reducing or eliminating feed grain price supports will not be great. It appears that the negative effects of price programs are strong enough to make it possible for feed grain prices to reach higher than current levels after the immediate shock of removal of supports is passed.

These seven considerations do not present a solution to the problem. They do establish a framework within which a solution must be developed. Attempts in the past to work out solutions without recognizing these fundamentals is what has led to our present difficulty.

Chapter Twelve

Market Potential for High-Protein Concentrates in Northwest Europe

1958

AUTHOR'S NOTE: I spent the summer of 1957 investigating the potential for high-protein concentrates in northwest Europe. It was an interesting opportunity to see European agriculture and the political factors involved in U.S. exports to Europe. It was at the time that the European Common Market was being implemented. Only a small part of the full report is included here.

The purpose of the investigation that I made was to explore the potential market expansion for high-protein concentrates, particularly soybean meal, in six northwest European countries.[1] These are the United Kingdom, Belgium, France, the German Federal Republic, Denmark, and The Netherlands. Excepting the United States, these countries are the most important users of high-protein concentrates for livestock feeds, and they import a very high proportion of their requirements, as cakes and meals and as oilseeds.

---

1. T. A. Hieronymus is associate professor of agricultural marketing, University of Illinois. Talk given at the American Soybean Association Annual Convention, Des Moines, Iowa, August 19, 1958.

CONSIDERATIONS IN EXPORT POTENTIAL

The export potential of soybean meal as such, or as soybeans, to the six northwest European countries depends on the size and potential of the market for high-protein concentrates within the countries. Any activities of the United States as a government or as individual firms in stimulating exports need to be directed toward exploiting the potential expansion that already exists; that is, in speeding up market development.

METHOD OF INVESTIGATION

The pattern of the study was to compile and examine the statistics pertinent to market size and then go into the countries involved to supplement the statistics, to obtain interpretation of the statistics, to discuss problems of expansion, and to obtain opinions about the expansion possibilities. In each country, Foreign Agricultural Service personnel of the USDA, government officials of various kinds, university specialists in various fields, trade association officials, importers, exporters, traders, oilseed crushers, and feed manufacturers were contacted. In all, there were conversations with about 200 people.

SIZE OF THE ECONOMIC MARKET

How big is the economic market for high-protein concentrates? Rough calculations indicate a potential increase of some 30 percent on the basis of current livestock numbers and kinds. Increases in population and per-capita consumption of meat and poultry meat add some 2 percent per year to the market size.

Livestock populations are increasing faster than protein production from forage. Because of the labor problems of increasing production, further increases in requirements of proteins will continue at a faster rate than production of forage proteins. Because the proportion of the total protein supply that is obtained from forage is much greater than that obtained from high-protein concentrates, there is a multiplier effect of the increase in requirements in relation to forage production. Not enough is known of protein sources and totals to calculate this effect on market size.

No precise calculation of the size of the market five to ten years from this time can be made. The several considerations involved suggest a market size some 50 percent greater than current consumption. Whether it is 50 percent, or 30 percent, or 80 percent is not of great consequence. The important conclusion is that the potential market size is substantially greater than current consumption.

The most rapid potential expansion is in France and Germany. These are the two countries with the greatest protein deficits in livestock rations and the greatest propensity to increase consumption of livestock products. The rate of expansion in these two countries will depend on continued consumer demand for increased meat consumption, improvements in the quality of protein concentrates, the rate of development of poultry meat industries, and the rate of advance in the technology of animal nutrition.

The United Kingdom presents an interesting case. The level of feeding efficiency is high, and the rate of increase in consumer demand for livestock products is low. Yet there is a continuing increase in the use of high-protein concentrates. It is apparently tied to the expansion of the mixed feed industry. The dynamics of this industry are such that it would be an error not to expect a continued expansion of use of the same general size as that of recent years.

In The Netherlands and Denmark, feeding efficiency is at a very high level. Substantial market expansion can be expected out of the decrease in butter production as compared to pork production and the shift to swine and poultry production.

The Netherlands and Denmark are livestock product factories, importing feed and exporting products. Market expansion for high-protein concentrates will depend, to a very great extent, on export volume. From a purely economic point of view, the export situation is favorable because these two countries hold a comparative advantage in livestock production. However, the political situations involved in the two countries are giving rise to very great pessimism about the possibilities of maintaining exports. Their policy makers greatly fear that the agricultural policies of the countries to which they export are freezing them out and that this will result in decreased animal production.

PROBLEMS OF AGRICULTURAL PRICE POLICY AND NATIONALISM

To this point the discussion has been mostly confined to economic considerations. But these alone will not determine market expansion. There are agricultural policies and programs and protectionist systems that retard market development and alter the structure of production and trade.

Generally speaking, agriculture is highly protected and subsidized. In part, this is done to maintain a home-produced food supply-an attempt to become as self-sufficient as possible. It is, in part, for the purpose of supporting agricultural income.

There is little support and protection for agriculture in Denmark. There is very little disposition to promote or protect agriculture in Belgium. There is increasing concern about the agricultural situation in The Netherlands, and measures have been taken to protect the domestic price level of grains. In turn, a system of subsidizing exports is being developed. In Germany, France, and Great Britain there are large subsidies to agriculture and very extensive protection systems.

By way of example of the effect, the case of Germany can be cited. The import of feed grains is closely regulated so that the domestic price of feed grains, barley in particular, cannot fall below certain minimum levels. This, in turn, supports the price of feed potatoes and raises the costs, hence the price, of livestock products. Meat production in particular would expand substantially if it were not for this policy. It is very difficult to expand market size by price measures if the market is protected in this fashion.

In Germany there is a policy and a program to get all of the feed needed on a farm produced on that farm. This seems to have the effect of slowing down the rate of advance in the technology of animal nutrition. There is a policy of keeping poultry enterprises small and nonspecialized. This may be a good policy, but it slows down the rate of poultry expansion. The large, specialized poultry operations that are developing in Germany must overcome the opposition of governmental policy.

There are people in Denmark who have computed that the net farm income in Great Britain is just equal to the amount of the subsidies of various kinds paid to support British agriculture. British economists do not contradict the statement.

As agriculture is expanded in Britain, the cost to the treasury is increased. The situation of large subsidies and high cost to the treasury cuts two ways with regard to the market for high-protein concentrates. On the one hand, it encourages importation of products from the colonies, mainly beef and butter from New Zealand and Australia, in the interest of keeping costs to the treasury down.

It appears that there is potential for increased poultry meat consumption in Europe. This does not mean that there is a great opportunity for the export of poultry from the United States. At this time poultry can be profitably exported form the United States and markets developed. Such a development has a short life expectancy. As the European market for poultry meat is developed, it will become protected for domestic producers. It is a kind of enterprise that fits in well with European agricultural conditions. The long-run benefits of the development of a market for poultry meat must be evaluated in terms of increased imports of feedstuffs rather than poultry meat.

There is no doubt that U.S. oilseed crushers are in a weak competitive position because of European protectionist policies. In the future, high-protein concentrates from the United States will be increasingly imported as oilseeds. This will continue until the market for oil is saturated with oil made from seeds and there is no oil export outlet.

Chapter Thirteen

Soybean Price Supports Should Be Reduced

1958

AUTHOR'S NOTE: Following the reduction of price support levels, the soybean industry, with the help of heavily subsidized exports of cottonseed and soybean oils under Public Law 480, avoided surplus problems for several years. With a large crop in 1958, a carryover problem again developed. I wrote a rather detailed (some 7,000 words plus 10 pages of tables and charts) argument for another price support reduction. It was published in its entirety in the January 1959 Soybean Digest. The version here is substantially reduced. The editor asked for comments and published some of them in the February Soybean Digest. The comments were about evenly divided between support and opposition. After reading many of them, I further commented, "I must confess an error in writing the price support article. Now I know I was not arguing for lower soybean supports but was arguing for no soybean supports. In the long run we need upwards of a billion bushels of soybeans. To achieve this volume during the next ten years, we must constantly keep our soybean acreage in balance. If we let soybean acreages become overextended right now and the industry falls into the clutches of the government, we will stop the long-run expansion of the industry."

Soybeans are in trouble.[1] There is not a large enough market to absorb current production. We are faced with the need to find larger markets or to reduce production. This must be done now, or government inventories will be built up. The examples of other crops—corn and wheat in particular—are sufficient to prove the need for immediate action and underscore the futility of remedies taken too late or in half steps. The soybean industry should take its medicine now and should take a large enough dose to effect a cure.

The soybean markets, export and domestic, are expanding rapidly enough to absorb current production increases, and the expansion can be continued for the indefinite future. If the expanding need for high-protein concentrates is to be met, there must be further expansion of soybean production. The trouble lies with the oil fraction. Oil production has been expanded past its market size at current prices. The market for soybean oil can be expanded further only by a major reduction in price.

Soybeans must be allowed to sell at prices that will permit the continued expansion of the market for soybean meal, and that will permit oil to compete effectively with other fats and oils for the existing world market.

Soybean production in 1958 is in excess of requirements. Part of the increase in production is the result of an increase in acreage, and part is the result of unusually favorable growing conditions. The problem has been brought on rapidly because of the weather. This may be fortunate because it clearly illustrates the nature of the problem as it will likely exist in the years ahead. Production in 1958 was estimated at 573 million bushels on October 1. Seed requirements from this crop will be about 33 million bushels. Exports may reach 95 to 100 million, leaving a crush availability of 440 million. A reasonable estimate of the potential use of meal in 1958-59 indicates a crush of 385 million bushels, leaving an increase in carryover of 45 million bushels from this crop if the very high October 1 yield estimates materialize. The yields forecast on October 1 were 3.4 bushels above the average of the last 10 years. Normal yields this year on the expanded acreage would

1. T. A. Hieronymus is associate professor of agricultural marketing, University of Illinois. Paper given November 12, 1958.

have produced 492 million bushels against a projected meal, seed, and export need of 515 million.

A crush of 385 million soybeans would produce 4,235 million pounds of oil. If we allocate projected production of lard and cottonseed oil between domestic use and exports, and if we assume that domestic use of edible fats and oils per capita will remain at the same level as it has in recent years, 2,689 million pounds of soybean oil will be needed in the domestic market. This would leave 1,543 million pounds to be exported. If we take into account the projected exports of 1,737 million pounds of lard, cottonseed oil, and soybeans, a total export of 3,280 million pounds will be needed. The average for the period 1952-56 was 1,894 million pounds. In 1956-57, exports of the three totaled 2,779 million pounds, and in 1957-58 about 2,422 million.

General world conditions in fats and oils are such this year that an export of the big three at the 1956-57 record level would be a very optimistic forecast. Such an amount would result in an export of 1,042 million pounds of soybean oil and require a crush of 339 million bushels of soybeans.

On the meal side, a crush of 385 million can be used; and on the oil side, 339 million. The result of this 46-million-bushel gap will be some kind of compromise. There will be continued downward pressure on oil and upward pressure on meal as a result of the support price for soybeans. The combined value of the two must be sufficiently greater than the price of soybeans to encourage processing.

The effect of the price of oil and meal pivoting around the loan will be a smaller crush than would exist without the loan. Without a support price on soybeans, we would produce the needed meal and let the oil price decline to a point at which oil would find its way into export and into domestic inventory.

A second effect will be to push meal prices up to levels that will restrict use below the amount that would otherwise be used and to reduce the export of fats and oils.

MEAL MARKET EXPANSION

Production and use of soybean meal in the United States have expanded at a very rapid rate during the past twenty years. Production of other high-protein concentrates has increased very little, and production per protein-consuming animal unit is at the same level as it was twenty years ago.

The increase in protein concentrate consumption per animal unit has been associated with a substantial and continuing increase in output per 100 pounds of feed fed. This increased productivity is especially notable in swine and poultry. Use of high proteins has increased greatly for these two classes of animals. The use of high-protein concentrates has been stable in the production of milk and beef.[2]

Wells estimates that substantial deficits in protein still remain.[3] He estimated that in 1955 about 198 pounds of high proteins were needed per grain-consuming animal unit, and the amount fed was 133 pounds, a deficit of 33 percent. Since 1955, consumption has increased by only a small amount.

In addition to the feeding deficit at the present time, it should be expected that substantially increased amounts of protein will be needed to supply increasing livestock numbers. Population is increasing rapidly. If current per-capita consumption levels of livestock products are to be maintained and expanded, livestock numbers will need to be increased.

When we combine all three of these market growth factors (current protein deficits, increased feed grain production and inventory liquidation), our estimate of soybean meal market potential becomes fantastic. It is clear that if meal production is continued at the same rate in the decade ahead as it has in the decade ending, a shortage of high-protein concentrates will remain.

THE OIL PROBLEM

Supplies of edible fats and oils are in very troublesome abundance in the United States.

---

2. C. M. Wells, The Expanding Market for Soybean Meal, University of Illinois Bulletin 620, October 1957, Tables 1 and 2.

3. Ibid., pp. 6-8.

Production of fats and oils is increasing at a much faster rate than use. Production of fats and oils other than soybean oil is stable. Therefore, increasing quantities of soybean oil are needed to maintain domestic per-capita disappearance. But these increased requirements are very small in relation to the increase in soybean oil production.

The limited domestic market for soybean oil, the expanding market for soybean meal, and the fact that one cannot be produced without the other make the export market for edible fats and oils of paramount importance to the further growth and development of the soybean industry.

THE EXPORT MARKET

Prior to World War II the United States exported minor quantities of cottonseed oil and soybean oil and major quantities of lard. At the same time the United States was a major importer of other fats and oils, particularly copra, so that on balance the country was a net importer. Following World War II and the expansion of the soybean crop, the United States became a major supplier of fats and oils for Europe. A record high was reached in 1950-51. Exports fell off during the following two years with the destocking following the Korean War and with the cottonseed oil buying program of the USDA. This buying program tended to hold U.S. oil prices above world prices, as well as generally to support world oil prices. In early 1954 the USDA initiated an oil sales program that liquidated its stocks in 18 to 20 months. This was mostly cottonseed oil. The sale of oil for foreign currency was initiated under Public Law 480 in the latter part of the 1954-55 crop year and got up to about 740 million pounds in 1957-58.

Until 1958-59 the problem of exporting the domestic surplus was solved by a dollar business of about 2 billion pounds per year and by P.L. 480 sales. The prospect that these two methods will accomplish the job in 1958-59 and the years ahead is remote. The exportable surplus production has jumped from a troublesome 2.4 billion pounds in 1957-58 to a huge 3.9 billion in 1958-59. If we assume a dollar export market for 2.0 billion pounds, a P.L. 480 export of 1.9 billion pounds will be needed to avoid an increase in the carryover of oil and soybeans. This program is 2.6 times as large as last year's. If the increase in meal use is projected to 9 percent, which appears reasonable in view of the normal market growth and increases in livestock numbers, a total export of 3.3 billion pounds will be needed.

It is quite clear that the need to increase exports of edible fats and oils is not a temporary one. The immediate problem presented by the 1958-59 situation must not be allowed to overshadow the long-term problem of increased oil exports.

EXPANDING THE EXPORT MARKET

The key to increased exports over the long term is a reduction in the price of fats and oils. Cheap oil will accomplish two things:

1. It will stop further increases in the production of competing seed oils.

2. It will facilitate increases in the consumption of fats and oils in areas of the world where per-capita consumption is low.

The areas of the world where per-capita fat and oil consumption is low and where incomes are low are also the areas that supply fats and oils in world trade in competition with U.S. exports. Oil needs to be priced cheap enough to retard competing production and make it possible for the world's poor people to afford to consume their own production. This would enable the United States to take a larger share of the import requirements of deficit areas.

The five oils—peanut, sunflower, coconut, palm kernel, and palm—compete most directly with soybean oil. They all come from plants that are produced primarily for their oilseeds. All move in volume in world trade, and all are within the same general price range. These five oils are the ones on which price changes in soybean oil can be expected to have an effect.

Production of almost all of the different kinds of fats and oils is up from prewar. The most rapid increases have been in the group designated as competing above. In the noncompeting groups, per-capita production was 12.8 pounds prewar, 11.6 pounds in 1950, and 11.8 pounds in 1956. In the competing group, production was 8.2 pounds prewar, 8.0 pounds in 1950, and 9.8 pounds in 1956. Put differently, world production of the noncompeting groups increased by 27.2 percent from 1950 to 1956, while production in the competing group increased 58.2 percent in the same period.

The current troublesome level of world production of edible fats and oils has developed since 1950 as the result of increases in production in the competing group. Production in this group continued upward at a rate greater than population growth during 1957 and 1958. Current levels of world oil prices are encouraging increases in production at a rate in excess of population growth.

It is especially interesting to note that palm kernel and palm oil production has been increasing at a very slow rate in recent years. The potential increase in palm oil production from these sources is very great. The palm trees are growing wild, and all that is needed is to harvest and market the seeds. All that stands in the way of much greater palm and palm kernel oil production is current prices that are low enough to retard harvest and marketing.

The essential point is that production of many of the world's fats and oils is price responsive. The most striking example is babassu. It is estimated that one Brazilian state alone has enough trees—if the oil from them were harvested—to produce 230 billion pounds, which is more than three times the current world production of all edible and soap fats and oils.

World exports are made up primarily of the group of oils designated as the soybean oil competing group. The difference between the competing and non-competing groups becomes more striking when we take into account the large amounts of cottonseed oil exported from the United States in 1954-56 as an aftermath of the cottonseed oil buying program.

Within the competing group, exports of soybean oil, coconut oil, peanut oil, and palm oil were up in 1956 from the 1950 level, and those of sunflower oil and palm kernel oil were down. The largest increase was in soybean oil, followed by peanut and coconut oils. Increases in world-retained production of edible fats and oils are much greater than increases in exports. That is, a high proportion of the increases in fat and oil production have been retained in the countries of production.

The significance of these comparisons is that the declining world prices of fats and oils since 1951 have caused a high proportion of the increases in production to be absorbed in the areas of production rather than moved into world trade.

What has been the effect of declining fat and oil prices since 1951? North European imports have not been affected. In that area the demand for fats and oils is extremely inelastic. The total size of the market for the world's fat and oil exports is affected only moderately by price. In southern Europe (Spain, Italy, Greece, and Turkey), consumption has been increased by price declines. Through the United States cottonseed oil sales program in 1954 and 1955 and since then through the differential pricing system of Public Law 480, prices of fats and oils have been decreased. Consumption has responded with important per-capita increases.

During the period of falling prices, imports and total supply in eastern Europe have increased. Eastern Europe and the USSR are relatively low-income, low-fat consuming areas.

Asia is an area of low incomes and low fat consumption. The failure of Asia to regain its prewar place in world exports is associated with the availability of exports from North America. It appears likely that, without the cheaper supplies from the United States, exports from Asia would have increased during the past decade.

This review of production, use, and export indicates that the price policy of the United States needs to be directed toward preventing further increases in production of peanut, sunflower, coconut, palm, and palm kernel oils. It appears that prices during recent years have succeeded in retarding production of palm and palm kernel oils. They are too high to retard the others. These are crops that are produced primarily for their oil. There is no doubt that some price level would put production of these several crops in an unprofitable position and retard or actually decrease production.

The review also indicates that cheap oil causes indigenous production to be consumed at home rather than exported. Home demand for edible fats and oils produced in Africa, South America, and Asia is sufficiently elastic to absorb much greater than current quantities of both.

By way of further example, a 23-cent-per-bushel reduction in soybean price will cost peanut growers 72 cents for an equal weight. While it is unfortunate that we are in a price war with peanut growers, the advantage lies on our side. If it is true that production of edible fats and oils is in excess of existing markets at current prices, there is not much doubt which commodity will win out.

ALTERNATIVES TO CHEAP OIL

There are alternative suggestions for maintaining U.S. oil exports. One is to expand sale for foreign currency; a second is to donate oil to charitable agencies abroad; and a third is to work out a two-price system. As short-term, one-shot operations, they are workable and have been employed with success. Whether they can be used in sufficient volume to cope with an exportable surplus of the 1958 size is questionable.

These measures will likely fail as permanent measures. The first weakness is that unquestionably they involve export dumping, and this is a practice that invites retaliatory measures that will eventually stop its effectiveness.

The sale of commodities for foreign currencies is a sophisticated dumping scheme. While the prices at which the different items are sold are nominally the same as dollar sales, the foreign currencies are not worth their nominal value. Hence prices are, in reality, reduced. This method not only differentiates between domestic and export price, but also differentiates among the prices charged to the different countries of destination. In the first place, the price is reduced only for those countries that are ruled eligible for P.L. 480 benefits. Second, the terms of the agreement vary by countries, and hence the effective price varies. Third, the different currencies have different real values so that, when all are accepted at nominal values, there are actual price differences. That the method is complicated will not permanently obscure the fact that it is export dumping.

A straight two-price system would be better than the P.L. 480 system because it would act to retard competing production and exports. But it has the disadvantage of being crude and obvious.

WHAT PRICE FOR OIL?

There is no way to estimate the level of oil prices that would be needed to enable the United States to export all of the fats and oils necessary to bring production and use into balance. Clearly, it is a price substantially lower than that of recent years. The guiding principle is to set the support price on soybeans low enough to give oil substantial downside room. The hour is late. Had we acted three or four years ago, there would have been time to experiment. Getting the support price too high gets the crop into trouble. Putting the support price below the equilibrium price has not proved harmful in the past-a support is not a ceiling when there is no surplus, as has been repeatedly shown in the case of soybeans.

During the 1957-58 crop year, the average price of soybean oil, tank cars at mid-western mills, was 10.8 cents per pound. A 20 percent reduction would be 8.6 cents. A 25 percent reduction would be 8.1 cents. A support price for soybeans, low enough to permit 8 cent oil is a good point of departure.

WHAT PRICE FOR SOYBEANS?

The support price of soybeans should be set low enough to permit 8 cent oil, $45-per-ton meal, and a processing margin wide enough to call forth a large crush. In 1957-58 soybean meal averaged $53 per ton in bulk at Decatur. With lower feed grain prices and lower livestock prices (particularly for hogs), $45 appears to be a price that will permit maximum meal market expansion.

At 8 cents, the oil fraction of a bushel of soybeans is worth 88 cents, and at $45 the meal fraction is worth $1.06, for a total of $1.94. During 1957-58 the difference between track price in Illinois of No. 1 soybeans and product values computed in the above way averaged 24 cents. During the period October 1952 to September 1957, the average difference was 15.5 cents. Say that 20 cents is allowed. For No. 1 soybeans this is a track price of $1.74 or a farm price of $1.69. The national average support price is currently 6 cents below the Illinois support price. The national average support price would thus be $1.63, scaled off for lower than No. 1 quality.

A reduction of 46 cents per bushel in the support price appears drastic. But it is justified because the situation is drastic. Very soon decisions are going to be made that will determine whether soybeans are going to return to being a commercial, competitive crop or whether they are going to become wards of the government. By historical standards a reduction of 46 cents in soybean supports has a fortunate precedent. In 1953 the support price was $2.56; in 1955 it was $2.04. The expansion in the soybean crop during the past five years was made possible by this reduction.

Chapter Fourteen

The Competitive Position of Soybeans

1959

AUTHOR'S NOTE: Exports under P.L. 480 became quite popular during the 1950s. Commodities were sold to Third World countries at current world prices, but the buyers were permitted to pay with their own currencies, which were not exchangeable for dollars. The currencies were held in the country of origin. It was a "write us a check but we won't cash it" scheme. Some of the funds were used for developmental projects, and some were used to pay for U.S. costs in the recipient country. The scheme was named "Food for Peace" and had a nice ring to it. An invitation to discuss the competitive position of soybeans provided an opportunity to label P.L. 480 for what it was: export dumping.

The soybean is two products rather than one.[1] It is a high-protein food and feedstuff and a relatively high-quality liquid oil, used for food and in industry. Virtually all of the American-produced soybeans are separated into the two component products, either in the United States or abroad. Nearly all of the meal is used as livestock feed, and about 90 percent of the oil is used as human food. The two joint products are generally equal in value.

---

1. T. A. Hieronymus is associate professor of agricultural marketing, University of Illinois. Paper presented at the Commodity Club of Chicago, April 16, 1959.

One of these two products, the protein feed, is in short supply and has a rapidly expanding market. The other, oil, is in abundant supply and has a much more slowly expanding market. In spite of the rapid increases in the size of the soybean crop, it has been very difficult to supply the market for soybean meal. Soybean oil is in burdensome surplus. During the current crop year nearly 40 percent of total U.S. fats and oils exports will be shipped under the P.L. 480 scheme of surplus disposal. This amount equals about 10 percent of the total U.S. production of edible fats and oils.

One product cannot be made without the other, so we are caught on the horns of a dilemma. Differences in market structure for the joint products make it difficult to evaluate the competitive situation. Evaluation is further complicated by the distortion caused by the oil surplus disposal program. The effect of this program has been to obscure the surplus situation.

THE POSITION OF MEAL

The fundamental strength of the meal situation is worldwide. In the world's food supply, the carbohydrates and fats are moving into a situation of abundance. Cereal grains and oilseeds are the world's basic food sources. An increasing proportion of the world's population is moving away from the specter of famine. An agricultural revolution is in progress that has enabled production to increase at an even faster rate than population. As populations, following the Western pattern of development, are brought under control, the gain will be rapid.

Much of the world now has an abundant supply of dietary basics and is concerned with upgrading the quality of the diet. The primary element in upgrading diets is the use of more protein, both directly and through animal products. This possibility points to more rapidly expanding markets for proteins than for carbohydrates and fats.

Production and use of soybean meal in the United States have expanded rapidly during the past twenty years. Production of other high-protein concentrates has increased very little, and production per protein-consuming animal unit is at the same level as it was twenty years ago. Use has not increased at the sacrifice of price. Prices of high-protein concentrates have increased in relation to feed grains in recent years. Dramatic examples of market growth have been noted in the past two years. About 12 percent more soybean meal was used in the year beginning October 1, 1957, than during the preceding year, and it was used at 12 percent higher prices. During the first half of the year beginning October 1, 1958, about 20 percent more meal was used at prices moderately higher than the year before.

How large is this potential market? Livestock numbers will increase at about the same rate as feed-grain production increases. During the past ten years, feed-grain production has increased at a rate of about 2.6 percent a year. If this rate of increase is maintained, somewhat more than a 30 percent increase in protein supplement will be required five years from now. Because soybean meal makes up only about half of the protein supplement and production of the other protein supplements is increasing slowly, soybean meal production will need to about double to maintain current rates of protein supplement feeding.

During the past ten years, substantial inventories of feed grains have been accumulated under price-support programs. If these supplies are used in the years immediately ahead, large amounts of proteins will be required to supplement them.

When we combine all three of these market growth factors (current protein deficits, increased feed-grain production, and inventory liquidation), our estimate of the market potential for soybean meal becomes fantastic. It is clear that if meal production continues to increase at the same rate in the decade ahead as it has in the past decade, the shortage of high-protein concentrates will continue. It appears that the need for meal from a billion-bushel soybean crop is less than a decade away.

THE POSITION OF OIL

Supplies of edible fats and oils are in very troublesome abundance in the United States. Fat and oil production is increasing at a much faster rate than use. Production of fats and oils other than soybean oil is stable. Therefore, increasing quantities of soybean oil are needed to maintain domestic per-capita disappearance. But these increased requirements are very small in relation to the increase in soybean oil production. Per-capita disappearance of the principal fats and oils is quite stable. Demand is extremely inelastic in current uses.

The limited domestic market for soybean oil, the expanding market for soybean meal, and the fact that one cannot be produced without the other make the export market for edible fats and oils of paramount importance to the further growth and development of the soybean industry.

The fat shortage is in the poor areas of the world. Need does not make a market. It is desire plus the ability to purchase that makes a market. But if world consumption of fats and oils in food uses is to be increased, it must be in the poor areas in the underdeveloped countries.

The poor areas of the world are also the areas that export fats and oils. It is with these areas that the United States competes. Consumption in these poor areas can be increased by reducing their exports. Price is a useful device for decreasing exports and increasing indigenous consumption. The declining world prices of fats and oils since 1951 have caused a high proportion of the increase in production to be absorbed in the areas of production rather than moved into world trade.

THE WAY OUT

The way to solve the dilemma of too little protein and too much fat is to switch from fat to protein.

In the first place, this has some implications for soybean breeding. Historically, soybeans have been bred for high oil content. As the unit value of protein increases in relation to the unit value of fat, and as more attention is paid to fiber in fabricating feeds, the breeding emphasis should be shifted. At $60 per ton, the protein content of 44 percent meal is worth 6.8 cents a pound. When we take into account the effect of export disposal programs on oil prices, we see that the unit value is nearly as high for protein as for oil at present, and perhaps higher.

But the major shift from fat to protein will be accomplished, by changing the relative production of the various oilseeds. Much of the world's fats and oils are secondary products, like lard and cottonseed oil. But more than half of the world's fats and oils are produced as primary products, from oilseeds. Chief among the oilseeds competing with soybeans are peanuts, sunflower seed, copra, and palm kernels.

Soybeans are in a strong competitive position. The advantage lies in their relatively low yield of oil and high yield of meal. The oilseed crops with which soybeans compete most directly have a much higher percentage of oil and a lower percentage of meal. Accordingly, reducing the price of oil in relation to the price of meal affects the competing seeds more than it does soybeans. For example, at current prices, reducing the price of oil by 20 percent while holding the price of meal constant would reduce the value of soybeans by 6.5 percent, peanuts by 15 percent, copra by 19 percent, and sunflower seed by 15 percent. By way of further example, a 23-cent-per-bushel reduction in soybean price would cost peanut growers 72 cents for an equal weight. Soybeans can stop further increases in production of competing oilseeds if prices are allowed to seek their own level.

DICTATES FOR PRICE AND TRADE POLICY

This way out of the dilemma has implications for U.S. price and trade policy. The soybean must be free to exploit the great strength of its competitive position. It is not now free to do so. Our export dumping schemes-specifically P.L. 480-result in an artificially high world price for fats and oils that encourages the continued expansion of production of competing oilseeds and retards the consumption of fats and oils in the poor areas of the world.

The sale of commodities for foreign currencies is a sophisticated dumping scheme. While the prices are nominally the same as dollar sales, the foreign currencies are not worth their nominal value. Hence, the price in reality is reduced. This method differentiates not only between domestic and export prices but also among the prices charged to different countries. In the first place, the price is reduced only for those countries that are ruled eligible for P.L. 480 benefits. Second, the terms of the agreements vary by countries; hence, the effective price varies. Third, the different currencies have different real values, so that, when all are accepted at nominal values, there are actual price differences. That the method is complicated will not permanently obscure the fact that it is export dumping.

In the long run, these measures will fail. First, export dumping invites retaliatory measures that eventually stop its effectiveness. Second, these measures compound an existing problem rather than contribute to its solution. And, third, they are expensive. From 1954 to mid-1958, some $4 billion worth of commodities were disposed of under P.L. 480. The immediately realized return to the United States was at most $978 million, or 24 cents on the dollar.

The soybean is in a very strong competitive position. The industry has great expansion potential. This potential cannot be realized under existing governmental policy. It cannot be realized unless P.L. 480 is eliminated.

Chapter Fifteen

Changes Needed in Futures Contracts

1959

AUTHOR'S NOTE: By 1959 futures trading in grains had recovered substantially from the suspension that existed during World War II. But trading was lethargic, and there was risk that trading would decline to negligible amounts. The primary cause was the influence of governmental price-support programs. The price-support programs for cotton had so limited price variations that the New Orleans Cotton Exchange had closed. The primary force keeping the Chicago Board of Trade in business was the soybean market, which had remained relatively free of governmental influence on price. Against this backdrop, a session of the first Agricultural Industry Forum at the University of Illinois was devoted to problems of the decreasing volume of futures trading. Officials of the Chicago Board of Trade were present and participated. The session provided an opportunity to suggest that the exchange look inward for problems other than the heavy hand of government. My recollection is that a quite vigorous discussion ensued.

In appraising the problem of a declining level of futures markets activity, we need to cast about in all directions.[1] My comments are limited in scope. The total of the causes cannot be ascribed to problems arising within the futures markets

1. T. A. Hieronymus is associate professor of agricultural marketing, University of Illinois. Paper given at the First Agricultural Industries Forum, January 1959.

mechanism. I do not want to give the impression of saying that if you will do this all of your problems will be solved; they will not.

The direction of my casting about is internal. It is a matter of introspection. We are always reluctant to consider that some of the fault may be our own. For this reason, this analysis is especially valuable. It is also valuable because it is a line along which we can take action. If we find something internally wrong with futures trading, we can correct it—that is, if the delivery terms of contracts are not the best possible, we can change them. But let us face it, the government is not going to get out of the grain business because intervention is hurting futures markets.

A second point I want to make at the outset is that I speak from a biased position. The assumption on which I have based my comments is that futures markets are useful economic institutions and that a decline in the level of futures market activity is undesirable. To me this is a quite valid assumption. My critical comments are intended to be constructive.

FUNCTIONS OF FUTURES MARKETS

In the interest of finding a common ground for discussion, some review of the fundamentals of futures trading is appropriate. Futures markets are devices for separating some of the marketing functions from others so that specialization is possible. Futures markets have evolved as devices by which the functions of risk bearing, risk financing, and the pricing of commodities are separated from the functions of storing, merchandising, conditioning, processing, etc.

The process of risk shifting and risk financing is well known and understood. The pricing responsibility of futures markets is much less well known. In fact, it is usually denied. When a hedger has shifted his risks of ownership, he is no longer interested in price level, only in price relationships and the prices of individual lots of a commodity in relation to the general level. The price level of a commodity is determined by the fundamental forces of supplies, requirements, and monetary values in the long run. But interim prices, particularly within crop seasons, are in part determined by inventory holders, by their willingness to hold or divest themselves of inventories and their reservation prices in their inventory actions. Inventory operations affect prices; speculators affect inventories, and, more important, the price levels at which inventories are carried.

In essence, futures markets are devices for facilitating specialization in risk bearing and pricing. This function is properly called speculation. A futures market is an institution designed to foster, encourage, and increase specialized commodity speculation.

The long-run level of futures market activity will be determined by

1. The need and desire of the marketing systems to shift inventory risks.

2. The effectiveness of the system in facilitating risk shifting.

3. The effectiveness of the system in maintaining specialized speculation.

To expand, or to halt the downtrend, the system must be so organized that it works to the mutual advantage of three groups of people; the risk-shifters, that is, hedgers; the facilitators, that is, brokers and scalpers; and the risk-bearers-pricers, that is, speculators.

Current declines in the level of futures activity can be traced to decreases in all three areas. Two factors are working to decrease the need and desire of inventory holders to hedge.

First, the government has taken over much of the inventory-carrying function and has tended to decrease price fluctuations by placing upper and lower limits on prices. It is easy to exaggerate both of these. In the main, the inventories that are held by government would otherwise not exist or would be held by growers. Grower inventories of grains are not usually hedged. Government activity affects hedging only to the extent that it affects stocks held by merchants and processors and by special export arrangements that reduce price risks in the exporting business. While extreme price fluctuations may have been reduced by government activities, a great deal of price variability has been generated by the caprice of government activity.

Second, the need and desire for hedging has been decreased by integration in grain marketing. As firms integrate all of the way from the country level to final consumption, they are in a position to absorb and average out price change. They become their own underwriters.

There are also potential increases in the need for risk shifting. Historically, farmers have carried most of our grain inventory risks. As farming operations become larger and a higher proportion of farm costs become variable as contrasted to fixed costs, the need to shift risks will increase. Because this is an area from which there has been so little hedging in the past, and because it is such a high proportion of the total inventory, a small increase in hedging has a big proportionate effect on the total of hedges.

The effectiveness of futures markets in facilitating risk shifting is declining. Markets are becoming less liquid. The volume of pit trading appears to be declining. Scalpers are finding it increasingly difficult to earn a living. One major cause is a decline in independent brokerage activity. The liquidity of the market has decreased as hedgers have increasingly handled and cleared their own trades.

The effectiveness of the system in maintaining specialized speculation is decreasing. Although speculation in futures contracts has not been a very profitable occupation in recent years, speculation in cash commodities has been reasonably profitable. The contrast in these two statements leads us to want to take a hard look at the futures contract itself.

WHAT IS NEEDED IN A FUTURES CONTRACT?

A futures contract must permit and enable specialization in speculation. It must successfully separate the risk-bearing and pricing functions from the other grain-marketing functions so that speculators can be speculators and nothing more. It must not be a merchandising device. Delivery must be rare. And when delivery is taken, there must not be transferred to the taker of delivery any need to merchandise. At the same time, it must be a commercially real contract, representing and thus pricing actual commodities as they exist and are used in ordinary commercial activity. A non-deliverable contract, as has been suggested at times, would be fiction and would have no real relationship to the marketing of commodities. The rights and obligations of delivery must be inviolate.

Neither of the two specialists, merchant and speculator, is doing his job when delivery is made and taken. The speculator is doing part of the job of the merchant, and specialization breaks down.

How is a contract a deliverable contract and yet one on which delivery is rarely made or taken? This is a matter of balance of contract. The contract must be such a perfect balance of advantage that both parties remain in their respective spheres of specialization and do not make or take delivery.

Essentially, the balance is between merchant-storer and speculator. Merchants are short, and speculators are long. In the context of contract considerations, we must consider the aggregate positions rather than the position opportunities of individuals. The net of hedgers' positions is almost always short. The net of speculative positions is, therefore, necessarily long. In a broader sense than futures trading, this is also true. There are inventories that must be owned, and whoever owns them is speculating on the long side of the market.

If the balance of contract terms is advantageous to one side or the other, specialization of functions cannot exist. If this specialization does not exist, the basic reason for futures cannot exist. If this specialization does not exist, the basic reason for futures trading will not exist. An institution without a basis cannot survive.

CONTRACTS ARE OUT OF BALANCE

It is my hypothesis that contracts in grain futures on the Chicago Board of Trade are out of balance in favor of merchant-storers. We are in the process of killing off one set of specialists—the speculators.

Only rarely in recent years have futures contract values got up to the going market price for the grains they purport to represent. For example, on January 21, 1959, January soybeans closed at 4½ cents less than the price of No. 1 yellow soybeans to arrive from Illinois and Indiana origin points. Last summer, with corn quite tight and stocks in Chicago negligible, No. 2 corn to arrive traded about 4 cents over the July contract until the final two or three days of trading. The March 1955 corn future expired 8 cents under the No. 2 bid to arrive price.

No. 2 corn to arrive, LP. and T.M. billing, and No. 1 yellow soybeans, high rate, Illinois and Indiana origin, are the standard commercial items of trade. If asked, "What is the Chicago price of corn and soybeans?" one should answer in terms of this kind of price.

We are trading in one kind of grain in our ordinary merchandising and processing activities. Futures markets are pricing very different items. These days it takes a very fancy squeeze indeed to force the futures price up to prevailing cash price for ordinary commercial items.

For a speculator to buy a futures contract, he must be very bullish. Suppose that on November 18, 1957, with the crop in store, a speculator decided that soybeans were cheap at $2.13 bid to Illinois farmers and so bought May futures at $2.41. By May 1, bids to farmers were up 12 cents. It would have cost a cash speculator 8¼ cents storage and about 4 cents interest. He would have just about broken even. But our specialized futures market speculator lost 14 cents. His ideas about soybean values were not bad. But he lost money because he started out trading in a standard commercial item and wound up threatened with delivery of a specialized commodity properly labeled Minnesota Out-of-Position Junk for Delivery Purpose.

Any similarity between the two was only by grace of coincidence of certain characteristics under federal grade standards.

On July 19, 1957, No. 2 oats, 36-pound test, were worth 1¼ cents more than the July future. By December 1 the same quality oats were 6⅞cents over the December price-that is, for a speculator to break even, the oats price needed to go up by the carrying charge shown in the July-December spread plus 5⅝ cents, not counting commissions. As a result of this kind of thing over the past several years, the oats pit is now occupying too much floor space. The exchange would make more money by renting the space to a peddler of candy, cigarettes, and headache powders.

For the average of the past six years, to-arrive corn on the next-to-last day of trading in the December contracts was 2.75 cents over the December future; and on the next-to-last day of trading in the May contracts, it was 4.42 cents, for a net gain on the futures of 1.67 cents plus the December-May spread.

For the average of the past four years, the to-arrive price of soybeans basis Chicago went from 1.53 cents under the November on the next-to-last day to 1.06 over the May on the next-to-last day, for a gain of 2.59 cents on the futures plus the November-May spread.

For the average of the past three years, the to-arrive price of 36-pound test oats went from 3.04 cents over the July futures on the next-to-last trading day to 6.04 cents plus the July-December spread.

These net gains tend to measure the extent of disadvantage the contracts have for speculators. Speculators cannot give away sums of this size and remain in a profit position in the long run.

ANTI-SPECULATOR BIAS

Generally speaking, futures markets have had an anti-speculator bias for a very long time. As we look at the history of governmental action regarding futures trading, four reasons stand out:

1. The courts and Congress do not understand a contract that is not intended for consummation. It appears necessary that a legal pretense be understood that, when futures contracts are created, delivery is intended. Obviously, this is not the case if the basic function of the market is to be fulfilled.

2. In the public, producer, and congressional minds, there is a feeling that speculators are evil, preying on producers, merchants, and consumers. They were once described by a prominent person as "gamblers in human misery."

3. The Congress and the CEA have always been fascinated by manipulation and have concentrated on its prevention. The period of extreme concentration on futures market legislation and regulation from 1920 to 1936 was one in which manipulation was associated with long-side speculative operations. In these deliberations, it appeared that hedgers were knights in shining armor who could do no wrong.

4. Because of these attitudes of government and the public toward speculators, the trade has defended futures trading from the numerous attacks on it by glorifying hedging and denying any effects of speculators on price behavior. How many times have we heard the statement, "The speculator has no effect on price because he must eventually sell that

which he has bought?"

The effects of these four influences have rubbed off on the way that futures markets are operated through governmental regulations and efforts of the exchanges to avoid poking a hornet's nest.

Time does not permit elaboration of the remarkable errors of these four concepts. Suffice it to say that they cannot be based on an understanding of futures trading as a system for specialized speculation. The position of the speculator needs to be strengthened. The first step in this direction is a general one. His role in the marketing system needs to be reappraised and the onus of the popular concept of evil removed from him.

The second step is to remove the position and trading limits that apply to speculators. The case for them was never reasonably proved in the first place. There are virtually no limits on anyone who has a cash position. Obviously, there is not a balance between hedgers and speculators when one is subject to position limits and the other is not. The best defense against bear-raiding of markets is a strong speculative interest. Speculators should not be forced to fight with one hand tied behind them.

CONTRACT CHANGES

The position of speculators can be strengthened by changes in the terms of delivery. The futures contract, and hence the futures price, should represent top-quality commercial commodities. They should represent the best of the commercially traded commodity, in the most advantageous location, and with the best possible freight billing associated with them.

The contract should represent a top-quality product, in most instances a U.S. No. 1. It is a shocking thing when oats are screened and the screenings shipped to Chicago so that 27-pound oats can be manufactured for delivery purposes. I am not critical of the firms that do that kind of thing. I am critical of a set of rules that permits it.

The standard commercial soybean is a No. 1. Why does the futures contract specify a No. 2? At this time the futures contract represents the lowest common denominator with regard to quality. It should represent the highest quality traded in significant volume. In such instances as the CEA requirement of trading on official grades interferes with this general principle, the exchange should work vigorously for tightening grade standards.

The exchanges permit delivery of less than contract qualities at discounts. This provision was inserted in the rules to prevent manipulation and to make corners more difficult. It is not necessary. In the first place, a corner is a pretty rugged proposition. Secondly, the world's largest grain merchant, the CCC, has an abundance of grain of all qualities available at a price. A contract should mean what it says. If it calls for No. 2 corn, it should mean precisely that.

If this suggestion that the contract should mean what it says is too much of a step to take all at once, then I suggest that the discounts be made punitive. If the normal market discount of No. 3 corn is 2 cents under No. 2, the delivery discount should be at least 6 cents. The legal principle of multiple damages is an old one. It should be applied here.

Delivery grain is very apt to be out of position. It is more apt to be in a high-tariff house than a low-tariff house. It is well and good for a house to set its own storage rates, but grain should be put on delivery at the lowest tariff existing in the market. The same principle should be applied to insurance. Instead of the current dollar limit, the limit should be approximately that of the lowest rate house. Here again the principle of the highest common denominator, rather than the lowest, should be applied.

One of the key problems in the extraordinary gain of cash corn on futures is the high cost of moving corn across town. Perhaps delivery corn should have a prepaid weighing and inspection and loading-out charge attached. This, plus a reduction in the very high cross-town switch rate, would make delivery corn contributory cargo and materially strengthen its price in relation to to-arrive corn.

The freight attached to delivery grain is a major factor in its value. The simple solution to this problem is to put all freight schedules on a ton-mile basis. It is not unlikely that freight rates are headed in that general direction. But in the meantime little can be done to improve the billing conditions of delivery grain.

In looking at freight structure, one is at a loss to understand why it costs more to move soybeans east out of Chicago than to move corn or wheat. The delivery situation in soybeans would probably be improved by a cheaper eastern rate.

The great white hope of Chicago as a delivery point is the establishment of an export rate. Such a rate would greatly increase the amount of grain that is price contributary to Chicago. At one time Chicago was the grain crossroads of the world. It no longer is. An export rate would restore this situation.

EFFECTS ON HEDGERS

That the various things suggested here are designed to strengthen the position of speculators does not mean that they are disadvantageous to hedgers. They are designed to make contracts more concisely representative of commodities trades.

They would also aid hedgers. In the first place, a market without healthy speculators is not an effective hedging medium. It is unwise to kill a goose that lays golden eggs.

In the second place, a futures market that is not representative of commercial values has an erratic basis. So long as the basis is consistently erratic in favor of hedgers, they benefit until they exhaust the existing supply of speculators. But it does not always occur that way. Years are encountered, as 1958, when most of the oats are high in test weight and the net gain of cash on futures is not obtained.

Last year we learned the basis effects of large Chicago stocks of soybeans. Until this time this crop year, the basis gain downstate soybeans has been very large. But this fancy basis may not last. The deliverable supplies this year are high-quality, Illinois origin. A brisk demand out of Chicago would break the downstate basis. In this situation a short hedge in Chicago futures is a precarious thing not conducive to sound sleeping.

The essential point is that a basis that involves something more than the going market price of storage is a capricious one and therefore not a good hedging one. We have reached the point of speculating in basis out-of-delivery considerations. It is not healthy; it can be stopped by tightening up delivery terms.

Finally, I want to make it clear that the primary basis of my concern is not the need to improve the hedgeability of the market. I rather think that, of the two major functions of futures markets, risk bearing and pricing, pricing is the more important. Risks exist and they will be assumed. The cost of getting risk carried is greater outside of a futures market complex than in it.

But the greater loss from a decrease in futures trading is in pricing. Commodity prices are speculative. The accuracy of pricing and the stability of prices is improved with a high-quality job of speculation. The quality of speculation is markedly improved by specializing in speculation.

With specialized speculation there is a much greater degree of competition in pricing than would otherwise exist. Protection of this competition is of primary concern in the storage, processing, and merchandising of grain.

Chapter Sixteen

Making Use of Basis Changes to Earn Income

1959

AUTHOR'S NOTE: The article "Making Use of Basis Changes to Earn Income" was probably the first detailed instructional statement directed toward teaching country elevator managers how to hedge. During World War II, there was no future trading in Illinois produced grains and soybeans. In the years following the war, elevators remained small and made a living from handling margins, storage for farmers and, most important, from storage of grain for the Commodity Credit Corporation. Merchandising and hedging skills had been mostly lost. Storage space increased rapidly to meet needs for storing surplus grains and, later, to accommodate the shift from harvesting and storing corn to corn combines. It involved the restructuring of the entire industry. This first effort of teaching about hedging was widely circulated among country elevators and used at area schools for elevator managers. It was followed by a long list of publications and "Basis Outlook" letters that were part of a decade-long program of teaching grain merchandising and hedging. In the process, we learned a great deal about the practicalities of hedging. The rather long and tedious paper is reproduced in full as illustrative of the effort.

There is a large and increasing amount of country elevator storage space in Illinois. Space has a cost depreciation, interest on investment, and general overhead. It must be used if its costs are to be covered and a profit realized.

Earnings from storage space are especially important at this time. Large earnings from storage space arising out of government inventory programs have been used to absorb losses arising from very narrow handling margins. Current handling margins are too narrow for all but a few elevators to operate at a profit. Space used exclusively for receiving and shipping grain cannot cover cost.

The supply of storage space appears to have caught up with requirements. Last year, the increase in carryover of corn was only 48 million bushels. It does not appear likely to be large this year. If the highly profitable government storage operations end in the near future, many elevator businesses will be hard put to show a favorable balance sheet.

Most elevator companies prefer to store grain for the accounts of farmers and government rather than for their own accounts. Storage for these accounts requires less capital and less skill and is more certain to earn a storage charge. However, a well-rounded storage program necessarily includes the use of hedges in futures markets because:

1. Only through the use of hedges can occupancy be maintained at maximum levels. An elevator must have a sufficient amount of storage space to handle the peak loads of harvests. If grain purchased and accumulated at harvest is shipped immediately after harvest, the space remains empty until the next harvest. Grain placed on store by farmers is frequently sold soon after harvest. Most of it is sold well ahead of the next harvest. If it is sold and shipped by the elevator, the space remains empty.

2. The going market price for the use of space offered by potential basis change is frequently greater than existing tariff rates. Therefore, space used to store hedged inventory will earn more than space leased to other parties.

3. A good merchandising program cannot be operated without house-controlled inventory. To realize the highest price for grain, an elevator must be in a position to withhold grain from sale when a good outlet is not available and to supply grain when a good sales opportunity is present. This is particularly true in the current period of rapidly changing rail freight rates and truck transportation.

In most literature, hedging is oversimplified. A good hedging program has certain requirements. The first is adequate capital and sources of credit. Hedged inventories must be owned and futures accounts margined. Credit for purposes of carrying hedged inventories can be obtained at a very high proportion of inventory value. However, relatively few country banks regularly finance such inventories, and for this reason it is often necessary for elevators to teach banks the rudiments of hedging or to seek alternative sources of credit.

Second, basis behavior is uncertain. When one owns an unhedged inventory, one is speculating in price. When one owns a hedged inventory, one is speculating in basis change. Because the basis change makes regular seasonal patterns, speculating in basis is much easier than speculating in prices, but to trade basis successfully requires knowledge, skills, and constant, thorough attention. The use of basis offers opportunity for substantial rewards, but not without the cost of substantial effort.

HEDGES ILLUSTRATED

To hedge is to assume a position in futures equal and opposite to an already existing cash position. One is either long cash and short futures or short cash and long futures. Hedges should be set up on a "T" account system, with one side of the account for cash and the other for futures. Very rarely will a country elevator make, and never will a country elevator take, delivery. Accordingly, the two accounts should be kept separate—cash transactions always closed out with subsequent cash transactions, and futures transactions with subsequent futures transactions.

Cash prices should be entered in the hedging account at selling prices rather than buying prices-that is, the amount of the handling margin should not be entered in the hedging account. If com is purchased at $1.07 on a 3-cent margin and hedged, it should be shown in the hedging account as purchased at $1.10.

Positions cannot be precisely balanced. Futures trading is done in contract lots of 5,000 bushels and job lots of 1,000 bushels. Hedges are always somewhat out of balance. The imbalance can be either long or short, as the hedger elects. It need not ever exceed 500 bushels.

Illustration 1 shows a cash inventory hedged in futures. There was a gain of 10 cents a bushel on the cash and a loss of 5 cents on futures before commissions. (Commission is roughly ⅜ cent per bushel for nonmembers.)

ILLUSTRATION 1

DATE	CASH ACCOUNT		FUTURES ACCOUNT	
Oct. 10	Bought 10,000 bushels	$1.00	Sold 10,000 bushels Dec.	$1.15
Nov. 15	Sold 10,000 bushels	$1.10	Bought 10,000 bushels Dec.	$1.20
		$0.10		-$0.05
		Gain $0.05		

Illustration 2 shows a short cash position hedged in futures. This hypothetical hedge was placed ahead of harvest and shows a cash gain of 12 cents and a futures loss of 7 cents.

ILLUSTRATION 2

DATE	CASH ACCOUNT		FUTURES ACCOUNT	
Aug. 15	Sold 30,000 bushels	$2.17	Bought 30,000 bushels	$2.29
Sept. 15	Bought 30,000 bushels	$2.05	Sold 30,000 bushels	$2.22
		$0.12		-$0.07
		Gain $0.05		

Illustration 3 shows how a hedge is moved forward as the delivery month in which the hedge was originally placed approaches.

ILLUSTRATION 3

DATE	CASH ACCOUNT		FUTURES ACCOUNT		
Oct. 15	Bought 50,000 bushels	$1.00	Sold 50,000 bushels Dec.	$1.18	
Nov. 25			Bought 50,000 bushels Dec.	$1.22	-$0.04
Nov. 25			Sold 50,000 bushels May	$1.29	
April 15	Sold 50,000 bushels	$1.29	Bought 50,000 bushels May	$1.34	-$0.05
		$0.29			-$0.09
		Gain $0.20			

Hedges should not be thought of as being placed and removed at specific prices. The hedges must be thought of in terms of basis. In Illustration 1, the cash was bought at 15 cents under and sold at 10 cents under for a gain of 5 cents. In Illustration 2, the cash was sold at 12 under and bought at 17 under for a gain of 5 cents. In Illustration 3, the cash was bought at 18 under the December future, the hedge moved forward at a May premium of 7 cents, and the cash was sold at 5 under for a gain of 13 cents plus 7 cents, or a total of 20 cents.

There are two reasons for thinking in terms of basis rather than price: (1) the arithmetic is much simpler; and (2) the hedger is concerned about basis rather than price. When he hedges, he decides not to speculate in price. When he thinks in terms of basis, he is helped to remember that price is no concern to him. If he thinks in terms of price, he is likely to regard all three illustrated hedges as losing money. True, in all three instances, more money would have been made by speculating in cash than in hedging. However, the hedges, per se, were successful.

SOYBEAN CHARTS

Following are basis charts for soybeans for the past five marketing seasons. The cash price of soybeans used was on track east-central Illinois shipping points. The cash price was plotted in relation to the November futures price until the last trading day in September—that is, if on October 1 the cash price was $2.40 and the November future was $2.55, the plot was made at 15 under the November. The line for the May future was located above the November future by the difference existing on the last trading day in September. As one can see from examining the different charts, this difference changed from year to year.

The charts are thus oversimplified. They assume that prior to November 1 all hedges are placed in the November future and that they are shifted to May future at the end of October. In actual practice, the hedger has a choice of futures to hedge in and to shift to. What he does will depend on what he expects to happen to the existing spreads as well as basis to fully exploit hedging potential.

-4-

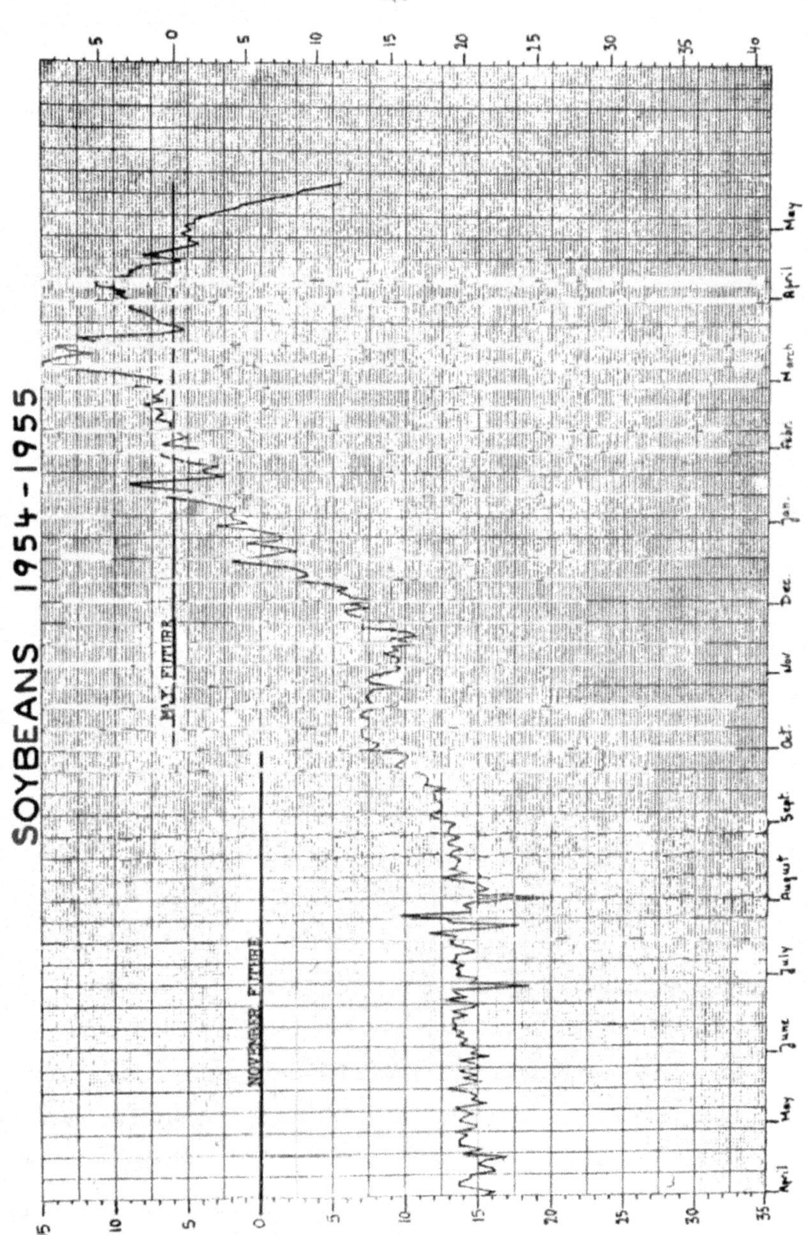
SOYBEANS 1954-1955
MAY FUTURE
NOVEMBER FUTURE
April
May
June
July
August
Sept.
Oct.
Nov
Dec.
Jan.
Febr.
March
April
May

-5-

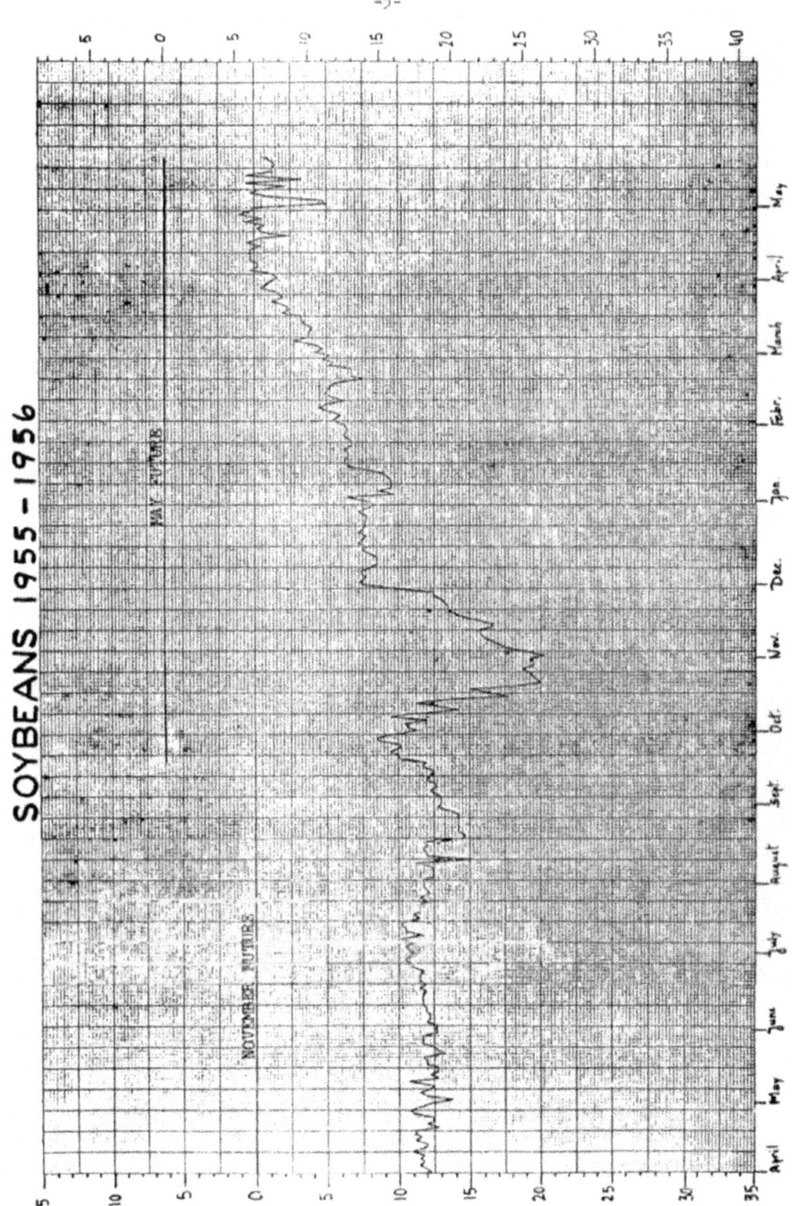
SOYBEANS 1955 - 1956
MAY FUTURE
NOVEMBER FUTURE
April
May
June
July
August
Sept.
Oct.
Nov.
Dec.
Jan.
Febr.
March
April
May

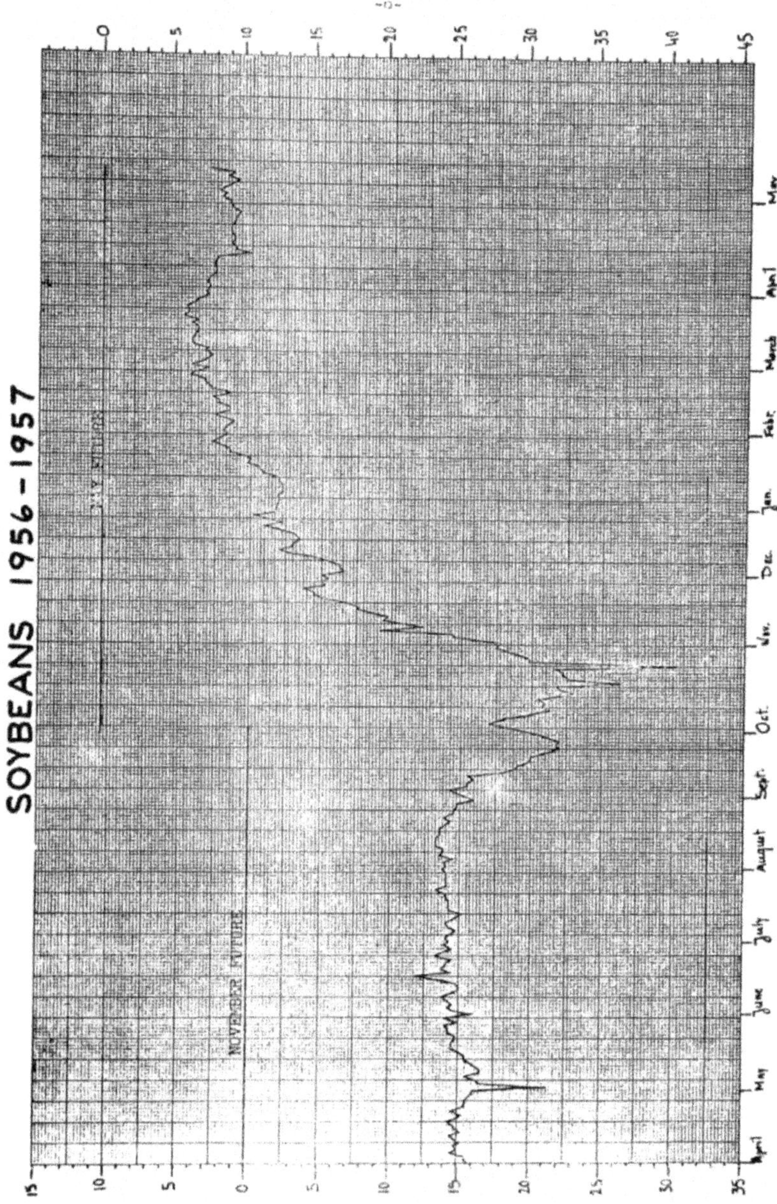
SOYBEANS 1956 - 1957
MAY FUTURE
NOVEMBER FUTURE
April
May
June
July
August
Sept.
Oct.
Nov.
Dec.
Jan.
Feb.
March
April
May

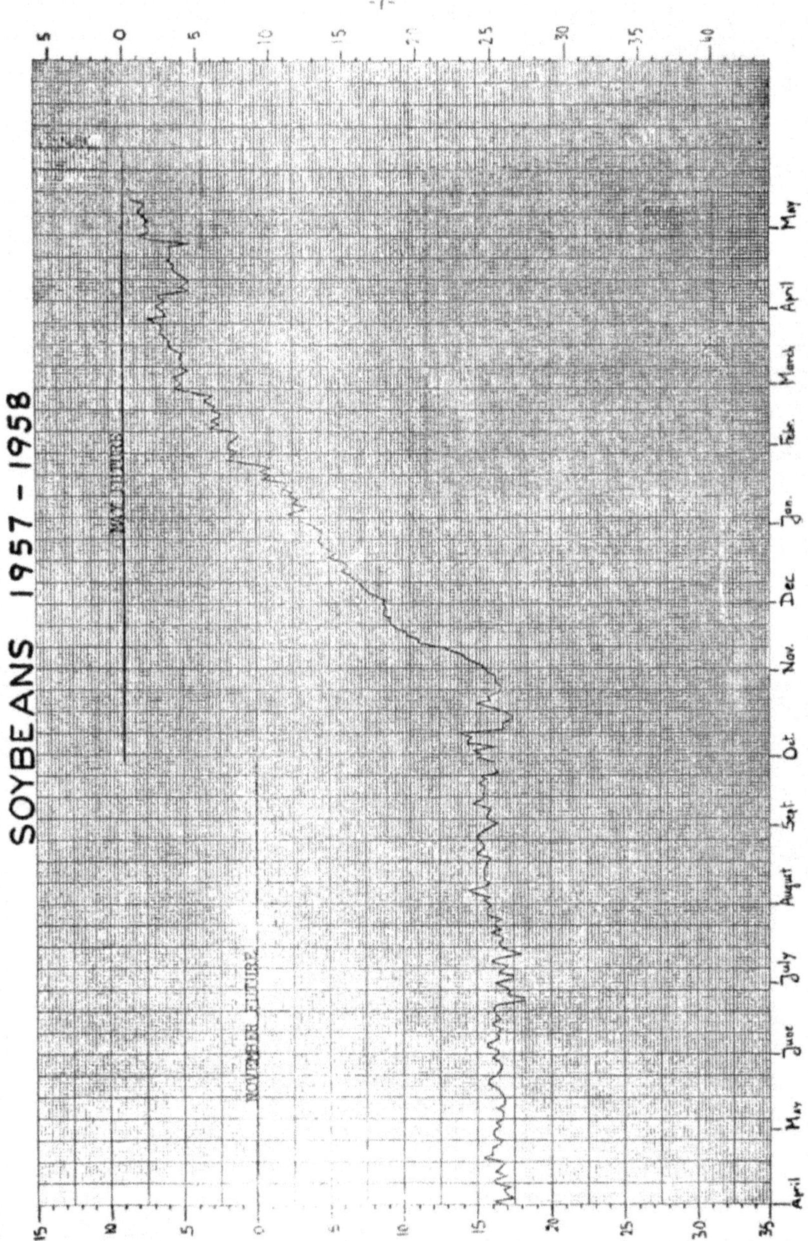
-7-
SOYBEANS 1957 - 1958
MAY FUTURE
NOVEMBER FUTURE
April
May
June
July
August
Sept
Oct.
Nov.
Dec
Jan.
Feb.
March
April
May

-8-

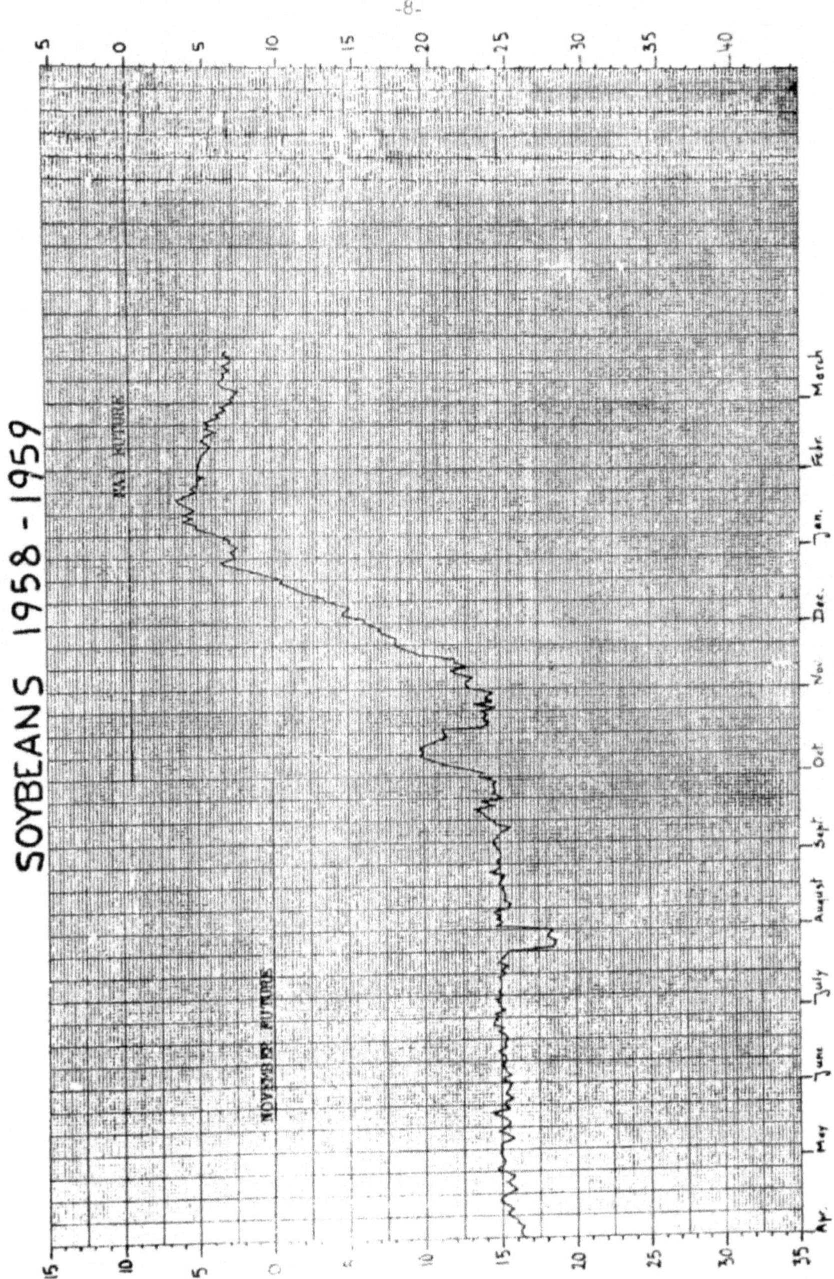
SOYBEANS 1958 - 1959
MAY FUTURE
NOVEMBER FUTURE
Apr. May June July August Sept Oct Nov Dec. Jan. Febr. March

1954-55

The first of the years shown is the most troublesome of the series. The basis was fairly stable at 13 to 15 cents under the November until the start of harvest. The basis narrowed during harvest. There was a vigorous holding movement by farmers that year and storage space was quite adequate to hold the crop. As a result, the available space was large in relation to the market supply of soybeans to put into it. The going price of storage, as indicated by the basis, went down, i.e., the basis narrowed. The basis was fairly stable to widening until the latter part of November, when it narrowed at a fairly rapid rate.

It is unusual for the basis to go above the May future, as it did from January through April. By May it had widened to an unusual discount in relation to the May. Why? The chart would appear more rational had the delivery months of January and March been included. The supply of soybeans at the delivery point, Chicago, did not build up to any appreciable size at harvest and subsequently was reduced to quite low levels. At the same time, the crop was substantially larger than the year before and generally judged to be more than adequate to meet all requirements. Throughout the year there was a chronic market shortage in the midst of plenty. The January future went to a substantial premium over the March future, the March to a premium over the May, and the May to a premium over the July. The market was saying through this succession of premiums, "There are plenty of soybeans, so an increase in price level is not justified, but more of them are needed now. In this situation, we must charge you for the privilege of storing rather than pay you for storing. Please sell now." When the May future became the current delivery month, the very small stock at Chicago forced the Chicago price (May future) up in relation to downstate price. This was the cause of the 20-cent basis loss from March to May.

1955-56

In the second year of the series, the preharvest basis was fairly stable at 10 to 12 cents. Just before harvest it widened to 15 cents and then narrowed to about 8 cents during harvest; then it collapsed to 20 cents under the November and 26 cents under the May, followed by a fast recovery to 15 under the May and a gradual rise to 6 under during May. Except for the harvest narrowing followed by the post-harvest collapse, this is a nice basis pattern, returning about 12 cents for the season's storage. If played correctly, the basis had a potential of about 20 cents. Why did it behave as it did?

The basis started strong as a result of the very narrow basis the preceding year. In early August, the potential yield per acre was estimated at nearly 23 bushels, sharply larger than the preceding year's 18 bushels. Note the accompanying widening of the basis. The crop deteriorated, accounting for the basis run-up during harvest. The price of soybeans increased sharply in September to a price that seemed high in view of the crop size and in relation to the loan. Farmers sold heavily, widening the basis. As soon as the crop was put away, the basis narrowed quickly some 14 cents during the month of November. The cash price of soybeans was stable during November. The narrowing of the basis was the result of a decline in futures.

1956-57

In the third year of the series, the basis was a stable 15 cents a bushel in the preharvest period. The acreage of soybeans was up 2.8 million acres, which was above average. The basis widened throughout harvest, reaching an extreme of 40 cents under the May at the end of harvest. The average during harvest was 28 to 30 cents under the May. It eventually went to about 7 cents under the May. A very high price was offered for storage in the fall of 1956. Note, also, that May was more than 10 cents over the November on October 1. After October 1, the cash price went up and the futures down.

1957-58

In the fourth year, the basis stayed between 15 and 17 under the November, slightly wider than during the preceding year. The November to May spread was 9 cents a bushel on October 1. Again, crop size was substantially larger than in the preceding year, but by 1957 a large amount of new storage space had been built, and the crop was taken care of without great difficulty.

The track country station price rose unusually high in relation to the May futures for a year in which the May future was continually at a premium over the March and at a discount under the July future. This was the result of a large stock of soybeans of very ordinary quality at Chicago. This stock kept forcing relatively large carrying charges between futures at Chicago and kept the price at Chicago low in relation to the downstate price. All of the 1957-crop soybeans were used up in Illinois. They were not used in Iowa and Minnesota. This tended to make Iowa and Minnesota tributary to Chicago, with Illinois at a high premium.

1958-59

This brings us to the current year's chart which is, of course, incomplete. The general pattern has been similar to 1957-58 except that further additions to storage have resulted in a stronger preharvest basis and substantial strength at harvest. During harvest, there was a strong holding movement by farmers, making it appear as if processors' storage bins would not be filled. This movement accounts for the 5-cent basis increase during harvest. But the crop turned out to be so large that everyone ran out of space, and the basis went back to its earlier level before the harvest ended.

The one-week break in basis in late July was the result of the crisis that occurred in the Middle East. Futures prices are more sensitive to events of this kind than are cash prices. When there is a sharp change in futures as the result of a single event, cash lags behind in making the adjustment, but it almost always catches up. In such cases, the best sale of cash grain is a hedge in futures.

Note that the November to May spread was on the general order of 10 cents a bushel. Again, a large stock of soybeans accumulated at Chicago.

The post-harvest basis gain was faster than usual, the cash reaching 5 under the May by early January. The basis has since widened. Last fall many farmers sold their elevator-stored soybeans as soon as the price reached $2. This occurred in mid-November. Note that from December 1 to January 15, the basis gain amounted to 12 cents. Elevators that sold and shipped the storage soybeans that they bought in the second half of November sat with empty space that earned nothing. Those who hedged have a 10- to 12-cent profit. The only extra cost was interest.

Where will the basis go from here? There is a large stock of soybeans at Chicago. It looks as if all of the soybeans in Illinois will be used up before harvest. These two factors suggest that the basis will narrow, but soybeans at Chicago are of higher quality this year than last. Further, the bulk of them are needed to meet Chicago processing requirements and export sales. It may finally become necessary to pull CCC-owned soybeans from Iowa and Minnesota. This would pull Chicago up in relation to downstate Illinois.

The basis will probably not get as narrow as last year, and there is a fair chance that it will widen in June and July. I would unhedge at 5 under the May and drop out.

SOYBEAN CONCLUSIONS AND RULES

These several charts of soybean basis lead us to some conclusions and rules about hedging:

1. The basis from harvest to late season was about as follows:

1954-55 ... 24 cents

1955-56 ... 15 cents

1956-57 ... 20 cents

1957-58 ... 21 cents

These gains should not be taken as a long-term expectation for the future. The amount of basis gain will reflect the interrelationship of supply and demand for storage. If the amount of storage increases in relation to the need for it in the future, the amount of basis gain will decrease. The amount of basis gain will be generally in line with other storage revenue arrangements. It is larger because costs are higher (interest on investment in inventory in particular) and because it is less certain.

The primary value of hedging to country elevators lies in the possibilities of increasing the percent of occupancy of storage facilities.

2. Generally speaking, the considerations that result in a small basis gain result in a large gain from speculating in cash soybeans, and vice versa. There is no chance for a large profit from hedging as there is from speculating in cash. At the same time, there is no chance of loss from hedging so long as the hedging basis is

greater than the cost of making delivery, which almost always is the case at harvest. Basis gains have averaged less than speculative gains during the past five years. At the same time, basis gains have exceeded speculative gains more than half of the time.

For comparison of hedging and cash speculation, it was assumed that hedges were placed in the May future on October 15 and removed on April 15. By years, the data and results were as follows:

	October 15		April 15			CASH GAIN
YEAR	CASH	FUTURES	CASH	FUTURES	BASIS GAIN	(LOSS)
1954-55	272	285 ¼	252	250	+14 ¼	-20
1955-56	217	236 ¾	281 ½	287 ½	+13 ¾	+64 ½
1956-57	216	248 ½	233	241 ⅛	+24 ⅜	+17
1957-58	216	241 ⅞	228	232	+21 ⅛	+12
1958-59	202 ½	223 ½	221 ½	226 ⅜	+16 ⅛	+19

Note the tendency toward an inverse relationship of basis gain and an increase in cash price. Because stocks are large, the basis gain tends to be large and the increase in the cash price less.

3. Obviously, one does not want to get short the basis after harvest except as it may be necessary for very short periods. Sometimes, elevators inquire about substituting futures for farmers' soybeans that are in storage when storage space runs out. All questions of legality aside, it does not pay. The cash gain on the futures is greater than the going farmer storage rate.

4. Hedges placed after the harvest is complete and the crop is put away do not earn as much per day of storage as hedges placed during harvest because the period of most rapid basis gain is immediately following harvest. However, hedges placed after harvest are more profitable than empty space.

5. The November-May futures spread varies from year-to-year. It tends to widen when stocks of soybeans at Chicago are large. Ten cents is a full carrying charge; that is, tariff rates plus interest and insurance are about 10 cents for six months. When spreads in futures approach a full carrying charge and stocks at Chicago are fairly large, hedges should be placed in nearby futures. There is a marked tendency for spreads to be greater at harvest than later in the season. Accordingly, it usually pays to hedge in the more distant futures.

6. A preharvest basis of 15 cents is normal. When the crop is smaller than expected early; that is, when it is adversely affected by weather, etc., the basis narrows into harvest. When the crop appears to be going backward, place hedges that are designed to earn storage early. When the crop develops favorably and is larger than expected, the basis widens into harvest. In this situation, place hedges late in the harvest period.

7. The track country station price usually gains to about 5 under the May futures. The basis on May is highly variable and depends on the Chicago stock and disappearance situation. It usually pays to remove hedges at any time the track price gets within 5 cents of the May futures unless there is some good reason for expecting further narrowing.

8. Hedges should not be taken into the delivery month except when the hedger is quite skilled. The basis during the delivery month is affected by actions of terminal merchants. Basis behavior in the delivery month frequently is erratic. The country hedger is in a disadvantageous position.

9. A preharvest basis as narrow as 10 cents can be sold except when the crop is deteriorating badly. Elevators can expect to profit by selling cash soybeans for harvest delivery and buying November futures with excellent chances of being able to cover the cash position and sell futures at a wider basis at harvest.

10. For inventories to be stored and hedged, the elevator should try to average the basis down from 15 cents. The elevator must buy, store, and hedge when farmers sell. How much choice one has regarding when to hedge depends upon how large harvest purchases are in relation to available space. If harvest purchases are twice as large as the amount the elevator has to store and hedge, there is a 50 percent selectivity, etc. It is almost always necessary to average. It is also prudent. The best time to hedge cannot be selected and could not be executed if it could be selected.

CORN CHARTS

The following five corn charts are organized in the same way as the soybean charts except that December and July futures were used. The price was track country station. The change in July futures was made on October 31.

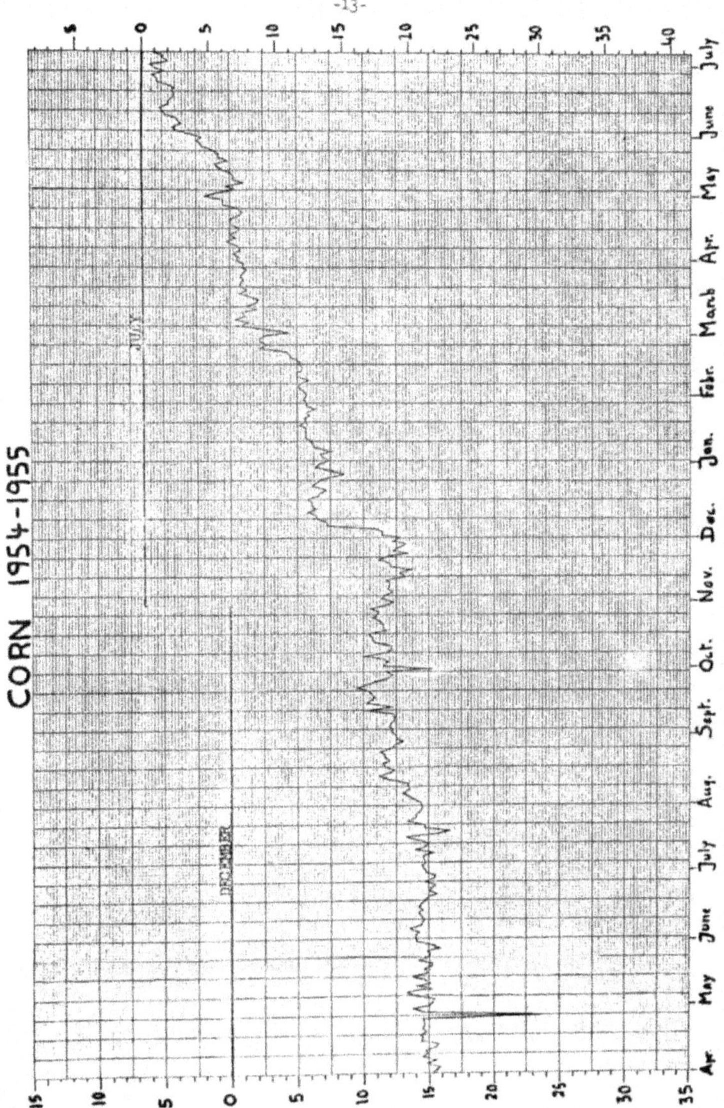
-13-
CORN 1954-1955
JULY
DECEMBER
Apr. May June July Aug. Sept. Oct. Nov. Dec. Jan. Febr. March Apr. May June July
15 10 5 0 5 10 15 20 25 30 35
5 0 5 10 15 20 25 30 35 40

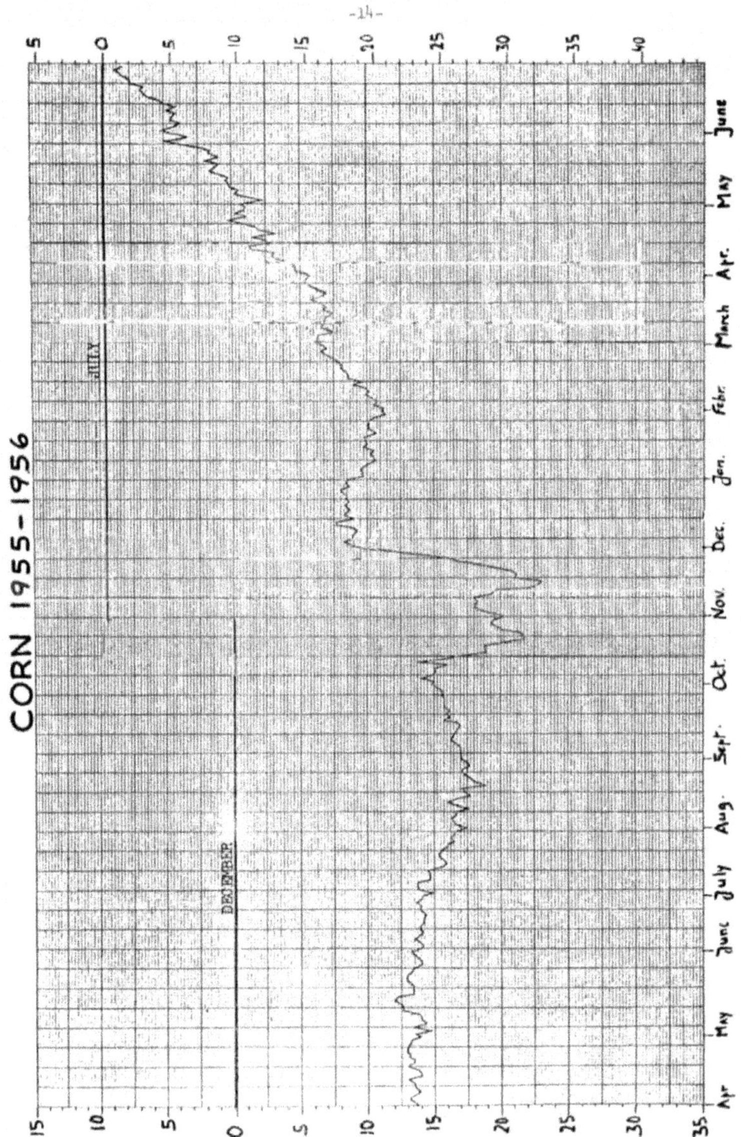
-14-
CORN 1955-1956
JULY
DECEMBER
Apr
May
June
July
Aug.
Sept.
Oct.
Nov.
Dec.
Jan.
Febr.
March
Apr.
May
June

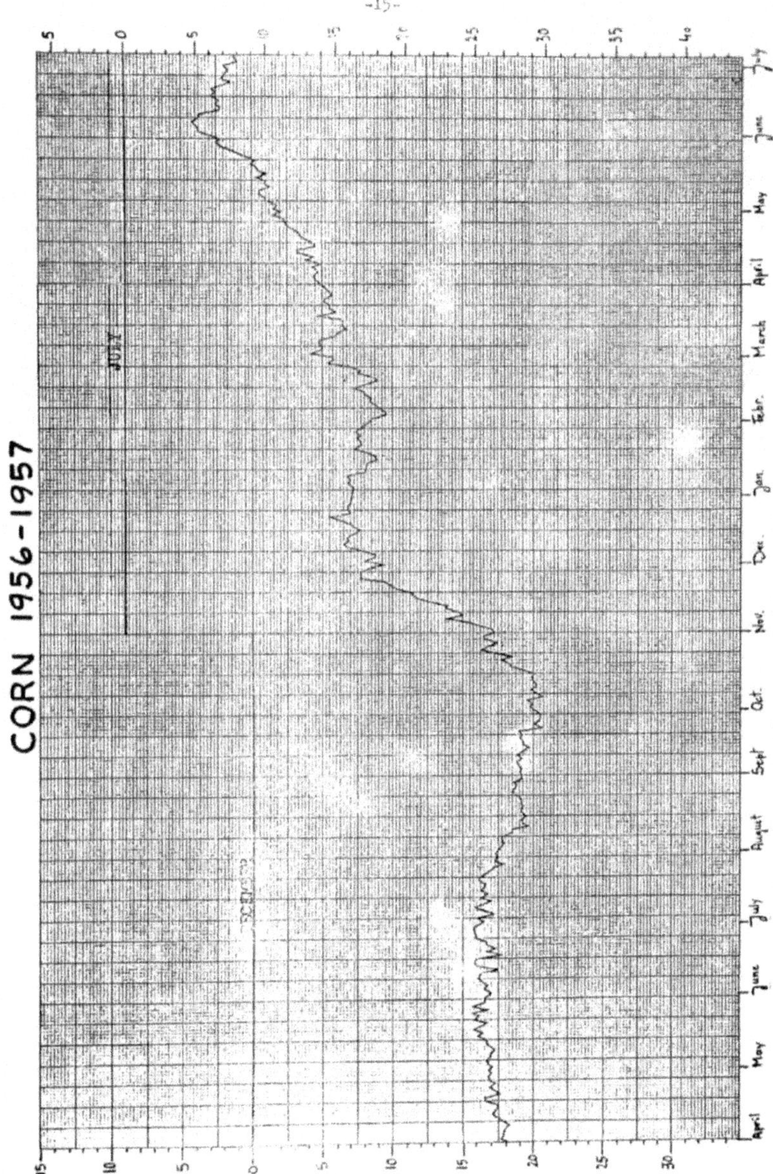
-15-
CORN 1956-1957
JULY
April
May
June
July
August
Sept
Oct.
Nov.
Dec.
Jan.
Febr.
March
April
May
June
July

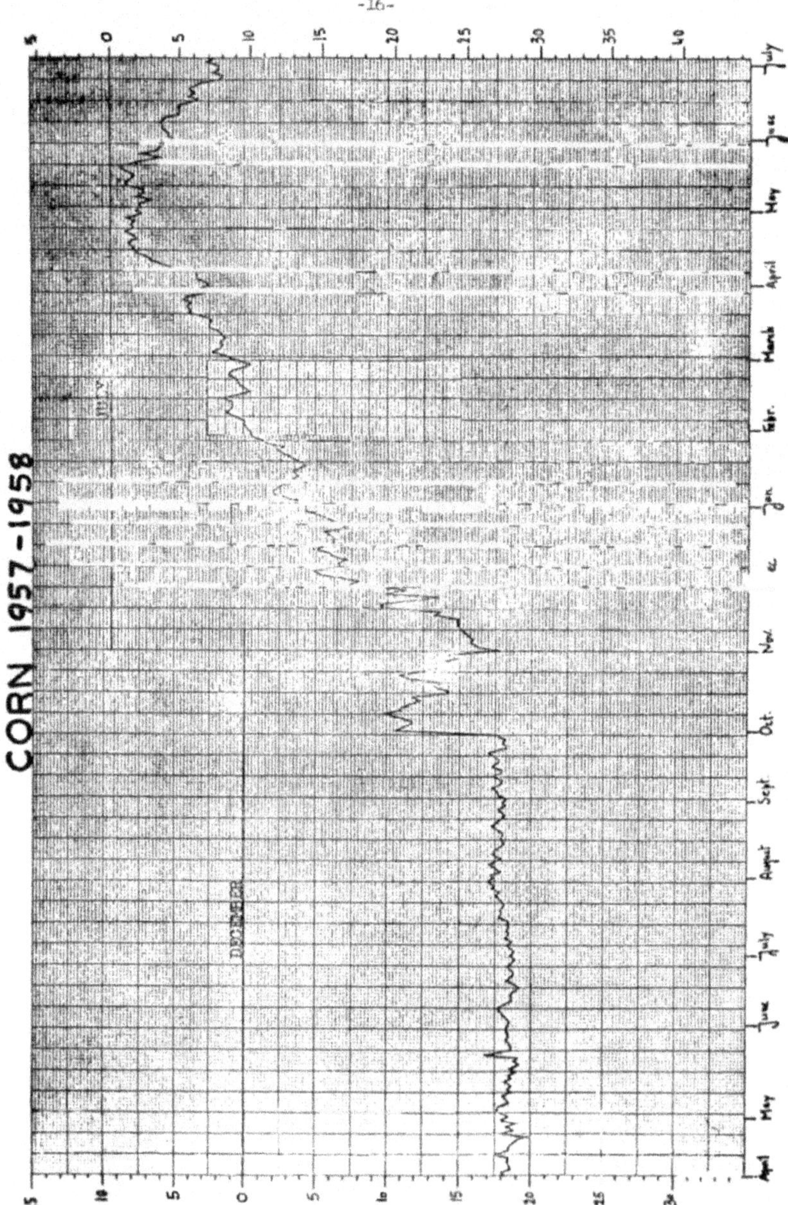
-16-
CORN 1957-1958
DECEMBER
JULY
April
May
June
July
August
Sept.
Oct.
Nov.
Jan.
Febr.
March
April
May
June
July

-17-

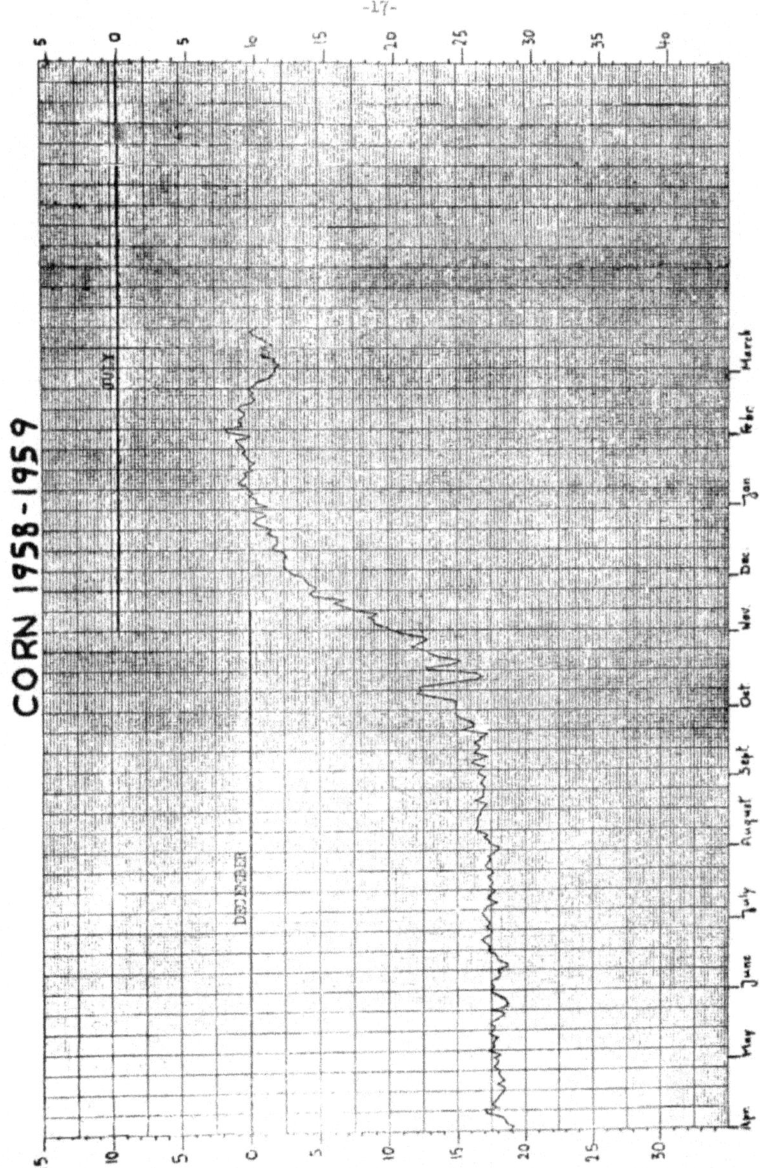
CORN 1958-1959
JULY
DECEMBER
Apr.
May
June
July
August
Sept.
Oct.
Nov.
Dec.
Jan
Febr.
March

1954-55

The spring and early summer basis in 1954 was stable at 15 cents. The moderate strength into and through harvest was the result of a decrease in estimated crop yield from 41.3 bushels as of July 1 to 35.2 bushels as of August 1. There was a sharp post-harvest basis gain of 5 cents, followed by a gradual basis gain of 13 cents. The December-July difference was 6½ cents at the end of October.

1955-56

In the second year of the series, the basis started at 15 cents and gradually widened until harvest, at which time there was a decline of about 7 cents. Post-harvest recovery was very rapid, the basis gain amounting to 13 cents in two weeks. There then followed a gradual gain of about 18 cents to the end of the season. It should be noted that during the five months beginning February 1 the basis gain amounted to 19 cents, or about 4 cents a month. The December-July switch was 9 cents.

1956-57

Here is a nearly classic basis pattern: 17 cents until harvest, widening to 20 cents during harvest; a quick narrowing immediately after harvest; and a gradual basis gain during the rest of the year. The February 1 to July 1 basis gain was about 12 cents, or 2½ cents a month. The December-July switch was 9 cents.

1957-58

The basis was a very stable 18 cents until harvest. A lot of corn sold for early harvest shipment and could not be bought. The result was a sharp basis gain at the outset of harvest. As harvest expanded, farmers sold the crib overrun, putting the basis back to its earlier level. After harvest, the only unusual development was a widening of basis in June and July due to extremely small stocks of nongovernment corn in Chicago. The Chicago price had to go high enough to draw corn out of Iowa for local processing and shipping.

1958-59

We seem to be in another classic year. The market accurately forecast the harvest basis throughout the spring and summer. The basis made a nice rise immediately after harvest, and the December and July spread was 9 cents at the end of October. The basis is now about 10 cents under July. Where is it going? Some further strengthening is a reasonable expectation. The non-high-loan corn appears to be fairly well cleaned up. Chicago free stocks are substantially above year-ago levels. There is an excellent shipping demand from Chicago. The basis will probably be within 5 cents of July corn.

CORN CONCLUSIONS AND RULES

The series of corn charts leads us to some conclusions and the establishment of some rules:

1. The basis gain from harvest to late season was about as follows:

1954-55 ... 15 cents
1955-56 ... 23 cents
1956-57 ... 22 cents
1957-58 ... 23 cents
1958-59 ... 16 cents to date

Basis gains similar to those of the past few years have a better chance of prevailing in the future for corn than for soybeans. Corn is harder to store than soybeans. It is likely that there will be an increased demand for off-farm storage of corn in the future as the use of picker-shellers and the grain bank expand.

2. For comparison of hedging and cash speculation, it was assumed that hedgers were placed in the July future on November 1 and removed on July 1. The data and results were as follows:

	November 1		July 1			CASH GAIN
YEAR	CASH	FUTURES	CASH	FUTURES	BASIS GAIN	(LOSS)
1954-55	143	162⅞	141½	142⅛	+19¼	-1½
1955-56	109½	139⅛	147	148⅝	18	+ 37½
1956-57	122	148¼	122½	129½	+18¼	+ ½
1957-58	103½	128¼	127½	135⅛	+17⅛	24
				(April 23)		
1958-59	97½	129½	118½	125⅝	+15⅞	21

The average basis gain was slightly larger than the average cash gain. The result was much more consistent. Again, the smallest basis gains tend to be associated with the largest cash gains and vice versa.

3. The same comments about going about the basis apply to corn as applied to soybeans.

4. The corn basis gain after the first of the year is generally quite substantial. It exceeds the usual custom storage rates by a wide margin and offers an opportunity to use otherwise empty space.

5. In recent years, there has been an opportunity to switch hedges from December to July futures at about a full carrying charge. This difference tends to be widest at harvest.

6. A preseason basis of 15 to 20 cents appears to be normal. It is influenced by the prospective crop.

7. The basis tends to gain to about 5 cents under the July. It is fairly safe to take hedges into July except when Chicago free stocks of corn are below 4 million bushels. However, 5 under the July is a good selling basis.

8. A preharvest basis of 12 cents can be sold except as the crop is deteriorating badly. The amount sold and the commitment for time of delivery must be based on the amount and timing of elevator purchases. The elevator must study the history of its own purchases, as these vary substantially by localities.

9. For inventories to be stored and hedged, the elevator should try to average the basis down from 20 cents. Purchases made from the middle to the end of harvest are usually the most profitable.

GENERAL CONCLUSION

Two points stand out: (1) the use of basis offers an opportunity to handsomely supplement country elevator income by making advantageous sales of cash grain, by increasing the average per-bushel storage rate, and by increasing the average rate of occupancy of space; and (2) careful study, strong capitalization, and skill in caring for cash grain are essential in a hedging program.

Chapter Seventeen

A Comment on Soybean Price Supports

1961

AUTHOR'S NOTE: "A Comment on Soybean Price Supports" was written on March 16, 1961, in response to a proposal of then Secretary of Agriculture Freeman. It was a sort of "here we go again" statement and was directed at the public, farmers, and farm organizations. It received rather wide circulation; some responses were "Amen," and others, "But we need high price supports in order to get a fair living for family farms." A good time was had by all.

Secretary of Agriculture Freeman has said that he intends to increase the support price for soybeans to $2.30 regardless of whether new feed-grain legislation is passed.[1] Raising the soybean price support would be a serious mistake. It is hoped that some reflection will lead him to change his mind.

There have been two major downward adjustments in the soybean price support. It was reduced from $2.56 for the 1953 crop to $2.22 for the 1954 crop and from $2.09 for the 1958 crop to $1.85 for the 1959 and 1960 crops.

The reduction made in early 1954 was in anticipation of a major increase in soybean acreage as the result of imposition of allotments on corn, wheat, cotton, and rice acreage. In the October 1953 *Soybean Digest* I wrote,

---

1. T. A. Hieronymus is professor of agricultural marketing, University of Illinois.

> It is not possible to accurately forecast the price effects, both short and long run, that an increase of 100 million bushels of soybeans would have. Taking the several factors into account and assuming a constant to growing livestock population and a constant level of consumer income, it appears that a decline of about 15 percent in the price would keep a large stock of soybeans from development; that is to say that a support price of 75 percent of parity would likely preserve an essentially free market for soybeans; would allow farmers to avoid acreage restrictions on soybeans... The choice to be made is fairly clear. If soybeans are supported at 90 percent of parity, there will likely be a sharp increase in acreage. Farmers with storage will receive a high price for a big crop. But the following year it will be necessary to restrict acreage and there will be a price-depressing surplus overhanging the market... If soybeans are supported at 75 percent of parity ($2.10), the increase in acres planted will likely be less. Returns from soybeans will likely be less the first year. Farmers will be able to keep productive land in high-value crops.

The choice was made in favor of lower price supports. Organizations representing soybean producers took the initiative and petitioned the USDA for a reduction in price supports.

The reduction in early 1959 was the result of the likely accumulation of a modest surplus in the hands of CCC from the very large 1958 crop. In the January 1959 *Soybean Digest*, I wrote,

> Soybeans are in trouble. There is not a large enough market to absorb current production at current prices. We are faced with the need to find larger markets or reduce production. This must be done now or government inventories will be built up. The example of other crops—corn and wheat in particular-is sufficient to prove the need for immediate action and underscore the futility

> of remedies taken too late or in half steps. The soybean industry should take its medicine now and should take a large enough dose to effect a cure.

> The soybean markets, export and domestic, are expanding rapidly enough to absorb current production increases, and the expansion can be continued for the indefinite future. If the expanding need for high-protein concentrates is to be met, there must be further expansion of soybean production. The trouble lies with the oil fr action... Soybeans must be allowed to sell at prices that will permit the continued expansion of the market for soybean meal and that will permit oil to compete effectively with other fats and oils for the existing world market.

Again, organizations representing soybean producers went in with a request for a reduction in the support price.

There was a carryover of 62 million bushels on October 1, 1959, of which CCC owned approximately 43 million. CCC has since sold its entire inventory at substantially higher support prices.

The growth in the market for soybeans has been tremendous. The total disappearance during the 1953-54 crop year was 278 million bushels. Disappearance during the 1959-60 crop year was 572 million, more than doubling in six years. Disappearance in 1960-61 will be about 570 million but limited to this amount by the supply available. The price, at the moment of this writing, is $2.76 bid to east-central Illinois farmers. The loan is $1.91.

A soybean supply essentially double that of ten years ago is a shortage! The wisdom of the policy that was initiated by soybean producers and executed by the USDA during the period 1954-61 is incontrovertible. It is extremely difficult to argue with success, particularly in an agricultural world as messed up as today's.

The essence of the policy has been to maintain a price support low enough that competitive market prices guided and regulated production and use of soybeans. The record proves the wisdom of this policy. I put a simple proposition, now proved: The wisdom of the marketplace is greater than that of government; therefore, the soybean industry can do a better job of directing production and use of soybeans than can governmental employees. However competent they may be, I cannot, in my egotism, but doubt that they are not, in these matters, but little more competent than I; and as a forecaster, I have assaulted the wisdom of the marketplace a sufficient number of times to gain a considerable regard for it.

The rationalization for an increase in the soybean support price is that we need more soybeans and farmers should be encourage to plant a larger acreage in 1961. I heartily agree that a larger acreage is called for in 1961. But there are other and better ways to encourage an acreage increase than with an increase in the support price.

There will be a larger acreage in 1961; this is true whether the price support is raised, held the same, or eliminated. It is not just the government that is saying we need more-the market is saying it as well. November soybean futures at the moment that this is written are $2.47. Last fall the bids to farmers were 13 cents under the November. The market guide to farmers planting is $2.34. The bids for 1961 crop corn are $1.00. The market's ratio is 2.34. A competitive price system does its job.

The reaction of farmers to the suggested $2.30 support is worth special note. I have had my ear fairly close to the ground in this matter. In Illinois an overwhelming majority of soybean producers think an increase in the support to $2.30 would be unwise. They clearly understand the difference between policies that have been applied to soybeans and other crops and are fully aware of the differences in results. We are now seeing the interesting situation in which the best way to lose farmer support is to suggest an increase in the support price! I rather suspect the best agricultural economists these days are farmers.

Chapter Eighteen

Agricultural Supply Management

1962

AUTHOR'S NOTE: This paper was a convoluted exercise in the use of an invitation to address one topic—to vent my dislike for the then popular price and income support programs. My recollection is that the talk was given at a dinner meeting held in the ballroom of the Waldorf Astoria with a large and influential audience. I did not have a recognized claim to expertise in matters pertaining to general agricultural policy, but the sorting out of the impacts of various price and control programs had led me to negative conclusions about existing and proposed programs. I constructed an opportunity to put current programs in broad perspective. My honorarium was an expense account that included transportation for my wife and tickets to the Broadway presentation of "The Sound of Music." Would that my comments had found as large an audience as "The Sound of Music."

We are starting this evening's discussion at odds with each other-it is my impression that you want me to talk about the price of corn this season and for the 1962 crop.[1] I want to talk about "supply management," or, to put it differently, the general nature of the farm programs advanced by the current national administration. These two seemingly diverse topics are closer to the same topic than they seem at first glance.

---

1. T. A. Hieronymus is professor of agricultural marketing, University of Illinois. Talk given to the Commodity Club of New York, May 17, 1962.

What I should like to try is to move from the current corn price situation to the situation for next crop year and finally to the broader aspects of agricultural legislation.

CURRENT CORN SITUATION

The price of corn until new crop is available will focus on the question of whether a sufficient amount of corn is tied up in inventory and under loan to force the price up to, near, or above the support price.

Finally, the general tightness that I have projected rests upon some assumptions about government sales. I think the government wants the price of corn to go up and will limit sales to the amounts I have indicated, but it has enough corn to severely depress the price if it elects to do so. This threat will continue to hang over the market.

In this discussion of the current corn price outlook, I have been talking about "'supply management." You will note that there is virtually no economics in it. It is a matter of trying to appraise the effects of the governmental manipulation of the supply, use, and price of corn.

Suppose that we repeat the feed-grain program over and over. At the outset, it becomes a supplemental price payment system with the government buying at one price and selling at a lower price to force compliance with the program the following year. Either the differential must be kept large, or the payment for retiring land must be large if a high level of compliance is to be maintained. All commercial corn channels through government with accompanying large losses.

As the inventory owned by government declines, the differential becomes increasingly difficult to maintain. If compliance with the program in the year ahead is as large as is currently indicated and CCC inventory is 300 million bushels less on October 1, essentially all of the inventory will have to be sold to maintain a differential. A further liquidation of stocks in 1962-63 makes it essentially impossible to maintain a price differential in the 1963 program. This reduces compliance in subsequent years, and the whole cycle is started over.

The only way to break out of this sequence is to increase the payment per acre in relation to the support price. What I am suggesting is that in the final analysis the feed-grain program comes back to a land rental scheme. Its effectiveness as a land rental scheme is hampered by the existence of a support price. The higher the support price, the more expensive land retirement becomes.

In central Illinois, the full cost of producing corn is about 85 cents a bushel. The marginal cost-the amount that can be saved by letting land remain idle-is on the general order of 37 cents: $1.20 minus $.37 is $.83.

This examination of the extension of a voluntary supply management scheme serves to illustrate two points: (1) land rental is a very expensive way to reduce production, and (2) the existence of a support price increases the cost of a program and the difficulty of making it operate.

THEORY OF "SUPPLY MANAGEMENT"

At this point, it is worthwhile to digress from the trees to a more distant look at the total forest of "supply management." The first problem is one of terminology. The question is often asked whether we should have supply management. It is a foolish question. We have supply management; we always have had supply management; and we always will have supply management. There is no such thing as un-management of supplies. The only question is, Do we manage supplies (and consequently utilization) by a system of market price interrelationships, or do we manage supplies by a system of governmental decree? The real question is whether it is desirable to manage by a system of administrative supply control. In some areas of agriculture, we have had systems of administrative control of supply for quite some time, but these have had a tendency to simply shift problems to other commodities. So, what we are really talking about now is a system of comprehensive administrative supply control.

This system is presumably designed to solve a problem or problems. During the past thirty years of tinkering with various schemes, we have not done a very good job of identifying problems. The first problem that seems to stand out is that incomes of people who are identified as farmers are lower than those of the rest of the population. We have not taken a careful look at which farmers get how much. We have dealt with averages, and they can be deceptive. We have never asked: What is the income situation of a farmer whose labor resources are fully and efficiently employed and properly balanced with land and capital inputs? The first crude look indicates that such a farmer has, and has had for the past twenty years, an income that very few people would consider low enough to be worthy of public assistance. For example, the average income of farm operator families in 1959 whose sales were $10,000 and over was $9,960. A gross sale of $10,000 is not much for a farming operation. It does not meet the minimum threshold implicit in the question above, nor does it meet most definitions of a "family farm."

What farm income figures really show is that there are a lot of low-income, semi-employed people who are identified as farmers. Obviously, the income situation of people who have nothing, or very little, to sell is not going to be helped by a system that increases prices.

The second problem is the high cost of past farm programs. Whatever the real merits of the matter, the large expenditures in the agricultural sector are causing a lot of criticism. To keep the record straight, I agree with the criticism.

A third problem is that, while income of commercial farmers is livable, it would be ruinously low if a system of market prices were substituted for administrative control of supply and price. Whether this is truly a problem is open to discussion. The point is that the administration has identified it as a problem.

The basic assumption underlying administrative supply control is that the demand for farm products is extremely inelastic. Therefore, a decrease in supply will result in a greater increase in price and, hence, an increase in revenue. It is said that food and clothing are necessities that command a high priority of expenditures, but once the food priority is met, increases in the domestic demand for food depend primarily on population growth. The human food requirements are only so large, and we will pay almost any price to meet them, but when this need is met we will buy no more and will spend additional income on other things.

If this assumption is true, then it follows that we must reduce prices a great deal to induce additional use, and this reduces farm income. On the other hand, by moderately reducing supplies we can materially increase prices and, hence, increase farm income. Reduced to its simplest terms, administrative supply control means extracting a monopoly revenue from consumers to be transferred to producers. This practice solves two problems. It alleviates the farm income problem that would result if we went to a system of market prices, and it essentially eliminates the governmental cost of income support for commercial agriculture.

The people who project this theory also project a long-term imbalance of production and use at prices that will yield equitable incomes to producers; that is, they see no end to this monopoly operation. A system of administrative supply control would become permanent.

The basic decision is whether such a scheme should be adopted or whether something else should be done. We have begged the question since the end of World War II. We have established a few monopolies for such products as peanuts, tobacco, and rice, while allowing agricultural production to expand in a different direction. We have taken halfway measures, such as with wheat, where we have said we will restrict production to maintain price but will not cut allotted acreage below 55 million and will exempt from restrictions farmers who raise fewer than 15 acres. We have supported prices of feed grain without production controls, etc. The high cost of agricultural programs appears finally to be forcing at least a partial decision.

PROGRAM OPERATION

The grand scheme, and the inevitable final result, is a comprehensive system of administrative supply control. We reach this final destination by a succession of commodity programs. The basic problem in a production control program is to allot production rights. Until this time, virtually every such program has been tied to land. One exception is the proposed turkey order, which would attach production rights to people.

There are several problems that develop out of commodity programs. The first is that the monopoly value of production rights gets capitalized into the item of input to which the production right is attached. Land on which there is authorization to produce tobacco is worth several thousand dollars per acre more than similar land without production rights. If we attached production rights to people, there would be a windfall capital gain. We must face the problem of transfer of production rights because people are mortal. If we withdraw production rights on death or retirement, we have the problem of licensing entry. If the government sells production rights, it defeats the income purpose of control, and the scheme becomes a tax on consumers to give value to the salable production rights. A basic point stands out. It is difficult, if not impossible, to avoid putting a market price on something of value.

A second problem is that new technology is not initiated because institutional and geographic patterns of production become frozen. For example, the production of cotton has been slow in moving westward because of acreage allotments. It is far from certain that we have the best locations for assignment of current production rights. We have been slow in increasing the scale of operation of cotton production. To the extent to which it has proceeded, the values of production rights have been included in rentals charged current operators. The large-scale cotton operations on the Delta are purely competitive and would not long be affected if the price of cotton were substantially reduced. Only the rentals would be affected.

Agriculture has an amazing record of advancing technology that reduces unit costs. The most outstanding instance is probably broilers. Improvements in feeding, medicine, and breeding have improved quality of product and reduced unit costs. It is a dramatic success story. Last year the broiler industry got into trouble. We are now contemplating a broiler marketing order that would, by law, restrict production to amounts that would clear the market at "fair" prices. Perhaps we have gone as far as we can technologically and should freeze current production and price. However, the situation is no more troublesome now than it was eight years ago. Just as good a case could be made then as can be made now. With the benefits of hindsight, we know that to have restricted production then would have been a mistake. Where would Georgia broiler producers be today if a rigid market order scheme had been established a decade ago?

The administration's food and agriculture program looks forward to 1980. Do we want to freeze today's agricultural production structure for twenty years? Perhaps, but the advances of the past twenty years argue to the contrary.

Third, productive inputs are not adjusted to optimal levels. Let us take the current corn situation. We have taken land out of production and greatly increased fertilizer and cultivation. We are wasting land resources. Land is, in and of itself, inherently productive at no cost. Not to use it is to waste it. To waste a natural resource makes no economic sense.

In a broader sense, production restriction wastes the labor and management skills of farmers. If it is successful in raising income, it tends to hold people in farming, and it certainly partly idles those people who are already farming. One of the factors creating income problems of rural people is only partial employment. We do not cure it by aggravating it.

Fourth, the opportunity to succeed or fail is denied. We hear a great deal about the loss of freedom of farmers as the result of control programs. We also hear the answer that not many farmers are concerned about whether they are told to put the south forty in corn or soybeans, and with this I would disagree only moderately. Comprehensive control programs do inhibit the opportunity of people to enter and succeed or fail by their own skill, energy, and venturesomeness. The opportunity to be good and succeed, or to be poor and fail, is important. It is important socially because it increases overall economic productivity. It is important individually because the very fundamentals of freedom rest upon the opportunity of a man to compete and better himself.

Let us take tobacco. The production rights have been reduced and spread around to the point where few men can make a good living as tobacco farmers. We have socialized poverty. Is this the model scheme that we would extend to the whole of agriculture?

Fifth, people other than farmers are affected by production controls. The volume of business of people who supply farmers with production materials and market their products depends on the amount of agricultural production. The restriction of agricultural production would act to further shrink rural communities. I might add parenthetically that these are people, too, and that their interests cannot reasonably be disregarded in the interests of reaping monopoly profits for farmers.

Sixth, adjustments in the nature and size of the market for farm products are slowed down if not entirely prevented. To this point, in talking about problems generated by production controls, I have assumed that they would actually work to transfer income from consumers to producers. This is far from certain in spite of the various studies showing an extreme inelasticity of demand. In fact, the logic of the matter is that they will not work.

The studies showing the price inelasticity of demand are based on annual quantities taken and annual average prices. They tell us nothing about secondary effects of supply changes. In current traffic, there are citations of four "independent" studies of the impacts of the absence of support schemes for agriculture. They all show "ruinously low" prices. The fact that all come out the same is not impressive. In these studies, similar assumptions, data, and analytical techniques were used. That the results are alike only indicates that computing machines respond similarly to similar stimuli. None of them is a proper study of long-term market reaction to varying levels of supply of different mixes of agricultural product.

In the food sector, the crux of the matter is the response of consumers to varying relative prices of different food items, to relative food and nonfood prices, and to changes in disposable income. The objective is to extract the maximum amount of money from the housewife in the supermarket. What happens if we raise prices? Before we do, we had better reckon with a hard fact: We are not in the business of selling necessities. The typical family spends several times as much money for food as it needs to spend for nutritionally optimum diets. This extra expenditure is for the higher quality foods.

When we first increase prices, housewives will grumble and pay, but quickly the press of keeping up payments on the television set and paying for Papa's Thursday night bowling will force these housewives to lower cost foods, and the contest will be a standoff.

The third effect of higher food prices is likely to be a decrease in food expenditures. Consumers equate the marginal utility of the last dollar spent in the various categories, such as food, housing, recreation, clothing, travel, education, etc. If the price level of one of these several categories is increased in relation to the others, the utility provided by the last dollar spent in that category will be less than the utility provided by the last dollar spent in other categories, and it will be withdrawn and transferred to some other category. The validity of this statement rests on the proposition that the utility of the last dollar spent for food provides nearly as much utility as the next to the last dollar, etc. The close relationship between consumer disposable income and food expenditures indicates that this is the case.

Put differently, the proposition is that when you sell a housewife a bargain, you can get her money; but when you charge her a high price, she will take her money where there is a bargain.

Food has stood the test of competition with other categories very well. As consumer incomes have gone up, food expenditures have also gone up. During the decade of the 1950s, food expenditures went up about 70 percent as fast as incomes. This per-capita increase from higher incomes, plus the population growth, resulted in an increase of about 3 percent a year in domestic market size. Agriculture is a growth industry. This fact argues strongly against freezing it or cutting it back.

Some agricultural products have expanded their markets at rapid rates. We have mentioned broilers. A second outstanding example is soybeans. This crop has increased from a World War II level of less than 200 million bushels to a current level of over 600 million. A good product, attractively priced, will move.

I recall an analysis of the competitive positions of soybeans and peanuts made at the end of World War II that concluded that soybean production would decrease and peanut production would increase. The opposite has been true. There are several reasons, but high on the list must be the fact that peanuts went the control route and soybeans went the competitive price route. Yet the peanut program is one of the examples cited in advocating extension of administrative supply control!

Let us take the prosaic crop corn. In 1952-53, total disappearance was 2.7 billion bushels. I have estimated total disappearance in 1961-62 at 3.7 billion. This is a 37 percent increase in nine years. Corn makes high-quality preferred foods and so finds a good market when consumers are prosperous.

In the final analysis, the size of the agricultural production plant will depend on the size of the market for its products; its growth, upon market growth; the number of family farms, if you please, on the size of the market. Agriculture had better take a long, hard look at programs that will restrict market size.

BROADER IMPACTS OF PROGRAMS

In looking at the detail of impacts of programs, we are in danger of overlooking the serious general impact of compulsory supply control. It is this: The overall economic efficiency of agricultural production is reduced. Human and land resources are wasted, and the resources used are improperly organized.

The first god that must be served in organizing and operating an economic system is production efficiency. The size of the pie that we have to cut determines the welfare of the people of a nation. The time was when three-fourths of the people in the United States were occupied in farming. Now, 1.5 million farmers produce most of the food and fiber for domestic consumption and export. This is a remarkable achievement. It has enabled us to move ahead of the rest of the world in production and consumption of other consumer goods. We will be well advised indeed to avoid changing a system that has worked so well, especially when we can so readily find examples of systems that work poorly. We should note, in passing, that such examples are state control systems.

THE ALTERNATIVES

We have finally gotten to our crux of the matter. It is this: How should we manage supply and utilization? Should we do it by a market price system or a state control system?

We have been looking at a system of state control all the way from the current corn situation to the very general impacts of comprehensive supply control. The goal of the state system is to stop the operation of a competitive market price system to a greater or lesser degree.

We have seen that when we follow regulation through to its logical conclusion, complete state ordering is involved. One suppression of a market pricing system leads to another.

Before we undertake to replace a competitive market price system, we should first review what it does when it is allowed to function. The first area of accomplishment of a competitive market price system is in ordering production and utilization. In a complex economic system, we have a myriad of jobs to do. Countless decisions are based upon price interrelationships. We cannot, here and now, begin to list them, but a few illustrations are in order.

With regard to agriculture, a first decision is how many people and which ones. Left alone, the relative attractiveness of employment in or out of farming will make the decision. The huge decrease in agricultural employment has been the result of attractiveness of employment elsewhere.

How much land shall be used for farming? How much machinery, fuel, and fertilizer? The most profitable employment as expressed through relative price will provide an answer.

What kinds and qualities of products? Fat hogs or lean hogs? Wheat or grain sorghum? Do we make starch or whiskey or chicken feed from corn? How much corn do we feed in Iowa and how much do we send to Georgia and Alabama? How much do we store, and how much do we use now? If we each in our own areas of familiarity let our thoughts range over the whole gamut of activity, we can quickly see the vastness of the job that price interrelationships accomplish.

What kind of job do market prices do? The quick answer is to say: Look at the tremendous productivity of our economic system. The more thoughtful answer is to say that competitive market prices order the economic processes in the way in which people spending the fruits of their own productiveness want them ordered. This is the most democratic of all possible procedures. People spend their money where they get the greatest satisfaction. It is not all on television sets and tail fins, or beer and bowling. It is also in sharing with less fortunate people and building for the future. It is also in saving versus consuming and in working versus leisure. Production will go where the profit is, and profit is where people want production. Anything other than a market price system is an infringement on individual freedom and a negation of democracy.

I do not want to paint a rosy picture of a competitive price system. It is a hard task master, imposing rigorous discipline on producers. There is not only profit, there is also loss. There are both lavish and niggardly rewards failure as well as success.

The second area of accomplishment of market prices is in allocating the fruits of production, in dividing up the product. Here, again, market prices are rigorous. If left alone, they will divide the product up on the basis of individual productivity. They will reward the productive and punish the unproductive.

In the thinking of some people, this is fair; in that of others, it is not. There are a lot of unproductive people in the world. In the aggregate social judgment, some of the unproductive people should be cared for, and others should be helped to become productive. The extent to which this is done is a difficult decision to make.

It may well be that, in the instance of agriculture, some redistribution of income from other sectors of the economy is desirable. A stronger case can be made for increasing the productivity of semi-employed agricultural workers than for direct income supplements.

If this is to be done, there must be a better way than the extensive impairment of the pricing system. The simple solution is to do it directly out of public funds. In this way, we can keep track of precisely what we are doing.

If we separate income support from commodity prices, we can then make deliberate decisions about the food stamp plan, school lunches, direct distribution, and foreign food aid. These should be considered on their own merits instead of as part of the farm income problem as they are now.

CONCLUSION

How do we get out of this maze that we are now in? The solution is perfectly simple: Eliminate price supports and commodity inventory activities of the federal government. In my opinion, the adjustment would be much less drastic than is generally thought. However, the longer we let the problem compound, the more drastic the adjustment will become. If we are afraid of the impacts, we can build in income safeguards, extend credit, and hold inventories where they are, but there is no gradual route to the elimination of price supports. It should be done immediately.

Chapter Nineteen

Lessons to Be Learned from Agricultural Policies of Other Countries

1962

AUTHOR'S NOTE: The paper, "Lessons to be Learned from Agricultural Policies of Other Countries," presented an opportunity to take my biases regarding price support programs of the United States to the horse's mouth. It is interesting that my discussion did not include Japan, which was then just becoming a major factor in U.S. agricultural trade.

In contemplating the subject "Lessons to be Learned from Agricultural Policies of Other Countries," two broad categories of lessons come to mind.[1] The first has to do with the transfer and application of policies and programs to U.S. agriculture, and the second with the impacts of policies and programs of other countries on the competitive position of U.S. agriculture.

Many countries have had extensive experience with agricultural programs, and these programs have met with varying degrees of success. In view of the problems

---

1. T. A. Hieronymus is professor of agricultural marketing, University of Illinois. Address before the Field Crops Conference of the American Farm Bureau Federation, Dinkler Plaza Hotel, Atlanta, Georgia, December 10, 1962.

that beset U.S agricultural programs and the great difficulty that we have had in solving our problems, it seems reasonable to look at what other countries have done. Perhaps we can find some successful things that can be applied to our own problems. They also have made mistakes. Examination of some of these mistakes should make it possible to cast new light on some of our problems so that our own mistakes come into focus more accurately.

A substantial share of U.S. agricultural products are sold abroad. The amount of the total U.S. production is now on the order of 14 percent. For some commodities, the export share amounts to more than half of the total disappearance. The protection of these markets is of prime importance to U.S. agriculture.

The size of our export markets is affected by the agricultural programs of other countries. The impacts are of two general kinds: (1) the restriction of imports to protect domestic markets for home producers; and (2) the stimulation of production, both in countries that are importers of U.S. farm products and in countries that compete for export markets with the United States. American farmers have a stake in the agricultural programs and policies of other countries.

The world is large and there are many countries. Each one has an agriculture, and, for the most part, they have specific agricultural policies and programs. To examine each and seek out its application to U.S. agricultural policies and programs is an unmanageable task. What I shall try to do here is to classify the kinds of countries involved and pick out specific countries in each group that can serve to illustrate kinds of policies and programs.

The four general classifications that I should like to use are (1) industrialized, import countries; (2) developed exporters; (3) "underdeveloped countries"; and (4) communist countries.

INDUSTRIALIZED, IMPORT COUNTRIES

The countries of the world whose agricultural policies and programs are most like those of the United States are the highly industrialized, high-income countries of western Europe and the United Kingdom. Important similarities are that (1) relatively small proportions of their populations are engaged in farming; (2) by the world's standards their agriculture is highly productive; (3) they enjoy high dietary levels; (4) they have great concern for the welfare of their farm populations and can afford to indulge this concern; and (5) a substantial proportion of their farm units are of less than optimum size in terms of area or volume of production.

There is one major difference: The United States is an agricultural surplus-producing country, whereas the others are major importers of agricultural raw materials. The import position of western European countries makes the implementation of a high price-income policy relatively easy. By restricting imports, domestic prices can be easily maintained.

UNITED KINGDOM

The specific example among the industrialized countries that I would like to look at is the United Kingdom, the world's largest importer of agricultural raw materials. About one-half, by value, of food materials consumed are imported. All tobacco and cotton requirements come from abroad. The United Kingdom is usually first or second in importance as a customer for U.S. farm products.

The exports, which pay for the imports, consist mainly of manufactured goods. Britain is a trading nation. She can survive only by importing raw materials and exporting manufactures. Much of the exports are re-exports of imported raw materials that have been processed. Exports must be made at competitive prices. Therefore, raw materials and labor costs must be competitive. The import cost of industrial raw materials and foodstuffs is an important part of the costs of manufactured export items. A cornerstone of British agricultural policy must be a moderate cost of food.

A second major consideration of British agricultural policy is a concern for the incomes of farmers. That farm income be maintained is an accepted national goal.

Third is a goal of maintaining a minimum domestic agricultural production. The islands have been nearly isolated twice in this century. During the post-World War II period, there has been a policy of maintaining food production at 60 percent above prewar levels. A second facet of this policy has been the conservation of foreign exchange. The more food that is domestically produced, the more exchange can be used for the import of raw materials for manufacture and subsequent re-export.

Unfortunately, the goals of income support and maximum self-sufficiency get muddled together so that it is difficult to identify the precise reasons for the payment of various subsidies.

Fourth, British agricultural policy is in part directed toward support of Commonwealth agriculture. British off-take of Commonwealth agricultural surpluses is very great, and the United Kingdom has an interest in maintaining its Commonwealth relationships.

Within the framework of these policy considerations, the United Kingdom has developed an agricultural program that consists primarily of direct treasury payments. The first of these is a system of guaranteed prices. After conferences with agricultural organizations, forward prices for a long list of agricultural prices are established. The primary considerations involved in establishing these prices are the effects on farm income, effects on production of the various products, and the cost to the treasury. Market prices prevail, and the difference between market prices and guaranteed prices is made by direct payments.

Import restrictions are kept at relatively low levels so that the interior price level is very close to the world price level.

The second system of direct payments is in production allowances. These subsidies have the effect of reducing input costs.

In addition to what I identify as commodity subsidies, there is indirect aid to agriculture in the form of credit, special tax treatment, education and extension, and land reclamation.

The cost of programs can be identified readily because it is a matter of treasury payments. In recent years, this cost has been held fairly constant. Sometimes, they miss their estimates of cost, but not badly. It is my impression that the United Kingdom has come very nearly to the point of setting aside an amount of money that can be paid out to agriculture. The way it is divided up is left to negotiation with farm organizations.

This system has much that is commendable. It results in relatively inexpensive food and is, therefore, desirable from a consumer point of view. It leaves a great deal of flexibility in the kinds of product so that inputs are used fairly efficiently. The cost is readily identifiable and so can be kept in reasonable bounds. It tends to maintain the status quo of agriculture and guarantee a minimum food supply level for whatever social values these things may have.

There are certain drawbacks to the system. If the subsidies did not exist and there were the same small import restrictions, the cost of food would be very little, if any, higher. Imports would be greater, and the size of the agricultural plant would be smaller. Resources would be freed for other uses. This more nearly optimum allocation of resources would increase the total economic output of the United Kingdom.

Further, the system of guaranteed prices results in a different production pattern than would a system in which competitive prices directed the use of resources. There is some deviation from optimal output.

It goes without saying that the cost to the treasury would be less. The cost is large, amounting to about 75 percent of the net income of farm operators.

On balance, we must conclude that if there is to be subsidization of agricultural income and production, the British have worked out a pretty manageable system for doing it.

GERMANY

For a contrast to the British system, we turn to Germany. Germany has lots of very small, unproductive agricultural units as well as some large, efficient units. Her agriculture, as a whole, is not as rationally organized as Britain's. Land is badly fragmented so that production tends to be inefficient. There is a small agricultural population that is politically quite potent. Germany is heavily dependent upon imports of agricultural raw materials, particularly food and livestock feed for making food. She has felt the squeeze of food shortage during two great wars.

The agricultural policy of Germany is to work toward an agricultural income that is at parity with the incomes of other economic groups. The most important segment of this policy is to increase agricultural income through a system of favorable price-cost relationships. The second segment is to improve, through technical rationalization, the productivity of German farmers so that they will more nearly earn the incomes that they get.

There are two devices by which agricultural income in Germany is maintained. First is a system of production subsidies. These subsidies include rebates on fertilizers; purchase of seed, particularly potatoes; improvements of orchards; improvement of milk quality; purchase of machinery for cooperative use and for land consolidation and settlement. These several things are done at a considerable cost to the treasury, but the share of net farm income that they represent is not large.

The primary device for the maintenance of farm income is import restrictions. Germany maintains very high import restrictions on many agricultural products, particularly feed. As the import restrictions on feed grains are high, the interior price of barley is high. As the price of barley is high, the price of feed potatoes is high. As the price of feed potatoes is high, livestock product prices are high, etc.

A country that is a net importer can maintain almost any price level desired by simply restricting imports. It can also make quite a profit on the operation out of which it can pay subsidies to agriculture. This is the essence of the German system.

This system has not solved the German farm problem. Many of the production units are so small and inefficiently organized that no feasible level of prices can result in parity income. The large, efficient units do very well, but they are not really a part of the German farm problem. It is a system whereby the poor stay poor because they are not productive, and the rich live off of the fat of the land.

The system has two things to commend it. It is of little cost to the treasury, and it raises farm income substantially above levels that would otherwise prevail. The real cost is borne by the German consumers. The prices of foodstuffs are a great deal higher than they would be in the absence of import restrictions. To what extent the raising of food costs to consumers for the benefit of the more productive farmers is social justice is a moot question. It is certainly worthy of consideration.

We must again raise the question of economic efficiency. Clearly, the overall productivity of Germany would be raised if they imported more, consumed more of the high preference foods, and diverted some of the resources now going into agriculture to pursuits in which Germany enjoys a comparative advantage.

German agriculture is currently confronted by a considerable problem as a result of the implementation of the Common Market. When fully implemented, the Common Market will present a common exterior tariff structure and equalization of agricultural prices and will allow the free exchange of agricultural products and flow of agricultural resources within the Common Market area. The effective protection of some countries will be increased. For others, it will be decreased. In the main, the protection of German agriculture will be decreased.

The decrease of protection of Germany is now causing important changes in the organization of German agriculture. In a capsule, many German farmers must either increase total production and productive efficiency or retire from the field. This is causing considerable political repercussion as well as economic change. It goes without saying that the change is to the benefit of German farmers.

COMMON MARKET

A word on the Common Market seems appropriate. This is a large area that may increase further and that will have a common agricultural policy. The system is to maintain a uniform set of target prices within the area and realize these target prices with variable import duties. There is also to be a uniform system of direct subsidies and somewhat uniform indirect aids.

The level of protection is considerably above current world prices for some important commodity groups. Most important of these are the food concentrates.

The consensus at this time is that the level of support and the freer trade within the area will result in a near balance of production and use of foodstuffs within the area. The position of the Common Market area as a major net importer will be greatly changed.

On the one hand, the system will result in greater agricultural output, greater farm income, and the retention of more resources in agricultural production, particularly people, than would be the case in the absence of such protection.

From a narrow agricultural point of view, one must rate these results favorably. It again points out the simplicity of supporting agriculture in a situation in which an area is a net importer of food.

There are, however, disadvantages. In the first place, it will increase the cost of food above levels that would exist if the Common Market countries had unrestricted access to the world's food supply. One must sometimes marvel at the tolerance (or political ineffectiveness) of consumers.

Second, the total resource allocation is different than would exist were prices at world levels. It is less efficient. The total productivity of the Common Market will be less than would exist in the absence of agricultural protection.

Third, this restriction policy invites criticism and retaliation from countries outside the Common Market. There is little question that agricultural imports from the United States will be reduced. The United States is not happy about this. This displeasure may well take a more potent form than conversation.

THE DEVELOPED EXPORTERS

Among the leading agricultural surplus nations of the world are Canada and the Argentine. The exports of agricultural products play an important role in their national economies. What are their policies and programs?

CANADA

Canada is heavily dependent upon agricultural exports and must necessarily relate her domestic farm progress to the need to export. The United Kingdom and the United States are the two most important destinations of Canadian exports. In addition, Canada is one of the import destinations of U.S. agricultural exports.

Canada has several types of assistance to agriculture, but Canadian agricultural production is essentially a free-enterprise operation. Programs have been designed with a view to maintaining maximum freedom of choice in land utilization. An important policy goal is the improvement of the quality of products, particularly those destined for export.

There is not parity legislation, but costs and incomes are taken into account in determining the amount of assistance to agriculture.

The primary device for intervention is the marketing board system. The wheat marketing board is the most suitable example. It is the buyer and seller of wheat, having complete control over transactions and shipments of wheat from delivery to the local elevator until the time it is sold to the domestic processor or until it is delivered for export.

The board sets a minimum price early in the season—which it pays out promptly on delivery. As the crop is gradually sold, supplemental payments are made until the total realized is paid out. On occasion, this has taken several years.

Other marketing boards are operated by the provinces and cover a long list of commodities including dairy products, hogs, fruits, and vegetables. The general pattern of the schemes is to gain control of the marketing of a commodity with a view to maximizing returns. They are, in effect, compulsory pooling schemes. They can bargain, regulate quality, divert surpluses outside of usual channels, including destruction, and require set-asides of funds to finance diversion schemes. These schemes involve virtually no direct production controls.

There are no federal government subsidies on acreage or production and no direct production control regulations. However, the payments on quality produce, grain freight subsidies, and losses on price-support operations amount to very substantial sums of money. There are indirect aids that include farm credit, insurance, education and extension services, and land improvement.

Canadian farm programs have been disciplined by the need to export into a pattern of prices that reflect world market values. They have been further disciplined by the inability of Canada to pay out large sums for the benefit of agriculture. The amounts have been held to known and manageable levels.

Canada has quite wisely avoided restriction of its agricultural production. At the same time, she has not maximized agricultural production. In the United States, we have had acreage restrictions on wheat but have encouraged the maximum implementation of technology by holding price supports at incentive levels. Canada has avoided such contradictory programs by holding wheat prices at world levels. The result is much higher wheat yields in North Dakota and Montana than in neighboring Saskatchewan.

It is important that Canada not restrict agricultural production. Here is where her comparative advantage lies. This is one of the basic sources of wealth out of which she must finance further industrial development.

The marketing board system of control of quality and marketing is interesting. It evolved from problems associated with selling in international markets, particularly wheat and hogs. The marketing boards have not met with notable success for most other commodities.

ARGENTINE

The Argentine is a rich agricultural land that has not succeeded over time in using this potential for industrial development. This nation gains its international livelihood from its agricultural exports of grains, vegetable oils, meats, hides, wool, and dairy products.

The articulated policies have been aimed at revitalizing agriculture to gain foreign exchange. In practice, the programs have had a contrary effect, and agricultural exports have tended to decline.

In years past when international commodity prices were high, the government collected products at rather low fixed interior prices and sold them as high as possible. While this yielded a profit for a time, it did not tend to call forth maximum production. At the present time, there is a retention of 10 percent levied on exports of most agricultural products other than meat. Meat producers pay a 4 percent tax on sales..

A further handicap to the agriculture of the Argentine is a price control system designed to hold down the cost of living in the rampant and chronic inflation that the country has experienced. This has been harmful to the effective organization and technological improvement of agriculture and the development of an efficient marketing system.

On balance, these policies have been exploitative of agriculture. In view of the need to develop the country out of agricultural wealth, this may be desirable, but certainly not to the point of strangulation.

There is a generally accepted school of thought that the agriculture of the Argentine is organized in too large units. The owners can live well as matters now stand and so have little incentive to improve. Behind this again lies the problem of inflation. Property is the thing of great value, not money or, for that matter, productivity.

The most important lesson to be learned from the experience of the Argentine is that national monetary, fiscal, and price policies are of very great importance in the development and welfare of agriculture; that is, the most important agricultural policies do not relate directly to agriculture. In my opinion, if monetary and fiscal programs that would eliminate inflation were implemented, if competitive market prices were allowed to function, and the tax structure were changed to de-emphasize the value of holding tangible property, the agriculture of the Argentine would grow, prosper, and serve as a base for industrial development.

"UNDERDEVELOPED COUNTRIES"

The term is not very accurate, but I would include in "underdeveloped countries" those areas that have recently gained independence from colonial rule. They fall into two broad categories: densely populated and fairly sparsely populated.

The countries south of the Sahara and north of South Africa are generally in the second category. These areas have a well-organized commercial agriculture and, with the exception of some mineral deposits, little else. Their agriculture has been 'developed out of trade with the European colonial powers. The acute nationalization that has developed now endangers the progress that has been made over most of this century.

If there is a road up for these countries, it is through education and agriculture. One of the most promising countries is Nigeria. Nigeria is putting a very high proportion of its governmental revenue into education and emphasizing agricultural productivity and exports.

These situations are very different than that of the United States. What lessons are to be learned? I see only one: To the extent that these nations succeed in developing, they will present export competition to the United States.

Another great "underdeveloped" area is India. At the top, it is a fairly advanced country. It falls in the densely populated category, but at the level of the masses it is very poor and uneducated. It has rather sophisticated schemes for development. India is trying to develop on three fronts: industry, agriculture, and education. To date, it has been a slow and discouraging process.

The primary emphasis in agriculture now seems to be in the education of individual farmers. The people most closely associated with this can see progress.

The lesson to be learned here is that the advancement of a nation rests on individual productivity and, further, that individual productivity rests upon the knowledge of new technology, a climate that encourages the application of knowledge, and upon the judicious availability of capital.

COMMUNIST COUNTRIES

It is currently popular for Russia to learn something from capitalism. So we should look at the communists as well. Our lessons, however, are more in terms of what not to do rather than what to do.

Russia has a severe agricultural problem. She cannot get her agricultural productivity up to desired levels. The European satellite countries have the same problem in greater or lesser degree.

So long as Russia must hold a high percentage of the population—about 40 percent—on the farms and the United States can release nearly all of its population from farming, Russia will fall further and further behind the United States in total productivity. One of the great sources of strength in the development of the United States during the last 150 years has been the ability to reduce the agricultural population from 75 percent down to its current low level.

Russia has three agricultural problems. First, her agricultural resources are limited. The combination of soil and climate that exists in Russia is not conducive to a high level of productivity. At best, it is a hard go.

Second, she has starved her agriculture for capital. Through state planning and direction, a disproportionate amount of capital has been allocated to industrial development and an insufficient amount to agriculture. In part, this appears to have been deliberate, intending to force rapid industrial development at the cost of a fairly low dietary level (in terms of quality). It also seems to have been, in part, a planning error. Getting the right things to be in the right places at the right times to maximize productivity is a very complicated matter. The Russian system of decree prices leaves them without a meaningful guide for allocating resources.

Third, the Russian system has not provided incentives to produce. From an American point of view, one of the more satisfying aspects of the Russian experience is the high proportion of output that is produced on the small plots allowed individuals. These are highly productive. The output is sold at good prices.

The Russian agricultural productivity could be significantly increased if resources could more readily flow to the places where they are in greatest demand and if the incentives to produce were increased. State socialism has proved to be a rather poor way to organize and operate agriculture.

However nasty a bone to swallow the change might be, the Russian agricultural situation is not beyond recall. It may be that China's situation is. The Chinese went through the classical communist procedure of destroying the peasant agriculture and establishing a collective system. This was designed to free resources for industrial development. However, the effect has been to decrease agricultural production; the strength of the population is so sapped that the whole program has come to a standstill.

The agricultural troubles in China were accompanied by a rapid increase in population. It appears at this time that the Chinese are moving back toward a peasant agriculture. Whether or not this will come in time to cope with the population problem is not clear. At any odds, this lesson is clear: Here is another example of the failure of state organization and operation of agriculture.

LESSONS AND THEIR APPLICATION

By this point, we have explored the agricultural policies and programs of eight countries and the Common Market. This runs the gamut of possibilities. My negative reaction to most of these is readily apparent. They all have one thing in common: They interfere with the effective operation of a competitive pricing system. These two things together point to the first and most important lesson: A competitive pricing system is a very effective means of generating economic efficiency, and for every group helped by modification of competitive pricing system, another group is injured.

The second lesson is that the general monetary, fiscal, and price policies are important considerations in agricultural productivity and welfare.

Third, there are many agricultural export areas of the world. These countries are heavily dependent upon such exports for the revenue out of which industrial development can take place. They are hungry exporters. If we are to hold our export place, we must be competitive. And, competition is in terms of price. Further, if we are to maximize agricultural exports, we must oppose the restrictions that other countries place on imports from the United States. We cannot effectively do so if we maintain an artificially high price level within our own country.

Fourth, only wealthy countries can afford real farm income-supporting programs. Note that only Britain, western Europe, and Canada do anything that is directly and immediately effective. This support is done in one or both of two ways—by direct payment from the treasury in the form of deficiency payments or production subsidies, or by operating a monopoly system that charges consumers higher food prices than would otherwise exist, an income transfer from consumers to farmers. We have further seen that this latter system is effective for importing countries, but it is not effective for exporting countries because of the need to meet world competition.

Fifth, programs that modify a competitive pricing system tend to direct productive resources in other than an optimal manner. This, in some cases, reduces agricultural productivity. In all cases it reduces the total productivity of the economic system.

Sixth, programs that interfere with the operation of a competitive pricing system tend to reduce agricultural adjustments to changed technology and to changed market conditions. If we assume that adjustments in line with economic efficiency must finally be made, it follows that the delay of adjustment increases the violence of adjustments when they are finally made.

Seventh, most price interference schemes have to do with increasing prices. This can have no effect other than to limit consumption. Such limitations must also limit production, reducing the size of the agricultural plant and the number of people engaged in farming except for importing nations.

Finally, what I have done is look at nine different ways to contravene the effective operation of a competitive pricing system and find them wanting. Thus, the burden of my remarks is that price supports should be eliminated. I leave the matter there.

Chapter Twenty

Elevator Adjustments to Corn Combines

1964

AUTHOR'S NOTE: This paper is an interesting example of an effective use of a land grant college integration of research, teaching, and extension (public service). It reported research results—research that was generated from addressing problems that surfaced out of extension programs that were in close contacts with business clientele. It was pertinent and timely research. Results were disseminated as they became available on a preliminary basis, making them available as operative business decisions had to be made. All of this fed back into modification in the subject-matter content of resident courses to students who would soon be making the pertinent business decisions on both farms and agricultural businesses. The paper was distributed to grain elevators, grain merchandisers and processors, and county extension agents, and was widely quoted and excerpted by numerous magazines and other trade publications, and eventually circulated throughout the Midwest. The operative title assigned to it by trade publications was "Hieronymus says, 'Get good or get out,' and few of you will survive." It was a fun experience and may have even had an impact.

My comments today are going to raise more questions than they are going to answer.[1] The general subject of change in the country elevator business is actually a whole series of topics, any one of which would take more time than is available. Further, I do not know the answers to all of the questions confronting elevators, yet the questions must be answered now. Thus I shall raise questions about a variety of subjects.

THE NATURE OF THE CHANGE

The rapid change from the harvesting of ear corn to the harvesting of shelled corn is resulting in major changes in the processes of conditioning and storing corn. The rate of change in harvesting method is not known. We do know that in the state as a whole the quantity harvested by mechanical pickers decreased from 76.0 percent in 1962, to 65.5 percent in 1963, the amount harvested by picker-shellers remained unchanged at 7.0 percent, and the quantity harvested by corn combines increased from 17.0 to 27.5 percent. These percentages represent a lot of bushels. The increase in the quantity harvest by corn combines was 90 million bushels and brought the total of shelled corn harvested up to 259 million bushels.

One cannot accurately forecast the rate at which the change in harvesting method will proceed. It has been suggested that farmers can economically change only at the rate at which existing corn cribs become unserviceable. I should expect the rate to be much faster. Regardless of the economics, farmers want to change and will proceed to do so just about as fast as, if not faster than, they can find something to do with high-moisture shelled corn.

The change to corn combines is greatly changing the job of conditioning and storing corn. Historically, we have waited to harvest corn until it was dry enough to keep and stored it in slat cribs where it automatically further conditioned itself for indefinite-term storage after it was shelled. A storable product was harvested.

1. T. A. Hieronymus is professor of agricultural marketing, University of Illinois. Paper presented at the Illinois Grain Dealers' Annual Convention, Peoria, Illinois, May 20, 1964.

Now we are changing to the harvest of a nonstorable product that is capable of nothing by way of self-conditioning or automatic improvement in keepability.

The change requires a new technology of conditioning and storage and very large capital investment in new equipment and facilities. From an economic point of view, it is important that this be done with the kinds of equipment and at the locations where it can be done the cheapest and that the correct decisions be made at the outset before large amounts of capital are sunk in the wrong kinds of equipment and at the wrong locations. Sunk capital must be used.

The choice of location is, I think, between farms and country elevators. I do not think it economically feasible nor likely that sufficient amounts of transportation will be made available to move the problem out of the country at harvest. The statistics of the number of boxcars available indicate that we have not had a boxcar shortage the past two falls. Rather, we have had the rapid harvest of large corn crops, in large measure wet, shelled corn. Further, I do not think that the conditioning and storage of corn can be done as economically at destination as in the country. The choice between farm and country elevator is not either all of one or all of the other. The fact is that part of the job will be done on farms and part in country elevators.

COSTS ON FARMS AND AT ELEVATORS

It is difficult to make a good tabulation of costs of conditioning and storing corn, either on farms or at elevators. Davis has calculated the farm costs that can be avoided by hiring elevators to dry and store, basis a 13,200 volume, batch-in-bin system.[2] These are fixed costs of handling and drying equipment, 2.37 cents; fixed costs storage structure, 3.80 cents; hauling and unloading, 1.45 cents; drying, 2.8 cents; insurance and treating corn, 1.40 cents; for a total of 11.82 cents of which 6.17 cents is fixed costs. To this should be added shrinkage of .5 cents and loss of weight from drying from 15.5 percent to 13 percent, 3.20 cents. The grand

2. V. W. Davis, "Costs of Storing Shelled Corn on Farms," Proceedings of the Sixth Agricultural Industries Forum, Feed and Grain Industries, January 23, 1964.

total is 15.52 cents. In point of fact, corn dried on farms is often taken below 13 percent so that the shrinkage factor is greater.

Other costs include interest on money invested in corn and personal property taxes. The first of these amounts to about 1/2 cent per bushel per month, and taxes are about 1.5 cents if corn is held past April 1. But these costs exist in the case of country elevator storage.

Two significant points other than the total stand out: (1) a high production of the total cost is fixed investment in facilities; and (2) the cost of the operation for the season is about the same regardless of the length of the storage period. The significance of the first is that once a farmer has made an investment in drying and storage equipment, he can operate fairly cheaply. He is a much easier competitor before he gets equipped than he is after. The point that costs are about the same regardless of the length of the storage period relates to the kind of charge structure that elevators might reasonably use.

Costs at elevators for performing the same services are somewhat lower. Gillfillan has estimated a total cost of 2.43 cents for the removal of 5 points of moisture from 500,000 bushels of corn with a 1,000-bushel-per-hour dryer.[3] As the dryer is used less, the cost goes up.

Cost of storage varies with the kind of storage space. Space equivalent to the kind of farm storage used above is minimal and can be provided cheaply, certainly as cheaply as on farms. The extra in-and-out costs are certainly as low as those encountered on farms.

There are intangible costs in the farm drying and storage operation that do not get into the tabulation. One is labor balance. The job must be done at one of the busiest times of the year and requires a relatively high degree of skill. Second, there is risk of quality loss that is not encountered when elevator services are hired. Third, unless the drying capacity is very large, the harvesting period must be extended to such an extent that a part of the gains from smaller field losses of combines are lost. Fourth, we have assumed that farmers dry corn just down to

3. R. A. Gillfillan, "Drying and Storing Corn at Country Elevators, Proceedings of the Sixth Agricultural Industries Forum, Feed and Grain Industries, January 23, 1964.

a keepable level. In actual practice, much of the corn is dried to lower levels with an accompanying greater weight loss than indicated. Finally, we should mention the heavy capital investment that farmers must make in the whole line of new equipment. There is a factor of capital rationing that may imbalance the farm business.

I have only a limited tolerance for the detailed arguments about where the job can be done more cheaply. There is no serious doubt in my mind that conditioning and storage of shelled corn can be done for substantially less at country elevators than on farms. There are several inherent advantages that elevators have.

First, there are economies of scale in drying. The total capacity required for drying a million bushels is less if concentrated in one unit than if scattered in many. It is less if the drying period can be extended than if it must be done all at once, as is the case on farms. The operating costs (fuel, labor, maintenance) are less in large units.

The quality of the drying job is greater if the time is extended and specialized personnel are used.

Second, there are economies of scale in storage. The history of grain storage is one of a few large units rather than many tiny units. I do not think anyone who had the job of storing one million bushels of corn would build 500 individual bins of 2,000 bushels each rather than a single large unit.

Third, a more minimal job of conditioning and storing can be done at elevators than on farms. The key problem is to do the least possible amount of conditioning and storage necessary to cope with the speed of harvest. On farms it is necessary to prepare the corn at the time of harvest to keep indefinitely without further supervision. In elevators it can be conditioned the minimum amount necessary to maintain quality for the immediate future. The full conditioning job need be done only for the corn that will be kept indefinitely. The use of temperature devices and specialized personnel and the flexibility of elevator operations enabling the quick removal of grain that is in trouble makes it possible for the elevator to walk a much more dangerous line of keepability than a farmer can.

Fourth, elevators can get a better space utilization than farmers can. A bin on a farm is used to store the corn produced on that farm when the farmer wants to store it. Otherwise, it sits empty and the equipment is unused. The elevator has access to several kinds of grain, and some com is going to be held back on farms until after harvest. Thus the average occupancy can be higher.

In addition, the corn is finally going to move through an elevator. This requires a substantial facility even if the off-farm movement is spread exactly evenly through the year. To a considerable extent, this loading part of the facility can have a storage use as well, further reducing the total storage required at central locations in contrast to that required on farms. In connection with better space utilization, it should be kept in mind that a high proportion of the cost of storage is in the fixed costs of investment and depreciation. Empty space is expensive.

Fifth, elevators can come much closer to meeting the quality for which the market is willing to pay than can farmers. Corn stored on farms has to be put in the highest possible quality and kept there. The market simply does not pay for this quality at all times. Because the elevator can hold higher moisture corn and can blend various moistures and quality, it can furnish each of the outlets for corn with the quality for which it is willing to pay. There is an inherent advantage in integrating conditioning, storage, and merchandising.

Sixth, elevators can do an excellent job of maintaining the quality of com. It is more difficult for farmers to do so. Much has been written and said about the effect of high temperatures and rapid drying on the quality of corn. Some market outlets do not want country dried corn because much of it is damaged. Country elevators can maintain market outlets better if they condition corn than if it is dried on farms.

In summary, conditioning, storing, and merchandising of corn constitute a major economic activity in which substantial benefits can be obtained from the economies of scale, application of advanced technology, and specialization.

THE OPPORTUNITY AND THE HAZARD

The conditioning and storage of corn is a major economic activity. The change from one system—slat crib storage of ear corn—to another is a major change requiring new technology and major capital investment. If a high proportion of this activity is transferred off farms, a large growth in the total activity of country elevators will occur. The country elevator industry has a great opportunity for growth. Add to the growth opportunity of taking on new functions the rapid increase in the total production and marketing of grain in Illinois, and we necessarily foresee a bright future for the industry.

To capitalize on the opportunity, the industry must move rapidly. The key consideration is to get the facility investment made in the right place, which, I think, is off farms rather than on farms. To the extent that the investment is made on farms, elevators are going to have to wait until that sunk capital is exhausted before getting that particular lot of business. I do not think that farmers are going to wait to get corn combines until elevators are ready to take corn from the fields. They are changing and will continue to change.

As is true of every major change, there is not only opportunity for growth of individual firms, but there is also a hazard to survival. The business is going to go to the elevators that can receive corn as fast as farmers want to bring it in. The experience of the past two years has made this quite clear.

The hazard in the country elevator field is doubly great because of the large number of elevators. Originally the distance between elevators was established by the distance that grain could reasonably be hauled from farms with horses and wagons. Obviously this has changed, and I think it is clear that if we were starting from scratch today the spacing would be quite different.

The density of elevators in Illinois is quite great. For example, there are approximately 47 elevators in Champaign County. The total sales of grain off farms per elevator in 1962 averaged 352 thousand bushels of corn, 132 thousand bushels of soybeans, 16 thousand bushels of oats, and 33 thousand bushels of wheat, for a total of 532 thousand bushels of grain. In Logan County, 33 elevators handled an average of 300 thousand bushels of corn and 100 thousand bushels of other grain.

Obviously, these volumes were not evenly distributed, and there are a lot of units that operate on a quite small volume.

I do not know what the minimum volume for survival in the new technology is, but I suspect that it is larger than the average now being handled. If so, there are many elevators marked for extinction in the future. By way of illustration, suppose that two million bushels of all grain handled per year is a viable number. Some thirteen elevators would be required in Champaign County. If this many elevators were spaced equidistantly, no farmer would be more than 5 to 6 miles from an elevator. Such spacing is not possible, but 5 to 6 miles is not very far either. I was tempted to work the exercise out on the basis of a 10-mile maximum haul, but it was too bloody.

The essential conclusion is that now is the time for each firm to look to the future, to make plans to get in a fully modern way or to get out, either now or by gradually dwindling. And in more cases the decision should be to get out than to get in. The blunt truth is that the economics of the situation indicate that territories need to be consolidated. Merging of territories is a more graceful and mutually profitable system than competitive extermination.

WHAT ARE THE ADJUSTMENTS?

Elevators need to make adjustments so that they can follow four basic rules. The first of these is to put themselves in a condition so that they can take farmers' corn at the time that they want to bring it in and give the farmers a choice between selling on delivery and storing at the elevator. Farmers are not going to tolerate waiting for long periods in line or stopping harvest for very long before they either take corn elsewhere or provide on-farm facilities for conditioning and storing.

Further, farmers generally want to be in a position to speculate in the price of corn. They do not want to be in a position where they have no choice about whether to hold or sell at harvest. The long-run average price change is just equal to the cost of storage. However, the difference between the harvest price and the subsequent season's high is usually greater than the cost of storage. There is money to be made from successful speculation, and farmers want the chance to try. In 1963 20 percent of the corn was marketed directly from the field, and only 3 percent was stored off farms. The percentage marketed was greater than traditional harvest sales have been. It was greatest where the harvesting of shelled corn was greatest. For example, in the east-southeast crop reporting district, 44.5 percent was harvested shelled and 30 percent sold from the field, while in the central crop reporting district 36.5 percent was harvested shelled and 20.5 percent sold from the field. For the past two years farmers have been quite tolerant of being forced to sell at harvest, but I do not think that this tolerance will be a thing of long life.

The second rule is to charge an amount for drying and storing that will price a maximum of the job off farms. It goes without saying that charges must be high enough to cover costs and return a profit. But the economics are sufficiently in favor of off-farm conditioning and storage that a price above elevator cost but below farm cost can be established.

It is possible to charge a higher price for services in the short run than will stand up in the long run. The pressure of harvest the past two years has made some rather large elevator charges possible. Yet the wisdom of charging all that the traffic will bear in a particular year is questionable. A study of farmer attitudes made by Richard Gillfillan and reported at the Agricultural Industries Forum this year indicates different attitudes of farmers toward on-farm drying and storage and elevator storage in different areas. They tend to favor elevator storage in an area where charges are rather low, and farm operations in an area where charges are higher. Elevators are going into this business for the long run and should maximize long-run rather than short-run profits.

In this connection, elevators have a major teaching job to do. Farmers frequently fail to add up all of the costs involved in on-farm operations and are rather quick to suspect elevators of charging too much. The real on-farm cost structure needs to be explained to farmers, and I am afraid that a lot of this explaining is going to be left up to elevator operators.

Third, elevators must walk a fine line of danger on the brink of corn going out of condition. The worst bottleneck in dumping corn as fast as farmers want to bring it is in the conditioning processes. A large share of the cost of drying is investment in the dryer itself. The objective is to minimize the drying capacity and yet get the job done.

The largest advantage that elevators hold over farmers is their ability to hold corn at fairly high moisture. On the one hand, this enables them to avoid the weight loss taken by farmers from drying below 15.5 percent, and, on the other hand, it enables elevators to extend the conditioning process out over a much longer period of time than the harvest. This extension reduces the amount of dryer capacity required and the dryer operation costs.

Fourth, the average percent of occupancy of space must be maximized. The space required is determined by the harvest receipts of corn and soybeans minus the amount that can be shipped out during the harvest. The aggregate need for space in the state declines as the season progresses and supplies are used up. The total amount that is in storage in all space farm, country elevator, processors, and terminals is determined by forces other than the actions of the storage industry. The aggregate percentage of occupancy is determined by immutable external forces. The objective of the individual firm is to get more than an equal share while, of course, getting paid for the use of space.

Individual firms can influence the percentage of occupancy above an equal share or let it fall below. In general, country elevators are in a better position than either terminals or processors; they get first chance at the grain and have a lower cost structure. There is a lot of skill involved in space management. The good managers are going to have a higher occupancy rate and obtain a higher return per bushel of grain in storage than are poor managers.

There are three main sources of income from the use of space: warehouse rental, hedging of owned inventory, and merchandising. The first claims on space are by farmer customers. This reverts to my first rule: the need to satisfactorily serve farmers.

On occasion, space can be rented to processors, but these opportunities have not been great in recent years. In addition, this business can be declined if more profitable opportunities appear, particularly through hedging.

Much has been said about the demise of CCC as a factor in the storage market. However, much as I might like to write them off, to do so would seem premature. It appears to me that there will be a substantial increase in the carryover of corn on October 1 of this year. The increase will be carried by CCC and stored, primarily, in warehouses. CCC is also going to acquire some soybeans. The prospective 1964 crop of soybeans now looks larger than use and implies a further buildup. If farmers continue to get corn yields as high as in recent years, the current loan of $1.10 is above market equilibrium, and inventories will accumulate.

The use of hedging-owned inventories as a means of selling space is a subject in itself. It seems sufficient at this point to suggest two things: (a) there is substantial variation in the results of hedging obtained by different operators, and (b) so long as prospective gross returns are greater than out-of-pocket costs, space should be filled with hedged inventories.

During the past two years the basic gain available from hedging has been less than in the several preceding years. This was caused by the rapid decrease in CCC inventories of corn. But I am optimistic about hedging opportunities at country points in the future. There are two principal reasons for my optimism. First, there is a tendency for the cash price in the country to gain in relation to the cash price at terminals. At harvest the country tends to be tributary to the terminal while later in the season it is not. Thus, the country has a better basis gain built in than the terminal. Second, there is a tendency for the basis to be set by terminal elevators. They are the people who deliver or move hedges forward during the delivery month. They try to operate at cost or higher. So long as the terminals can make cost, the country can make a profit because of lower costs.

Storage space is essential to a good merchandising program and, conversely, a good merchandising program can make the ownership of space profitable. One aspect of merchandising is the blending of various qualities and moistures of grain. If there is opportunity to have a variety of qualities and moistures of grain on hand and this opportunity is used, profits can be obtained from blending operations. The country grain trade in Illinois has learned to do this out of CCC corn sales.

In the future, there will be a wide range of moistures of corn available most of the time. There will be just as high moisture from combined corn as elevators will let farmers bring in, lower moisture from combined corn as harvest progresses, picked corn at about 20 percent moisture, and moisture content of dried corn ranging down to an over-dried 9 or 10 percent. Elevators will hold corn at various moistures until summer so that blending opportunities will always be present.

A second aspect of merchandising is picking a time to sell when the local market is high in relation to other locations. The market directs the flow of grain by increasing the price at the points from which it wants to draw grain and decreasing the price at others. Thus, at any given point the price of a grain is like a cork on a lake, continually rising and falling in relation to the general level of the lake. Only out of an existing inventory can the opportunity to make premium sales be used.

HOW MUCH AND WHAT KIND OF STORAGE?

In view of the major adjustments that confront elevators, the pertinent question is not how much space can be effectively used, but what is the minimum amount of space that will accomplish the job of taking corn as it is harvested.

The minimum, in addition to the necessary soybean space, is equal to the harvest receipts minus the amount that can be shipped during harvest. During the harvest last fall, we tabulated the receipts of five central-Illinois elevators. During the nine weeks ending October 5 through November 30, they received three million bushels of corn. Receipts the week ending October 5 were 100 thousand bushels, and receipts the week ending November 30 were 27 thousand bushels. The peak was the week ending October 26 at 750 thousand bushels. Inasmuch as the year is not yet completed, we do not know how large the total receipts from 1963 will be, but it appears that on the order of 40 percent of the year's receipts were in the nine-week period.

An ordinary kind of boxcar allocation for shippers of the size in the study might well be 10 per week per elevator, or a total of 450 cars for the nine weeks. This number of cars would move about one-third of the harvest receipts and leave an accumulation of two-thirds.

I do not think that this rudimentary data can be applied to other elevators. I use it only as an illustration of method. Each elevator should now look back on last fall's receipts and shipments, adjust these for the losses from its usual trade territory because of closed time, and for amounts shipped by abnormal transportation procedures.

The experience of last fall is not a reliable guide to next fall. The harvest receipts last fall were a higher percentage of the receipts for the year than the year before, and it appears likely that there will be a further peaking of receipts next fall as the use of combines continues to expand.

Some estimate of the long-run requirements can be made for individual territories by making assumptions about the ultimate percent of the crop that will be combined and the share that will be stored on farms. The balance should be delivered to the elevator. From this, the potential shipments can be subtracted. The balance is the corn storage space requirement.

While at the university we are attempting to work out some norms for the state as a whole; the adjustments in capacity of elevators should be based on studies of individual trade territories.

The kind of space that should be erected is a much-discussed question. Arguments develop between upright concrete and flat space, and each has advantages and disadvantages. The answer may well lie in some balance between the two.

Upright space has the advantage that grain can be moved quickly and cheaply. As the number of times that space is filled and emptied each year increases, the value of this advantage increases.

A second advantage of upright space is that as problem spots in corn develop, they can be eliminated more quickly and cheaply. This could prevent a major financial loss. Corn of much more questionable keeping quality can be put in upright rather than flat space.

One can envision the problem encountered if a heating spot is detected in the center of a flat bin of 120 thousand bushels of com in the middle of a busy harvest!

A third advantage of upright space is the flexibility in binning various moisture and qualities of corn and in blending operations. In this connection a substantial amount of upright space appears essential.

The primary advantage of flat space is the cheaper construction cost. This reduces capital cost and, presumably, depreciation. Capital and depreciation cost on flat space is calculated at 3 to 3½, cents per bushel per year compared to 6 to 6½ cents for upright concrete storage space. Offsetting the lower cost of flat space is the high cost of putting grain in and out. The in-and-out costs vary substantially from elevator to elevator, depending on the physical situation.

A second advantage that flat space may have is in the ease with which grain can be held under aeration. It is suggested that the smaller distance that air must be pulled through corn in flat space increases the ability to hold high-moisture corn. Offsetting this is the difficulty of moving hot spots. I think the fact is that we do not fully know what can be done with aeration, either in flat or upright space. A lot of people are gaining experience this year.

The debate between flat and upright space must also relate to the question of drying capacity. It seems fairly clear that the flat space must relate to once in and once out each year because of the cost of moving corn. Thus, it follows that corn that is to be put into flat space must be put in adequate condition to hold at least until spring under aeration.

On the other hand, it seems to be possible to do a limited amount of drying of corn that is to go into upright space on the first pass through the dryer. This may well extend to simply blowing cold night air through the corn and holding it under aeration until the flush of harvest is passed. To the extent that drying capacity can be reduced, the higher capital cost of upright space is offset.

There is a system of holding and conditioning corn from corn combines that I should like to see experimented with further. It is to accept corn at harvest only as the moisture content is under 25 percent, take the moisture down to 18 percent on its first trip through the dryer, hold it in upright tanks under aeration until the press of harvest is past, and then gradually bring the moisture of the whole house down. By this process, the drying capacity and operation is minimized, and the elevator is in the position of always selling maximum-moisture corn. There is always moisture corn available to mix with corn of less than 15.5 percent moisture that comes in from farms. It should be kept in mind that a key advantage that elevators have over farmers is that they can avoid the weight loss associated with drying corn below 15.5 percent.

THE CHARGES TO MAKE

There is a great range in the charges that elevators make for drying and storage of corn. This is to be expected in a fast-changing situation; however, it is to be both hoped and expected that the charge structure will stabilize into a fairly uniform pattern.

The key consideration in the charge structure is to charge enough to make a profit but to keep charges low enough to prevent farmer investment in on-farm facilities. The charge structure should relate to the cost of performing the various services; that is, some services should not be priced below cost and others above. In the country elevator business we have seen handling margins falling well below cost so that elevators could obtain corn to store for CCC. Once these distortions get institutionalized, they are difficult to correct.

The charge for drying can be related to the implied charge in the market discount schedule. At one-cent discount for each half percent above 15.5, the market charge is the equivalent of .6313 cents per bushel per point of moisture at a price of $1.10 per bushel, or .7557 cent per bushel per point of moisture at $1.00 per bushel. This assumes that the elevator takes 1/2 percent invisible shrinkage.

A charge of .75 cent per bushel per point seems to be common around the state. It is high enough to be moderately profitable and definitely low enough to price the job off farms. At a cent per bushel per point of moisture, a substantial number of farmers will be encouraged to own dryers.

Storage charges are more variable, covering a wide range of prices from lump sums for the season to daily charges. One guide to storage charges is the cost of storage. Gillfillan arrived at a storage cost of 6.13 cents per bushel for the period of October-March and 8.54 cents for October through August for storage in upright concrete space storing one million bushels and fully occupied. These costs include allocating expenses among drying, storing, and merchandising, and require assumptions about other grains handled. They do not include property taxes on corn or interest on the value of corn.[4]

A very high proportion of the cost is fixed, that is, is incurred regardless of the length of time that corn is left in storage. Most of the 6.13 October to March cost is attributed to the first month. The cost structure suggests a season's charge or certainly a charge that has a high minimum payment.

Another guide to the appropriate storage charge is the market price of storage as it is indicated by basis patterns. I calculated the basis change, east-central Illinois points, nearby contract, from the first day of each month to the last day for the period October 1958 through April 1964. The results follow on the next page.

The basis pattern is much as we should expect; there is a rapid basis gain (high price for storage) at and immediately following harvest, and a quite slow basis gain (low price for storage) later in the year. The price of storage is high when the quantity of corn is large in relation to the available space, and the price is low when part of the crop has been used up and some space stands empty.

I adjusted the basis gain downward by 1/2 cent per bushel per month because of the interest cost that the elevator avoids if it stores for farmers rather than

4. R. A. Gillfillan, The Effects of Field Shelled Corn on Country Elevators, M.S. thesis, University of Illinois, 1964.

stores hedged corn. I have thus arrived at an opportunity cost of storing corn for farmers. The cumulative total for the first three months averaged 7.4 cents, and the average per month thereafter through July was approximately .4 cents per bushel per month. The cumulative total through July was 10 cents.

	1958-59	1959-60	1960-61	1961-62	1962-63	1963-64	5-YR AVG	MINUS ½ CENT INTEREST	CUMULATIVE TOTAL
Oct.	2.125	2.750	-3.375	1.750	1.500	-3.750	0.950	0.450	0.450
Nov.	6.625	2.625	0.750	5.875	1.250	4.750	3.425	2.925	3.375
Dec.	1.750	3.375	11.125	2.125	4.250	6.125	4.525	4.025	7.400
Jan.	-0.375	1.375	0.375	2.250	0.875	-1.125	0.900	0.400	7.800
Feb.	-0.875	0.250	0.562	1.500	-1.125	1.500	0.075	-0.425	7.375
March	2.250	2.875	0.125	-0.625	0.625	0.625	0.850	0.350	7.725
April	2.125	-0.250	3.875	0.625	-1.250	1.375	0.825	0.325	8.050
May	0.375	0.500	-0.500	3.625	1.750		0.950	0.450	8.500
June	0.250	3.375	0.250	1.250	2.000		1.425	0.925	9.425
July	0.250	0.500	3.625	-1.125	2.000		1.050	0.550	9.975
Aug.	0.250	0.625	-0.750	0.125	-1.875		0.000	-0.500	9.475
Sept.	-8.250	-4.500	3.875	2.250	-8.875		-5.125	-5.625	3.850
Total through July	14.500	17.375	16.875	17.250	12.000				
Total through August	14.750	18.000	17.625	17.375	10.375				
Total through September	6.500	13.375	21.500	19.625	1.500				

The data shows a rather small basis gain during October and the largest basis gain in December. As the use of corn combines increases, we should expect the harvest pressure to occur earlier.

This data suggests that a rate of, say, 2.5 cents for October, 2.5 for November, 1.5 for December, and ½ cent per month thereafter would be a reasonable charge system. Such a rate system should price the storage job off farms. The rate is high when farmers least want to store corn, the charge for the first three months is a low total so that there is no clear gain to farmers for erecting storage, and the ten-cent total for the year seems to be an acceptable figure.

These numbers that I use here are tentative suggestions rather than firm recommendations. There is one aspect of the problem about which I wish to be quite emphatic: because of the high proportion of the costs that are fixed and are thus incurred when the space is made available and because of the structure of opportunity costs, the rate charged for the harvest and immediately following period should be much larger than that for the balance of the year and should be large enough to cover all of the fixed costs for the season.

SOME WAREHOUSE RECEIPT PROBLEMS

The development of corn storage operations along lines that I have been discussing may necessitate some changes in warehouse rules and law. One problem is the permissibility of a charge schedule such as I have just been discussing. Frankly, I do not know nor have I looked into the question of its legality or permissibility. It makes economic sense. If it contradicts the law or regulations, then it will be necessary to change the law or regulation.

A more difficult problem is the quantity and moisture content for which warehouse receipts should be written. Suppose that a general practice develops of taking in 23-percent-moisture corn and gradually reducing the moisture content of the whole houseful to 14 percent by summer. How shall warehouse receipts be written? If the delivered quantity is receipted at 23 percent, the house will not have enough corn to cover the receipts. If the receipt is issued for a lesser amount of 14 percent moisture, the house will not have the right quality. It rather appears to be a question of which crime the warehouseman would prefer to be convicted. Yet he will be performing as a prudent and efficient warehouseman.

One solution that occurs to me is to issue receipts at three different times. One might be issued for 18 percent corn at harvest, the first one called in in January and a new one issued for a smaller quantity at 15.5 percent. Finally, the second might be called in May 1 and a third one issued for a still smaller quantity at 14 percent.

A simpler solution would be to write a receipt that would specify different quantities at different moistures for each month, and the quantity and moisture that the farmer would receive would depend upon the time that the receipt was presented. These automatically declining balances would, of course, be based on a constant quantity of dry matter.

Chapter Twenty-One

The Desirability of a Cattle Futures Market

1964

AUTHOR'S NOTE: In the early 1960s, the Chicago Mercantile Exchange proposed the development of a live cattle futures market. It drew a lot of negative response from ranchers and cattle feeders and their trade associations. It was of the "don't turn the fate of our industry over to gamblers in the futures markets" type. An invitation to address the subject at a meeting of the American Meat Institute seemed a fun outing and an opportunity to bring the facts of economic life to a group who should already know them. It was another lesson in why economists should not take themselves seriously. I presented the paper and was asked to leave the room so they could discuss the question. When we reassembled for lunch, I discovered that they had voted unanimously to use their influence to oppose the development of a cattle futures market. But, it was a good lunch featuring martinis and filet mignon, and the inevitable market did develop and prosper. It was a lesson in economic inevitability.

The general question of having some kind of cattle and beef risk-shifting system is not new.[1] I note that there was an article in *Illinois Farm Economics* in January 1952 entitled "Hedging Cattle Feeding Operations," by Hieronymus,

---

1. T. A. Hieronymus is professor of agricultural economics, University of Illinois. Talk presented to the American Meat Institute, August 13, 1964.

Scott, and Wills. It has been a long time since I read that article, but my recollection is that we explored the possibility of hedging cattle on feed in various existing media (commodity futures and securities). We were not successful. There has been forward trading in various kinds of products for a very long time. The history of futures trading in hogs goes back at least thirty years.

I think that the fundamental conditions for futures trading in the cattle complex are present and that some form of forward contracting is likely to develop. The most sophisticated and efficient system of forward contracting is futures trading, and so I expect that futures trading will develop if an effective contract can be worked out.

WHAT MAKES A FUTURES MARKET?

At the cost of oversimplification, I would answer this question by saying that futures markets evolve when there are risks present that the holders need and desire to shift to other people. Futures trading develops in the presence of risk shifting. All else—the speculation, the contract terms, and place of trading-falls into place around this central consideration. Futures markets are sometimes started where major risk shifting does not occur. In the past, these markets have faded and disappeared. I think that futures markets cannot exist if they do not serve the useful economic function of acting as a risk-shifting medium.

On the other hand, some kind of forward contracting system will evolve if a risk-shifting need is present. It may or may not take the formalized futures trading form, but it will nonetheless exist and be real. The question at hand, therefore, is not whether a futures market in the cattle complex is desirable, but what form of forward contracting in the cattle complex is most desirable.

We can best see the real nature of a futures market as we look at the structure of the open interest. There are hedgers on one side and speculators on the other.

Hedgers sell for deferred delivery, and speculators buy for deferred delivery. Hedgers are predominantly short, and speculators are predominantly long. In well-established futures markets, the total of the open interest tends to equal the amount of inventory that is in hedgeable position. In the grains, the open interest varies seasonally as the inventories vary, rising to a peak at harvest and reaching a minimum just before the next harvest.

Forward contracting in grains and other commodities preceded formalized futures trading. The establishment of futures markets has been nothing more nor less than codifying already existing trade practices.

The second major aspect of futures trading is that of establishing prices. In the hedging process, speculators gain effective control of inventory. Either they take today's price, encouraging the outflow of inventory, or they hold for a higher price at a later time. Thus, the job of establishing the short-term price is in the hands of speculators. Futures markets tend to become the central focus point of the pricing system. This arrangement has worked out satisfactorily in commodities in which there are viable futures markets. This proposition is necessarily true because an unsatisfactory pricing arrangement will not be used. Thus, futures prices are necessarily real commercial prices.

ARE FUTURES TRADING CONDITIONS PRESENT IN THE CATTLE COMPLEX?

We must look at the cattle complex in four parts: stocker and feeder cattle, cattle on feed, dressed beef carcasses, and boneless beef. The question is where the inventory risks exist. On January 1, there were 79 million head of beef cattle in the United States. In addition, there are typically 200 to 250 million pounds of beef in storage. The prices of cattle and meat change substantially over time-there is no question but that there are large aggregate risks.

The logical hedgers in stocker and feeder cattle futures market would be ranchers, but I would be surprised to find that they would make substantial use of such a market. Primary producers are logical risk bearers—I have particularly observed this fact in grains. They do not really have a great interest in shifting risks to speculators and thus, in effect, producing to contract. The basic reason is that they have a 100 percent equity in the product they sell. Price variation is usually moderate in relation to the total value. Thus, the gross returns are not greatly affected by price variation.

Cattle move from ranges and farms into corn-belt farms and feed yards for fattening. The total tonnage of beef produced in feedlots is large. The length of the feeding period varies, but the average length of time is long, and for the higher priced animals it is quite long indeed. Thus, the total inventories carried by feeders are large. Fed cattle prices are variable. The combination of large inventories and variable prices makes feeders subject to large risks.

Cattle feeders buy and sell cattle. They operate on a feeding margin. Their gross revenue is much less than the total value of the product. This is especially true for short-fed cattle. Although the proportion of produced values in calf programs is high, the feeding program is quite long, and the chances of price variation are thus great. It follows that cattle feeders are more logical hedgers than are ranchers.

The processor—and here the analogy applies to the cattle feeder—can shift his risks to someone else while proceeding with his ordinary manufacturing processes. The flour miller, for example, must carry large inventories of wheat which vary by season. In the absence of a hedging opportunity, he must concentrate on speculation as the major determinant of his gross margin. In the presence of a hedging opportunity, he can compute his operating margin quite closely, concentrate on technical efficiency in manufacturing, reduce his financing costs substantially, and operate on lower margins than would otherwise be feasible.

If cattle feeders could effectively fix their selling prices at the outset of the feeding period, they could make tight calculations of their raw material cost (feeder cattle), feed costs, and operating costs, and concentrate on efficient cattle feeding. As matters now stand, the biggest factor in contemplating a cattle-feeding operation is the uncertain selling price of cattle.

Cattle feeders are logical hedgers. I think that they are becoming more so and that this trend will continue. The reason for the change is the increasing scale of cattle-feeding operations. The operators of large feed yards and of large scale farm cattle feeding operations are less logical risk bearers than are the small-lot feeders. The northern Illinois farmer who owns and operates a 240-acre farm and feeds sixty cattle a year is in a much stronger position to assume the risks of price change than is the operator of a commercial feed yard. Although painful, losses of the sort taken during the past year do not seriously endanger his financial position or make a huge difference in his gross income. If he feeds six hundred cattle on the same basis, the increasing need to shift risk becomes readily apparent.

I think that the increase in scale of cattle feeding and the accompanying need to shift risk are such that some kind of forward contracting system for fed cattle will evolve. Thus, the question at issue is not "if" but, rather, what kind.

A comparable basis for shifting risks on dressed carcasses does not seem to exist. I doubt that meat packers have a serious risk-shifting problem. The inventories of dressed beef are not large, and they are fairly constant over time. Price variations can be isolated and absorbed with a modest inventory reserve. A last-in-first-out inventory system seems to work well.

The boneless beef inventories are not large in relation to total beef production. The price is fairly stable and shows a predictable seasonal variation. On the basis of the domestic situation, there seems little need for a hedging medium.

There is a large volume of international trade in boneless beef. The inventories in process at any given time are large. The question of whether an international futures market in boneless beef could be made to work is an interesting one but is apart from the present discussion.

CAN AN EFFECTIVE CONTRACT BE DEVELOPED?

We have traditionally tended to impose a list of conditions that must be met before a futures contract is feasible. I am not convinced that the matter is so troublesome. If a commercial contract for deferred delivery is feasible, so is a futures contract. Commercial feasibility for deferred delivery implies only the need to be able to accurately describe the commodity. The only condition beyond commercial feasibility that I would impose is the absence of monopoly conditions on either the supplier or user side of the market; that is, the price must be competitive. Clearly, the large number of suppliers and users makes control of price impossible.

It appears that under present arrangements, live cattle cannot be effectively traded by description. Yet, it is the very market that has a real need for a risk-shifting medium.

It does appear that cattle carcasses can be traded on the basis of description. There is a substantial amount of trading by description now in the market. Most of it is on the basis of buyers' standards. Generally speaking, it is at the low-choice quality level. This quality level includes a large amount of feedlot beef.

It also appears that a stable bridge exists between carcass beef prices and live cattle prices. That is, cattle prices are a nearly constant percentage of the prices of the carcasses they will make.

These considerations indicate that a live cattle futures based on carcass quality standards is feasible. My inclination is to recommend that all segments of the cattle industry concerned proceed with the development of a workable contract.

Beyond making these general comments about the contract terms, I do not wish to do more than state a general principle about futures contracts: they must not become a medium of exchange but, rather, must be a hedging and pricing medium. At the same time, they must be deliverable so that the prices will be commercial prices. The ideal contract is one that is so perfectly balanced in advantages of making and taking delivery that delivery is neither made nor taken. Markets that are consistently delivered are not good hedging markets.

Chapter Twenty-Two

The Collins Letter: Tino De Angelis

1964

AUTHOR'S NOTE: A major and often determining factor in soybean prices during the 1954 to 1963 period was the P.L. 480 sales program for surplus soybean and cottonseed oils. Upon taking office in 1953, the Eisenhower administration found itself the owner of a large quantity of oil that had been accumulated under price-support programs. There was an export market for the oil, but the countries that needed oil did not have the dollars to pay for it. Export companies were authorized to sell oil for foreign currencies and trade them to the U.S. government for dollars. The foreign currencies were used to pay U.S. costs in the recipient countries and to finance development projects. What the USDA was doing about P.L. 480 allocations was a major factor in soybean prices.

Allied Crude Vegetable Oil Refining Company, owned and directed by one Tino De Angelis, was a major player in the export program. Tino was the focus of attention he seemed to be able to undersell his competitors and mystified the market for a long time. What he was doing became clear when the De Angelis house of cards was brought down in bankruptcy. The series of events and their culmination were the major commodity event of its time. Norman C. Miller, of the *Wall Street Journal*, was awarded the Pulitzer Prize for a series of stories he wrote about the affair. He subsequently wrote a book entitled *The Great Salad Oil Swindle* (Coward-McCann, 1965).

De Angelis's bankruptcy was triggered by a margin call on the massive futures positions held. As was to be expected, a strong antifutures trading cry went up, and further regulative power was proposed in Congress.

On June 3, 1964, I received a letter from Warren Collins, Assistant Director, Commodity Division, American Farm Bureau Federation, asking for my views on proposed legislation and my thoughts regarding how the salad oil scandal developed and how this might have been prevented. Thus, the Collins Letter.

June 3, 1964
Mr. W. E. Collins, Assistant Director
Commodity Division
American Farm Bureau Federation
Merchandise Mart Plaza
Chicago, Illinois 60654

Dear Warren:

I have not yet seen S. 2859. I have asked for a copy, but if you have one available perhaps you should send it to me.

There is not any brief way to describe the vegetable oil scandal, nor are all of the facts known. About 1954, the United States started exporting substantial amounts of soybean oil to Spain under P.L. 480. A substantial share of the business was handled by Allied Crude Vegetable Oil Refining Company. As exports of various fats and oils expanded, this company became a very important market factor. They seemed to be able to undersell the competition and to get the bulk of the business. From the mid-1950s until last fall, conversations about the probable price trends were dominated by speculation about the position and actions of Tino De Angelis of Allied. He was known to have built up a very large cash position in expectation of export business. In the spring of 1961, the price of oil increased rapidly and for no apparent reason except that Allied was buying heavily. I was quite surprised by the price increase at the time. As exports failed to materialize, the price declined sharply into the fall of the year. About that time, the United States Department of Agriculture purchased some 500 million pounds of oil for charitable donation. It is my impression that Allied was the principal supplier.

The price of oil was rather low and draggy from the fall of 1961 until the fall of 1963. It was apparent that Allied was carrying huge inventories, paying large storage charges and high rates of interest, and was doing a lot of export business at prices that appeared to be below cost.

As the Russian wheat business developed, stories of prospective oil exports circulated and the price increased sharply into November.

Quite suddenly, Allied declared bankruptcy. It was not surprising that the high costs of carrying oil and transactions at losses should finally catch up and cause a failure, but it was surprising that it should occur on a rising market. It was also surprising that one firm could stand such costs and losses for so long. How they did it was subsequently to become clear.

Following the bankruptcy, the people who presented warehouse receipts found that there was practically no oil. These were American Express warehouse receipts. It now appears that there were warehouse receipts out for about 800 million pounds, an amount nearly equal to the whole U.S. supply, and a far greater amount than could possibly have been at the New Jersey tank farm. It is clear that the costs and losses were paid out of fraudulently acquired funds involving warehouse receipts. Corruptions, counterfeiting, bribery, etc., were obviously rampant. This is the core of the scandal.

When Allied and De Angelis started trading in cottonseed oil futures and soybean oil futures is not readily apparent. Their market actions were apparent to the trade for some years, especially from 1961 on. Their market position seemed to be basically long. Their actions appeared to be the opposite of hedges; they appeared to go long futures to lend strength to a large long cash position.

By last November, Allied had accumulated a huge long position in cottonseed oil futures on the New York Produce Exchange and in soybean oil futures on the Chicago Board of Trade. Even though it did not have access to the position records, the Chicago Board of Trade raised margin requirements. De Angelis could not come up with the money and went into bankruptcy. Ira Haupt had extended De Angelis credit for margin as a hedger and, consequently, went bankrupt as cottonseed oil futures prices declined. The forced liquidation at Chicago was picked up by other traders, and the price quickly stabilized and recovered. The large ownership was diffused quickly, and the price did not change greatly. No funds of futures market customers were endangered, and all losses of the longs were paid.

Three things seem reasonably clear:

First, a large cash position was built up to the point of dominating the market and could be construed as manipulative. This is quite legal. I know of no way to prevent someone from engrossing a cash market if he wants to, and has enough money. It has proved to be stupid in the past because a price that is put above market value will finally come back down at the expense of the person engrossing the market. The history of these is a pretty good preventative. De Angelis blames the government for his troubles. This blame is misplaced. However, I doubt that the whole thing could have happened in the absence of surplus disposal programs of the USDA. Also, the history of speculation about what De Angelis was doing often suggested something less than purely competitive actions by officials of governments who receive P.L. 480 allocations.

Second, there was extensive fraud, corruption, bribery, etc., in warehousing. Possibly, some closer warehouse supervision is desirable. American Express Warehousing Company performed very badly. It did not have enough money to guarantee the quantities of product that it attempted to guarantee. The parent company, American Express, has only limited liability. Warehouses take on a public utility aspect. It is important that receipts be valid. In this connection, it is worth noting that none of the missing soybean oil was in warehouses regular for delivery on the Chicago Board of Trade. For years, the exchange supervision of warehouses regular for delivery that duplicates supervision by the federal government has looked a little silly. It looks less so now.

Third, DeAngelis and Allied Crude turned to futures market operations to bolster cash operations. This was finally their undoing. The Chicago Board of Trade got worried about how good the financing behind soybean oil contracts was, and took action to make it good. This action unstuck the house of cards and it fell. They took this action soon enough that the contracts were financially sound. No customer lost money because of invalid contracts or financial insolvency of any other customer or any agent through whom he traded. No exchange lost money or had to assume customer losses. De Angelis and his assortment of companies was in trouble with the courts, the federal government, and the trade for years; and no one seemed able to do much about it. When his actions threatened the validity of futures contracts, the commodity exchanges clobbered him. He successfully dominated the cash vegetable oil markets for years, but when he tangled with the futures markets he lost.

A lot of people lost a lot of money out of this affair. One must certainly sympathize with those who held American Express warehouse receipts that proved to be worthless and wonder if better warehouse supervision is needed.

Past this point, I have a limited amount of sympathy for the losers. Ira Haupt Company, for example, lost heavily. They extended huge credits to Allied on the basis that it was hedging, which it obviously was not. One can only explain such imprudent behavior on the basis of greed for commissions. There is an interesting sidelight in the Haupt facet of the scandal. It is my understanding that the company used securities that it held for customers to finance the Allied trades with the Produce Exchange. It was this loss that the New York Securities Exchange made up. The Produce Exchange (the futures market) already had its money and did not lose because it had been hard-nosed about margins. Also, Haupt did not use futures customers' funds because these must be held in segregated accounts.

It seems reasonably clear that other firms that lost money were fairly active participants with De Angelis to the extent of collecting big storage and interest charges, both directly and indirectly, and trading commissions. One must ascribe a substantial share of their losses to greed and be only moderately sympathetic.

When De Angelis went down, many things came up stinking. There are two notable exceptions. One is the USDA. In view of the heavy involvement of the USDA in oil surplus disposal programs since 1954, it is a substantial tribute to the integrity of USDA personnel that they are out of this clean.

Second, the institution of futures trading was clearly financially responsible and not corrupted. On November 21, 1963, two days after the collapse, I wrote Bob Liebenow, president of the Chicago Board of Trade, "One should expect some sharp repercussions, both immediate and over a prolonged period, as a result of the "soybean oil fiasco and the accompanying break."

The situation dates back several years. The essence of it was a concentrated cash position with strong manipulative overtones that was, at least in part, a by-product of governmental surplus disposal programs. In my judgment, the futures markets in soybean oil and soybeans diffused and reduced the impacts of this manipulation and were instrumental in breaking it up. As significant, these markets are currently important and useful in diffusing the concentrated holdings of the now defunct combine over a large ownership so that they can be carried and disposed of in a more orderly fashion.

Instead of being criticized, the futures markets should have an award for superior performance. I would not defend but would attack. There is a real story to be told, and I would not be bashful in telling it.

What I said then has been fully borne out by subsequent disclosures. There is no rational basis for making futures markets a whipping boy in the De Angelis scandal. Rather, the whole affair is a clear indication that futures markets are adequately governed and regulated by themselves and the Commodity Exchange Authority at the present time.

I hope that this long letter is not too confusing, but, as I said at the outset, the affair defies simple description.

Sincerely,

T. A. Hieronymus

T. A. Hieronymus, Professor
Agricultural Marketing

Chapter Twenty-Three

New Concepts in Futures Trading

1966

AUTHOR'S NOTE: I was invited and did present a mundane paper at a study conference sponsored by the Chicago Mercantile Exchange. But as I prepared the paper, some less than flattering things about the operation of exchanges and commission houses occurred to me. Although I did not include them in the mundane paper I presented, I wrote them down and supplied them to officials of the exchange in an attempt to remind them of their longer-term responsibilities. The initiation of futures trading in nonstorable commodities, such as cattle and hogs, opened up new problems in contract terms and new concepts in the functions of futures markets. First among these was the role of speculators. If markets were to fulfill their new role in ordering and guiding production, an improvement in the quality of speculation was needed. The paper "New Concepts in Futures Trading" was an attempt to point out the new role, the need for emphasis on speculation, and the responsibility of the exchanges in the development, care, and feeding of a new, improved breed of speculators.

Cattle, hog, and fresh egg futures markets are new departures in the field of futures trading.[1] Two of these new markets established by the Chicago Mercantile Exchange are working, and the third is not. I wish to look at some of the new concepts and at the things that may be needed to assist in the success of the new markets.

At the outset, I should like to commend the Chicago Mercantile Exchange for the innovations made in recent years. These have been forward-looking steps that have already enhanced the position of the Exchange (and the value of the memberships). You should continue to look ahead, to change, and to improve.

NEW CONCEPTS

Although we have long looked at futures markets as risk shifting and pricing arrangements, they are, in the final analysis, financial institutions. Their business is furnishing equity capital. Historically, futures markets have been mainly concerned with furnishing capital for carrying inventories of stored commodities. This has been accomplished by hedging, by which risks of price change associated with stored commodities have been shifted from hedger to speculator. This shifting has enabled the hedgers to borrow from the banks at prime rates of interest. The equity capital with which price changes are absorbed is furnished by the speculators who buy the hedges.

The new game, recently started, is the equity financing of production. It has been brought about by the increasing commercialization of agricultural production that has greatly reduced the ability of primary producers to carry the risks of price change.

Agriculture is changing rapidly. Production is becoming more specialized, concentrated, and commercialized. Out-of-pocket costs are becoming a higher proportion of total costs. Producers are using an increasing proportion of

---

1. T. A. Hieronymus is professor of agricultural economics, University of Illinois. Paper NOT presented at Study Conference, Livestock and Meat Futures, sponsored by the Chicago Mercantile Exchange, Chicago, November 30, 1966.

borrowed capital. Farms, those engaged in poultry and livestock production in particular, are becoming factories that buy a high proportion of their inputs. They are operating on increasingly thin margins. Thus, change in the selling price has a major effect on net return. A moderate change in price can easily halve or double the net profit. Because of these changes, primary producers are losing their ability to carry risks of price change and are looking for ways to produce at firmly contracted prices.

The method of accomplishing the objective—reducing producer risks—which is coming to the forefront is forward pricing through futures trading. As this system grows and expands, products will be produced to firm prices for delivery at the completion of production. As this occurs, the capital to finance production will be forthcoming at minimum interest rates.

The equity capital necessary to carry the risks of price uncertainty and variability is furnished by speculators. Studies of the older futures markets indicate that speculators furnish this capital at very low or even negative rates of return. It appears that speculators, as a group, lose money or at best break even minus the cost of commissions. They do this because of the leverage that minimum margin requirements makes possible. They hazard a small amount of money in exchange for the chance to make a large amount.

As capital to finance producers is furnished at minimum rates, the competitiveness of producers is increased. They are freed to concentrate on efficiency of production. A workable system of forward pricing of productions will lower costs, just as a hedging system for stored commodities has increased marketing efficiency. This is economic progress and contributes to the welfare of the nation.

The most important single problem in agriculture is the expansion of markets. As markets for products expand, more resources, particularly people, can be retained in agricultural production. Our agricultural markets are no longer based on the necessity to consume food; rather, they are based on the desire to eat better food. The markets into which we sell no longer need to consume only those foods that can be efficiently produced but, because of our productive capacity, their prices can direct the marketing and production system to furnish the products that are wanted. We must now produce to orders from consumers.

At this time, market growth is dependent upon good merchandising and new product development.

Price stability is essential to good merchandising programs. One problem that we have had in the past in increasing consumer expenditures is variable prices. This has been and is particularly true of the livestock and poultry sectors. Price stability should be maximized. It is not possible to totally stabilize price. There are vagaries of nature, changes in technology, changes in consumer behavior, and inadequacies of knowledge that make some price variation inevitable if prices are to direct the production-consumption system. Yet maximum price stability must be our goal. The fundamental goal of futures trading must be a set of prices that so effectively guides production and consumption that prices remain stable.

Futures markets live on price variability. Their goal must be to put themselves out of business.

SPECULATORS

The equity capital for production is furnished by speculators to the extent that producers forward-contract through futures markets. By doing this, the speculators gain control of production. The forward prices that are established by trading between producers and speculators order and direct production. As the distant future prices are bid up by speculators, production is increased. And as they fall, production is retarded. Speculators control prices to the extent that producers and buyers contract forward.

The responsibility for price stability rests on speculators in futures markets. The quality of the job that they do will ultimately determine the success or failure of the markets in achieving the broader objective of price stability.

It is true that speculators will carry the risks of price variation, sometimes profiting and sometimes losing, whether they do a good job of pricing or not, but this only partially improves the performance of the system. Major attention must be paid to improving the quality of the job that speculators do.

The intention of every speculator is to make money. The success of the speculator depends upon his ability to forecast prices. There are other considerations in successful speculation, but the forecasting of equilibrium prices is fundamental and determining in a fully competitive market. Speculators must analyze the quantities that will be consumed at a series of prices at specified times in the future—specifically the delivery months. They must analyze the quantities that will be furnished at a series of prices in the future. They must not be unduly influenced to the extent that they project the current supply, demand, and price situation into forecasts of prices at future times. In contrast to the inventory hedging markets, these new markets are truly forward contract markets; they are supply determining.

To the victor belongs the spoils; to the more skilled forecasters will go the profits and to the less skilled will go the losses. As the speculators, as a group, become more skilled, the less it will be necessary to adjust prices as the forward contracts mature and the prices become more stable; and the less will be the remaining profit opportunities.

WHAT THE MARKET MUST DO

All of this is by way of a preface to what the market must do to achieve its full potential. I shall list three principal things. First, it should teach forward contracting through futures trading to producers, buyers, processors, and distributors. The history of most futures markets is that they are built on forward contracting hedging; the need to shift risks comes first, and where there is risk and price variability speculation follows.

This is a big teaching job and requires a large and continuing effort. Producers, in particular, must be taught how to contract forward, the way in which their trading activities are related to their production operations, the relationship of their cash prices to futures prices, and how to account and relate profits and losses. This is what this study conference has been about. More important, they must be taught not to speculate. The Exchange and public agencies, such as the Cooperative Extension Service, can do some of this teaching, but the bulk of the effort must be made by the commission merchants. They are the only ones who can do the job because they are the ones who directly profit from the generation of new business.

Second, the market must help speculators make money. Speculators must be furnished a flow of information that can be used in forecasting, and they must be taught to use the information in making forecasts. Unfortunately, before these things can be accomplished someone must learn what information is pertinent and how to use it. Then the speculators must be taught to avoid mistakes in capital management, of letting mistakes in forecasting become too expensive, and overtrading. This latter is necessary if the lives of the speculators are to be preserved long enough for them to learn to forecast; keep them alive first, and then teach them to forecast.

Third, the market, the members of exchanges in particular, must continually and carefully examine contract terms, trading procedures, and business practices of commission merchants to see that all facets of the futures trading mechanism are operating in the best long-run interests of the outside customers, both hedgers and speculators. In making this comment, I am not levelling criticism against existing terms, procedures, and practices on the Chicago Mercantile or any other exchange. Rather, I want to suggest that the exchanges have a semi public-utility role to play and that there are many things about futures trading and commodity exchanges that are not fully known, and some of the things that are known are not fully understood.

To achieve its maximum potential and to fulfill the financing mission, a high proportion of the total production of cattle, hogs, eggs, and, eventually, other products must be brought within the forward-contracting system. If the objective of achieving sophisticated price forecasting and discounting is to be accomplished, a large and skilled group of speculators must be drawn in and retained. The market must operate in the best interests of these two groups. This may not serve the profit maximization objectives of all of the members of the exchanges.

Exchanges must not be run for the benefit of their members but for the benefit of commission house customers and speculating members. These are not mutually exclusive. Those things that serve the best interests of hedgers and speculators also serve the best long-run interests of most of the membership. The achievement of the semi public-utility role places a heavy burden of responsibility on the exchanges. They are democratic bodies, run by the membership. The high degree of democracy present in the government of commodity exchanges makes them somewhat resistant to change. They must continually prod themselves to take a careful look and change where change is needed. Improvements often hurt some of the membership, particularly in the short run.

I should like to suggest some areas in which more knowledge is needed. The results of such research may vindicate existing rules and practices, or they may suggest changes that can better enable the markets to fulfill their roles. I am not suggesting critical investigation, but constructive research.

First, I should like to suggest careful study of the structure of the open interest in the various commodities traded, particularly cattle, hogs, and pork bellies. Prior to the inception of cattle futures trading, I argued that the success of trading would depend upon the use of the market by feeders as a forward-pricing system. I thought that it would be so used. I should now like to know the extent to which feeders use the market, how the use relates to their feeding operations, and the trading results. These things would be useful in directing further educational and promotional efforts.

I have long since been fascinated by the large open interest in pork bellies in relation to storage stocks. A detailed knowledge of the structure of the open interest in bellies would yield totally new and unique insights into futures trading. Similarly fascinating is the failure of skinned hams to trade in volume even though the commercial situation and price variation is closely comparable to that of bellies.

Second, a study of the trading results and methods of operation of the speculator customers of commission houses would be useful in evaluating and improving the pricing usefulness of the market. There are many opinions about how speculators operate and fare, but little is known. If there is a large turnover of customers, the pricing usefulness is probably less than if there is a small turnover. One cannot be around markets for long without hearing innuendo about churning accounts and hustling for commissions. It would be well to know the facts. More than any other group, commission merchants must operate with special circumspection. The position of account executive is a semiprofessional one.

A third kind of study might be called a flow of funds analysis. The clearinghouse breaks even; for every long there is a short, and for every profit there is a loss, but several kinds of traders exist. One list of kinds might be small hedgers, large hedgers, combined hedgers-speculators, scalpers, floor traders, professional speculators, large-scale speculators, and small-scale speculators. A careful study of who wins and who loses would be useful in evaluating contract terms, trading rules, and commission-house practices.

None of these comments are meant to imply that market use should be restricted in any way. It is each person's own peculiar business if he wishes to trade. Markets must remain open and competitive. Nor do these comments imply any wrongdoing or questionable practices. It is quite as important to illustrate that which is good and correct as it is to search for things that need improvement. Nor are my comments applicable to the Chicago Mercantile Exchange alone. It does seem important to me that the Mercantile take leadership in market analysis consistent with the leadership that it has taken in the development of the new concepts in futures.

CONCERN WITH GROWTH

I think that my concern with the future of futures trading is readily apparent. I trust that I have made my enthusiasms for the new developments equally apparent. It is incumbent on all of us who work in the area to promote widespread use by producers, processors, and distributors as well as to assist in the development of a large group of competent speculators.

There are three routes we can go in pricing of agricultural products in the increasingly commercial agricultural world-three routes in the search for greater price stability: first, toward government price establishment; second, toward vertical integration and dominance by a small number of large firms; and third, toward larger futures markets. I think in the third direction lies the maximum competitive efficiency and the maximum individual opportunity and freedom.

Chapter Twenty-Four

Statement to The Domestic Marketing and Consumer Relations Subcommittee of The House Agriculture Committee

1966

AUTHOR'S NOTE: The De Angelis affair did, indeed, spawn legislative proposals. An invitation to appear before the pertinent subcommittee was a welcome opportunity to educate the Congress about the fundamentals of futures markets and to express faith in a competitive economic system that congressmen generally profess but deny in their approach to regulatory legislation. Did it have an effect? Who knows? But, it was a fun "in your face" game.

April 6, 1966

A proposal for the extensive amendment of the Commodity Exchange Act has been placed before both houses of Congress and the United States Department of Agriculture. If enacted into law, these changes may have major effects on the operation of existing futures markets. More important, they will have major effects on the development of futures markets for additional commodities that, as a result of the nature of the commodities, need to take on quite different characteristics than the older markets. Some of the provisions of the proposed legislation are salutary and should receive support. Others contain possibilities of causing severe damage and should be rejected.

PHILOSOPHY OF THE PROPOSALS

An understanding of the proposals first requires a look at the philosophic concepts involved. First, the bill is massive and comprehensive. For many years, the Commodity Exchange Act has been amended in a piecemeal fashion, and the Congress has considered small suggestions for change in such a way that the law, as it now stands, has gradually evolved. The proposal for massive change implies that this procedure has been inadequate. It casts critical reflection on the legislative history of the existing law. However, the economic effectiveness of existing futures markets supports the historic process and casts doubt on the need for great changes.

Second, the proposals would invest sweeping powers in the hands of the Secretary of Agriculture. He would have great discretion in control of businesses and individuals and, indeed, over the market mechanisms. Philosophically, I suggest that economic affairs should be regulated by markets and by law. They should not be regulated by administrative fiat.

Third, the proposals are concerned with the same two major aspects of futures trading with which all of the legislation since 1921 has been concerned: (a) manipulation and excessive speculation, and (b) protection of the public from malpractice and fraud. I have no quarrel with the latter of these and will not speak of the parts of the bill that pertain to commission futures merchants, financial responsibility, etc.

The USDA has long been preoccupied with price excesses in futures markets and, thus, with manipulation and excessive speculation. The underlying concept seems to be that futures markets exist for hedging and that speculation is a necessary evil, that hedging is good and speculation is bad, and that speculation should only be tolerated to the degree necessary to absorb the risks shifted by hedgers.

A good example of this attitude is found in some comments of the Joint Committee of the Economic Report in December 1947. Mr. Mehl, who was then administrator of the Commodity Exchange Authority, said, "I believe that if we are to maintain the present system of marketing, with the incident of hedging which enables processors and dealers to transfer the price risk from their shoulders to speculators who are willing to assume these risks, we will have to tolerate some degree of speculative trading in order to take up the slack between the merchant and processor who wants to buy for hedging purposes, and the one who wants to sell for hedging purposes." In immediate response, Representative Rich said, "I am not interested in trying in any way to stop legitimate business; I want that to proceed. But, I thought if there [were] anything that you could suggest to our Committee whereby we might, from your experience, stop speculation pure and simple, and let legitimate trade go on, I wish you would make that recommendation."

Hedging serves useful economic purposes that have long been understood and appreciated. The legislative record is replete with testimonials; the textbooks describe and extol the merits of hedging; and the Commodity Exchange Act has been changed from time to time in the direction of more considerate treatment of hedgers.

In fact, hedging is the lesser beauty of futures markets. These markets are competitive pricing institutions operating in a highly uncertain and, thus, speculative context. The futures prices established in these markets are speculative prices established by the trading activities of speculators. In addition to absorbing the risks shifted by hedgers, speculators serve the necessary and useful purpose of establishing prices that regulate the flow of stored commodities onto the market and that guide future production.

Thus, the two major functions of futures markets are risk shifting and pricing. In my judgment, the speculative pricing function is of the greater importance, and it is performed better as the level of speculative activity is greater.

Commodity prices have certain jobs to do. Most important among these are the guiding of production and the regulation of the rate of consumption. The prices that will result in an equilibrium between demand and supply forces are uncertain and, thus, speculative. Equilibrium prices continually change as the underlying factors affecting supplies and requirements change. The market is continually searching for that single price that will just equate supply and use. If the market were all knowing and all wise, there would be no price variation. As the balance of judgments in that market is that the price should go up, it is quickly bid higher. The converse is, of course, true. All things foreseen are quickly discounted into current prices so that, at any given time, the judgment of the market is that price will not change.

These speculative functions must be performed whether in futures or in cash markets. There are futures markets for only a few of the many commodities that move in commerce. The question is whether the speculative job is accomplished better in futures markets than in cash markets. A perfect job would be no price variation. This is not possible because some things are unforeseeable, such as drought, floods, etc.

Careful examination of futures markets—comparisons of the price variation in actively speculated markets and the less actively speculated markets, and comparisons with price variation of commodities in which there are no futures markets—suggests a stabilizing influence of speculation. Most certainly, the actively speculated markets do not have any consistent pattern of price variation. Variations in prices are random.

For every long, there is a short, and, thus, for every dollar gained, there is a dollar lost. Speculation, then, is a zero-sum game in which speculators vie with each other for profits that they, in the aggregate, cannot achieve. Competition in the major futures markets is so highly developed that the theoretical model of perfect competition is closely approached. Speculators compete with each other, and each competes against the market. When a speculator takes a market position, he is saying, "I am right and the market is wrong." The thing that he thinks he is right about is that price which will just equate supply and use. And this is also what the market thinks it is right about.

The speculators who are accurate in their forecasts make money, and those who are wrong lose. In his quest for profit, the speculator is guided to making the best price forecast of which he is capable. He then hazards his money in support of his judgment. Thus, speculation is what futures markets are truly about, and speculators are very skilled. First, tremendous efforts go into price forecasting. The most advanced techniques are employed. The network of information is extensive. For example, the recent rain in South Africa was quickly registered in Chicago corn futures prices.

A second indication that futures markets are good is the difficulty that price forecasters have in being right. Over the years, I have achieved some stature and reputation as a forecaster of soybean and soybean product prices. I do not want to do anything to destroy this concept, but I have looked back and must recognize that, at best, I have batted only slightly better than five hundred. This mediocre record does not indicate that I am incompetent, but rather it is mediocre because I have been batting against major league pitching. The market is a tough competitor.

The USDA does a lot of price forecasting. The several Situation Reports such as Fats and Oils, Feed, Wheat, etc., are competently prepared and very useful. However, their record is no better than mine. When power is granted to the Secretary of Agriculture to control excessive speculation that is judged at a given time to have put prices too high or too low, someone has to decide when the existing price is too high or too low. Price excesses can be judged by hindsight, but I do not know of anyone who is qualified to make such a judgment with sufficient accuracy to dictate the market price. If there is such a person in government, he should be moved to price outlook work. I doubt that there is such a person; government salaries are not that high.

The point that I wish to emphasize is that the wisdom of the market is great. If this were not so, it would be possible for every reasonably competent technician to make a fortune. This obviously does not happen.

The burden of what I have said is that the philosophic concept, that hedging is good and speculation is a necessary evil, is wrong. Competitive speculation in major futures markets is a thing of beauty and a joy forever. Legislation with regard to futures trading must recognize this.

ANCESTRY

I should next like to speak to the ancestry of the bill. Some of the current proposals are orphans who have been looking for a father for a long time. The request for authority to control margin requirements was associated with the efforts to prevent inflation and reduce the high price of grain in December 1947. In 1948, the case for control of margin requirements was related to the severe decline in grain prices in February 1948. In 1950, the request for control over margins was attached to the Defense Production Act of 1950. None of these fathers claimed the orphan.

The alleged father of the current set of changes is Mr. Tino De Angelis of Allied Crude Vegetable Oil and sundry other companies. It is fitting that the amendments should be on a massive scale because certainly the De Angelis affair was massive. But never has a less likely parent been chosen. The single most important argument against the current bill is the tremendously successful performance of futures markets under the impact of the De Angelis assault. In early 1964, Mr. Warren Collins, of the American Farm Bureau Federation, asked me for my opinion about the proposed changes in the Commodity Exchange Act and, in the same letter, "how the soybean oil scandal developed and how it might have been prevented." I replied under the date of June 3, 1964. It is a long letter and for this I apologize, but it tells a story about futures markets that badly needs telling.

FOUR OBJECTIONS

Finally, I would like to comment on four specific provisions of the bill. First, the abolition of the Commodity Exchange Commission. The most important function of the CEC is the establishment of speculative position limits. In 1936, the Congress reserved authority to limit positions to the commission composed of the Secretary of Agriculture, the Secretary of Commerce, and the Attorney General. This put a desirable brake on precipitous action. I cite an example. In 1953, the USDA proposed speculative limits of fifty contracts per person on soybean oil, cottonseed oil, and lard. These were amounts of about 2 percent of the open interest then existing. It was argued in opposition that such small amounts would inhibit the growth of the young soybean oil market and impair its use. The CEC adopted the amount but suspended the implementation indefinitely. The limits are in existence today but remain suspended. On March 17, 1966, the open interest in soybean oil futures at Chicago was 17,023 contracts. The 2 percent standard applied to this amount would be 340 contracts. I think that had the fifty contract limit been put into effect, the market would not have grown and developed into the very useful hedging and pricing mechanism that it now is. An unwise action was prevented by the CEC; it should not be abolished.

Second, cease and desist orders, and injunctions. These two things would permit the Secretary of Agriculture, directly or through the Attorney General, to compel traders to comply with his notions of what price behavior should be. It presupposes that the Secretary can recognize incipient cases of price distortion. A basic criticism of these provisions goes back to the difficulty of anticipating price changes. Seemingly erroneous courses of prices often, if not usually, turn out to be quite correct when we gain the advantage of hindsight. Speculative actions that seem most misguided usually turn out to be correct and profitable.

Were such power placed in the hands of the Secretary, there would be a great temptation for him to act frequently and closely control markets. His slogan might well be: "When in doubt, prevent-because we cannot afford to have failed to take action when evidence of illegal action subsequently comes to the fore." It is difficult enough to be a speculator without being subject to precipitous action of the Secretary. The Secretary now has great powers of persuasion because he has power to bring action when violations occur. To grant the power of cease and desist and of injunction is to grant the power to punish. This does not belong to a regulatory agency but rather to the law and the courts.

Third is the definition of manipulation. The bill says that "the word manipulate shall be construed to mean the exacting, causing, or maintaining of an abnormal or artificial price by any course of action which raises, depresses, fixes, pegs, or stabilizes the price at or to be a level different than that which would otherwise prevail." As I read this, it says that at any time an artificial price is judged to have existed; that is, if a price declines subsequent to a rise or rises subsequent to a decline, everyone who had a part in the move is guilty of manipulation. Everyone who makes a trade, even the smallest job-lot trader, has an effect on price and causes it to be something different that otherwise would have prevailed. Thus, every trader would be guilty and those selected by the Secretary would be punished. Accusations of manipulation have been brought by the Secretary on numerous occasions during the past thirty years. Some of the accused have been found guilty, and some have not. I do not think that the law should be changed to define all of the accused guilty.

The word *manipulate* was not defined in the Commodity Exchange Act of 1936. Definition has been left to the courts. Over the years, a fairly clear concept of the nature of manipulation has evolved. This concept contains five considerations: (1) an artificial price, (2) intent, (3) effective control of the cash supply, (4) a dominant position in futures, and (5) causation of and responsibility for the artificial price. Each of these is subject to investigation and judgment. Manipulation cases are not simple. They are not simple because the forces affecting prices and of competitive power in markets are not simple. They cannot be made simple by definition in the law.

Fourth is the control of margin requirements. As I have pointed out, this proposal has a long history, and the Congress has wisely refused its passage. The alleged purpose of the proposal is control of excessive speculation. To use margins for this purpose requires that the Secretary identify excessive speculation when it is occurring. We can only tell in retrospect whether a given price change is warranted or not.

An important reason for not granting margin control is that it would not work. Suppose that the longs do get overly exuberant, the price goes up sharply, and this is recognized by the Secretary. He imposes higher margins. The longs will not have any trouble; they already have profits and experience no difficulty. The shorts will have difficulty since they have losses; it is their capital position that is extended. An increase in margin requirements will force them to buy in short positions, lending further upward impetus to prices. Long speculators do not mind a margin call in a rising market; the shorts do. I have long been intrigued by CEA thinking on this matter.

Margin requirements serve the necessary and useful purpose of guaranteeing contracts. The exchanges keep them at levels adequate to accomplish this purpose. The De Angelis affair makes this clear. The validity of contracts is essential to the effective functioning of futures markets. This function of margins should not be endangered by giving some other purposes to margins.

Margins should be kept at minimum levels consistent with contract guarantee. Capital for carrying inventories is furnished to markets by speculators at a very low or negative rate of return. If speculators are impaired from furnishing capital, the cost of obtaining funds from other sources will be greater and the cost of markets increased. Money to finance inventories that are hedged can be obtained at prime rates. This is true because there is almost no risk of loss. There is no risk of loss to banks because speculators assume the risks of ownership.

Margins should be kept at minimum levels to maximize competition in markets. Margins affect ease of access to markets. The markets' best defense against dominance by a few, monopoly, manipulation, or overexuberant speculation is competition provided by other traders who detect and defeat such efforts and mistakes. This is the stuff that successful speculators are made of. Their ability to enter the market and compete should not be impaired.

CONCLUSIONS

The four provisions that I have singled out are not the only ones to which I object, but they are sufficient to make my basic point: the underlying philosophy of the bill is wrong. It is based on a misunderstanding of the nature of speculative markets. The bill reveals a failure on the part of the USDA to appreciate the function of commodity futures markets in providing risk capital and in the establishment of interim prices.

The bill fails to recognize the high order of competition that exists in futures markets and, in fact, denies the effectiveness of competition in market regulation. Its central thesis is that competition is not a sufficient means of price establishment and that competition is not a sufficient means of controlling market excesses, dominating power, and manipulative efforts. In essence, the bill is a denial of the effectiveness of a competitive economic system.

Legislation, with regard to futures trading, should have as its basic objective an increase in the competitiveness of the markets. The function of the law in economic matters is to establish a framework of rules within which competition can flourish and be maximized. Past this point, we must have faith in the system.

My fundamental plea is for an appreciation of futures markets as belonging to the highest order of competition and for an expression of faith in the wisdom of the market. In this piece of legislation, you are faced with a choice between the wisdom of the Secretary of Agriculture, whoever he may be, and the wisdom of the market. I think it best to choose the wisdom of the market because this wisdom is the essence of our competitive economic system.

Chapter Twenty-Five

Where Are We in Modernizing Our Grain Markets?

1969

AUTHOR'S NOTE: The paper "Where Are We in Modernizing Our Grain Markets?" is something of a cry of frustration. At a five-year checkpoint time, the neat package that I thought should develop was developing at a slow rate and only partially in the direction that I expected. It is illustrating the tedious ways in which major economic evolutions take place.

My quick answer to the question posed in the title is to ask another question: In relation to what? If it is in relation to where we were five years ago, I should observe that a limited amount of progress has been made.[1] If it is in relation to where we are going, I should say that there is a long, long way to go. Quite frankly, I am surprised that so little progress has been made during the past five years.

My comments today are brief and will touch on four areas: (1) developments in country grain marketing, (2) technology of conditioning and storage, (3) transportation, and (4) quality and its evaluation. They are much more a recitation of unknowns than knowns.

---

1. T. A. Hieronymus is professor of agricultural economics, University of Illinois. Talk presented at Grain Sessions, Eleventh Agricultural Industries Forum, Urbana, Illinois, January 29 and 30, 1969.

IN THE COUNTRY

I recently reviewed comments that I made five years ago. At that time I said that I thought the job of conditioning and storing corn harvested as shelled corn rather than ear corn would be done in the country, either on farms or at country elevators. While I expected a part of the job to be done at each, I thought that the economies of scale and specialization greatly favored the country elevator and that elevators should gear up to do the job. I further said that to survive in the long run required elevators to (1) dump corn as fast as farmers wanted to bring it in, (2) allow farmers to retain ownership of conditioned and stored corn so that they would not be forced to sell before or at harvest, (3) perform the storage and conditioning jobs cheaply enough to price them off the farms, and (4) change firm and plant technology so that the receiving, conditioning, and storage functions would be sufficiently profitable to attract new capital.

My biases have not changed during the intervening five years. The long-run survival of the country elevator system depends upon successful expansion activities in receiving, conditioning, and storing field-shelled corn.

I have tried to briefly quantify the developments from the 1963 through the 1969 crops in the following table. Production increased rapidly and shows every promise of continuing to increase. The amount of the crop that was harvested shelled also increased rapidly. The striking thing is that the amount harvested by conventional pickers has not gone down rapidly. The decrease from 1963 to 1964 was significant, but it appears that a limited number of pickers have since been retired.

The amount of corn marketed from the field increased through 1965 and has since declined. Offsetting this decrease in harvest selling has been an increase in warehouse storage by farmers. This bit of information tends to make the point that farmers are not going to be tolerant of a system that does not permit them to retain ownership past harvest.

Storage in corn cribs necessarily parallels the use of corn pickers. The existence of corn cribs perhaps explains much of the continued use of corn pickers. The high cost of conditioning and storing shelled corn is delaying the rate of change to corn combines. But the existing corn cribs are mortal. Replacing them is very expensive, and they will not be replaced as they fall down, blow down, or burn down.

CORN: HARVESTING, DRYING, STORING IN ILLINOIS
(figures in millions of bushels)

	1963	1964	1965	1966	1967	1968
TOTAL PRODUCTION	770	740	919	827	1,092	902
Harvested shelled[1]	312	352	505	485	704	600
Harvested ear	458	388	414	342	388	302
STORAGE						
Marketed from field[2]	143	179	224	148	177	149
Warehouse[3]	22	28	53	83	148	95
Total commercial	165	207	277	231	325	244
Crib	437	372	391	325	369	287
Bin and silo	168	161	251	271	398	371
Total farm	605	533	642	596	767	658
Percent farms	79	72	70	72	70	73
DRYING						
Custom, returned to farms	13	19	8	9	14	10
Custom, warehouse storage[4]	22	28	53	83	148	95
Other commercial[5]	143	179	224	148	177	149
Total commercial	178	226	285	240	339	254
Natural	513	417	494	401	400	329
Artificial	79	74	195	225	352	329
Total farm	592	491	689	626	752	548
Percent farms	77	66	75	76	69	72

Source: Reports of the Cooperative Crop Reporting Service, Illinois, and USDA

1. Combines, picker-shellers, and stational sheller in field.
2. Assumes all corn is stored.
3. For farmers.
4. Assumes all warehouse storage was custom-dried.
5. Assumes all corn moving at harvest was dried.

The drying data first tells us that not much corn gets commercially dried and returned to farms. At least in this instance, data confirms expectations.

There has been a fairly rapid increase in commercial drying of com—from 178 to 339 million—an increase of 161 million bushels. The numbers overstate-some corn that moves off farms at harvest is not dried but is held under heavy aeration, and not all of the corn that's dried is dried at country locations.

It is interesting to note that natural air drying exceeds the crib storage. Some corn that is field-shelled is stored under natural air.

Artificial drying on farms increased from 79 million bushels in 1963 to 352 million bushels in 1967, an increase of 273 million.

In summary, I would make three points: (1) the increase in off-farm storage has been substantially less than the increase in on-farm storage; (2) the increase in on-farm drying has been substantially greater than the increase in off-farm drying; and (3) there is still a large amount of corn harvested and stored in the ear that will eventually be harvested and stored as shelled corn.

From these data it follows that I was wrong initially, or that country elevators have not and are not expanding to take advantage of their opportunities, or that farmers are acting irrationally. Most likely, it is some combination of all these: that a part of the job belongs on farms, that elevators have not adjusted, and that farmers have acted irrationally. But I remain disappointed in the relative rates of expansion on farms and at country elevators. A few explanatory observations are in order.

First, developments vary widely by areas of the state and by elevator territories within areas. There are territories in which elevators have expanded; the on-farm conditioning and storage is limited; and elevators are profitable. At least in some areas, the job can be done to the satisfaction of both elevators and farmers.

Second, there is a serious lack of knowledge about relative costs on farms and at elevators. For one thing, we do not know costs, and for another, the decision makers have not been taught that which is known. For this, we at the university must take much of the blame.

Third, some elevators are charging too much. I can point to elevators that charge one cent per point for moisture removal, shrink corn to 14 percent, and charge 1½ cents per bushel per month. Customers of these elevators are forced to either sell at harvest or go to on-farm operations. I would not be critical of such elevators if they were making money, but they are not.

Fourth, there are inherent problems in shrinking an industry that is composed of many firms. It is clear that there are far too many country elevator plants in the state for them all to expand and operate efficiently. There is a great deal of sunk capital, management, and labor that is not mobile and must be consumed in place. These sunk resources operate very cheaply while they last and furnish severe competition. This requires a very high level of efficiency of new capital and management.

Fifth, the long-run development of the system may be accompanied by a major change in ownership and management form. In the main, country elevators have been small, independent businesses operating with local management and capital. This applies to both independents and cooperatives. The huge amounts of capital required, the changes in technology, and the enlarged managerial function may require vertical integration that extends down to the country from processors, exporters, and large, horizontally integrated firms. If the capital and management is not forthcoming locally, it will move in from the outside.

TECHNOLOGY

A key problem in adjustment to field-shelled corn is the lack of development of new technology. The most efficient ways of receiving, conditioning, storing, and shipping corn are not known. What is the optimum size, in capacity or volume, of the country elevator plant? What combination of aeration and drying is most efficient? What is the maximum feasible moisture removal? What is the best combination of handling and dead-storage space? What traffic layout will maximize speed at lowest cost? These are some of the unanswered questions. We lack systems engineering for country elevators.

In addition to these physical problems, there are organizational, capital, and managerial problems that have not been solved.

TRANSPORTATION

Uncertainty about transportation developments in the future has had a retarding influence on modernization of the grain marketing system. It would be desirable if we knew what kind of transportation system and rate structure would exist a decade from now. Most particularly, it would be desirable to know what the real inbound and outbound transportation economies are. It appears that large outbound shipments are of lower cost than smaller ones. But as the distance from farm to country elevator increases, so does inbound transportation cost. At some point efficiency is offset by inefficiency, but the point is unknown.

Rapid progress has been made in modernizing the transportation system. Large trucks move cheaply on the improved highway system. Barge rates have declined to quite low levels. These declines have been accompanied by loud cries of losses, but I do not note a decrease in the offering of service.

The rail rate structure has changed more rapidly during the past decade than might reasonably have been expected. The basic change has been from a value of service to a cost of service and from a package of services to minimum services basis.

The transition is far from complete. There is much further to go before rates are fully rationalized with cost.

QUALITY

Almost nothing has been done by way of modernizing our quality standards or the measurement of quality. There are especially urgent problems relating to corn quality.

It appears that the system has gone backward in the maintenance of the quality of corn. The changed harvesting, conditioning, and storage methods are literally beating corn to pieces. This appears to start at the combine and continue through all points to final use.

A great deal of difficulty is encountered in making the measurements of quality as described by current grade standards. A major problem is the measurement of foreign material in high-moisture corn. The confusion with regard to moisture testing has not been reduced. There is a need for a device that measures not only the average moisture of a sample but the range of moistures as well. There is a significant difference in test weight between high and low moisture content of corn.

Revisions in corn quality standards are under consideration. Possible changes relate to allowable moisture, seed coat damage (stress cracks), and foreign material. It appears likely that foreign material will be divided into two parts: small and large. The latter may well be known as "large broken kernels."

We may be approaching a time when several different marketing and quality tracks for corn develop. Quality and its measurement relate to cost of marketing and value in use. It may be that the system is not really beating corn to pieces and reducing its value but, rather, increasing its value by pregrinding it.

What I am suggesting is that the different uses of corn require corn of different specifications. The pregrinding that may be desirable for feed manufacturing may be highly undesirable for long-term storage and ruinous for dry milling.

It may be that the cheapest way to harvest, condition, store, and transport corn creates a large proportion of large broken kernels and foreign matter. This may not be greatly damaging for some purposes but may be very serious for others. If these things are true, then corn intended for different uses must go over different tracks and be evaluated against different quality standards.

There are currently several kinds of corn: normal, white, high amylase, waxy maize, and flint. The development of high-lysine corn may lead to many kinds of corn, each of which must be put over a different marketing track. Quality and measurement problems will become increasingly serious in the future.

CONCLUSION

Modernization of the grain marketing system is taking place. It is taking place at a rate slow enough that there appears to be an increasing rather than a decreasing need for modernization. It seems that the most profound conclusion that I can reach about where we stand in modernizing our grain markets is that it is unlikely that we will run out of problems in the near future.

Chapter Twenty-Six

Government and The Soybean Situation

1969

AUTHOR'S NOTE: "Government and the Soybean Situation" was a "here we go again" review of the need to look at real market forces in establishing governmental policy. A problem had developed out of a misguided policy and needed to be cleared up. Governments are slow learners. The article was published in The Soybean Farmer, February 1969.

Soybeans are in troublesome surplus. The carryover in the fall of 1966 was a minimum pipelines stock of 35 million bushels. In 1967 it was 91 million, high enough to weigh on the price but not a large proportion of the crop. In 1968 it was 167 million, which is clearly more than a prudent reserve and properly called a surplus. Current forecasts are for a carryover of about 300 million bushels in the fall of 1969.

Two decisions must be made in the near future—one of them immediately. The 1969 loan rate must be set prior to planting time, and it should be announced by February 15. At the time of this writing, it looks as if the announcement will be delayed until after the new administration takes office.

Second, longer-range price and production policy will be established with new agricultural legislation. The existing legislation for feed grains, wheat, and cotton expires with the 1970 crops. The 1970 wheat crop will be planted in the fall of

1969. Thus, Congress should write new legislation in the session beginning in January. The question at hand is what the soybean provisions should be.

HISTORICAL POSITION

In the October 1953 *Soybean Digest*, I wrote, "For the past several years soybean prices have been supported at 90 percent of parity ... there are indications that a support level of 90 percent for 1954 crop soybeans would be unwise ... A support price of 75 percent of parity ($2.10) would likely preserve an essentially free market for soybeans. It would allow farmers to avoid acreage restrictions." In the January 1959 *Soybean Digest*, I wrote, "Soybeans are in trouble. There is not a large enough market to absorb current production ... The soybean industry should take its medicine now and should take a large enough dose to effect a cure ... A reduction of 46 cents per bushel in the support price appears drastic. That the support price should be set at $1.63 does not mean that the average price will be that low." This bit of violence drew substantial irate response to which I replied, "I must confess an error in writing the price-support article. Now I know that I was not arguing for lower soybean supports but was arguing for no soybean supports ... In the long run we need upwards of a billion bushels of soybeans ... The more we compromise the economic balance of the soybean industry with support schemes having to do with other crops, the less likely we are to achieve our long-run goals."

The position that I took then and have continued over the years is based on two primary notions. First, the markets for soybean meal and soybean oil, both domestic and export, have expanded at a rapid rate so that production and revenue have increased. It has been possible to have a rapid rate of expansion at profitable prices. Soybeans have a comparative advantage over competing oilseeds because of their high protein-to-fat ratio. Freely fluctuating market prices have made it possible to exploit the potential market growth and to compete effectively with other oilseeds.

Second, it has been possible to take land out of other crops and put it in soybeans, holding farm income up. But land taken out of soybeans has no alternative use; better to sell soybeans at a lower price than to have nothing to sell.

This historical position is worth mentioning here because it was the generally prevailing attitude of the industry. A review of the price-support levels makes this clear. The long-standing policy of the industry called for a decrease either in anticipation of or following the increase accumulated from the 1966 crop.

PRICE SUPPORT LEVELS SINCE 1953

1953—	$2.56	1961—	$2.30
1954—	2.22	1962—	2.25
1955—	2.04	1963—	2.25
1956—	2.15	1964—	2.25
1957—	2.09	1965—	2.25
1958—	2.09	1966—	2.50
1959—	1.85	1967—	2.50
1960—	1.85	1968—	2.50

COMPETITIVE POSITION

We cannot review here the detail of the market situation for soybean products. A few generalizations are in order.

The domestic market of soybean oil is expanding at a rate faster than population. Total fats and oils consumption per capita is essentially static. Production of other fats and oils is not expanding as rapidly as population, hence an increase in soybean oil disappearance of about 4.5 percent per year. The price elasticity of demand for soybean oil is very low; oil can be priced at nearly any level without affecting consumption.

The export market for soybean oil is made up of two parts: dollar exports and Public Law 480 programs. The dollar market has had an excellent growth rate during the past decade. Most of the increase is in the form of soybeans. This market has been subjected to severe competition during the past two years from sunflower seed oil, mainly of Russian origin; and rapeseed oil, mainly produced in Europe under large subsidy. At this moment competition from Russia has subsided. Whether or not it will be resumed is conjectural. The answer is probably related to price. If soybean oil prices go back up to the levels of 1966, the Russians may be back in the market. The general level of world prices of edible fats and oils during the past decade has been low enough to prevent rapid increases in products competing with soybean oil, such as peanut oil, palm kernel oil, coconut oil, and olive oil. Dollar exports of soybean oil are price-sensitive, particularly in the long run.

The soybean oil surplus gap has been bridged since 1954 by shipments under Public Law 480. Currently, the largest of these go to India and Pakistan. Generally speaking, the USDA has maximized these shipments. Recipients are hard to find; our shipments compete with domestic production, such as peanut oil in India.

The domestic market for soybean meal has expanded at a moderate rate during the past decade. The rate of increase appears to have slowed in the past two years. The expansion has taken place in spite of rising and rather high prices. It thus appears that the growth potential is not fully exploited.

The domestic market for soybean meal is experiencing competition from increased use of three main substitutes: (1) fish meal, (2) urea, and (3) synthetic amino acids. Severe competition may develop from high-lysine corn. All of these are price-related; lower meal prices lessen competition and vice versa. The price of soybean meal has gone from very low to very high relative to the general group of feedstuffs.

The export market for protein has grown dramatically during the past decade. From 1958 to 1967 it increased from 3 to 9 million tons-from 25 percent of the protein market to 46 percent. Six million tons of meal requires 255 million bushels of soybeans.

The expansion of the export rests on the general increase in economic development, in consumer incomes, and in the resultant demand for animal products which require protein feed. This market has tremendous growth potential as economic development proceeds and expands to new areas.

European markets are not price-sensitive to the aggregate of protein prices, but they are sensitive to individual protein prices. U.S. soybean meal has been subjected to sharp competition with fish meal during the past two years. Fish meal production is price-sensitive. It is the primary product of fish and is related to the cost of fishing, particularly off the coast of Peru.

GUIDELINES

If we accept these sweeping generalities, we can develop some guidelines for establishing production and price policy. First, the rate of growth of the soybean industry may be slow in the future, but it appears that all four segments of the market have a substantial amount of growth potential left; the market is not saturated. It does appear that the period of dramatic increase may be at an end; thus, the soybean industry cannot absorb additional acreage pulled out of other crops.

Second, the domestic market for soybean oil will continue to grow at a fairly rapid rate; and it is not price-sensitive. Any scheme that will increase domestic oil prices will be reflected in higher soybean prices or lower meal prices without market damage.

Third, current soybean meal prices are high enough to retard domestic consumption in the short run and, if continued, will encourage the substitution of other protein sources in the long run. High meal prices do more long-run than short-run damage.

Fourth, relatively high soybean meal prices do little short-run damage to protein exports but will seriously reduce long-run growth potential.

Fifth, the long-run rate of expansion of soybeans in world competition with other sources of protein feeds and fats and oils will be increased as world oil prices are low and decreased as world oil prices are high.

POLICY CHOICES

In the very short run, the balance of the 1968-69 crop year, the best policy seems clear. The USDA should maximize exports of soybean oil under Public Law 480. This will tend to increase oil prices, enabling lower meal prices at the fixed soybean price. Lower meal prices will increase consumption, both domestic and export, and minimize the September 1, 1969, carryover. But not much can be done this year.

A lower level of price supports will result in a lower price of soybeans and lower income. How much lower income depends upon how much the price support is reduced.

On the other hand, lower prices will increase disappearance. How much of an increase depends upon how much the price support is reduced. It is not possible to accurately forecast the consumption response to a given price change.

The answer to the question depends on the long-run solution. If the industry is going in the direction of high prices and eventual production control, there is no compelling reason to reduce the price support. If the industry is going in the direction of competitive prices and long-run growth, it is imperative that the process start now before any more damage is done to growth, that of meal in particular.

It is interesting that this choice must be made now, just after a new administration takes office. The tone and general philosophy may be set by this decision. It will probably be a compromise with a moderate reduction.

In the long run there are several possibilities, some opposed and some complimentary. At one extreme is mandatory production control and a fairly high price. This could be done only at the expense of further growth of the industry. Further, there is not an escape crop into which one can put idled land. This choice is academic. The strict-control route has been considered and rejected several times and most likely died permanently with the wheat referendum in 1963.

At the other extreme is to let the market function. The question here is the price that would prevail. Certainly, it would be lower than current prices-else an inventory would not have been accumulated. But, it might not be so awfully low. Eight-cent oil is cheap by every reasonable comparison. Meal prices were fully competitive at $55 in the second half of the 1950s.These prices yield a soybean price of about $2 to $2.10 in the central belt. It is unlikely that both sides of the equation would sell so low at the same time. A policy of letting the market function would hold acreage in check and might reduce it.

Chapter Twenty-Seven

Commodity Speculation as An Investment Medium

1970

AUTHOR'S NOTE: By 1970 I had long been a defender and advocate of commodity speculation as an essential part of a smoothly and productively functioning economy. In addition, I had been exposed to the results of speculation, both anecdotal and quantitative. I was drawn, like a moth to a flame, to address the topic of how to speculate when the opportunity arose. It was another fun trip to New York, much appreciated by my wife. There is a broader lesson in the survey results presented: most of us are doomed to mediocrity, some more than others.

Morton Shulman begins the commodity futures chapter in his book *Anyone Can Make a Million*, "Commodity futures represent the quickest possible way to get rich or go bankrupt amongst all forms of market trading ...Comparatively few speculators participate in this form of gambling...This is a pity, because here is probably the only completely honest form of pure gambling in the market. Commodity futures are neither investments or speculations ..., but an exciting form of gambling from which small amounts of money can turn into huge fortunes." This is a strong statement of what is fairly typical of the prevailing attitude toward commodity futures trading.[1]

Obviously, I would not have foisted the topic of commodity speculation as an investment medium on this seminar had I intended to take a negative stance. Yet, some of what Mr. Shulman says is true. Commodity trading is exciting; it can be used as a remarkably honest gambling device with a relatively small house take; and it is a way in which unimportant amounts of money can be turned into important amounts. But commodity speculation is much more: it is a vehicle for exercising the prudent investment techniques that enable one to get a larger than common interest return on invested capital. It is a vehicle of great flexibility that can be adapted to the circumstances and objectives of all kinds of investors. At the same time, it is a demanding vehicle that offers maximum opportunity for dramatic failure. It is, thus, a singularly honest game in which victory goes to the best players and defeat to the worst.

MOTIVATION

The many motivations for commodity speculation can be generalized into three. First, successful speculation can be used to increase a relatively unimportant amount of money into an important amount. Some important amounts of money are inherited, but few of us have an opportunity to choose our parents. Others are accumulated out of earnings by such people as excel in sports, entertainment, the professions, business entrepreneurship, and the like. But only a few reach the top. Other important amounts are accumulated out of speculation. Speculation takes many forms but generally involves selling property at higher prices than those at which it is purchased. Gold, uranium, and oil are sold at higher prices than mining rights are purchased; the trick is to locate and purchase the right rights. Large fortunes have been accumulated from real estate speculation. Pre-

1. T. A. Hieronymus is professor of agricultural economics, University of Illinois. Talk before Seminar/70, New York Coffee and Sugar Exchange, October 22, 1970.

cious jewels, art objects, and rare coins are popular speculative media. Securities are probably the most popular medium in the United States.

Second, speculation is a means of supplementing income and gaining a return on a constant capital investment. Here, the motivation is not to accumulate but to make money to spend or save. There are professional speculators, particularly in commodities, who do not intend to use markets for capital growth but as an income-producing system and who plan to accumulate wealth by saving. This is a different game than using the markets in quest of capital growth.

Third, some speculators are attracted by the stimulation of the game. People trade in the same way that others are baseball or football fans. Sports fans appear to get a vicarious thrill from associating themselves with a team and its fate. The exuberance of winning and the dejection of losing are real. The thrills from speculation would seem to be greater because profits and losses are real; the trader is a participant. But for some, the money made and lost is not of consequence; money is only the way the game is scored.

APPEAL AS A SPECULATIVE MEDIUM

Commodity futures markets have much appeal as a speculative medium. First, the mechanics are simple and clear-cut. Information is abundant and readily available; price quotations are abundant; and the market is liquid. The commodity trader is not concerned with the dividends, options, splits, proxies, conversions, etc., that clutter up trading in securities. It is easy to keep score in commodity trading; one buys and sells and wins or loses.

Second, minimum capital requirements for entry into commodity trading are small. Contract units and margin requirements are small enough that only a few hundred dollars are required to finance an initial transaction. Commodity trading is one of the very few roads to big money open to the shoestring investor.

Third, commodity trading has appeal because of the realism of prices. Contracts mature and go out of existence by the end of the delivery month and are exchangeable for the cash commodity on first delivery day. Contract maturities are frequent—five to twelve times per year. The securities analog to this would be to declare XYZ Corporation bankrupt five or more times per year and auction off the plant, equipment, patents, goodwill, etc. Speculative fictions in securities can be long perpetuated, but speculative excesses in commodities, up or down, are soon pricked by the test of the first delivery day auction block.

Fourth, commodities are relatively low-risk speculative media. This notion is a contradiction of standard doctrine and widely accepted concepts—commodity trading is said to be the fastest track of them all. Commodity trading can be made a fast track, but it is not inherently fast and need not be made so.

The degree of riskiness is a function of price forecastability and price variability. Commodity prices are relatively easy to forecast because of the vast amount of information that is universally available. There just is not inside information. Further, the realism of prices forced by delivery yields a solid value base for forecasting.

A test of the relative variability of commodity and security prices made in 1968 yielded an average coefficient of relative dispersion of securities prices 1.65 times that of commodity prices.

Fifth, the great appeal of commodity speculation is leverage. This is the way that the track is made fast. Margin requirements tend to be 5 to 10 percent of the contract value. Thus, a 5 to 10 percent move in the price is either double or nothing of the investment required. Because of the great leverage, the doubling of one's capital in one year is not out of a realm of reasonable possibility. Now, $1,000 doubled in each of ten successive years expands to something over $1 million. A successful speculator can turn an unimportant amount of money into an important amount.

THE GAME SPECULATORS ARE IN

A first step in playing a game is to understand it. Speculators need to understand what markets are, how they work, their economic basis, and how they are used by commercial interests. Here, we can only underscore a few features of the markets.

First, the clearinghouse breaks even; it pays out the amount that it takes in. Futures trading is a zero-sum game minus the cost of doing business. In the aggregate, the participants break even gross and lose net by the amount paid in commissions, brokerage, and clearing fees. Thus, when the speculator enters the market, he is attempting to take money away from someone else who, in general, is most reluctant to lose.

Second, price variations in the major, highly developed futures markets, are random. Successive price changes are independent; that the most recent price change has been up does not increase the likelihood that the next price change will be up, etc.

Third, the speculating public must compete with a large group of professionals. These include the professional speculators—people who have gotten good enough at the game to make a living at it. They also include the facilitators at the markets whose primary purpose is to furnish liquidity. These are the scalpers, pit traders, and floor traders who trade in large volume for small price changes. And they include commercial interests whose market actions are partly based on their judgment about prices. The competition is tough.

RESULTS OF SPECULATION

Little is known about how well the speculating public makes out. The lore of the market suggests that 85 to 90 percent lose money. I recently took a look at the trading results of a group of 462 speculator customers of a large commission house for 1969. These were all of the customers of three offices. The information consisted of the profits, losses, and commission paid by each. On quick examination the data suggested a need for some classification. Accounts that had only profits or losses suggesting one or a series of trades were separated. Second, a group was designated as regular traders. The standard for regularity was low: (1) commission paid of at least $250 indicating at least ten contracts traded, and (2) both profits and losses, each of which was $500 or more. This left a group of "other traders." The results were as follows:

	REGULAR	ONE TIME	OTHER	TOTAL
Number of Accounts	193	170	99	462
Number of Profits	80	44	40	164
Number of Losses	113	126	59	298
Profits	398,839	37,237	26,337	462,413
Losses	421,030	461,659	244,666	1,127,355
Net	-22,161	-424,422	-218,329	-664,942
Commissions	364,646	21,403	20,295	406,344
Gross	342,455	-403,019	-198,034	-258,598

There are a lot of people who come into the market, lose a lot, and go away or make a little, breathe a sigh of relief, and go away. The occasional traders are big losers.

Second, a lot of money falls through the slot in the table—commissions. Commodity commissions are small in relation to the value of the contracts and in relation to price variations, but they take a lot of money out of the game and their cost should be kept in mind by would-be speculators.

Third, even at the low criteria established, the regular traders did better than is generally thought. A frequency distribution of their results is as follows:

	RANGE	NUMBER OF ACCOUNTS	GROUP TOTAL
Loss	15,000 and over	7	143,063
	10,000-14,999	6	75,273
	5,000-9,999	7	51,598
	3,000-4,999	14	53,883
	1,000-2,999	39	75,753
	0-999	40	21,460
Profit	0-999	26	13,948
	1,000-2,999	21	40,035
	3,000-4,999	11	45,142
	5,000-9,999	11	81,714
	10,000-14,999	5	67,426
	15,000 and over	6	150,574

Fourth, a high proportion of regular traders neither made nor lost substantial sums; 126 of the 193 were within the plus or minus $3,000 range. This apparent lack of results obscures a lot of activity. For example, one account made $27,000, lost $23,000, and paid $5,000 in commissions. His gross trading results were a modest profit and his net a modest loss, but it was an active game.

Fifth, a few people made substantial sums, and a few people lost substantial sums. The game was quite expensive for a few of the regular players, just as it was quite lucrative for a few. The game is played and won by some people; it can be done.

HOW TO SPECULATE

To trade successfully, the speculator must do three things well: manage capital, forecast prices, and avoid speculative suicide.

The purpose of commodity speculation is to make money. It is not to make cents per bushel of soybeans, cents per pound of copper, or dollars per ton of soybean meal. It is not to make X thousands of dollars. The purpose is to make a given amount of capital grow into a larger amount to obtain a return on investment.

The potential profits are a function of the risks of loss that are accepted. Every commodity investor should establish a fund of capital that he is willing to hazard. He should next establish his objectives in trading in terms of returns on capital; if his objective is 20 percent per year, he establishes one kind of program and level of risk, but if his objective is 50 to 100 percent he needs a different program and risk level. All trades and positions should be related to the capital position and their potential contribution to the objective.

Commodity prices fluctuate, and it is out of these fluctuations that profits and losses are made. Commodity prices are real, responding to market forces of supplies and requirements so that an equilibrium price is established. Thus, the essence of successful commodity speculation is price forecasting. The market as a whole forecasts prices, and the current price is the composite forecast of the market participants, weighted by the size of their positions. To take a position in a market is to challenge the aggregate judgement—to say that the market is in error. It is from the mistakes of others that speculators make money and from their own mistakes that they lose money.

There are numerous kinds of forecasts that apply to different time periods. The scalper is interested in the next tick—whether the next order will be to buy or sell. At the other extreme, an economic analyst may be interested in a twelve-month equilibrium. There are all gradations in between. Each kind of forecast requires a different style of trading and different capital management. Each speculator should know his own forecasting skills and limitations and stay within them.

The forces affecting the price of a commodity are numerous and subtle in their effects. Information about them is never absolutely complete or accurate. Many of the forces are nonrepetitive and change over time. Thus, an analyst must be completely and thoroughly familiar with the commodity or commodity group that he trades, and no one can possibly know enough about a large group of commodities to challenge the wisdom of the market in them all.

Price forecasts vary in their level of certainty; all are uncertain, but some are more uncertain than others. The level of certainty must be appraised and related to the allocation of capital to market positions. One might be worth, in size of move and certainty, one-half of the capital in the fund, while another might be worth none at all.

This interplay of forecasting and capital management requires a great deal of patience. All systems have to be A-Okay before the start button is punched, and once the start button is punched, the hand must be held over the abort button. But the prospective speculator should be consoled; speculative opportunities abound. Were a speculator to take advantage of even 20 percent of the moves in a relatively dull commodity, he would soon have most of the money in the game. The problem is not finding something to do but avoiding doing the wrong things. Needless to say, this is a game that requires talent, hard work, and discipline.

Finally, the speculator must avoid committing suicide. There are numerous ways to louse up, and the novice speculator manages to find most of them quickly. These include (1) undercapitalization of individual trades so that forecasts do not have a chance to work out, (2) trading for small moves so that the account is eaten up by commissions, (3) trading outside of the speculator's competence, either for small moves or in commodities that he does not understand, and (4) taking profits too quickly and letting losses run until capital is seriously impaired.

Behind these mistakes lie four weaknesses: the lack of strength of character to challenge the market, the lack of sufficient cowardice to run from the market, the lack of sufficient hard work to master a commodity, and greed. Commodity speculation is not a fast way to get rich; it is a hard way to make an easy living. It is a way to combine money, work, and skill to get a larger return than common interest; this is the essence of investment.

Chapter Twenty-Eight

Futures Markets and Equity Capital

1971

AUTHOR'S NOTE: Economists of my era of training have a strong bent toward theory. I think that we subconsciously envision ourselves as reincarnations of Adam Smith and Alfred Marshall. In the piece "Futures Markets and Equity Capital," the development of a theoretical base was irresistible. It was built on observation of the worlds of both futures trading and changing agriculture. As was then my strong bent, the discussion led to advocacy of more and better systematic speculation in futures markets.

The purpose of this first presentation of this program is to set the theoretical framework into which the more applied aspects of the place of futures trading in agribusiness finance should be placed.[1] The basic point that I want to make is that futures contracts are financial instruments, and futures markets are financial institutions. This concept of futures markets is in sharp contrast to the more usual view that they are glorified crap games that, happily, have a useful economic spin-off in the provision of a risk-shifting hedging medium.

The traditional discussions of futures trading describes its origin and development out of the need to shift risks, the generation of short futures positions by

---

1. T. A. Hieronymus is professor of agricultural economics, University of Illinois. Paper presented at the Agricultural Industry Forum, February 2, 1971.

inventory holders, and of off-setting long positions taken by speculators. It is clear that the need to shift risks was the original impetus for the development of the markets and that, for more than a century, the hedging of price risks has been the dominant force in determining the size of the markets and the fluctuations in the level of trading. However, this description does not explain why the activity takes place—why some businessmen involved in commodity production, marketing, and use have a compulsion to hedge risks while others do not. To observe the practice is useful and adequate for understanding the past and present. It is necessary to inquire into the motivations of hedgers and the institutional arrangements lying behind the hedging activity if we are to fully understand the why of that which has taken place and to make progress in charting the course that lies ahead.

FINANCIAL INSTRUMENT

A futures contract is a financial instrument, and futures trading is a financial institution engaged in gathering and using equity capital. It is not a financial institution in the sense of a bank in which money is received from one group of people and loaned to another. Rather, it is a means by which loans made by banks or operating money otherwise secured by businesses is guaranteed against loss. When a bank loan or capital from other sources can be protected from part or all of potential losses, it is more readily forthcoming than when it cannot. Operating businesses acquire debts that they add to their own net worth to build a total operating capital structure. By this process, they can control capital without owning it, and the people from whom they obtain funds can own capital without administering its use. The financial system is the means by which the ownership of real capital is separated from its control. Futures markets are a part of the system. In this context, a futures contract is the exchange of a monetary obligation, or debt, for a commodity obligation, or debt. The long speculator exchanges his own monetary obligation, or debt, for a commodity obligation, or debt. The long speculator exchanges his own monetary obligation to pay for the commodity for the obligation of the hedger to deliver the physical commodity. The short speculator exchanges a monetary obligation to buy and deliver for the commodity obligation of the hedger to accept and use the commodity. Thus, the hedgers remove themselves from financial debts by substituting commodity debts for them. The financial obligations are assumed by the speculators.

This process of debt exchange through the financial system enables resources to be used more productively, and from this the social benefits of the financial system flow. The consolidation of resources through the exchange of debt enables the increased productivity associated with large-scale enterprises. The ownership of scarce resources is widely diffused, and if it were not possible to consolidate their control, production would be quite as diffused as ownership. This would result in small-scale production, limited technological advance, and less total productivity. Control of capital needs to be consolidated into the hands of the people who can use it most efficiently, and people who can operate businesses most efficiently need access to capital beyond their own equity.

Historically, we have tended to look on speculators as the people who accommodate the hedgers in a null fashion, appearing when and only as needed. As we turn to borrowing money from banks to finance stored inventories, we tend to merely note that warehousemen who have their inventories hedged can borrow more money than those who do not. This does not do justice to the speculator. By committing his wealth to commodity futures, he influences the warehousing activity and its cost and, thus, becomes an important financier.

FINANCING PROCESS

The process by which equity capital is raised through futures trading can best be seen by some examples. First, the importance of hedging in financing stored inventories of grain has long been recognized. Terminal elevator operators, cotton merchants, grain processors, and, to a lesser extent, country grain warehousemen are able to borrow in excess of 90 percent of the value of stored commodities at prime rates of interest, providing that the inventories are offset by short positions in futures markets. Warehouse receipts serve as collateral for the loans so that the general balance sheet and liquidity of the company are not affected by the inventory ownership except for the small difference between the value of the cash commodity and the amount of the loan. In some cases in which the capital position of the company is so fully extended before borrowing to buy inventory that the commodity loan would restrict financing of noninventory activities, separate warehouse companies are established or a system of field warehousing is used. In such cases, the commodity inventory does not enter the balance sheet.

The inventory loans are sometimes worked up to quite high levels. Banks frequently loan the margin deposit on the futures transactions as well as a high proportion of the current value of the inventory. Or they loan the full value of the inventory on the basis that the margin deposit is quite enough protection. In general, the value of stored commodities tends to increase in relation to the futures price as the storage season progresses. For example, corn in country locations may sell 25 cents under the July futures price at harvest and typically sell for 4 cents under the July on July 1. There is thus a highly probable 21-cent storage profit in a hedging operation. Armed with this information, the country elevator operator may go to his banker and ask for the full purchase price of the corn, the margin requirements, and even a part of the storage earnings and thus finance part of his operating costs in addition to the inventory. Bankers are not inclined to go so far, but the operator may get away with the full purchase price and margin plus a promise of the storage earnings as they accrue.

As time passes, the price of the commodity and, hence, the market value of the warehouse receipts, changes. If the price goes down, the bank reasonably wants part of its money. It is readily available out of the increased value of the short futures position. The warehouseman asks his commission futures for the money the bank wants. If the price goes up, the short futures position shows a loss, and the commission house calls for margin. The value of the warehouse receipts has increased, and the additional margin is forthcoming from the banker.

The point of this is that ordinary bank financing is readily available for the purchase and storage of hedged inventories. This is not the case for unhedged inventories. The transaction is put on the balance sheet, and a normal liquidity margin is required. The proportion of the loan may be 60 percent or so—certainly a great deal less than for hedged inventories. The equity capital that the operator must furnish is very much less for hedged than for unhedged inventory. The uncertainty of the warehouseman's return is reduced by hedging, but the total uncertainty of the storage venture is not. The fact remains that the market value of the commodity may decline so that the return to storage may be less than zero, or it may increase so that the return is much more than the cost of storage. Losses are taken out of someone's equity, and gains are paid into someone's equity. On the other end of the hedges stand the speculators. The flow of funds from commission house to warehouseman to bank or from bank to warehouseman to commission house as prices decline or increase, flows further to the clearinghouse and then from or to the speculators, decreasing or increasing their equity. The speculator is thus a financier, furnishing the equity capital required to absorb changes in price level.

This process of financing is roundabout and specialized. It would be theoretically possible for the warehouseman to go directly to individuals for the money, selling them warehouse receipts and charging them storage. The individuals would, in turn, go to banks and borrow, on the basis of their net worth, the money to buy receipts. It would be a clumsy system, with banks making very small loans to speculators instead of a few large loans to hedgers. More important, it would have little attraction to speculators because they would be furnishing the total of the funds rather than the equity necessary to finance price variations. Further, it is difficult to visualize such a scheme sufficiently sophisticated to afford liquidity comparable to that of futures trading. More likely, the warehousemen would reorganize the financial structure of their businesses in a way that would make the assumption of equity financing possible.

Futures markets originated out of a need by country grain merchants for equity capital, just as egg warehousemen turned to their friends for the equity capital to carry inventories. It is worth noting they did not necessarily lack the net worth to obtain funds from the banking system; in the case of eggs, net worth was more often adequate than not. They simply preferred not to endanger their capital structure to the extent they judged the price risks of a full inventory would endanger it. The system evolved over a long period of time as the most attractive among the alternative ways of gaining access to equity capital.

A second example relates to cattle feeding. The production of market beef is a two-stage process. The animals are raised from breeding herds on the grazing lands of the West and South and moved into specialized feeding yards or onto grain-producing farms for further growth and fattening. The traditional pattern, now much modified by the development of large, specialized feeding yards, was from the forage-producing lands of the plains and mountain states to the corn-production lands of the central states, particularly Iowa and Illinois, and then on to the central markets for slaughter and shipment to eastern consumption markets. Farmers buy feeder cattle, feed them grain and other concentrates, and sell them for slaughter. Their profits and losses depend on their skills in feeding cattle and on the price of fat cattle in relation to the purchase cost of feeder cattle and the cost of feed. They are part cattle feeder and part cattle speculator.

Some cattle feeders follow the same pattern, year in and year out, buying the same size and quality of feeders at the same season each year and feeding them to the same weight and quality for sale. For these people, variations in the feeding margin average out over a number of production cycles so that, in the long run, they get the industry average returns (plus or minus their own technological skills in relation to those of the industry). But the long run may be several years so that a large reserve of equity capital is necessary for survival. This group of people are speculative nulls. Most cattle feeders, however, vary their operations on the basis of existing and expected prices and price relationships, becoming active participants in the speculative game. They buy different sizes, kinds, and qualities of cattle and sell at different weights and qualities in different production cycles. At times, they leave their lots empty and sell part of the feed supplies that they have produced on their own farms and, at other times, they increase the size of their operation and buy additional feed. The extent to which programs are varied differs greatly within the cattle-feeding fraternity. Some of the members are more speculator than feeder.

On the farm that the operator owns, which produces a surplus of feed, and on which one or two carlots of cattle are fed each year, the money to purchase feeder cattle is readily forthcoming from usual financial institutions. On smaller farms where more cattle are fed or on tenant-operated farms, money for the purchase of cattle is more of a problem. The equity position of the feeder influences the size and kind of operation. With a small equity, they feed small droves of small cattle. When calves (300 to 500 pounds) are bought and fed to 1,100 to 1,200 pounds, variations in the fat cattle price endanger the security of loans used to purchase feeder animals less than in the case when 900-pound cattle are fed to 1,100 pounds. Who feeds what size of cattle is partially determined by the equity position of the feeder, just as entry into the business is limited by the availability of equity capital.

When cattle futures trading was started in 1964, the game changed. Suppose that a young tenant farmer approaches his banker for a loan to purchase a drove of 700-pound feeder cattle; he already owes the bank for a loan to pay part of his operating costs in feed production. He shows the banker the purchase cost of the cattle, operational costs in feeding, the current price of fat cattle, and the profit margin. The banker says, "If the price of fat cattle goes down, you can't pay off; your equity is too small. I won't make the loan. However, if you will sell cattle futures, you will be guaranteed a profitable operation. On this condition I will make the loan." Without the sale of futures contracts the equity is inadequate, while with it, it is. From whence cometh the equity capital? From the purchasers of the contracts—the speculators.

PYRAMIDING OF CAPITAL

The command of resources can be greatly increased by hedging inventory risks or by pricing finished product before operating costs are committed. A loan rate of 90 percent on hedged inventory enables a firm with $1,000 of equity capital to contract and use, in a storage and merchandising activity, $10,000 worth of a commodity. A loan rate of 60 percent is two-thirds as much; however, it enables the control of only $2,500 of inventory. Thus, the increase in the borrowing rate from 60 to 90 percent enables the control of four times as much capital. This is illustrated here at a 60 to 90 increase so that the numbers remain finite. As we have seen, a 60 to 100 increase is feasible. In this case, the equity capital requirement for price protection is zero, and the multiplier is infinite. Constraints on the growth of the business are from sources other than equity capital for inventory control.

The impact of equity financing through fixing sales prices of products ahead of production is equally impressive. Suppose that a corn producer is operating 1,000 acres and is contemplating expanding to 2,500 acres by leasing additional land. Assume that his lease cost is $40 and his operating cost other than return on fixed investment in machinery and equipment is $40 per acre, his anticipated yield is 100 bushels, and the net price that can be obtained is $1 per bushel. He thus has a prospective operating margin of 20 cents, or a total of $50,000 compared to a current $20,000. He will use up virtually all of his balance sheet liquidity in the purchase of additional equipment. He has to furnish a bank guarantee for payment of the lease. How much of his own equity must he hold for operational costs? It depends on the percentage loan. Price-vulnerable, the bank may loan 60 percent, requiring $40,000 of operator equity, but not price-vulnerable, the bank may go 90 percent, requiring only $10,000. This latter amount is not really a price vulnerability equity but rather a guarantee of the organization and management skills of the operator in the production process his technical ability. If his past performance record is excellent, the bank may loan the whole of the operational cost and the lease guarantee.

The ability to obtain the operating capital is not the only consideration in fixing sales prices. It protects the operator from his own mistakes. The market may not offer a price as high as $1, making the expansion less attractive or possibly unprofitable. The operator may optimistically—as is the nature of farmers—expect the price to eventually turn out to be $1 or more, commit his own equity, and fail. If the futures market will not furnish the equity and he cannot otherwise obtain it, he, the operator, is protected.

More important, the process protects the equity capital of the operator. He may not elect to make the expansion if it must be done at the hazard of the equity that he has built up. He may be willing to hazard his net worth on his ability as a corn producer but not as a corn speculator, especially if he recognizes that he is tied to the long side of a speculation with no flexibility. He would be long 250,000 bushels of corn throughout the production period and thus a speculator on the price of corn. The old 100,000-bushel level may be more attractive. If it is, the expansion may not be made. Equity capital from futures markets may affect the business structure and efficiency of corn production. This is but one example. Others can be drawn from any of the commodities actively traded.

ATTRACTION OF THE SPECULATOR

There is something ridiculous about explaining to a member of the speculating public who is a chemist or a private detective that he, fine and noble entrepreneur, is furnishing the equity capital to feed cattle or produce plywood. Told so, he is apt to reply, "Who, me? I'm just trying to make a fast buck in a market where I can get high leverage on money that I am willing to lose (heaven forbid)." Shades of Adam Smith; not only is he led by an invisible hand to increase total productivity, but he thinks it is a quite different one.

This process of equity capital flow from speculative markets is an example of commercial specialization among financial institutions. The process of gathering up money is separated from hazarding equity. One is the business of the banking system, while the other is that of speculators.

The division and specialization is the thing that attracts speculators. Had they to furnish the whole of the operating capital to produce corn or buy feeder cattle, there would be little attraction. They are only interested in furnishing the equity and taking the risks. A high proportion of commodity inventories for which futures markets exist are hedged. But only a small part of the production of corn, cattle, plywood, orange juice, etc., are forward-priced in futures markets: the equity capital is otherwise forthcoming.

This gets us to the question of the adequacy of futures markets, regarding both size and cost. Futures markets are larger financial institutions than is generally recognized. In 1969, there were 11,206,685 contracts traded on U.S. exchanges. The average value of each contract was on the general order of $11,000, so that the total dollar value was on about $123 billion. But this is not the most meaningful measure of the size of the markets. A more meaningful one is the open interest. It represents the quantities and values that are at hazard, the amount of risks that are outstanding. Some are hedger to hedger (or, more accurately, trade interest to trade interest), some hedger to speculator, and some speculator to speculator.

In most markets, a fairly high proportion of the open positions are opposite cash positions and thus represent actual commodities. The average number of open contracts for the regulated commodities (about 80 percent of all trading) in fiscal 1968-69 was about 240,000. Their value was approximately $1 billion. Not all of this was at hazard because price variations are less than 100 percent. If we think in terms of price variations on the order of plus or minus 10 percent, some 20 percent of the value, or $380 million, was truly at hazard.

These are interesting and impressive numbers, but they are not very meaningful unless they are compared to something. In the context of the effectiveness of the system in providing equity capital, the germane comparison would seem to be with the total risk load. Production, average stock, and average open interest for five commodities for fiscal 1968-69 were as follows:

COMMODITY	PRODUCTION	AVERAGE STOCK	AVERAGE OPEN INTEREST
Wheat (mil. bu.)	1,570	1,346	215
Corn (mil. bu.)	4,375	3,011	246
Soybeans (mil. bu.)	1,080	707	167
Cattle (thous. head)	14,063	5,920	897
Hogs (thous. head)	94,496	57,205	67

These are some of the oldest, largest, and most highly developed markets. They are used extensively by producers and commercial people and are widely regarded as useful tools in production and inventory management. But as we compare the total risk load, as measured by either production or stocks, it is clear that only a small proportion of the total risks ever get involved with futures trading. One must be impressed not with how large the markets are but rather with how small they are relative to their potential.

NEED FOR MORE SPECULATION

The structure of agriculture is changing from small units to larger units, and an increasing proportion of inputs is variable costs in contrast to fixed cost on land. The need for equity capital per unit of output is increasing rapidly. I should thus expect a rapid growth in futures markets. The total volume of trade doubled in the decade of the 1960s. There should be a much greater growth in the 1970s.

These markets are an excellent source of equity financing. Extensive studies of price variations in futures markets have been made. The conclusion is that in the developed, successful markets, variations are random. From this it follows that returns to speculators are zero minus the cost of doing business commissions. In hedged inventory and production operations, there is a zero or negative interest rate on the high-risk capital that finances price variations compared to a usual bank interest note on the nonrisk capital. It is difficult to think of a better source of equity financing than one that furnishes it free.

From this notion that equity financing flows from futures markets, it follows that speculators are truly investors in the production and marketing processes.

From the smallness of the markets in relation to the total risk load, it follows that there is need for much more speculation. The great weakness of futures markets is that they are grossly underspeculated.

Chapter Twenty-Nine

Statement to The Domestic Marketing and Consumer Relations Subcommittee of The House Agriculture Committee

1972

AUTHOR'S NOTE: In the 1960s, potatoes were a significant feature of politics in Maine. The plight of potato producers got to be associated with the potato futures markets. Politicians won, and lost, elections on the basis of who could most effectively beat up on potato futures. Several bills to ban futures trading in potatoes were introduced, and I got an invitation to address the subject. It presented an opportunity to revisit the onion legislation debacle of 1958 and, at the same time, brag about the superiority of midwest agricultural knowledge of futures. It was a somewhat harrowing experience. There was a substantial audience of irate potato farmers behind me as I faced the Congressmen on the dais. In my mind's eye, they were armed with spears that might be unleashed at any time. Fortunately, none were, but I left the room as soon as possible.

March 16, 1972

My name is T. A. Hieronymus. I am a professor of agricultural economics at the University of Illinois. I have been employed there since 1946. Much of my time has been spent in teaching and research in commodity futures trading. My writings on the subject are fairly voluminous. I appear here today in opposition to H.R. 7287, a bill to ban futures trading in potatoes.

The central point to which I want to go is that there is no case to be made in opposition to potato futures trading that is any different than can be made against futures trading in any or all other commodities, and that I suspect that much of the hue and cry against potato futures trading is related to unsatisfactory speculation on the part of growers and shippers. The market has been a useful pricing tool for growers and shippers who have used it properly in connection with their business. I suspect that their speculative experiences in cash potatoes and potato futures have been less satisfactory and that here lies some of the root of disgruntlement.

I have been this way before. I did quite a lot of work on the onion futures market before appearing before a congressional committee in the spring of 1957 in opposition to a bill to ban futures trading in onions. I repeated the process before appearing before the Senate Committee on Agriculture and Forestry in 1958. I subsequently spent quite a lot of time assisting with legal proceedings to test the constitutionality of the onion futures ban. The onion futures market was an institution that contributed to marketing and pricing efficiency and benefited onion growers.

Prior to the trading of onion futures in volume, dealers bought onions at harvest at substantially reduced prices-at prices low enough to make them willing to assume the attendant risks of ownership. Prices regularly increased during the storage season by more than the cost of storage to the disadvantage of the growers. During the period of active futures trading, the dealers hedged and speculators bid prices high enough at harvest that the seasonal increase in price above the cost of storage disappeared. Speculators, as is true in other markets, assumed the risks of price changes at no cost to the market and to the benefit of the growers. In the years immediately following the demise of futures trading, the dealers went back to buying at reduced harvest prices. They could do so because the competition of speculators was no longer present. They needed to do so because they could not afford to carry the risks of ownership at higher prices.

The banning of futures trading in onions clearly worked to the disadvantage of the growers. It did not greatly disadvantage the dealers, who simply went back to their old ways—one suspects, more profitable old ways. The Chicago Mercantile Exchange was temporarily disadvantaged, but it soon developed in new directions and has since expanded and prospered almost sensationally. The onion speculators went elsewhere and traded in other commodities. It was no big deal except to marketing efficiency and those people whose businesses were directly related to the actual onion production and trade.

In the year of the greatest debacle and the generation of the greatest negative hue and cry, the price of onions was quite high in the fall during harvest. Large hedges were placed in the market, and hedgers were net short by a wide margin. Behind these hedges were large sales of actual onions by growers, some for spot delivery and some in storage for deferred delivery. Opposite the hedgers were the speculators who were net long by a wide margin. The price of onion futures declined drastically, held steady for a time, and finally completely collapsed at the end of the season when the new crop in Texas came in early. The growers who sold early received excellent prices. Those whose market judgment told them to hold did not do so well. They were understandably frustrated and lashed out at the most convenient whipping boy, the futures market. The simple fact was that there were too many onions, and the price went where it inevitably had to go. The speculators, as a group, lost heavily. When I looked at who the speculators were as the occupational identity of traders was revealed in a market survey made by the Commodity Exchange Authority, I found the single largest occupational group of long speculators were onion growers. Onion growers, as such, sold at advantageous prices. Onion growers, as speculators, fared poorly indeed. I strongly suspected then, and continue to think now, that much of the opposition to onion futures trading arose out of unhappy speculative experience on the part of onion growers.

In this connection, I note with interest from the CEA market survey of November 27, 1970 that there were 247 members of the potato industry who were identified as speculators, who were net long by a substantial margin, and that there were 163 members of the potato industry identified as hedgers, who were net short by a comparable margin. I note comparable patterns in the surveys made on October 29, 1965, and on October 27, 1961. It is typical of every survey result that I have looked at.

The economic difficulties of Maine potato producers have been well documented in these hearings. They arise out of increased potato production in other regions and the highly inelastic demand for potatoes. They are lamentable, but they can in no way be ascribed to the existence of a potato futures market, or to speculation in potato prices. Nor would they be alleviated if futures trading were to be eliminated.

It appears to me that the long campaign against futures trading in potatoes is the result of four things: (1) general frustration arising out of an unfavorable economic position; (2) frustration resulting from having timed the sales of cash potatoes poorly; that is, having speculated poorly in cash potatoes; (3) unhappy speculative experiences in futures losing speculators are notorious alibiers and misuse of futures in connecting with growing and shipping operations; and (4) misunderstanding of the operation of futures markets.

I do not doubt the sincerity of the people who are testifying in support of the bill, nor do I suggest that any of them are losing speculators in futures. Rather, I am looking for the root of the support. The kind of thing that I am describing is like that which I have observed in many years of teaching the role and use of futures markets to farmers, interior merchants, and bankers. I am pleased to report that a great deal of progress has been made in developing an understanding of futures markets in the agribusiness community of the Midwest. Each year, more farmers and marketing firms make effective use of futures as management tools, and I hear less and less blaming of futures trading for price problems. In twenty-five years, I have seen the attitude of the agricultural community toward futures change from predominantly negative to predominantly positive.

I think that, as in grains and livestock, an active and expanded futures market in potatoes can be a useful instrument in restructuring the potato industry to a more profitable level. The potato futures market is a useful forward pricing and hedging medium for growers, shippers, merchants, and processors that has been well documented in these hearings, and I will not restate the case. I particularly commend the statement of Mr. Caldwell of the CEA. The point that I would like to make is that speculative markets, if used extensively by the industry concerned, particularly producers, are useful in readjusting production to profitable levels.

Speculators are in the business of anticipating events to come and discounting their impacts into forward prices. They put money at hazard in guaranteeing those forward prices. If producers contract their services forward when futures prices are at profitable levels and decrease production when futures prices are not at profitable levels, production is adjusted to amounts that speculators, in the aggregate, judge to be appropriate. If the speculators are right, they may make money, and if they are wrong, they lose. The profit-loss results of speculation tend to improve its quality and, thus, its effectiveness in guiding production to appropriate levels.

Producers of commodities that are actively traded on futures markets need never produce at unprofitable prices. As futures prices are at profitable levels, they can contract their services forward, and as they are at unprofitable levels, they can refuse to produce until prices rise appropriately. If they go ahead and produce when forward prices are below profitable levels in the hope that prices will rise, they have only themselves to blame if they lose money.

My suggestion to potato growers is: rather than blame futures markets for their competitive problems, they should make effective use of the markets.

I thank you very much for the opportunity to be heard.

Chapter Thirty

Note on The Soybean Price and Speculation

1973

AUTHOR'S NOTE: In August of 1972, I wrote a soybean price outlook paper for the Midwest Outlook Conference. Fortunately, it has been lost. Fortunately, because it turned out to be totally wrong. But, unfortunately, I remember it well. It was a mundane thing: the prospective crops were large and doing well so that there was no prospect of supply shortage, livestock numbers were large, and export sales looked good. A large crop would be used down to comfortable carryover levels, and prices would remain within ranges of recent years. It was a good forecast. Soon after the forecast was made, an unprecedented series of events took place. As harvest started, the rains came and continued, finally turning to snow so that field losses were huge and some of the crops didn't get harvested until the following spring. There were numerous other unusual events that resulted in huge price increases and price volatility. In anticipation of the usual criticism of futures markets and speculators, I made a note of the situation in retrospect. It is an interesting look at market misbehavior. The problems were in cash markets, not futures. The problem existing in June was solved in part by export licensing (mainly to Japan) and cash buy-backs. There was a subsequent major decline.

The price of 1972-crop soybeans has gyrated wildly for some months, mostly upward, and has reached levels without precedent and higher than seems believable.[1] It appears to be a level which cannot be sustained by consumption demand for end products, meal in particular. Intra-day price ranges are very large, reaching $1.00 on June 5. Abnormal demand forces appear to be in operation.

The price action in old-crop soybeans appears to be having an impact on new crop soybean prices, pulling them to levels higher than would otherwise prevail. Old crop prices are disruptive of the orderly movement of limited supplies into consumption; they are also disruptive of the orderly achievement of a production use balance for the 1973-74 crop year as well. Some appraisal of the reasons for the dynamics and an offering of suggestions for quieting the market down seem a reasonable exercise.

The market has done a remarkably bad job of discounting all the price-making forces into the current price in a way which would hold price variations within a reasonable range for the season. What went wrong? Three principal factors are involved.

First, it appears in retrospect that the market had an extraordinarily difficult task. The supplies were not only unknown at the outset of the season but also remain unknown even now. Further, reasonable supply estimates changed as the season progressed. The production of fish meal (the principal competitor of soybean meal) started in the fall season and was suspended. It was again started with excellent results in March but was re-suspended in April. What appeared to be a very high-yielding soybean crop was severely damaged by heavy rains in October and subsequent abnormal weather. There is a major and as yet unresolved discrepancy between the crop estimate minus known disappearance and the April 1 stock report. The market could not reasonably be expected to know how fast it could prudently allow the use of protein supplies when it did not know what those supplies were.

There appears to have been an unusually large increase in demand. This was probably the result of rapidly increasing economic production and consumer incomes that increased the demand for livestock products, hence, for food, hence, for protein supplements. On a world scale, anticipating and appraising the impact

1. Paper prepared on June 5, 1973.

of the demand changes as they worked through the system was extraordinarily difficult.

The amounts of both supply and demand changes were outside of historical experience, which added to the difficulty of measuring their impact, to put the matter mildly.

A further addition was a series of changes in the relative values of currencies. The U.S. dollar was twice devalued and currencies were allowed generally to float. And there was an increase in the worldwide rate of inflation.

In the face of this extraordinary set of difficulties, a large fluctuation in prices is not surprising.

Second, imperfections in the pricing system have likely contributed. These are in the nature of lags in registering current market prices at the consumption level. It has been, and is, necessary to reduce soybean meal use from optimum protein-carbohydrate balance in rations and to restrict or reduce animal numbers. Feeding was quite profitable early in the season, and consumption was at quite high levels. It was, and is, necessary to reduce use from early season levels. Price, and price alone, can do this. But, price can be effective only as it operates at the consumption level.

In the United States, feed manufacturers do a fairly good job of keeping feed prices current with replacement costs of ingredients. But, to some extent, they do buy ahead and do fail to increase feed prices fully as fast as ingredient prices rise.

In soybean and meal destination countries, forward cover of requirements is much more extensive, and feed prices are not kept current with replacement cost of ingredients. There is extensive vertical integration, from importer to processor, to feed manufacturer, to livestock producer, and to livestock and poultry buyers. Long-term contracts were made in the summer of 1972 for animals and poultry to be delivered in early spring of 1973, and costs, soybean meal in particular, were covered at the then-existing prices. In France, there is a system of ceiling prices on mixed feed which is based on ingredient costs. It is changed only as actual cost of ingredients changes. Ceilings were established early in the summer of 1972 and ingredients requirements covered through as late as May 1973. Thus, high meal prices have simply not existed at the consumption level for much of the market.

Third, the soybean futures market for contracts relating to the 1972 crop (November 1972 through September 1973 maturities) has been underspeculated. The level of speculative participation has been low, and this has contributed to the violent price variations and poor job of discounting new information into the price.

The single meaningful measure of speculation is the number of open contracts, not (as is often thought) the volume of trading. It is positions taken that are significant. For the past three years, the May 31 open interest by contract was in millions of bushels.

YEAR	JULY	AUGUST	SEPTEMBER	TOTAL OLD CROP	TOTAL NEXT CROP
1971	68.9	35.8	27.2	131.9	128.4
1972	106.1	43.1	16.8	166	151.4
1973	40.4	27.8	15.3	83.1	211.1

In spite of price volatility, open interest in old-crop positions was relatively small at the end of May. This, in part, reflects the small inventory, but it also reflects a relatively low level of speculative interest. Positions pertaining to the 1973 crop were unusually large (of record size by far) at the end of May. This reflects forward purchases, particularly exporters, and forward sales by farmers in response to high prices.

The structure of the open interest is more revealing. Each market participant who has a position of 200,000 bushels or more is required to report daily to the Commodity Exchange Authority and declare whether he is a hedger or a speculator. If a hedger, he must show the offsetting cash position. People whose positions are smaller than 200,000 bushels are identified as "nonreporting traders," and their positions are derived from those of hedgers, speculators, and the total open interest. Special cross-section studies indicate that the bulk—say, eighty to ninety percent of non-reporting traders are speculators. These are the speculating public.

The positions of the three categories on April 30 for three years were in millions of bushels (net open being total open interest minus reported spreads). Unfortunately, the data are not reported by crop years.

	HEDGERS			SPECULATION			NON-REPORTING TRADERS			NET
YEAR	LONG	SHORT	NET	LONG	SHORT	NET	LONG	SHORT	NET	OPEN
1971	118.1	97.3	20.8	15.0	15.9	-0.9	59.7	79.6	-19.9	192.8
1972	104.7	128.6	-23.7	14.6	14.5	0.1	128.1	105.0	23.9	247.6
1973	172.4	155.0	17.4	18.4	20.9	-2.5	54.6	69.5	-14.9	245.5
				PERCENT OF NET OPEN INTEREST						
1971	63.1	50.5		7.8	8.2		31.0	41.3		
1972	42.4	51.9		5.9	5.9		51.7	42.4		
1973	70.2	63.1		7.5	8.5		22.2	28.3		

The thing of particular note is that the proportion of the open interest held by commercials, both long and short, is unusually large. (In passing, it is worth noting that, going into the very rapid price rise in May, both reporting speculators and the public were net short. This has been typical of the crop year as a whole.) Without confirming data, I think that were the old and new crop structures to be separated, the percentage held by commercials would be even larger.

Commercials are not price-responsive; speculators are. The long positions held by hedgers are of two main types: processors long against sales of soybean oil and meal and exporters long against cash soybean sales. They have firm commitments into consumption, generally at very much lower prices. The rising price of soybeans in no way encouraged them to sell; they are not affected except as futures profits generate large cash balances. The short positions held by hedgers are presumably against physical inventories of soybeans that have not yet been moved into consumption positions. What they lose on futures is gained on the cash inventory, so that the only effect is on cash balances they must post as margin as prices rise.

Note that hedgers were net long. The speculators are necessarily net short. They have no way to get out of the short position except as hedgers complete cash transactions and leave the futures market. Individual speculators can get out, but only as they can find others to take their places.

Speculators are responsive to price changes. Different speculators respond differently, and how they respond is not known. When speculators are active, they have a cushioning effect on price change. A rising price brings out profit-takers and vice versa. A price change doesn't accomplish anything if only commercials are in the market. The longs stay in even though they think the price is too high.

Losses of shorts do not force them out because they have offsetting profits. When cash interest has to meet cash interest, in futures, prices become quite volatile.

These three things explain the reasons for extreme volatility of price and how we got where we are. They do not point to the ultimate outcome nor to a solution of the problem.

We shall probably never know the nature of the impasse or how it is solved. There appears to be a strong possibility that the soybean supply has been oversold, that more cash soybeans have been committed to use than actually exist. Some cash commitments are offset by physical possession and others by cash commitments to receive and buy. Clearly, the commitments by hedgers in futures to buy and take delivery are greater than those to sell and make delivery. The difference is the net short position of speculators. In the ordinary course of events, speculators would go to holders of uncommitted cash soybeans, buy, and make delivery to the long hedgers. However, it may be that there are not enough uncommitted cash soybeans to cover the difference.

The alternative is to buy back commitments. The only ways long hedgers can liquidate positions are to buy cash and to buy back commitments. Say that an exporter has sold cash soybeans for August shipment to a French processor, who has sold meal to a feed mixer, who has sold feed to a broiler producer, who has sold broilers for October delivery. There is a price at which the broiler commitments can be bought back, etc., so that the short can get loose. This is about the longest buy-back route, but it does illustrate the kind of problem the market may face. Someone must give up soybean products that he has fully expected to use. Some price will do it. There is not only the price problem, but a communication problem as well.

It may be that the exchange can facilitate the communication problem. If the hedgers' longs and shorts are identified, and the longs encouraged to buy back some commitments, the logjam can be broken.

There is another side to this coin. It may be that the basic oversold amount may not be large, say 5 percent. The buy-back could easily exceed such an amount, and reach, say, 10 percent, before it became apparent. The market would then have inventory available for new commitments.

It appears that there are not now, at current prices, new commitments. There is probably a big price gap between getting someone to give up a long-standing commitment and getting someone to make a new commitment for consumption.

Should an over buy-back occur, there could be a price debacle. Most likely, speculators would be accused of causing it. The essential point is that this is basically a commercial market, and the problem will be solved in cash markets.

Chapter Thirty-One

A Note on Being a Commodity Registered Representative

1973

AUTHOR'S NOTE: "A Note on Being a Commodity Registered Representative" is a July 1973 letter that got out of hand. A friend who was working for a branch office of a commission house in a clerical capacity asked what I thought about becoming a registered representative, what the job entailed, and how to function as an RR. The note drew on many discussions with commission houses, registered representatives, and involvement in disputes between houses and commission house customers. It was written to be used by students who were job hunting, for operating RRs, and for commission houses.

The largest employment area in the field of commodity futures trading is with commission houses. There is a lot of money spent on commissions; in fact, a strikingly large share of the money that changes hands goes to pay commissions. The commission house industry is, itself, large.

There is an assortment of types of jobs available with commission houses. We can appropriately think in terms of three major categories: (1) the mechanics of communication, order placement, and execution; (2) the confirmation, accounting, and margin accounting functions; and (3) the functions relating to securing and servicing of clients. This third group of people includes those in price research, preparation of market letters, assembly and communication of current market information, monitoring of client success/failure, prospecting and development of new clients, and servicing client accounts. The activities of registered representatives fall in the third category.

The job of being a registered representative (RR) has substantial appeal. The income possibilities are excellent; with performance at quite ordinary levels, the job pays competitively. But earnings are quite closely correlated with success. A highly successful RR has a very high earnings potential. Second, the job is participatory. Clients succeed and fail in varying degrees in attaining their commodity trading objectives. The RR affects the success/failure of his clients and vicariously succeeds and fails with them. A job well done is rewarding in ways other than income. Third, being an RR is good training for becoming a commodity trader. It is a way to make enough money to start trading, to get a firsthand look at both successes and failures, to evaluate systems of trading, to explore pitfalls, and to develop a method of operation. One can be both an RR and a trader. The job can support living costs and provide a flow of information and analysis while trading capital and method are being developed. Trading is not for everyone, so that a career as an RR is a thing in itself, but trading is for a lot of people and combines well with the business of being an RR for some people and can, for a limited number, lead to full-time trading. Fourth, experience as an RR can lead to the management of an office of a commission firm and higher management positions. It can also lead to commodity trading and inventory management positions with commercial firms.

COMMISSION HOUSE STRUCTURE

The commission house industry is highly diversified. There is a wide range of kinds of firms in the commodity commission business. Some classification is useful for illustrative purposes. One, there are national wire houses with numerous offices whose primary business is in securities. Some of these have a major emphasis on commodities, others only an incidental emphasis—or as a convenience to customer interest.

Two, there are commodity houses, some of which become large enough to enter the securities business. Some are tied fairly closely to a single market, as is the Chicago Board of Trade or the New York Mercantile Exchange. As they grow and develop, they pick up working arrangements with other exchanges and, if they are successful enough, become clearing members of several or all exchanges. In the main, these firms have developed from partnerships formed by commodity traders who go into the commission business as a greater or lesser adjunct to their trading activities. These firms have a wide range in size and a wide range in emphasis on nonmember commission business as compared to their own or member business. Some mainly clear trade for members, including members with floor rates; some clear mainly for themselves; and some put major emphasis on nonmember business.

Three, there are commercial houses which are engaged primarily in cash commodity trading and processing business such as flour milling, corn processing, and meat packing. In the interest of reducing their own trading costs, they become members of one or more exchanges, and then (if they are large enough) clearing members. It is but a short step to qualifying to handle customer business. Some handle customer business as a convenience to people with whom they do cash business (as processors handling commission business for country elevators) and for friends and relations. Some of these firms do very little customer business, but for others the business becomes sufficiently large to warrant major attention; some form subsidiaries and go into the commission business in a major way as operationally independent firms. One leading example is ContiCommodities, a subsidiary of Continental Grain Company.

This broad range of kinds of firms and their histories results in a wide range of methods of operation, terms of employment of RRs, and support and supervision of RRs. A few RRs are salaried employees of commission houses. More are salaried employees with bonus arrangements. Some are paid for performing jobs (research, accounting, preparation of promotional material, etc.) and earn commissions on commissions they generate. Many RRs are on a straight production basis, some with a drawing account and some with a minimum guarantee. While there is a wide variety, there is, throughout the industry, a very heavy emphasis on payment for production.

A look at the sharing of commissions is useful. Almost from the beginning, exchanges have had rules establishing the minimum commissions houses must charge members and nonmembers and rules prescribing, in part, the way commissions are divided among functions. While some firms are fully integrated and perform all functions, there are enough firms and individuals specializing in the separate functions that a stylized description of the sharing can be made. Typically, an RR paid on a production basis gets one-third of the commissions he generates. Some clearing members work through independent agents on a fully disclosed basis, and others have branch offices in various cities which are essentially independent agents. These agents and branch offices get (typically) 45 percent of the commission from which the RR share is subtracted; thus, a net of 11 percent. Sometimes the accounts of firms are consolidated and traded on an omnibus basis. The nonclearing omnibus house typically gets 55 percent from which it pays the RRs. On the other end of the line, brokerage is 10 percent of the round-turn commission. Thus, the sharing of a usual thirty-dollar round-turn, nonmember commission is as follows:

Registered representative	$10.00
Agent function	$3.50
Omnibus function	$3.00
Clearing and execution function	$10.50
Brokerage	$3.00

t should be kept in mind that there is a wide variation of arrangements among firms and some range within firms.

Minimum commission rules have run into legal difficulties both under antitrust law and from class-action suits. At this time, the antitrust problems are pending but class action suits have apparently been settled. A formula has been worked out for a gradual phase-out of minimum commission rules over a four-and-one-half year period, at which time they will be fully competitive. It is not clear what the impact of this change will be. One probable result is that commissions will be increased for small accounts and traders and decreased for large. A reasonable guess is that the payment for the RR, agent, and omnibus functions will be little altered. There is currently ease of entry, and people and firms come and go. This suggests a competitive balance which will probably not be disturbed in the total amount of earnings. There will be changes in rates and sharing, but the income opportunities for RRs and agents will probably remain much as they currently are.

Because of the diversity of the industry, being an RR is a different thing from firm to firm; yet there is a centrality. In the main, a client is a client of an RR rather than of a firm. Some clients want only execution and accounting service, but most people expect a great deal more and have their first allegiance to an RR. RRs move about from firm to firm as they can make better deals, and, in large measure, they take their customers with them.

OBLIGATION OF THE HOUSE AND AGENT

The branch office or agent office is the place the RR works. He is furnished with certain tools and services. Who works for whom in this situation is an interesting question to ponder. The RR is hired by the house and usually, in a technical sense, is an employee. Policy and details of operation are specified by the house or agent. But the RR originates the business from which the income of the agent and house flows. The operation takes on aspects of a partnership arrangement.

Some of the working arrangements are as follows:

The branch office and house furnish office space, price quotation system, often a display board, and a communications system. The RRs have a say in the prices which are displayed on the board, as no board can contain the whole of the commodity world. Most typically the agent and house pay for communications with the central office and with clients; telephone bills are quite large and a poor place to economize. By paying the bills, the house encourages RRs to hustle for business.

Execution, reporting, and accounting are commission house functions that are especially important to RRs. They must be able to get orders into the pits and reports back with utmost speed. How much real difference there is in quality of execution among houses and brokers is not known; the differences are probably smaller than they seem to the RRs and clients. In addition to possessing execution skill and speed, the house should be able to "read" the pit and make an estimate of the prices at which various quantities can be traded. This is useful to the RR in advising clients in order placement and is good for RR-client relations whether or not it is useful.

The accounting system is important to the RR in his supervision of the accounts of clients. All orders and executions are confirmed in "writing" overnight.

In addition, account sales statements usually include not only debits, credits, and balances, but also the value of open positions and account values as well. Some printouts also include margin requirements and unobligated balances. The more nearly complete this information is, the better the RR can counsel the client about the client's progress and suggest trades.

Not only is it useful that the information should be complete; it should also be fast and fairly frequent. Some houses render account status reports monthly, while others report weekly. For large, active accounts, daily reporting is not unusual. There are quite enough errors and disputes arising out of a day's trading as the result of (mostly) telephone communication between RR and client and between RR and central office without letting those errors and disputes drag on. The RR and, to the extent possible, the client, should have written confirmation and account status reports in hand before the opening of the next day's trading. This helps keep disputes at minimum levels.

Account supervision is a joint responsibility of the house and the RR. Some houses have "know your customer" rules and place limits on the size of positions and losses individual clients may take. Others leave this to the RR, and still others to the client him/herself. The effectiveness and desirability of "know your customer" rules and measures for the protection of clients is uncertain. The practice of selectivity of customers and limiting losses certainly reduces the incident of legal action by clients. Losers often claim they have been defrauded and sue or complain to exchanges. And there are many instances where accounts are poorly handled, so that losses are greater than the client can afford or should be permitted. Also, clients are allowed to put back profits when closer supervision would prevent some of the losses that inevitably follow a winning streak.

Rules can be too rigid in their application to all clients alike. As will be developed, client accounts are highly individual in their purpose and trading. The ultimate responsibility must rest with the client him/herself, but both have important roles to play in account supervision. The area of client-RR-house relationships is delicate and needs to be spelled out.

Debit balances, their prevention and collection, is a troublesome concern. Under the margin rules of exchanges, these can occur only very rarely, for example, when prices make limit moves for close to open, usually for more than one day, and it is impossible to close existing positions. But rules are bent and there are lags in getting margin calls made, and "reasonable" times are allowed for customers to post additional margin. Many clients do not like to be forced out of markets and procrastinate about either closing positions or putting up additional money. RRs and houses are reluctant to risk the loss of a client by either forcing liquidation or demanding money in hand. Further, a client occasionally defrauds a house deliberately by managing to get opposite positions (one long and the other short) in different houses and underfinancing both trades. If it works, he takes the profit and refuses to pay the debit. And there are other ways. It seems unlikely, but it has happened. So debit balances do occur, and their incidence and collection constitute a problem in the RR-house relationship.

One method of preventing debit balances is one of automatic liquidation when a client is close to a debit balance, regardless of the status of margin calls. A computerized accounting system can be set so that the point at which a debit balance will occur as the result of a given adverse price change can be determined in advance of each day's open and execution orders written. If such a policy is arrived at, its enforcement becomes a responsibility of the house.

Because the client's written agreement is with the house, the collection of debits by legal process is a responsibility of the house. Most of such proceedings are settled out of court at less than the full amount, partly to reduce risk, partly to save legal costs, and partly because of adverse publicity. In addition, because the house operates the accounting system and margin calls, it is, at least in part, responsible for the occurrence of debit balances.

The RR also has a responsibility for debit balances. Only a mishandled account lands in a debit position, and the RR not merely wants, but necessarily has, discretion in handling clients. Responsibility for debits is a part of the independent entrepreneur nature of the RR position.

What all of this seems to say is that losses should be shared by RR, agent, and house. The logic of the matter suggests that the proportionate shares should vary among and perhaps within houses. It is a gray area in commission house operation that needs to be spelled out more completely than it has been.

The house responsibility in providing research in prices and sales tools is another matter varying highly from house to house. Some houses, the large ones in particular, have substantial research staffs which develop forecasts of prices and make position recommendations. This includes the publication of weekly market letters and, often, daily wire advice to branch offices. Often such houses are quite firm in telling RRs that "this and only this will go to clients."

At the other extreme, some houses, particularly those who operate through agents rather than through branch offices, furnish virtually no market information. There are all gradations in between.

It is important that RRs be knowledgeable about commodity price behavior and the current supply-demand-price situation. It is not necessary that they have market opinions about all things at all times, but it is necessary that they know current facts, recognize danger signals, and be able to appraise trades clients suggest. It is highly desirable that they have in mind possible trades which are adapted to the needs of individual clients. If they haven't any possibilities to suggest, clients will be inactive or go to another RR; in either case, commissions are lost.

To be so knowledgeable is a tall order. There are many commodities traded, and no one can have much expertise in all of them. There is something lacking when an RR simply reads off the house opinion. To sell well, he must be genuinely knowledgeable. This tends to suggest a division of labor among RRs in one office and with clients. There are groups of commodities that are reasonably self-contained and interrelated, such as the grains, livestock, oilseeds, metals, import foods, and so on. Oftentimes, individual RRs become and remain quite well versed in one of these groups. Specialization and sharing of knowledge is one approach to the problem. In addition, every office needs a technician to fly danger signals and to furnish conversation for other RRs to their clients.

The coordination of research and opinion development is a house and agent responsibility.

The development of new clients is an ongoing necessity to the success of both RR and house. There is a high rate of client turnover. Some come into commodity trading, lose money, and leave. Many more people try a while and leave than remain commodity traders for a long period of time. And the stayers are pretty mobile; they move from house to house frequently, particularly as they lose money. Some people maintain accounts in more than one house.

Finding new prospects is a problem. While there are many commodity traders who come from all walks of life, not a very high proportion of the total population either trades or should trade commodities. The identification of commercial prospects is relatively simple. Every commercial producer, warehouser, processor, and so on is a prospective user of futures markets. The RR goes to where they are, usually with house financing-to cattle markets, grain conventions, their places of business.

The identification of prospective commodity speculators is more difficult. One group is the security customers of wire houses. But security sellers are reluctant to let them go, so it takes strong action by the commodity house.

One method is newspaper advertising. Coupons to fill out and send in for a sample of a market letter or special situation study are placed on commodity pages of local newspapers. These are prospects which can be followed up with telephone calls and personal visits. But not many newspapers have good commodity coverage, and the people who read commodity pages are usually already traders.

Another is to offer commodity seminars which include free dinners or cocktail parties. These are usually far from resounding successes. Or some news stories are written regarding commodity situations that tie back to a house and include a telephone number.

The point of this is not to outline methods but rather to point out that the house and agent have a place in developing prospect lists.

WHAT IS A REGISTERED REPRESENTATIVE?

Having established the working parameters of an RR, it seems worthwhile to form a concept of what one is. There are three other names in general use. One is "broker," which is a spinoff from security terminology. A broker, an RR is not. A commodity broker executes orders in pits.

Another name is "salesman" which is an accurate description of what many RRs are. They sell people on commodity trading and stimulate them to trade actively after they open accounts. Behind this term is the somewhat cynical view that most people who trade commodities lose money, and the name of the game is continually to find new traders and get them to trade actively, taking small losses, and eventually leaving their money with the house in the form of commissions.

Such sales work is a part of the job, but it is not the whole of it and is the most dismal part. An RR needs to be part hustler, but he will not succeed if he is too much of one or if he is nothing else.

The third name is "account executive," which should be construed as meaning financial or trading counselor. In this context the RR is in the business of considering the investment, inventory management, and pricing problems of people who have surplus funds and people who are engaged in the commodity trades. Here, being an RR is a service job for which one is paid for helping clients solve problems. It is analogous to being a trust officer of a bank, implying a physician-patient or a lawyer-client relationship. In a sales sense it is emphasis on repeat sales and word-of-mouth or reputation advertising.

Looked at realistically, an RR is part salesman and part counselor. He must strike an appropriate balance to be successful, and he has significant ethical problems in arriving at a method of operation.

KINDS OF CLIENTS

There is a substantial amount of specialization within the general field of registered representative. It appears that the more successful RRs specialize to some extent. The major division is between commercial and speculator accounts.

It is generally accepted that a business based on commercial accounts is both more stable and more lucrative than the other. For the averages this may be so, but averages can be quite concealing. Commercial specialization has limitations. The strictly commercial use of futures is fairly small in relation to the value of cash commodity handled, and many commercial firms are quite small. Furthermore, the larger commercial firms tend to find ways to greatly reduce or nearly eliminate commission costs by becoming members or clearing members of exchanges. A farmer who produces and sells 50,000 bushels of wheat or 300 head of cattle is probably going beyond the use of futures in a strictly commercial sense if he trades more than 100,000 bushels of wheat or 600 head of cattle per year. It would take a lot of farmer clients for an RR to make a living at existing commission rates. The fact is that RRs who put major emphasis on farmer customers make money from them as speculators rather than as farmers.

The handling of commercial accounts requires specialization by kind of firm and by commodity group. One kind of specialization is in country elevators that are merchants and warehousers. The RR must understand the merchandising and warehousing business in general and must know the operational problems of each of his clients. He must be a careful and continual student of price relationships, and cannot handle very many clients and still do an adequate job for each.

The road to becoming a commercially specialized RR is to develop a high level of knowledge about one group of commodities handled by one class of firms. This knowledge must relate to the cash commodity trading, production, storage, processing, and distribution, and must include a thorough grasp of price relationships, both cash and future, and their changes. Then one must find a limited number of firms, each of which is large enough to generate sufficient commission business to make the special attention worthwhile.

The great redeeming thing about commercial accounts is that they speculate. It seems almost universal that good cash traders find some amount of speculation irresistible. The key consideration for the RR is to get the trader to recognize the difference between speculation and the use of futures in connection with business. This speculative business is good business. These people tend to trade in fairly large units, to be constantly in touch with markets and actively trading, and to be sufficiently knowledgeable as to have a good chance of speculating successfully. To the extent that they come out ahead, they keep at it and grow, and this is the best of all worlds for the RR.

In a realistic contemplation of the field, it must be recognized that the bulk of trading is done by speculators, and, hence, the bulk of commissions is generated by this group. Also, rather long experience and study are required before an adequate volume of commercial business can be generated. A beginning RR should think in terms of handling speculative business first and then seeing if he can or wants to develop a commercial specialization. Go where the numbers and the money are.

HANDLING SPECULATOR ACCOUNTS

There are two extreme ends to the theory of handling speculative accounts. One says that because speculators inevitably lose money, the first emphasis should be placed on sales; get new accounts to replace the losers and keep them trading. The other says that they are born losers, and the way to go is to tell them what to do, make money for them; they will trade bigger and pay more commissions. The emphasis is on client success. There is doubtless a more meaningful center ground.

Three facts form something of a framework. First, finding new clients in large numbers as a rapid turnover implies is a difficult task. It is also the kind of sales task that is not the "cup of tea" of the kind of people who make good RRs in the account executive sense. Second, a majority of the people who try commodity speculation fail and go away quickly. Perhaps the failure rate can be reduced, but we must be skeptical that it can be reduced very much, given people's natural inclinations and the fact that the clearinghouse breaks even and commissions take a lot of money out of the game. Third, many people persist in commodity trading over long periods of time. Some of these are losers but incurable optimists. If losses are at not very painful levels and there is an occasional taste of winning with the vision of the big win that could have been "if only I had," they stick around. Trading is exciting and an ego trip; people get hooked. And they may be right. I once had an army corporal who allotted nearly all of his money home and took the rest into the monthly crap game and lost it. This went on for a couple of years, and I chided him for it. But finally he hit it big and sent all of the money home to buy the filling station at which he had pumped gas before the war.

More important, there are successful commodity speculators. There are people who trade consistently, win year in and year out, and sometimes accumulate and leave enough money to eventually trade on a substantial scale.

With these thoughts in mind, the RR must take a hard look at a new client and form a judgment about whether that client is a winner or a loser. If he is a winner, he gets long-term careful treatment as an investment in future earnings. If he is a loser, the game is to keep him from gross losses that put money into the clearinghouse and absorb his money in commissions.

But the matter is not all that black or white. Potential success or failure is not easy to judge. Firm evaluations cannot be made until after the trader has been on the track a while to see how receptive he is to trade possibilities, how subtle in his thinking, how hard he is willing to work, how he responds to both adversity and gains. The RR must keep two things in mind: a lot of clients are going to lose and leave, and he must insulate himself from letting this get to him, and some are going to succeed and be his meal tickets for the future.

The key consideration in handling clients is adaptability to the needs of individuals. They are all different in knowledge, skill, willingness to work, psychological makeup, and objectives. There is no single method of operation which is suited to all clients.

An RR who is best for one client may not be the best person to handle the account of another. The more adaptable an RR to the diversity of clients who come his way, the larger business he can build. This is where "know your customer" really comes into play. There cannot be hard-and-fast rules. The RR must not only know how much money the client has and how much he can reasonably afford to lose, but must also know his objectives in trading, how painful it is for him to lose and, conversely, how much pleasure he gets from winning, how bold he is, how much he wants to lead or to follow.

One of the most difficult areas of the RR-client relationship is the extent to which the RR influences the action of the client. Again, there are two extremes. On the one hand is the information-supplying order taker. He keeps abreast of the flow of information, tells the client what the house thinks if it has opinions, clams up completely when the client asks for any sort of personal opinion, and places orders at the direction of the client. An RR who follows this approach develops tendencies to find out the ideas of the client and reinforce them. If, by subtle inquiry or careful listening, he thinks the client wants, e.g., to buy corn, he feeds him the bullish case.

On the other hand is the handling of managed accounts. Some houses accept accounts for management and take full responsibility for them. The client is a spectator. Some RRs do essentially the same thing, either with formal management agreements or with informal understandings. In the main these are RRs who also trade for their own accounts. Observation of trading records indicates that the clients of a given RR generally trade as the RR trades and succeed or fail likewise. In addition, these houses usually hold relatively firm opinions about prices. The accuracy of house decisions seems to run in streaks, good and bad. Usually, as the house goes, so go the RRs and the customers. When the RRs differ from the house, the customer tends to follow the RR.

If the RR is all that good, why does he bother with clients? It may be that he is using commissions while building up trading capital or using them for income so that there is not the pressure for earnings from trading. Further, some people are pretty good market analysts when they do not have a position but lose poise under the pressure of gains and losses.

There are all gradations between the extreme methods of client management. Two rules seem to be almost universally applicable. First, the final decisions should be made by the client. This includes most importantly the placement of orders. Disputes arise about orders and their placement; a rather large proportion of these relate to substantial independence of an RR based on generalized instruction by a client. Much of this is because clients are not always in touch with markets and with RRs. Every conceivable contingency can be covered by a contingent order. No matter what general conversation goes on and what plans are discussed between RR and client, actual trades should be made by written orders; noted down from telephone conversation, yes, but read back as an order.

Second, the RR should always monitor client behavior in terms of adverse possibilities. There are standard errors speculators make, such as being too quick to take profits or too slow to accept losses, trading for the sake of trading and taking positions with risks too great in relation to profit potential, and getting too confident and trading too big following a run of successes. Speculators fail to form complete game plans or to follow the game plans they work out. The RR must watch client behavior for mistakes and point them out, must help the client to maintain his poise. There is a tomorrow, and tomorrow the client will want to trade and the RR will want him to pay commissions.

NUMBER OF CLIENTS

In considering the number of clients an RR should aim for, there is, again, no single answer. The amount of time an RR has is finite. The amount of time required per client is highly variable and is not closely related to the amount of trading done or commissions paid. Some small accounts are valuable because they take little time. Others are not worth their cost in time even though they trade in fair volume. There is also the future to think about; an account which has promise of lasting and growing is worth more time per dollar of commission than an account with little promise.

The key to the earnings of an RR is the amount of money managed. The RR can well establish his own income goals and work from there. There are no published studies of the commissions paid per dollar of account value. An RR should look at the accounts of a house and relate account value to commissions paid. Doubtless, this varies widely among customers, some being long-term position traders and others short-term, even day-traders. The ratio probably also varies with the degree of traders' success, some trading too little and others too much. A look at a very few accounts suggests that conservatively traded position-type accounts pay on the order of 25 percent of the average account value per year in commissions. The industry average is probably greater. If the RR gets one-third of the commissions generated, then there is a twelve-to-one ratio of money managed to RR income. If the RR's income goal is $25,000, accounts with an average value of $300,000 are required. The best of all possible worlds is to have a fairly small number of accounts of fair size operated for fairly conservative returns. Operating for conservative returns involves small risks and the likelihood of greater longevity.

There are two sources of money to manage: new accounts and earnings of existing accounts. New accounts tend to be small; a new client may have quite a lot of money and thus be a potentially valuable account but is apt to try the commodity trading game on a small scale. In more cases, a client has but little riskable money and great aspirations. This combination is one main reason why such a high percentage lose money and go away. An emphasis on sales and the chewing up of clients' money in commissions is not a very appealing way to go.

It would be interesting to know how much of the money successful RRs supervise has been accumulated out of earnings. It is probably a pretty large share. The game is to find new clients, help as many of them as possible grow to respectable size, and then get them to trade conservatively. A client who starts with

$5,000, runs it to $30,000, and then tries to make $5,000 per year from it should be good for a regular flow of commissions for a long period of time. It is not so much how many new sales can be made that counts but how many new sales can be turned into long-run business. It thus seems that the RR should establish an objective of developing a fairly small group of successful and consistent traders. That the average speculator loses money is not all that meaningful. Some make money, and those are the ones for whom the RR is looking.

CLIENT SUCCESS

From all of the foregoing, it appears clear that the success of the RR is closely associated with the success of the RR's clients. It would seem, then, that the objective of the RR is to make his clients successful. But, again, it is not that simple. What makes traders succeed or fail is not known; many of the reasons for failure have been identified, but why some people succeed is not as clear. We also know that many people can be successful RRs and yet unsuccessful traders. To some extent, winning traders are born, not made. No football coach can be a success if he hasn't got the horses; hence the emphasis on recruiting. But coaching is also important, and a first rule of coaching is to identify and exploit the natural talent of the athlete.

How can RRs teach clients to be successful? The textbook on coaching has not been written, and I am certainly not qualified to write it. But certain things seem to stand out. First, the trader must play his own game. He must select his trades and place his orders and assume responsibility for the results. (This is not without exception. An RR who has established himself as a successful speculator can reasonably take client money and trade it as he does his own, but in such cases he is not really an RR as the concept is used here.) There are two outstanding reasons the trader must play his own game. Each trader is different, with different objectives and talents. More important, commodity speculation is both an investment and an avocation. One aim is to make money but another is to win a game and commodity trading is a participatory rather than a spectator sport.

Second, the essence of the game is to make money, and the measure of success is the return on money invested. Each trader should be made to understand that he is trading money first and commodities second. A trader who puts $5,000 into an account and in twelve months builds it up to $7,500 has made 50 percent on his investment and has accomplished quite the same thing as a trader who puts ten times as much in an account and builds it up to $75,000. When the client evaluates a prospective trade, he should think, "I am putting X percentage of my available funds into the trade at the risk of losing Y amount in the expectation of gaining Z amount. I like the odds and think this is the best way to use the available money. If the trade goes bad, I will not have lost so much of my capital as to seriously impair my trading in the future." He should think first about the money he is using, second about the risks he is taking, and third about the money he may make.

Before he opens an account, the prospective trader should review his financial situation to decide how much money he should put into the commodity game. This is a standard review of income and its regularity and certainty, liquid earnings for emergencies, life insurance, long-term investments for education and in living-home mortgages, payments on household goods: a retirement program, savings, securities, real estate, and so on. The standard review of this tends to yield the conclusion that when living expenses, liquid savings, life insurance, and home mortgage requirements are met and there is money left over, some of it can reasonably be risked in commodities.

This is not the correct kind of review for everyone. If an individual has all of these things, why bother trading? A contrasting view is that the commodity markets are things to take money out of rather than things to put money into. They can be the sources of funds to back home mortgages, retirement programs, and the like. If a trader has what it takes, he will make enough money to trade in substantial volume, and if he does not, he will lose what he puts in, so it should be kept fairly small. "Fairly small" is highly variable among individuals. It should be an amount sufficiently large to keep the attention of the trader and to hurt if it is lost so he takes the matter seriously. But it is important that the amount of money be one that the trader can trade with poise.

One great fault of traders is in letting losses run, and one defense is to keep the funds in the account small enough to cover only margin requirements plus room for small losses. Thus, one is forced to face one's losses and make decisions. But as a general proposition, traders are probably best off if they make fixed investments and are resolved to neither add to nor subtract from them for a protracted period.

The question of meeting margin calls always comes up in discussions of how to speculate. A common rule is "never meet a margin call but cut losses." A better rule is "never get a margin call." The trader should know his margin and loss situation and remain in charge by acting ahead of the house.

At the cost of being redundant, we should again observe that traders trade money, not commodities. They should think in terms of increases and decreases in the account value, not in cents per bushel gain or loss on a corn position. A large gain per bushel is not meaningful if it is on a small position relative to the account value; a small profit on a large position is much more meaningful. Every trader is going to win some and lose some. If losses are on small positions and profits on large, he will probably be a winner on balance. The client should be encouraged to count his money frequently and evaluate its use. The count must include both the credit balance and the current position value. Most house account sales statements include this information so that the RR, from his copy, can keep close touch of the account progress. A good rule is that a client should count his money every day and make a formal record of it for long-term review each week.

One important facet of opening a new account is to establish the client's objectives. This seems an obvious thing but appears to be done but infrequently. Prospective clients sometimes have ideas about a specific commodity and want to know the margin requirement, or have heard of someone who has made a lot of money and want to know what to buy. Rarely do they think in an investment context or take a long-term view. The result is that they tend to trade frantically and greedily, and lose more.

If one asks a trader how much return he expects to make on commodity investment money, the answer often indicates that the trader hasn't thought about it. On being pressed, he is apt to be reluctant to answer in terms of more than 20 percent. But experienced RRs say that clients trade as if they are trying to make 800 or 1,000 percent a year.

A client should be forced to think through carefully what he is trying to accomplish. If his goal is to play an exciting game without too great a cost, it is one thing, but if he wants to build a small sum into a large, he must recognize that he will be running a large risk of losing his investment. If he is attempting to make substantial returns on investment—say 25 to 50 percent—he will be running smaller risks. If a client establishes an objective in terms of return on money, he will do a better job of appraising positions and will be less greedy; both results will enhance his chances of success.

Frequently, RRs are asked by clients what should be done about a given position. The typical RR asks, "At what price did you get in?" This is a mistake. The client is in at the current price, and the gains or losses to date are not germane to the decision. Plenty of additional money is lost by people trying to get out even.

How many and what commodities should a client trade? Again, there is no single answer. Some people trade a large number of commodities and succeed, and others limit trading to one or a few and succeed. It is important that a trader have confidence in his market judgments. He can be confident only if he knows something about the commodity he is trading and has reasons of his own to expect the price to go up or down. These may be based on technical chart information or house opinion so that he can hold opinions about a lot of commodities. But such opinions can be held only tenuously. Fairly complete knowledge of a commodity, its price history, and its price behavior would seem essential to developing a high level of confidence in position taking. This suggests a limited number of commodities, probably within a commodity group, i.e., feed grains, oilseeds, livestock, metals, etc. Observations of trading patterns and market cross-section studies suggest that traders tend to stay within commodity groups and that the geography of speculative interest is related to the geography of the crop production. The geographic concentrations are decreasing with time but remain.

In the matter of the number of commodities traded, an effective compromise is a willingness to take small positions in a variety of commodities but to limit large positions to one or a few the trader knows best. It is difficult for most traders to stay out of markets; they have a compulsion to have something going. This argues for the suggested compromise. It is also quite good for the generation of commissions, which is the name of the game.

A key factor in assisting clients to come out on top is the prevention of mistakes. This puts the RR in the position of monitor, often forcing him to discourage trading and thus act against his own short-term interest. One of the hardest things to do is to get clients to take losses soon enough, to recognize mistakes before the mistakes impair capital. One method is to have a careful plan, including a line of retreat. If a client agrees before the position is taken that he will cut his losses at point P or decide that he is wrong if the upcoming crop estimate or stock report deviates from amount Q, he is much easier to handle. The RR tends to get his vanity involved too. If he has suggested or agreed to a position, he may encourage the client to stay when the latter should get out. Clients hate to lose money, and forcing them to take losses may cost the RR a client. Also, there is the danger that the point of advising the client to take a loss on a long position may be the low point of the market. Here, again, the concept of money management is useful. It is possible to say to a client, "We got out at just the wrong time, but even so we traded smart." And it is true, too.

Clients tend to find profits irresistible, saying such things as, "Shouldn't we sell now, taking a profit, and buy the reaction that is bound to follow?" To say no is to turn down a commission, but it may also cost the client the bulk of a major move. Here, an appraisal of the temperament of the client is important. If he can be pulled back in if a further rise takes place, for instance, instead of the expected reaction, it may be well to let him get out; if not, he should be discouraged. Here again, carefully articulated advance plans are important.

Clients over-trade. They get hooked on trading and find it very difficult to be out of markets. They see major moves in which they have not participated and think of all the money they might have made. The RR must accent the positive. If a client has doubled his money in six months, what is the difference if he might have quadrupled it? If a trader cashed in to the maximum in every market, he would soon have all the money in the game. Progress toward modest and reasonable objectives is a good preventive for overtrading.

Clients also become overconfident. They make a few good trades, get well ahead of the game, and take questionable positions that are too large. Some professional traders scale down the size of their position after a successful run because they know they tend to put it back. Clients need to be told to rest and enjoy victory for a while before seeking new worlds to conquer.

All of this seems to put the RR into a negative, scolding role and makes him quite vulnerable to being wrong. But it is an important part of his job. Probably the best approach is to ask plenty of questions. These best take the form of, what are your plans? Is this consistent with your plan? Why do you think that? Haven't you lost a dangerously large amount of money? What are you going to do if ...? He can also remind the client of the facts about production and use, upcoming relevant critical reports, price history, and market opinion. The purpose of all this is to force the client to manage his own account.

ON GENERATING COMMISSIONS

RRs must keep accounts active and commissions flowing in, but they must not do this at the expense of costing clients too much money; keeping accounts active is good, but losing them is bad. The RR must be forever throwing up danger signals but must also make some money. Relatively few clients will be happy unless they are active. From these things it follows that the RR needs to offer position suggestions which have good possibilities or at least carry small risks. These can be developed by the RR himself, from house suggestions, from discussions with fellow RRs, and from clients. The RR needs to know individual clients sufficiently well and keep close enough track of individual accounts to develop a sense of when to respond favorably to a client suggestion and when to call a client with a suggestion or to simply discuss the market situation.

Clients should be asked for opinions. For example, if a client has a record of success as a belly trader, he should be asked what he thinks of the price level, or the technical situation or the next report. Keep in mind that some clients are going to be winners in and good students of markets and individual commodities. One thing that should be in the back of the mind of every RR is to learn from successful clients to be able to advise other clients and perhaps, one day, to trade. Spreads are good low-risk commission generators. They are a way to keep people active with little risk. They can also be good money makers. They tend to appeal to the more studious clients. Every office should have someone who is spread conscious to furnish suggestions to other RRs.

TAX SPREADS

One much-overlooked commission generator is tax spreading. (There are numerous articles on how to; see especially Harry Jiler's in *Guide to Commodity Price Forecasting*, Commodity Research Bureau, New York City.) It is possible to carry profits from one year to the next, postponing the payment of taxes, and it is possible to convert short-term capital gains to long-term gains, saving taxes. The postponing and minimizing of taxes is important to successful commodity traders because the tax system is loaded against the trader. The government is a willing partner in all profits but will share in only the first $1,000 loss in a particular year. Further, past winnings on which taxes have been paid cannot be carried forward against new losses for a tax rebate. Successful traders learn to carry profits forward as a defense against losses. It should also be kept in mind that taxes on commodity trades are assessed at the taxpayer's marginal, not average, tax rate.

Tax spreading has a special appeal over and above its real value: it is a fairly intricate game. People as inherently acquisitive as commodity traders especially like to minimize and postpone taxes.

ON ACTIVE TRADING

Should the RR trade? One school of thought says no because he should be a dispassionate observer and adviser, and he cannot if he is involved. He is apt to limit his attention to the commodities he trades to the detriment of his service to clients interested in others, and to mold the trading of all his clients to his peculiar requirements and talents, when theirs may be quite different.

On the other hand, some clients prefer RRs who trade; this is especially true of clients who want to follow advice closely. But, also, there is the thought: who is he to advise me if he can't do it himself? The concept has validity.

On balance, these things seem to indicate that some RRs should trade and others should not. Once the beginner has become a successful Registered Representative, he is past the need of this advice.

Chapter Thirty-Two

A Comment on Review of Futures Trading Legislation

1973

AUTHOR'S NOTE: A request from the staff of the Senate Committee on Agriculture and Forestry presented another opportunity to beat on the same old drum of opposing more government intervention and promoting a better understanding of the positive role of speculation. In addition, I tried to open a new door of raising questions about the performance of futures commission merchants. Numerous subsequent telephone conversations reflected much less of a witch-hunting attitude and a more sympathetic posture than I had encountered in earlier Congressional contacts.

Mr. James Thorton of the staff of the Senate Committee on Agriculture and Forestry asked the question (as I summarize it from our recent telephone conversation): What improvements should be made in futures trading, and what changes should be made in existing legislation to facilitate such improvements?[1] This is not a simple question because there is much that is not known or understood about futures trading and about what makes markets succeed or fail; neither is the place of government regulation fully understood.

---

1. T. A. Hieronymus is professor of agricultural economics, University of Illinois. Statement prepared for the Senate Committee on Agriculture and Forestry, September 26, 1973.

I am an enthusiast about the growth and development of futures trading as an institutional system for financing, inventory management, and pricing in the U.S. economic system. Trading in commodity futures is the closest approximation to a system of pure competition that exists. A competitive economic system is an ideal toward which we should strive because of the efficiencies and equities such a system affords. Competition is the key factor that has made the American economic system so tremendously effective. The institution of futures trading has long been associated with a limited number of raw agricultural commodities, the grains in particular. It has expanded to other agricultural commodities, such as hogs and cattle, and to an increasing number of nonagricultural commodities, e.g., the metals. There are studies under way to extend the system to petroleum and its products, ocean freight, and home mortgages. Recently futures markets in international monies and stock options were launched.

Existing futures markets are not very large. I cite particularly pages 287-289 of my book *Economics of Futures Trading* (a copy of which I sent to Mr. Thorton). Corn is the oldest futures market and one of the most successful, yet it is quite small. The current open interest is on the order of 325 million bushels, as compared with a crop of 5,761 million. Cattle futures have done quite well since trading was started in 1964, yet rarely does the open interest get as large as 10 percent of the cattle on feed. The economic forces that give rise to futures trading are changing in ways which will result in major growth in markets during the years ahead if markets are organized and operated in ways which facilitate growth and development.

In looking at legislative proposals, we should take a broad view of the developmental problems. Futures markets are fragile. The long record of attempts to develop markets which have subsequently failed underscores this point. At least three major attempts to establish an effective grain sorghums market have been made. Two have failed, and the third, at the Chicago Mercantile Exchange, is disappointing. There are many more exchanges where futures trading is authorized than where there actually is trading. We do not really know what makes a futures market succeed or fail. We should, indeed, be very careful that legislative changes do not endanger existing markets, and that they do foster the growth of these markets and the development of new ones. I would like to see what a viable speculative futures market in petroleum could do to the monopolistic structure of the petroleum industry. I think it would force it to be a great deal more honest.

I am not sure the current climate is optimum for the consideration of major legislative changes. The past fifteen months have seen unprecedented turmoil in commodity prices and price relationships. These have attracted wide attention and criticism. As has always been the case, futures trading has been identified and castigated as a cause thereof. Speculation in futures markets has nearly always been blamed when prices are too high, too low, or too variable. There is now a large amount of Congressional and journalistic attention being paid to futures trading. The speculative pricing performance of markets during the past fifteen months has left a great deal to be desired. Part of the reason is that the job of price forecasting has been extremely difficult. *And part of the reason is that markets have been underspeculated.*

As you may know, I have paid close attention to the supply, demand, and price situation in the soybean complex for many years. Soybean and soybean product prices have been gyrating most wildly during the past year. On June 5, 1973, I made a note of prices in the soybean complex.

As the traffic, both in person and by telephone, has come through my office in recent months inquiring about the place of speculation in futures markets in price gyrations, I have thoroughly enjoyed pointing out that part of the problem is underspeculation. This is somewhat akin to swearing in church and then demonstrating that what I say is correct.

The crux of the matter rests on the method by which speculation is measured; this is usually done by the volume of trading. It is an error. The huge increase in the volume of trading is noted and associated with speculation. The appropriate measure of speculation is the size of positions held by speculators. One speculates by taking a position, not by trading. If I buy one contract of May 1974 corn at 11:01:05 a.m. on September 26 and sell it at 11:01:10 a.m. the same day, I have not speculated very much, nor affected prices very much, but I have contributed to the volume. If, on the other hand, I buy one contract of May 1974 corn on September 26, 1973, and sell it on April 15, 1974, I have committed my judgment and financial resources to putting the price of corn up and keeping it there. I have assumed risks and affected prices during the period when the contract remained open. It is open interest that counts.

The structure of the open interest which I cited in soybeans applies in other markets as well. On August 31, 1973, reporting speculators were long 159,200 bales of cotton and short 8,400 bales for a net long position of 150,800. Nonreporting traders were long 472,500 and short 458,200 for a net long position of 14,300. Reporting hedgers were long 1,042,600 bales and short 1,207,700. Note that the market was primarily commercial. If we assume that all nonreporting traders were speculators, the total net position of speculators was long 165,000 bales. This is not very much out of a crop of 13 million. We must look elsewhere for the cause of price gyrations in cotton and in other commodities.

Beginning with the Grain Futures Act of 1922, we have had more than fifty years of federal regulation of futures trading. Federal legislation, the Commodity Exchange Act of 1936 in particular, has been amended continually. The last major overhaul was in 1968. Looked at in total, regulation has been successful. I think that legislation and regulation have had too much of an anti-speculation bias and been too much concerned with minor variations in prices. Market self-regulation works much better than is generally thought.

Many, if not all, of the current proposals have been considered before and mostly rejected. Without going into these in detail, some reaction to a few of them may be given. First, Paul Findlay of the House is introducing a bill to include all commodities under the CEA. This started last year out of the scandals associated with options trading in nonregulated commodities—illegal in regulated commodities. It is a good addition to the law. There is no reason to regulate some commodities and not others, the arguments of the New York exchanges notwithstanding.

Second, there is a proposal to broaden the representation on the boards of directors. Steps have been taken by some exchanges. The makeup of most boards of directors is a balanced representation of the membership, ranging from commercials to locals to commission houses. Exchanges are great democratic institutions; they are quite sensitive to the interests of outside trade because that is where business stems from. I sometimes think that they are too democratic; they have great difficulty getting needed changes made. For example, the Chicago Board of Trade is underfinanced. It has been trying for some time to get a clearing fee through which would be comparable to the Chicago Mercantile Exchange's but has had limited success. Last year there were changes made in delivery terms for soybean meal futures; they were a step in the right direction but not enough. The committee making the proposal took the change just as far as they thought they could get a favorable vote from the membership. Broader memberships on the board of directors might do more harm than good.

Third, there is an attempt to make the CEA an independent agency or at least take it out of the USDA. I am not enough of a student of government to comment intelligently. Commodity futures are losing their agricultural identity but remain largely agricultural. My midwest agricultural biases tend to show when I consider a change.

Fourth, there are those who wish to give the CEA power of injunction, to let it determine that a given situation is out of line and order liquidation only, to instruct individuals and firms to liquidate, and to set price limits. This was turned down in 1968. It is dangerous. Markets deal in uncertainty. There is no way of knowing what real value is until the advantage of hindsight is gained. It exchanges the rule of competitive forces for administrative judgment. I don't know who is all that smart.

Fifth, there is again a suggestion that the CEA should have control over margin requirements. This has been brought up many times and turned down as many. The proposal makes no sense to me. I spoke to the subject fairly extensively in my book (pages 318-322). Existing margins have worked quite well during the turmoil of the past year.

Sixth, it is proposed that control of delivery points be turned over to the CEA. The Chicago Board of Trade was too slow in changing delivery terms for oats and may have let the market die. It has been too slow in changing the terms of the wheat contract. (I would be more critical if I could figure out what the wheat delivery terms should be.) I think that the soybean delivery location will need to be changed in a few years; the exchange is working on the problem. The corn delivery terms at Chicago should be adequate for quite some time.

Problems of hedgers during the past year, particularly in corn, have been attributed to delivery terms. I think this is an error. The problems have related to transportation limitations in delivering such huge amounts for export. Price relationships have been badly distorted. The same distortions would have existed had delivery locations been different. Other people would have had the delivery problems, but those difficulties would not have been any less. The transportation tie-ups are rapidly moving toward solution.

Delivery points should be held at a minimum consistent with a representative price. A multiplicity of delivery points tends to weaken the price structure which, again, offends my midwest agricultural bias. It also tends to make price differences more erratic, which works to the disadvantage of hedgers.

As I have said, we do not really know what makes markets succeed or fail. However, it is clear that delivery terms are important. There is a note on this on page 326 of my book. Delivery terms are a delicate matter and are highly technical. I would be very reluctant to turn them over to a government body. The CEA has quite a lot of power already for general rule supervision. It is a major force in the ongoing wheat delivery terms discussion.

So much for the things at hand. What urgently needs to be done is to take a long view of the growth and development of futures markets. An adequate amount of high-quality speculation is what I think is most seriously lacking. By accumulation and disbursion they help establish prices which will just equate production and use and generate a product flow into markets that helps maintain price stability at the necessary level. By forward pricing the next year's crops and future production of such perishable commodities as cattle, hogs, broilers, and eggs, they assist in determining the amount of production. They thus provide equity capital for the production and marketing system. As they perform this discounting of events to come well, they contribute to the efficient allocation of resources and the efficiency of the production and marketing processes; in addition, they make money. As they do it poorly, they lose money. They have a powerful incentive, and only the most competent survive. The more extensively markets are speculated, the greater are the opportunities for producers, processors, and marketing firms to operate efficiently and with minimum risk. As I have noted, the markets are really quite small in relation to the size of the jobs to be done, and one must have reservations about the quality of much of the existing speculation. A second weakness in the system is the slowness with which contract terms are adjusted to changes in marketing conditions.

The first major step toward remedying weaknesses is to increase the amount of research in the area of futures trading. During the period 1922 to 1936, the Grain Futures Administration made quite a few landmark studies which contributed toward the writing of the Commodity Exchange Act of 1936. Basic study of market operation by the CEA has been limited since World War II. Cooperative research projections into what really makes markets tick would be useful. More information needs to be generated before regulation can be effectively changed. Major research must be done in contract terms.

I think that the area of commission house behavior in getting and handling customers is one in which there may be a place for a new kind of regulation. Because they receive the revenue (commissions), futures commission merchants bear the main responsibility for finding, training, and taking care of speculators. I am not at all certain that they understand their mission or know how to proceed with it. The exchanges have taken a few steps toward commission house supervision, but this is difficult because many houses are members of more than one exchange. Guidelines for the operation of Futures Commission Merchants need to be established, as does some supervisory procedure. I think this is probably the most useful line of inquiry the Senate Committee on Agriculture and Forestry can pursue at this time.

Chapter Thirty-Three

The Use of Fundamental Analysis and Price Forecasting

1973

AUTHOR'S NOTE: An invitation to address the use of fundamental analysis and price forecasting provided an opportunity to vent the frustrations of years of attempting to forecast the prices of midwest agricultural commodities. It also provided an opportunity to dispel the notion that feeding a sufficient amount of data into a computer and pushing the right buttons could accurately describe the future. When will we stop questing for the Holy Grail? We won't, because such is human nature. What is really apparent is that advanced speculative markets are tremendously efficient at gathering pertinent information and processing it into current prices.

INTRODUCTION

The title under which these comments are flying is somewhat misleading.[1] It implies that there is something which differentiates fundamental analysis from other analysis, generally described as technical. There is no sound basis for such differentiation. So-called fundamental analysis can be quite technical, and good

1. T. A Hieronymus is professor of agricultural economics, University of Illinois. Remarks at the Third International Commodities Conference sponsored by New York University in Chicago, Illinois, November 15, 1973.

technical analysis involves measuring the impacts of underlying economic forces. The second implication is that I am going to tell you how to forecast prices. Even if I really knew how, time would not permit it; there are books written on the subject.

What I shall try to do is identify some of the problems encountered in price forecasting and to put these in the context of the current agricultural commodity price situation. It will probably sound like an apology for what those of us in the trade cannot do. But it is important that at the outset we recognize that careful analytical work can cast some light and improve the odds in taking speculative positions, but there is no engineering-type system for forecasting prices accurately.

A basic premise of my comments is that price change is the process of adjustment to the inevitable. There is one, and only one, price that will exactly equate the supplies available to the requirements for them. This equilibrium price is the value which the market is continually seeking and towards which current prices are continually moving. This concept of an inevitable price makes price forecasting interesting because it is easy to grade price forecasters: they are right, or they are wrong.

THE NATURE OF THE GAME

There are five generalities about the game of price forecasting which are useful to an understanding of the problems involved. First, price forecasts are made for the purpose of speculation. To speculate is to contemplate the future and take a position in anticipation of gain. This is more or less successful as price forecasts are more or less accurate. There are numerous speculators forming the market; in futures markets these include all of the commercial interests as both direct and indirect participants, professional speculators, and the speculating public. They all contemplate the future and take positions, long and short. The weight of these positions forms prices. Current prices, then, are the aggregate judgment of the market of the prices that will exist at various times in the future. Current prices in consumption are conditioned by expectation about futures prices. The price forecaster is participating in a speculative game in competition with other forecasters.

Were the aggregate judgment of all the participants omniscient, capable of foreseeing and discounting all events to come accurately, there would be no changes in prices. Price changes are the result of changes in the judgments of market participants a confession of error. To forecast a change in price is to challenge the judgment of the market, to say, "The market is making a mistake; I know more than it does." Thus, it is necessary not only to forecast the inevitable equilibrium price but also to identify the error the market is making. One should not be so cavalier as to be unconcerned about why the market thinks as it does, for many times (not most, one hopes) the market will be right and the forecaster wrong. Error identification is an important part of price forecasting.

Second, the forces affecting the price of a commodity are numerous and subtle in their effects. Information about them is never absolutely complete or accurate. Many of the forces are nonrepetitive. As a result, the use of advanced statistical techniques and econometric models as sole forecasting techniques is not sufficient.

Third, there are many kinds of forecasts and many things about which forecasts are made. Different people have different speculative problems, and price forecasts must be adapted to the problem. In substantial measure, these differences relate to the length of time a market position is held. At one extreme is a scalper in a futures market pit. He is concerned with the next order that comes into the pit, whether it will be buy or sell, whether the price will move up or down the minimum trading unit, say, 1/8 cent per bushel. A meat packer may be concerned about whether to buy heavily on Monday or anticipate buying heavily on Tuesday. A feeder with a drove of cattle weighing 1,000 pounds each has a month-long period within which he must pick the time to sell. A farmer who is planning how many acres of corn and soybeans to plant is concerned with the relative prices over the whole of a production and marketing season. It takes about one year to produce a hog after the decision to breed, rather than sell, a gilt is made; the producer is concerned with the price a year forward. A firm contemplating building a plant to make synthetic amino acids must make a very long-range forecast of soybean meal prices.

There is a sequence of information that flows into the market. This consists of acreage estimates, yield estimates, stock reports, movement into and out of storage, cattle on feed, etc. Much of this information is furnished by the federal government on a schedule that is known in advance. The market forms its own opinion about what the next report will show and adjusts the price, in advance, to its expectation. If it is correct, there is no effect on price, but if it is wrong, the price changes, and the change may be substantial. These adjustments tend to be instantaneous. The impact is in the market before a trade can be made. Thus, two forecasts are necessary: one of what the report will be and one of what the market expects the report to be.

Prices develop and change as the information becomes available in sequence. The market forecasts and responds to many things having short-term effect while en route to its long-term goal of discovering the equilibrium price for a longer period, such as crop year. Thus, forecasting is a continuous process made up of a succession of bits and pieces which finally form a whole.

Different forecasters have different skills. The pit trader is skilled at reading the flow of orders and forecasting price changes within a trading session. An analyst working for a com processor may be skilled at predicting a season's average prices and price patterns. Or one may be a long-term analyst who works with consumer incomes, expenditures for food, export demand, and producer supply reactions for purposes of projecting prices several years ahead. It is important that each forecaster identify his own skills and limit his speculative activity to the things at which he is skilled.

Fourth, markets respond to pressures which are not readily quantifiable and which are recognized by very few people. These pressures may be selling at a faster-than usual rate before or during harvest and reflect a larger-than-estimated production. Or, the flow of hogs may be smaller than expected on the basis of production reports, reflecting an error in estimation. These pressures are more apt to come from the demand side, as demand information is less readily available and more difficult to appraise than supply information. The price of cattle during the past year has been a case in point. Prices were forecast on the basis of supplies which turned out to be right and the usual patterns of consumer buying, but consumers shifted their demand schedules to the right faster than their incomes increased. Real market forces assert themselves whether or not they are foreseen.

The market response to unseen pressures has given rise to a school of thought on the omniscience of markets, which says that the wisdom of the market is greater than that of the sum of its parts; that, somehow, the market obtains and weighs all the information and seeks its own level. This is a persuasive argument, particularly to people who have encountered difficulty in forecasting prices, but the forces which move prices can always be understood, and the nature of forecasting mistakes determined, with the benefit of hindsight. The fact remains, however, that the things that seem to be market errors when they are occurring turn out afterwards to be not errors at all, but, rather, things that were overlooked. In such cases, realizing rather than anticipating markets exist.

The existence of realizing markets presents a problem to the forecaster. His role is to challenge the wisdom of the market, yet he must recognize that the market may be right and he may be wrong. Accomplished forecasters tend to develop a sense of danger they cannot see—which seems to arise out of experience in dealing with adversity. Much of forecasting is a science based on hard information and its interpretation, but some aspects of it remain an art.

Fifth, the forecaster must possess a large amount of information about a commodity, have that information systematically collated, and be experienced in forecasting the commodity's price. There is a tremendous store of information about every commodity that is actively traded, often so much that it is difficult to see the forest for the trees. However, one weakness of speculative markets is that relatively few people systematize information sufficiently well to put it in perspective. It is said that the market has an excellent memory for yesterday, a week ago, and a year ago, but has little knowledge of other times. This is the case because reports tend to refer to yesterday, a week ago, and a year ago.

There is no substitution for experience in forecasting the price of a commodity. The forecaster must live with a market to understand it. Each commodity has its own personality and subtleties. One key consideration in this regard is identification of important forces. Out of the multitude of things affecting a commodity price at some given time, there may be one of overriding importance; that will make or break the forecast. The problem is to identify and estimate the influence of the important forces, to ask the right question. Again, there is a major element of artistry in price forecasting.

PLACE OF SOPHISTICATED STATISTICAL TECHNIQUES

There are immutable laws governing price. Under a given set of quantities, uses, incomes, costs, expenditure preferences, and technological circumstances, there can be but one price or series of prices. There exist functional relationships among the various forces affecting prices. For example, supply schedules slope upward to the right, demand schedules downward to the right. Most of the forces can be quantified, and the information is readily available. Thus, it is conceptually possible to put together pertinent data and, from them, to develop systems of equations which measure existing functional relationships and to project the results into the future. Much progress has been made in developing such systems. One quickly envisions a time in which one feeds numbers into a computer and correct answers come out.

However, we are a long way from such a happy situation. These studies must be tied to the past, and we live in a dynamic world; dynamics are necessarily introduced, and this involves projecting the status quo. Forces affecting prices are numerous, and the mass of data is huge; a lot of pulling together is needed to make the problems manageable. This pulling together extracts information from the real world and makes simplifying assumptions. As these are greater, we depart further from reality. Complex models for many commodities have been developed. These are quite useful for describing structural relationships but are of limited application toward making specific forecasts, particularly for the short time periods with which most operational decisions are concerned. Their most important use is in establishing frameworks within which shorter-range studies can be placed.

In the commodity world, there is a plethora of data. A quite high proportion of it is generated by the federal government. It is of a very high order of accuracy and is universally and simultaneously available. Commodity analysts are in the pleasing situation of competing in a world in which they are on a nearly equal raw material (data) basis. The data, though, are less than perfect. We never really know just how large a corn crop is or precisely what stocks were where on a given date, such as October 1, 1973. We calculate feed and residual disappearance of corn, which is an important number in forecasting prices, but we must recognize that the residual part is largely an error term related to inaccuracies in measuring production and stocks. We estimate sows farrowing and from this forecast hog slaughter; the relationship is imprecise. One reason is that the estimate of sows farrowing is imprecise. It is important that the analyst always view his data with skepticism.

As the result of aggregation and data imprecision, structural relationships need always be looked at in a probability context. There is always a range surrounding a definite forecast, and the chances of the real value falling within some given range can be established. The size of the range is inversely related to the odds; if one wants favorable odds, he must accept a wider range.

I think that what all of this gets us to is a system of forecasting from bits and pieces, from numerous studies of small things that fit together into a continuum of fairly short-range forecasts. From structural studies, the analyst finds a broad range of prices which should contain the intrinsic value toward which the market is moving. As time passes, the range is narrowed as information and market response become firmer. A lot of not-very-sophisticated small statistical studies go into the making of a continuum of forecasts, all set in a probability context.

Chapter Thirty-Four

Current Supply-Demand Situation for Food and Fiber

1974

AUTHOR'S NOTE: On August 13 and 14, 1974, I participated in the Midwest Outlook Conference at Ames, Iowa. It was a very uncertain and volatile time. We were in the midst of a severe drought which threatened shortages. The 1972-74 period was one in which agriculture moved from surplus to shortage and prices experienced a quantum leap from a level dominated by government programs and price supports to a new and unexplored ground. The political air was filled with talk of price controls and export restrictions. Upon arrival at my office on the morning of August 15, I found a telephone request from the day before to go to Washington on the 15th to attend a hearing before the Subcommittee on Agricultural Production, Marketing, and Stabilization of Prices. My assignment was to listen and to critique outlook statements of the USDA. A fortunate plane service made it possible. Senator Hubert Humphrey was present part of the time, and much of the talk of protecting consumers from shortage and exorbitant prices had come from his office. A couple of staff people and I had a conversation in a side room with the senator. He was talkative, and we heard about his youth running a drugstore, the career of his son, his teaching of moral values, etc. But at one point I was able to get a word in edgewise and said, "Senator, the planting of corn and soybean crops was late in Minnesota, and if there is an early frost, farmers will need high prices to survive." He looked directly at me and said, "That's right, isn't it?" I returned home knowing there would be no price ceilings on corn and soybeans. Such is politics, and it says something about the relative importance of politicians and economists.

HEARING BEFORE THE SUBCOMMITTEE ON AGRICULTURAL PRODUCTION, MARKETING, AND STABILIZATION OF PRICES OF THE COMMITTEE ON AGRICULTURE AND FORESTRY UNITED STATES SENATE

August 15, 1974

Statement of Dr. Thomas A. Hieronymus, professor of agricultural economics, University of Illinois, Champaign, Illinois

DR. HIERONYMUS. I am T. A. Hieronymus, professor of agricultural economics at the University of Illinois.

SENATOR HUDDLESTON. Do you have a statement, Dr. Hieronymus?

DR. HIERONYMUS. No, sir; I do not. I came in late last night and found on my desk at 7 a.m. this morning the request that I come down here. I know the general subject matter.

I have just come back from two days at a Midwest Outlook Conference reviewing the total price outlook.

SENATOR HUDDLESTON. Could I suggest that you give us a summary of that review, describing what your studies indicate, and further, if you would care to comment on any of the testimony that you have heard so far today, feel free to do that. Then we will proceed with whatever questions we have.

DR. HIERONYMUS. My responsibilities at the Outlook Conference were to deal with the outlook for wheat, feed grains, and, to some extent, soybeans.

In the matter of wheat, the production plus the carryout, minus the domestic requirements for wheat, leave an exportable surplus of something over a billion bushels. This is an amount that is a little bit less than we have exported the past two years. It is a very great deal more than we have been able to export in the preceding years. From the 1972-73 crop year we exported a tremendous amount of wheat. In this the Russian wheat purchase was of major importance. The very strong export demand this past year was a result of increasing world demand and crop problems in various places, and, I think, some restockpiling.

There are a lot of uncertainties in world wheat crops remaining. The Canadian wheat crop is late. No one knows how well the Russian wheat crop is turning out. The weather in the wheat areas of China has not been very good.

SENATOR HUDDLESTON. Are your figures substantially close to those given by the Department?

DR. HIERONYMUS. I think so; yes. I work with the same numbers; it is a balance sheet problem, and it comes out very much the same.

So I think that we face a good export demand for wheat. I think that the price of wheat will not stay as high relative to feed grains as it has been in the last couple of years. I think we are quite comfortable with wheat unless there are severe crop problems from this time forward, particularly an early frost in Canada.

In soybeans, I worked this out to a soybean crush of about 795 million bushels, and an export of about 490 million bushels. I am using a little bit larger carryover than the USDA because I do not really believe we will get it down below the 60 million again of a year ago. This goes for oil and meal. On the meal side of it, I think we are going to be quite comfortable. We can export 5½ million tons of meal, which is about the same as this year. I think we face a little bit weaker demand. The Peruvian fishmeal production is up. The livestock industries in Europe are in trouble and will not be as good customers. It will leave us with, I should say, about 13.3 million tons to consume domestically. This is a quite liberal supply.

The trouble area is feed grains. Here we face a shortfall in the amount of feed grains that will be available. This is partly because of the restricted com crop and partly because of the shortfall in grain sorghums, which was rather substantial.

To me, it looks like a total production of 174.7 million tons. If I take off of that a minimum carryout, which I think is 16.6, a normal of food, seed, and industry use, and exports that I currently estimate at 30.8, it leaves a feed availability of 129 million tons. To put that in context, this past year, or the current year, the year ending September 30, we are apparently using about 159 million tons. So there is a substantial decrease in feed grain availability—19 percent.

In 1972-73 we used 156 million tons. So compared to the past two years it is a substantial cut in feed grain availability in the United States. This is assuming an export of com of 850 million bushels.

In 1971-72 we used 149 million tons. These were the big years. In 1970-71 we used 138.9. So the shortfall this year was not large compared to 1970-71. It is very much in line with the availability for years prior to 1969-70. On the basis of animal numbers, the bushels of com-per-animal are substantially smaller than the last three years but bigger than we ever used in any year preceding that. So it is sort of like someone asking a man how his wife was, and he says, compared to what? Now, compared to recently, it is a tight fit on feed grains.

How do we cope? The first line, you cut down the rate of concentrate feeding to cattle. This means putting cattle in the feedyard at heavier weights and keeping them a shorted period of time and putting less finish on them. What this really will do to the total supply of beef is not clear, because cattle numbers have been increasing very rapidly. They are troublesomely high. Feeder cattle prices are low. We may consume a lot of grass-fed cattle. If we run into forage problems, we will liquidate some cattle numbers and raise the consumption of beef.

The second way to cope is in cutting back on hog production. This will take time. Like everyone else, I guess, I will watch the September pig crop estimate very closely. The general consensus at Ames yesterday was that the spring pig crop, May 1974-75, would be down about 10 percent. I think it might be down somewhat more than that. So it will cut back on pork availability.

I do not think we will cut back broiler production as much as we do cattle and hogs, because broilers are extraordinarily efficient converters to feed. I think we will probably use scarce feed there.

I think what this adds up to ...

SENATOR HUDDLESTON. Would that be true with eggs, too?

DR. HIERONYMUS. Yes, it is, because, you see, eggs—we have faced a declining demand for eggs for years, declining per-capita consumption because people prefer other things. But when it gets right down to trying to get an adequate amount of proper food at the lowest possible cost, eggs are a very good way to do it. I think the market will behave in a way that will make this possible.

What it gets down to as a matter of consequence, I think, is that we probably face some reductions in per-capita consumption of meat. It may go as low as the level of 1968 or 1969, which were at that time of record size. It will be very much above the 10 years ago per-capita meat consumption. So I really just cannot get greatly alarmed about the nutritional consequences of shortfalls in feed grain supplies. It may be helpful to the cattle industry. We have got very big numbers, and any time we top out cattle prices there is going to be trouble. So if we have to slaughter some light cattle, this will solve some problems.

SENATOR HUDDLESTON. What is the net result to the feeder if he sells light animals for slaughter? He is selling on a per-pound basis. There are going to be less pounds even if the price is up a little bit per pound. Is he still going to receive essentially the same return?

DR. HIERONYMUS. No, he will take a lesser return.

SENATOR HUDDLESTON. He will feed less, of course.

DR. HIERONYMUS. Yes. The feeder cattle in Kentucky have been lately selling much cheaper than earlier. There simply is not a demand for them to go into feedyards because feed costs are high. It is necessary to get feed costs high enough to squeeze the feedyard operators down enough so that they will restrict feed use to the available supply. Somehow we have got to discipline the use of concentrates down to the available supply. This puts the squeeze on feeders. We have got to force some hog producers to market more sows and breed fewer sows. They get stubborn about this and let their margins get down pretty low.

SENATOR HUDDLESTON. What does that do to the demand and the available supply after they have reached the point where they are feeding fewer and breeding fewer? Are they going to create a shortage?

DR. HIERONYMUS. Of meat?

SENATOR HUDDLESTON. Of meat.

DR. HIERONYMUS. A shortage compared to 1972? Yes. I do not really think a shortage compared to 1973. It will be abundance compared to any year prior to 1969. Now, I guess the biggest unknown besides what the next crop report is going to show is how consumers will react. Consumers have been over a rocky road in the past two years. For the first time in 20 years we did cut back in 1973 on the availability of meat per capita. They fought this with great vigor, they chased the—there was no way that they could consume as much because there was not as much—they chased this with great vigor and drove prices up. We got into consumer boycotts in the spring of 1973. Then we kicked the whole thing into a welter of confusion with an assortment of price controls. So consumers lost their good sense of how to spend their money, and went after things before they ran out. They filled up their freezers. The cattlemen held the cattle back and got them too heavy, and the hog growers held hogs back until they got too heavy. Then the whole thing hit the market, and crashing down came prices.

I do not know how consumers will react to the next go-around. They can take their reductions gracefully, and get by at moderate prices, or they can aggressively pursue a restricted supply and bid prices up. They have got to make some choices.

In some exasperation last October, at a question-and-answer session at a meeting, I said I really thought consumers might behave with reasonable good sense, that when [a housewife] went down the meat counter and found that a T-bone steak cost as much as a bottle of Scotch—she would make a wise choice—pass up the meat and buy the Scotch. The fact is that we do not need to consume so much meat.

SENATOR HUDDLESTON. Do they get the same amount of protein that way?

DR. HIERONYMUS. I do not think people really buy meat for its protein. Hamburger will solve the problem.

SENATOR HUDDLESTON. Do you characterize the Department's statement today as optimistic, pessimistic, or realistic?

DR. HIERONYMUS. I might say with fingers crossed that the release on September 11 stands up for one thing. Reading between the lines in it, I think they obviously expect higher agricultural prices and higher food prices than they expected before adverse weather came into being. I think that this can be coped with by the market rather simply.

SENATOR HUDDLESTON. We have had suggestions that corn may go to $4 a bushel. Do you have any comments?

DR. HIERONYMUS. Before I went out to Ames—I had to do this before the crop estimates came out—I was using 5.1 billion bushels of corn, and I was kicking around the $4 a bushel as a kind of a workable price of com. It comes out, to put it to a feed cost basis, and this comes out $44.50 for hogs, and that is about an 82-cent pork loin. I think above 82 cents the consumers balk. Four dollars is a good ball-park figure, yes.

SENATOR HUDDLESTON. I think that is all the questions I have.

DR. HIERONYMUS. If I might, in hearing what I have since I have been down here, the crux of this matter may well relate to export restrictions. I think there should be no export restrictions. More important, I think it should be made clear at this time so that markets can function without this additional kind of uncertainty. I would list four points.

First, I think that it is in the best interests of U.S. foreign policy to maintain free international trade.

Second, I think it is important to U.S. agriculture that long-run exports be increased; we need export markets badly. Any reductions at this time will hurt us in the long run.

Third, I think farmers have a right of access to the highest profit markets that are available. If these are exports, then they should have them. They need higher prices this year to compensate for lower yields.

Finally, I think that reductions in feed grain use are not nutritionally serious. They will cut meat consumption moderately, but it will remain quite high.

SENATOR HUDDLESTON. Thank you very much. I appreciate that fine presentation.

Chapter Thirty-Five

Things Learned About Cattle Futures Trading

1974

AUTHOR'S NOTE: Back to the American Meat Institute ten years later. There was an element of "I told you so." The review of ten years' experience showed growth, but still a small market when compared to its potential. The mystery of the smallness of markets was still intact.

We are approaching the end of the first decade of futures trading in live beef cattle contracts.[1] It has to be labeled an outstanding success. Please keep this thought in mind as I comment, because much of what I will say is critical. I don't mean to belittle the market; rather, I want to say that we have seen only the beginning, and the big growth is yet to come.

In the same vein, I would also comment that, while we have learned a great deal about cattle futures trading, there is much that is unknown, and much, if not most, of the opportunity to study and learn has not been used. There is need for more study that can lead to market growth and development.

---

1. T. A. Hieronymus is professor of agricultural economics, University of Illinois. Remarks at the 68th Annual Meeting of the American Meat Institute, Chicago, Illinois, October 14, 1974.

SOME STUDIES

Among the things that have been learned that I would first mention is that it is possible to have a successful futures market in a highly perishable commodity. There were grave doubts about this a decade ago. It was necessary to unlearn one of the oldest principles of futures trading that only storable commodities could be successfully traded. Cattle was first, and it opened the door for numerous others, to the general betterment of the industries concerned.

One of the early significant studies of cattle futures was made by Kirtley in cooperation with the Chicago Mercantile Exchange (1). He reviewed the trading from December 1964 through May 1968 and did a cross-section survey of positions on July 28, 1967. The market had grown to substantial size by that time; it was used extensively for both short and long hedging (more short than long). Speculators played a significant role and came from all kinds of occupations, but were predominantly cattle producers and others associated with the cattle industry, and the risks picked up from hedgers were carried by many people in rather small units. Kirtley noted that, while there had been rapid growth, the open interest and the short hedges were quite small in relation to the number of cattle on feed.

In May 1970, the CEA published the results of a cross-section study made May 29, 1969 (2). The study reviewed the commitments of traders from July 1968, when cattle futures trading first came under CEA regulation, through October 1969. It found the same pattern that we were long used to finding in grain. There were hedgers opposite hedgers, but short hedges were much larger than long hedges. Long-side speculative positions were much larger than those on the short side. Risks associated with cattle feeding were shifted to speculators. It also showed that the bulk of the open contracts were held by nonreporting traders, both long and short.

The reporting level in beef cattle futures is 25 contracts. At the time the survey was made, the contract size was 25,000 pounds, about 23 head of fed cattle. The reporting level was about 575 cattle, a rather large amount. On the current 40,000-pound contract, the reporting level is 950 head. It is likely that a substantial share of the nonreporting positions are hedgers. On May 29, 1969, 34 percent of the non-reporting shorts were hedgers, and 10 percent of the nonreporting longs were hedges.

The survey found the same wide distribution, both geographical and occupational, of speculators and the same concentration of hedgers that the Kirtley survey found.

The results of both surveys show that the cattle futures market is basically a risk shifting vehicle for cattle feeders. The risks go to the speculators. In addition, the market is used fairly extensively by meat packers as a means of fixing procurement prices.

Leuthold (3) examined the pricing performance of the cattle futures market and found that futures prices were less accurate as forecasters of prices at delivery times than were current spot prices. The performance less than six months forward was better than the more distant months. There was a downward bias in futures prices; that is, futures prices generally rose as the time of delivery approached. The cyclic nature of cattle prices and the newness of trading left some doubt about the result.

This study as well as observation of price patterns generally, strongly suggest that the events to come are not well discounted into current prices. The market is not a good forecaster; the quality of speculation is not high. Such a variable market price does not send good signals to producers about the amounts that should be planned for marketing at future times. For a market to work optimally, prices for future delivery should serve as guides that get just the right amounts produced and, thus, contribute to price stability.

MARKET GROWTH

The volume of trading is frequently cited as a measure of the rapid growth of the cattle futures market. From a monthly average of 4.9 thousand contracts in 1965, it increased to 14 thousand per month in 1966; to 25 thousand in 1967; 83 thousand in 1969; and finally to 129 thousand per month in 1973. But much of this growth is illusionary. A more appropriate measure of the size of the market is the open interest.

It represents positions, that is, the amount of risks shifted and the amount of money at hazard. The monthly average open interest increased from 3.3 thousand in 1965 to 19.8 thousand in 1967; declined to 12.9 in 1968; rose rapidly to 25.7 thousand in 1969; fell to 14.5 in 1970 and 14.9 in 1971. It averaged 24.0 thousand in 1972; 28.1 thousand in 1973; and 24.7 during the first eight months of 1974. Two things are apparent: first, the market increases in size when prices are volatile and decreases when they are stable, and second, a comparatively stable plateau has existed for three years.

How large is the market? At the end of August 1974, total open contracts were 24,394. This is approximately 927,000 fat cattle. The short hedges were 11,604, and the short positions of nonreporting traders were 9,049. If we assume on the basis of the 1969 survey that 34 percent of the latter were hedges, the total short hedge position is 558,000 head. There were about 10 million cattle on feed on July 1. About 5.6 percent were hedged. The long hedges amounted to about 110 thousand head. Cattle slaughter during July 1974 was 3.1 million head.

It is readily apparent that only a small proportion of cattle producers, feeders, and slaughterers make use of the cattle futures markets. Rarely is the total open interest as large as 10 percent of the cattle on feed.

Perhaps more important, there is not much systematic speculation in cattle prices. On August 31, 1974, the long-side speculative positions were 867,000 head, and the short-side speculative positions were 290,000 head. This covers a whole 12-month period of maturities. Slaughter during the next 12 months will amount to about 35,000,000. Not very many cattle are involved in the speculative pricing process.

To press the point a bit further, on September 27, 1974, the open interest in August 1975 cattle was 612 contracts, about 23 thousand head. Not very many cattle, people, or money were involved in the judgments that put the price at $45.25. It is not at all surprising that the far-out cattle prices eventually prove to be quite inaccurate. Not much goes into their formation.

USEFULNESS AS A HEDGING MARKET

While the market may be small in relation to the total risking-financing job of the industry and the speculative price formation is of fairly minor significance, the market is a useful tool for those cattle feeders who elect to use it. As is well known, the past year has been one of serious losses for cattle feeders. One must sympathize with cattle feeders. But our sympathy is blunted when we recognize that losses were avoided by those feeders who elected to hedge their operations.

While I have not done the detailed arithmetic, I am certain that most of the time during the past 12 months it was possible to buy feeder cattle and feed, and sell fed cattle simultaneously, at profitable feeding margins. Most of the losses incurred were the result of speculating on the short side of the feed market and the long side of the cattle market.

For those periods of time during which the package of feed, feeder cattle, and fed cattle prices did not offer a profit, the cattle feeders had the option of refusal, of sitting on the sidelines, until price relationships were forced back into line.

One lesson that should have been learned from the experience of the past year is that hedging should be seriously considered as a strategy alternative to speculation in feed and cattle prices.

A thing that is interesting to consider is: What would have happened had the whole of the cattle feeding industry decided to hedge profitably or stand aside? If we think in terms of 10 million cattle of feed during the year, it becomes readily apparent that short hedges would have averaged about 263,000 contracts. For the market to be liquid, the open interest would have to have been at least 50 percent greater, or 395 thousand. This is 16 times more than actually existed. Had everyone decided to hedge all at once, I do not think that it could have been accomplished. The necessary speculation would not have been forthcoming. Feed and feeder prices would have been forced up, and fed cattle prices forced down, so that feeding margins would have been unprofitable. Had cattle feeders insisted on profitable margins in hand, or stood aside, the industry would have ground to a virtual halt.

What this exercise does is demonstrate that the whole of the cattle-feeding industry cannot divest itself of price risks until the speculative fraternity is greatly enlarged. Perhaps the necessary speculation would have come forth, but I doubt it. If the goal of a cattle-feeding industry free of price risk is to be achieved, it will have to be done gradually over a period of time. It will be necessary to recruit and train a lot of new cattle speculators. This is not cause for great alarm. Cattle feeders will be slow to learn that they really should keep their risks at manageable levels.

CAN AN OPERATIVE PACKAGE BE PUT TOGETHER?

The total package involves four futures markets. First, fed cattle. The growth and development of the past decade suggests that the speculative potential is present. It will take time. Second, feeder cattle. The open interest in feeder cattle futures was twice as large on September 30, 1974, as it was on September 30, 1973. This is rapid growth and quite encouraging, but it is still a very small market. I doubt that it will become as large as the fed cattle market. There is not the compelling need to sell feeders forward that there is for fed cattle. It will be very difficult to develop a large short speculative position, for speculators have a predilection toward the long side. Nor is it necessary to have a feeder cattle futures market as large as the fed cattle futures market. Cash feeder cattle prices can be forced into line if feeders insist on profitable, locked-in margins or stand aside. Third, grain sorghums. Futures markets for grain sorghums have been tried by the Chicago Board of Trade, the Kansas City Board of Trade, and the Chicago Mercantile Exchange during the past quarter of a century, and none of them have worked. It appears to be too specialized a commodity, and the corn futures market works too well. The necessary speculation does not come in. But corn is the applicable commodity for much of the industry and is reasonably usable for the rest. Fourth, soybean meal. This market appears to be quite capable of absorbing all of the long hedging that the cattle-feeding industry is apt to do.

A total package can be put together, and it appears to be in process.

CONCLUSION

Some conclusions stand out. First, there is a viable futures market in fed cattle that can be used effectively for risk shifting and financing.

Second, the market is not used very much, and the recent history of the cattle feeding industry suggests that it should be used more. Encouraging to the growth prospects is the fact that there is a great deal of contract feeding. Reduced to its essentials, contract feeding is a clumsy and nonliquid system of separating feeding and speculating in cattle prices.

Third, there is little evidence that the development of cattle futures trading has resulted in improved price formation. The quality of discounting events to come into current prices—and directing the output of the industry in a way that stable prices result—is not high.

Fourth, I think that the reason that speculative pricing is of ordinary quality is that there is not much of it. We need more and better speculation. The development of this is the biggest task that confronts futures-trading institutions.

LITERATURE CITED

(1) Kirtley, M. B. *Users of Livestock Futures Markets*, Department of Agricultural Economics, University of Illinois, AERR 94, October 1968.

(2) Nash, D. G., and Schaurbach, Duane. *Trading in Live Beef Cattle Futures*, CEA, USDA, May 1970.

(3) Leuthold, Raymond M. "The Price Performance on the Futures Market of a Nonstorable Commodity: Live Beef Cattle." *American Journal of Agricultural Economics*, 56:271-279, May 1974.

Chapter Thirty-Six

A Definition of Hedging for Administrative Purposes

1976

AUTHOR'S NOTE: Soon after it was established, the Commodity Futures Trading Commission appointed several study committees to hold hearings and recommend policies and regulations. I was asked to address the question of a definition of hedging. It was not simple. Out of the years of working with various commodity-related industries, I had become aware of the complexity of futures activities that different kinds engaged in. I tried to describe the complexity and the difficulty of drawing a line between hedging and speculation when, indeed, all commodity activities are more or less speculative. The conclusion was that hedging can best be described in very broad terms of risk reduction and that identification can best be made by exchanges.

INTRODUCTION

In the preface to a book I wrote in 1971, I said, "If this book makes only one contribution, it is the thorough lousing up of a standard doctrine of hedging."[1] I think that the CFTC is now in the process of substantially adding to the de-

1. T. A. Hieronymus is professor of agricultural economics, University of Illinois. Comments before CFTC hearings, New York, New York, January 8, 1976.

struction of standard doctrine. Hopefully, there will flow from this an improved understanding of the use of futures markets in the management of commercial risks.

The definition of hedging in the context of the CFTC Act is extraordinarily difficult, if not impossible. The definition is for the purpose of granting exemption from limits on the size of speculative positions permitted in futures contracts. This assumes that "hedging" and "speculation" are at least different, if not opposite. They are not. All hedges are more or less speculative, and all speculative positions are more or less hedged. There is not a simple solution to the problem of establishing a process for granting exceptions from speculative position and trading limits.

I am tempted to cop out on the assignment by saying that the solution is to not impose any limits on speculation. It would not be much of a cop-out because it is what I truly think is the best solution. But such would not be of use to the Commission at this time.

HEDGING

Hedging can and is defined in various ways, depending on the purpose. Three definitions seem appropriate: (1) to hedge is to assume a position in futures equal and opposite to an already existing or immediately anticipated cash position, (2) to hedge is to shift the risks of price level change while retaining the opportunity to speculate in changes in price relationships, and (3) to hedge is to use futures contracts in managing risk exposure associated with commodity ownership and commitment and with variable price relationships among commodities and related commodity products to levels consistent with profit maximization and/or profit regularization and with capital preservation and expansion. The first definition is descriptive of a process of risk aversion. The second is descriptive of a process of highly selective risk assumption. The third is descriptive of commercial uses of futures in a broad spectrum of activities in which capital and earnings are subject to risk exposure resulting from variation in commodity prices and price relationships. It opens the door to a long list of legitimate exemptions to speculative limits.

One thing is common to the three definitions: They all imply a reduction in risk exposure from levels that would otherwise exist or the maximization of profits from variations in cash commodity or commodity product prices or price relationships. The test, then, of whether a specific futures activity is a hedge is: Does it reduce risk exposure? Or does it contribute to an attempt to maximize profits from business activities associated with cash commodities? On the other hand, if an activity in futures contracts is designed to obtain earnings from price or price relationship changes in futures, it is speculation. Or, if it increases risk exposure, it is speculation.

DEVELOPMENT OF EXEMPTIONS

When the law providing for speculative limits was originally passed in 1936, the list of exemptions was quite short and was strictly equal and opposite in the same commodity, plus one year's production of a farmer. By 1968, it was expanded to include product hedging and the accumulation of up to one year's production requirement. The list has recently been further expanded to include wheat against prospective flour requirements, corn against prospective production of dry-milling products, corn against sales of seed and sweet com, and product futures against raw material positions. We are now on a middle ground with the door open for a long list of equally valid cases for other exemptions. It would seem that there would be no stopping point so long as a trader had some cash commodity base for his operations.

In looking at the broad definition of hedging, it is clear that more kinds of futures activities should be added to the exemptions list. It also seems that some things are now included in the list that need not meet the criterion of risk reduction. As it now stands, there are opportunities for taking large positions that are not offset by cash commitments.

SPECIFIC COMMENTS

Several kinds of futures activities are under discussion regarding their classification as hedges. I will comment on some.

GROSS HEDGING

I construe this term to mean the hedging of one cash commitment while not hedging an opposite cash commitment. An example is that of an exporter who is long 20 million bushels of cash corn and short 10 million cash corn, and who sells 20 million futures. He has added to his risk exposure in the amount of 10 million bushels. Half is a hedged position, and half a speculation. But this is true only so long as the cash corn positions are truly opposite. If one is of one crop year and the other a different one, they may or may not be opposite, depending on the relationship of old and new crop prices.

A more delicate question relates to the organization of the company. If it establishes separate profit centers by divisions, each with its own accountability, so that one entity is long 20 million cash and the other short 10 million, then the 20 million hedge may be truly risk reduction for the one division. How much the other speculates is its own affair (so long as the speculation is in cash rather than futures). It can well be said that such divisionalization is a subterfuge, but this is not necessarily true. A company may have soybean processing, flour milling, feed manufacturing, and merchandising divisions. It need not be expected that the soybean processing division know and relate to the soybean meal positions and requirements of the feed-manufacturing division or the merchandising divisions, etc.

A company should have to prove up its special case for not netting cash against cash to determine the risk exposure to be hedged.

PREHEDGING

The restricted definition of prehedging is the sale or purchase of futures in the anticipation of purchases or sales during the hours that the exchange is closed. This is a risk minimization process, hence hedging. A question arises about the size of expected overnight business. Expectations do not always materialize. Suppose an exporter intends to respond to an expected overnight tender that he expects to be 100,000 tons and for which he expects there will be five firms tendering. What is a reasonable prehedge?

How long a time span can a prehedge legitimately cover? The last ten minutes of the session? The last hour? Or a week? It depends on the size of the prehedge and the liquidity of the market.

ANTICIPATORY HEDGING

By this is meant the purchase of futures against expected sales of products or the sale of futures against the expected requirement of raw material. Whether the purchase of futures against anticipated sales of the cash commodity or products from the cash commodity is risk reducing depends upon the relationship of buying and selling prices. When raw material and product prices move up and down together, purchases without offsetting priced sales add to risk exposure and so are not hedges. But if product and raw material prices do not move together, anticipatory purchases may be risk-minimizing. Flour and wheat prices move together. Thus, wheat purchases in anticipation of eventual flour sales are not risk-reducing. But behavior within an industry is not uniform. Proprietary brands of margarine have quite sticky prices, so that advanced purchases of soybean oil to the amount of stickiness of prices are risk-minimizing. When to cover is a speculative decision that cannot be avoided. In this instance, the decision that now is the time to fix raw material cost is speculative, but it is also a hedge. On the other hand, prices of private label brands of margarine relate closely to soybean oil prices. To take forward cover is to speculate rather than hedge.

In the corn wet-milling industry, there is a saying, "If you are not long, you are short." Cornstarch prices are sticky and do not relate closely to corn prices in the short run. I once saw a calculation by a wet miller of his automatic short position; the size of the long corn position that he needed to minimize his risk exposure. It was three months corn requirement in a rising com market and one month in a declining market. How large a position was a hedging one depended on whether the price of corn was going up or down.

The current exemption from speculative limits appears to permit the purchase of a full year's raw material requirement. I doubt that very many firms avail themselves of the opportunity. For virtually all commodity users, it would be the grossest kind of increased risk exposure. No meat packer in his right mind would buy enough cattle futures to cover a year's kill. The anticipatory hedging exemption needs to be tightened up.

PARTIAL HEDGING

Partial hedging is the use of futures to cover part of an existing cash position. I prefer the term *selective hedging*. One hedges when and to the extent that he elects not to speculate. Selective hedging is also selective speculation.

Partial hedging is a legitimate risk management practice. In some circumstances, to be partially hedged results in less risk exposure than being fully hedged. It also enables the hedger to reach a balancing point between risk avoidance and profit maximization.

A farmer is a good example in making the case for partial hedging. One construction of his least-risk program is to space sales at frequent intervals across the whole time spectrum of a crop season. If he does this, he takes the average price for the season. At the other extreme, he may attempt to maximize his return by attempting to select the single best time (highest price) to sell. By the same construction, this is his highest risk policy. He usually makes a compromise. If he is short futures, it is usually in an amount less than his total production.

Partial hedgers can reasonably change the size of their futures positions. If the price offered by futures is a highly profitable one and there appears to be substantial risk of adverse price change, he may elect to be fully hedged. But if the price changes substantially so that it unprofitable and there is little risk of further adversity, he may elect to remove all or part of his hedges. Trading in and out is a legitimate activity and should be permitted.

I know of no rule that requires hedging. A firm can speculate with cash commodity inventories or obligations to whatever extent that it elects. A soybean processor may carry a five-year inventory of crush if he wants to and can arrange the financing. But this election of hedging or not is fraught with problems in futures market regulation. Suppose that a soybean processor accumulates an inventory of six months' crush of soybeans. He thinks prices are low, so he does not hedge. Prices rise to what he judges to be dangerous levels, so he hedges. They decline, so he unhedges, etc. If he has a large enough commercial base, as many processors and exporters do, he can trade in and out of the futures market in large amounts at will. This activity is conceivably disruptive of prices, and there may well be this kind of trading operative in futures markets at the present time.

It would appear that the only way to prevent such disruptive activity with position and trading limits is to require that firms that are granted exemptions follow policies of being fully hedged or hedged to some fixed proportion of risk exposure. I doubt that this is an acceptable suggestion, but I do think that regulations regarding exemption from limits should recognize and cope with problems associated with partial or selective hedging.

CROSS HEDGING

The concept of cross hedging has not been brought into the exemptions list. It should be. To cross-hedge is to assume a position in futures opposite to an existing cash position in a different but price-related commodity. This may be done because there is no futures market in the commodity on which market risks are outstanding, or because existing futures markets are not sufficiently liquid, or because the use of futures in a different commodity is judged to be a better hedge than one in the same commodity.

In the matter of using futures in a different commodity, a good example is hedging soybean meal inventories by selling soybean and buying soybean oil futures. Price relationships are sometimes such that a soybean oil hedge involves less risk or greater profit opportunity than a direct meal hedge. It is equal and opposite and risk-reducing, hence a hedge.

There are not futures markets for many commodities. When a wheat miller buys wheat and books flour at firm prices, he is long millfeeds. Millfeed prices fluctuate, and there is not a futures market. Prices fluctuate in relation to other feed prices—such as corn, oats, and soybean meal—and risks can be hedged. By the same token, cottonseed oil can be reasonably hedged in soybean oil futures, corn gluten feed in a combination of com and soybean meal futures, and pork inventories in live hog futures.

The problem in the matter of cross-hedging exemption from speculative limits is how far afield the hedger may be allowed to go. Some degree of covariation of prices is essential for a cross hedge to be legitimate. How close the relationship need be is related to the degree of risk. When prices of the commodity to be hedged are fairly stable, the covariation needs to be fairly close lest the operation be risk increasing rather than risk-reducing. But when prices are highly volatile and risks of adverse price changes are great, covariation can be very much less-any old port in a storm.

Legitimate cross hedges go far afield. Bakery wastes are collected and processed into animal feeds. They are bought on long-term contracts—up to several years—at firm prices. The product is priced date-of-shipment on the basis of the current price of corn. The sale of corn futures is a nearly precise hedge. The hedging of bakery wastes in corn futures should be exempt from speculative limits.

Every position is a hedge against something. A long position in a commodity future is opposite a long position in money, just as the ownership of real estate is a hedge against a decrease in the value of money. And a short position in commodity futures is a hedge against an increase in the value of money. Some commodities, such as gold, are widely judged to be storehouses of value. If a holder of an inventory of money is apprehensive about inflation, he can trade it for gold in an attempt to preserve its value in real terms. But he may judge that gold has been already bid up to levels that make it a poor hedge for money, but that wheat is very cheap relative to gold. He thus hedges money in wheat. The record of the price of money in recent years lends legitimacy to cross-hedging of money and commodities.

Bonds can be hedged in silver spreads. Bond prices go down as interest rates go up, and vice versa. Silver spreads widen as interest rates increase. Thus, if one is long bonds and fears an increase in interest rates, he can buy distant and sell less distant silver futures as a hedge against his bond position. The gain from the silver spread should offset his bond loss if interest rates increase, and the gain in bonds offset his silver spread loss if interest rates decrease.

The point of all of this is that cross hedges are a bona fide hedging use of futures; but it is difficult to draw a line between what is and what is not a cross hedge, and it appears virtually impossible to specifically list all exemptible cross hedges.

LENGTH OF PRODUCER SALES

The twelve-month production restriction (eighteen months for sugar) on sales by producers may be too restrictive. The marketing season for annually produced crops, such as corn and soybeans, extends from the time that resources are committed until the end of the crop storage season. For crops to be produced in 1976, the period is from late 1975 to late summer of 1977—the length of the trading span of December 1976 and July 1977—deliveries of com. A farmer is always in the process of marketing two crops. It seems reasonable to extend the exemption to two years.

In a broader sense, it seems reasonable to permit producers to sell as far forward as they have committed resources. A man bought a piece of land in the fall of 1974 at a quite high price—a good investment only if the price of corn remained high. The land was heavily mortgaged. The price of December corn was $3.50, an amount that, if it lasted through the duration of the mortgage, would make the investment profitable. The man sold enough com to equal the value of the mortgage, guaranteeing his ability to repay. It was several years' potential corn production. A bona fide hedge? I think so.

RAW MATERIAL AND PRODUCT SPREADS

The soybean complex is unique in that there are active futures markets in a raw material and its products, and that raw material and product prices are closely related. Processors can sell cash products against cash soybean inventories, sell product futures against cash soybean inventories, sell cash products forward against soybean futures positions, and sell product futures against soybean futures positions. Soybean processors are in the business of selling the service of processing soybeans into meal and oil. They do this at a margin described by the difference between soybean and product prices. Margins are variable, and only rarely are they as wide as the cost of processing. These are highly developed and highly speculated markets. The objective of the processor is to sell his services at as wide an average margin as possible. The industry has had a history of operating below cost profitably. They do this with trading skill. It is skill in the timing of putting on and taking off the crush and skill in basis—cash to futures—operations. The whole operation is a remarkable tribute to the efficiencies forced by a fully competitive pricing system. Fully competitive is essentially synonymous with highly speculative.

If soybean processors are to continue to operate at such remarkable efficiency, they must be allowed to have a full range of opportunities to use their skills. This should include not only the putting on of crush by buying soybeans and selling products but also the taking off of crush by selling soybeans and buying products. In their operations, processors are opposed by speculators who have long since learned to trade in processing margins.

So long as speculators are restricted in the size of positions that they are allowed to take, it seems reasonable to restrict the crush positions of processors to the size of their crush capacity. Defining crush capacity is not simple. Restrictions should not be limited to the quantities of capacity for the months in which offsetting positions are taken because the shifting back and forth among months is a part of the trading game. Further, the operation is assumed to have a perpetual life so that positions can be rolled forward indefinitely and there are no capacity limits.

The cattle-feeding complex is as complete as soybean processing with futures markets in feeder cattle, feedstuffs, and fat cattle. However, trading is less highly developed and used, and price relationships are not as closely related. But it is developing.

Approaching these two are the hog and broiler production activities in which there are futures markets in feeds and finished products. These markets, too, are developing and expanding as producers make increased use of them.

The use of futures on both sides of these several processing activities are risk reduction operations, hence, bona fide hedging. They should certainly be exempt from speculative position limits. It is to be hoped in the interest of productive efficiency that these kinds of fore-and-aft futures operations with full speculative participation can be extended to many more parts of the economic system. The only reasonable restrictions would be related to production capacity.

TOWARD A SOLUTION

From this, three things stand out: (1) to qualify as a hedge, a position or set of positions should be risk-reducing; (2) in gross hedging, anticipatory hedging, and partial or selective hedging, there are opportunities for abusive practices if large positions do indeed enable abuses; and (3) it appears to be virtually impossible to specifically enumerate the kinds of positions that exemptions from speculative limits will be automatically granted. There will be risk-reducing activities left out, and there will be included room for the taking of positions that are risk-increasing rather than risk-reducing or that permit the trading in and out of markets on a large scale.

A reasonable solution to the problem is twofold. First, to exempt strictly equal and opposite cash-to-futures offsets in the same commodity, with the promise that all cash transactions be kept essentially fully hedged. Second, to broadly define hedging in the context of risk reduction and earnings and financial management and require that firms seeking exemption apply for it. The application should include justification in terms of the general definition, a statement of policy, a description of proposed operational practices, and proposed position sizes. Each application would then be judged on its merit and the allowable practices and positions described. It would be necessary to establish a system of auditing to assure compliance.

An alternative would be to require exchanges to establish a system of position limits and exemptions for commercial users based on the same general standard. This might be the better way. If there is merit in speculative position limits, the appropriate size of limits and exemptions to them varies by commodity and exchange and from time to time. It may be that the high level of trading expertise needed to judge the appropriate size and weigh the merit of applications for exemption is most readily found among the membership of exchanges.

Chapter Thirty-Seven

Designation of Delivery Points

1976

AUTHOR'S NOTE: The next month, February 1976, it was back to a study committee to address the question of designation of delivery points. It was an important political issue in the act that established the CFTC. The thrust of my comments was in the direction of protection of the longs; however, after extensive study of the issue, little, if any, intervention would occur.

If the CFTC finds that the delivery terms for a commodity are inadequate to prevent or diminish price manipulation, market congestion, or abnormal movement, it is empowered to change delivery terms, particularly by designating additional delivery points.[1] This charge of the Congress to the Commission has a ring to it that troubles me. There is an implication that there is currently a need for changes in designation of delivery points. The implication is not true; it cannot be, for markets that have the wrong delivery terms disappear.

The implication of the law is that there is congestion that causes upward price distortion. There is another side to the coin. It is possible for delivery to be so restrictive that there is congestion, but it is also possible for delivery to be loosened up to the point that markets are damaged and go out of existence. It appears to me

---

1. T. A. Hieronymus is professor of agricultural economics, University of Illinois. Comment to the Commodity Futures Trading Commission, Kansas City, Missouri, February 19, 1976.

that over the years, the pressure put on exchanges to avoid congestion has resulted in weaker than optimal delivery terms. I think that the mill feeds futures market at Kansas City and the turkey futures market at Chicago died because of too easy delivery. It is important that at least as much attention be paid to seeing that delivery terms are sufficiently restrictive as to seeing that they are loose enough to avoid congestion.

The power of the commission must be exercised with great care. There is in it danger of the destruction of markets. Futures markets are fragile things; many are started and fail, many more fail to grow to viable size, and even the best are small in comparison to the jobs that need to be done. I have said many times that instead of being impressed with an open interest of 400 million bushels of corn, the market should aim for four billion. One basic principal is that if a market works, leave it alone.

One of the most difficult tasks in starting and operating a futures market is establishing the terms for delivery. A futures contract is a temporary substitute for an eventual cash transaction. In markets that work, delivery is rarely made and taken; futures contracts are entered into for reasons other than exchange of title. Markets where there is a large amount of delivery fail and go out of existence because extensive delivery is an indication of an out-of-balance contract, one that favors either the longs or the shorts. When a contract is out of balance, the disadvantaged side ceases trading, and the contract disappears.

The objective in writing a futures contract is to obtain such even balance that only an amount to test the price is delivered, to make the contract so readily deliverable and receivable that there is no incentive to make or take delivery. The terms of the contract must be precisely representative of the commercial trading practices of the commodity. When contracts are written, their terms are as closely descriptive of existing practices as a committee of knowledgeable people can make them. The commercial circumstances surrounding a commodity change as the production, marketing, processing, and consumption change. The delivery terms appropriate at one time are not appropriate at another, so that changes, sometimes frequent ones, are necessary.

There are several terms of futures contracts: commodity, amounts, price, quality, place of delivery, time of delivery, terms of payment, and provision for default.

All of these, except price, are standardized. The terms are simple to write except quality and place of delivery. Both have been the source of continuous problems for exchanges, but quality issues have remained out of the public sector.

For the first century of futures trading, deliveries were almost entirely at the central markets where the futures markets are located. Nearly all trade was in raw agricultural commodities, and a large proportion of each moved to central markets for storage and processing and then into distributive channels. The amounts that flowed naturally to and stored at central markets were large enough to be fully representative of value and to prevent congestion in delivery months. Following World War II, the marketing system was decentralized as the result of numerous changes in the commerce of commodities. A high proportion of wheat now moves from areas of production to export points. Livestock slaughter moved from central markets, as Chicago, to the interior. Trading in new commodities developed, and many of these have never moved through central markets. The soybean processing industry developed in the interior near points of production, and oil and meal moved from the dispersed processing plants to equally dispersed points for further processing. It was thus necessary to designate multiple delivery points at interior locations. The questions continually at issue are not single versus multiple delivery points, but are of how many points at what locations.

Commodity exchanges are great democratic institutions, and they make changes slowly. It is a clumsy matter to change delivery terms. It takes a lot of committee work and consultation with all affected parties. Contracts for which trading has started must be continued with the old terms until they expire. It either takes a year to implement a change, or there is overlapping so that there is trading in, say, "Old March Wheat" and "New March Wheat." Exchanges have had a record of changing slowly, sometimes too late. Trading in rye futures expired. One reason, doubtless, was the failure to recognize that Chicago was no longer a viable delivery point. Trading in oats futures nearly stopped before Minneapolis was made an alternate delivery point.

It is easy to be overly critical of exchanges. The establishment of delivery terms is often quite difficult. The soybean meal futures contract has been a problem since the beginning of trading in 1951. The delivery terms have been changed many times. There is a new contract starting with the March 1976 delivery. How well it will work is uncertain, but we must give the committee involved excellent marks for effort. The Chicago Board of Trade, in response to criticism of the existing wheat contract, launched a thoroughly researched and carefully designed Gulf wheat contract in 1974. It failed to trade. A lot of work, information, and wisdom of experienced people goes into the development of contracts. The motivation is to make the contract work. The record shows that it is an involved and difficult process.

Delivery on futures contracts is a sampling of value process. The objective is to take a sample from the flow stream of the commodity, test it for value, and return the sample to the stream. There must be a sufficient amount of the commodity to move to and through the delivery points to provide a representative sample. Note that I stress movement to and through rather than stock at the delivery point. The great apprehension about starting futures trading in perishables such as live cattle was the lack of a deliverable supply. But the sampling of the flow stream principle has worked quite well. The amount of flow and stock must be large enough that the price is representative of the value of the commodity generally, so that the relationships with other points of commerce are rational. These are minimum requirements, and the minimums should be maximums. The delivery process must be kept as simple as possible. Speculators will not participate in markets in which delivery is complex, and great merchandising skill is required to know what market value is and to dispose of the commodity received on delivery.

Speculators are the most scarce and precious resource in making markets work. When delivery terms are disadvantageous to them, they have a simple solution: they simply go away and trade something else. No speculator is tied to corn when there is a pork belly market. But a corn producer or corn merchant is tied to corn, and he has to have speculators present.

A strong case can be made that the terms of futures contracts should lean in favor of speculators. Delivery terms should be a premium item in terms of quality and location, a No. 1 quality grade instead of fair, or average, quality. The top of the line is easier to identify and relate to than are other qualities and locations. If it is necessary to broaden the delivery base to prevent congestion, it should be done on a moderately punitive basis. If the normal Toledo corn price difference is

4 cents under Chicago, the Toledo discount should be 8 cents, etc. The delivery location should be a strong location from the taker's point of view.

Proliferation of delivery points results in distortion of price relationships over space. Delivery is made at the point of lowest value, and cash prices at other points are above this by commercial value differences. Delivery goes to the least common denominator, and the identity of the least common denominator is continually changing. When delivery hops from point to point, cash-to-futures price differences at all other locations become erratic. This makes hedging difficult, if not impossible. There is not only danger of losing the speculators but of losing the hedgers as well. Primary producers and interior merchants have a tendency to want delivery points close to their operations so they can make delivery when they cannot readily merchandise the commodity. It is a simplistic notion that has appeal: delivery at the entry point to the marketing system. However, on more careful consideration, such a system would be disadvantageous to the hedgers because of the erratic basis behavior. It would be useful to the least common denominator only when it was his turn to be the least common denominator.

An incident in the corn market in July 1973 was of major influence in getting attention focused on the delivery point question and inclusion of the delivery point legislation into law—exports of all grains were extremely large that summer. Movement of wheat to the Gulf tied up rail cars so that movement of corn among interior points and to the Gulf for export was difficult and limited. Where there was transportation to move it, corn was valuable; and where there was not transportation, the price was unusually low in relation to other markets. In early July, the cash price at interior Iowa points was unusually low relative to Chicago. The interior Illinois points price was above Chicago, rather than a usual 10-cent discount. And the Gulf price was much higher than usual in relation to Chicago. The cash price at Chicago was above the futures. It was an abnormal spatial price structure caused by a huge export movement and limited transportation. The price of July futures rose from $2.33 on July 12 to $2.49 1/2 on the 17th, and $2.59 1/2 bid on July 19. Trading limits were removed, and the price spiked up to close at $3.70 to $3.90 on July 20, which was the last day. It appears that the primary shorts were interior hedgers west of the Mississippi, and the primary longs were exporters who were counting on corn from Chicago for Great

Lakes shipment. Until the last day of trading, the July futures price lagged under the cash prices at Chicago, interior Illinois and Indiana, southeastern United States, and Gulf prices. Cash prices continued strong, and relationships distorted following the expiration of the July futures.

The interior hedgers not only went into the delivery month without foreseeable means of making delivery, but they stayed until the end. The abnormality was basically caused by transportation problems rather than inadequacy of delivery points. More immediately, the abnormality was caused by imprudent and poor hedging technique. Had interior Iowa and Minnesota points been deliverable, the futures price would have gone to the Iowa level and all of the other points would have gone to huge premiums over the future. The spatial disequilibrium would not have been corrected. That which would have been a good deal for some hedgers would have created a very difficult situation for others. Most important, the predictability of basis would have been reduced, hence, the usability of the market by hedgers.

It is easy to look at the corn incident and become more concerned than justified. The July futures price spiked up to a very high price in one day. Other futures prices were not affected; there was not congestion in the September delivery. It expired quietly and weak relative to the December. The cash price was not affected. It appears that price relationships over space were not affected.

What this really raises is a question about the extent to which market participants should be protected from themselves. I suspect that part of the reason that the hedgers stayed imprudently short for so long was that they had confidence that there would be sufficient pressure brought on the longs to prevent a sharp run-up. Perhaps it would not have happened had there been a less regulated atmosphere.

So much for the general guidelines. The problem of the Commission at this time is to develop a system of monitoring delivery terms to comply with the charge of the Congress. How can inadequate delivery terms be identified? (Note that I have broadened the question to include the totality of delivery terms other than just delivery points. It is not possible to look at just one part.) The problem is one of identification of a distorted price or set of price relationships.

Identification of a truly distorted cash price that is the result of a market corner is easy and should not be a part of the delivery point question, but a part of a manipulation investigation.

A substantial research effort is needed for the monitoring of the effectiveness of delivery terms and needs to be developed. It is an ongoing process that is a permanent part of the activity of the Commission. The problem is conceptually simple but quite difficult to implement. The procedure is to establish normal price differences over space on the basis of historical differences, then measure deviations from normal that are the result of changes in commercial forces affecting locational differences, and finally relate remaining unexplained differences to the situation in the futures market.

The development of normal differences is not easy because data are not readily available nor notably accurate. There are secular changes over time that need to be taken into account in developing normal differences. Accounting for deviations from normal that are the result of commercial forces is complex. There is a concept of a spatial equilibrium that will result in just the right flow of a commodity from the many points of origin to the many points of consumption. But for any given time the spatial equilibrium is uncertain. Differences approach equilibrium but never achieve it. They are constantly in motion. Sorting out the differences that are "proper" because of commercial forces from those that are "improper" because of activities in futures is difficult.

Some effective work can be done on narrow ground relating to futures markets. These relate to the size and composition of the open interest, particularly near the expiration of trading in a given month and in months near the end of the crop years. They relate to the degree of price volatility near the expiration of trading. Finally, they relate to the amount of delivery made and taken.

As a final comment, I would caution that at least as much, if not more, attention should be paid to the possibility of excessive short positions and excessive delivery as the possibility of long-side congestion. I suspect that more damage has been done to markets by too easy rather than too difficult delivery.

Chapter Thirty-Eight

Toward a Definition of Manipulation

1977

AUTHOR'S NOTE: Having participated in the defense of several firms and people accused of manipulation of futures markets by the CEA and the CFTC, I responded positively to a request from the Hofstra Law Review to write an article on the subject of a definition of manipulation. It was published in the fall 1977 Hofstra Law Review, Volume 6, pages 41-56. As published, the article is extensively footnoted (twenty three times). It is reproduced here without the footnotes in the interest of readability. While I was involved peripherally in others, the article is based on four cases, two accused of short-side manipulations and two of long-side. One ended in a draw and both sides withdrew from further warfare—the CEA probably because it saw a strong possibility of defeat, and the accused firm because of rising time and legal costs and because it was offered cessation of battle without sanction. Two were won on the basis that they acted as prudent merchants. The fourth was the most interesting. Two speculators were long when there was a sharp price increase on the last day of trading. As it developed, the principal short position was also speculative. The central question came down to "When you have got your opponent in your grip, how hard are you allowed to squeeze?" In the article, I again came down on the side of "Let the market trade out," that there is greater wisdom in market forces than in regulatory bodies.

INTRODUCTION

A central focus and important purpose of the CFTC Act and its predecessor on legislation dating back to 1922 is manipulation, its punishment and prevention.[1] Manipulation is prohibited by the rules of exchanges. But the law and the rules of exchanges do not define manipulation, and the only guidelines are the results of legal actions in which specific behavior patterns and actions associated with specific price movements were judged to be or not be manipulation. The legal actions are a matter of record and can be examined, but the judgments and actions of exchanges in suspected manipulative situations are not a matter of public record.

The legal actions and decisions have not resulted in a clear set of guidelines for traders in markets to use when contemplating a given market situation and course of action. There is a line someplace across which they dare not step, but the location of the line is uncertain. There is a need to draw the line for the guidance of traders, both commercials and speculators.

There are two possible approaches to such line drawing. One is to trace decisions of courts and exchanges and the other is look toward that which should and that which should not be tolerated in the context of market effectiveness in price formation and risk management. Their comments are in the direction of the latter approach.

The results are somewhat extreme in the level of tolerance of the use of market power suggested. They stem from the notion that market prices are the result of competitive forces and that competition is a contact sport. The line is put in the direction of tolerance of the use of power and countervailing power to a greater extent than will gain immediate acceptance, and it is recognized that there is a place for the thinking of people of more moderate persuasion. It is hoped that the result will be the beginning of more consideration of the problem than there has been in the past.

---

1. T. A. Hieronymus is professor of agricultural economics, University of Illinois.

STANDARD DOCTRINE

Section 9b of the CFTC Act provides: "It shall be a felony for any person to manipulate or attempt to manipulate the price of any commodity... or corner or attempt to corner any such commodity." The Congress discussed in hearings or debates from 1936 onward various definitions but deliberately left definition to the courts. The implications are twofold: first, a definition of manipulation is difficult, and second, the circumstances surrounding instances of sharp price variation are so diverse and have so many elements of causation that it is necessary to look at each instance in detail to determine whether manipulation existed and, if so, who was responsible. No manipulation case is ever simple. This is true because the forces that go into the making of prices are numerous and complex, and uncertainty always exists. Prices are the result of interplay of market forces such that the forces toward strength are always in balance with the forces toward weakness. As the relative strengths of market forces change, prices change, maintaining the balance.

A definition of manipulation by Arthur B. March, then president of the New York Cotton Exchange, before a Senate Committee in 1929 has been preserved and generally accepted: "Manipulation is any and every operation or transaction or practice ... calculated to produce a price distortion of any kind in any market either in itself or in relation to other markets. If a firm is engaged in a manipulation using devices by which the price of contracts for some one month in some one market may be higher than they would be if only the forces of supply and demand were in operation ... and any and every operation, transaction, or device employed to produce these abnormalities of price relationships in the futures market, is manipulation." This has been shortened so that in common usage the generally accepted definition is: Manipulation is causing, with intent, the price to be something other than it would have been under the "ordinary" force of supply and demand.

The word "ordinary" gets to be important. The price is the result of forces of supply and demand, and in futures markets this is the supply of and demand for contracts. The whole notion of manipulation is that some forces are ordinary and some are manipulative. It implies a price distorted from the price that would have existed in the absence of the operation, transaction, or practice that is manipulative.

The basis for the initiation of an investigation of possible manipulation is usually a sharp variation in price, such as a major move on the last day of trading in an expiring contract. In the succession of cases that have been tried under the CEA and CFTC Acts, the elements of manipulation have been reduced to (1) a distorted price, (2) a dominant or controlling position in deliverable supplies, (3) a dominant or controlling futures position, and (4) manipulative intent.

A manipulation may be either a long-side or a short-side operation. In the classic concept of a long-side manipulation, the operator buys futures in excess of the immediately deliverable supply, accepts the delivery that is made, and exacts a high price from the shorts. The futures price and the price of cash commodity certified for delivery are forced above the current bids for noncertificated supplies in the delivery market, above the prices of other futures contracts, abnormally high in relation to other markets, and high in relation to prices immediately following liquidation of outstanding futures contracts. The longs control the deliverable supply and force the shorts to pay an arbitrary price.

In the short manipulation, the operator puts an inordinant quantity in deliverable position, sells more futures contracts than the quantity of the cash commodity owned, and hammers the price down with delivery. The deliveries fall into weak, unsuspecting hands who must not only redeliver but must sell long positions as well, adding to the debacle.

Such is the standard doctrine of manipulation, its investigation, and prosecution. A suspect price is identified; and if it is a price increase, the identity of a large long is determined, the size of the long position is compared to the open interest and to the certificated deliverable supply, and charges are brought. If the suspect price is a decrease, the large short is identified, his position, trading, and delivery actions are examined in relation to the open interest and certificated deliverable supply, and changes are brought. The futures price is compared to the price reported from transactions between commercial suppliers and users and, if there is a digression, the price is said to be distorted. The intent aspect is treated lightly. If an individual is big enough to do it, he is assumed to be knowledgeable enough to know what he is doing, and the making of money is proof of intent.

For the most part, the material presented in prosecution is confined to the activities of the individual being prosecuted. Comparisons are made with positions and actions of other large-scale operators, but only for purposes of establishing dominance of futures and/or certificated deliverable supply. Only a limited examination of events leading up to and following the climactic situation is made. The questions asked and answered are simple: Was the position large in relation to the open interest? Was the position large in relation to the technically deliverable supply? Was the price of futures different than the reported commercial price? "Yes" answers establish guilt.

The defense in manipulation cases has tended to be simplistic-first, that the prosecution has not established "yes" answers, and second, the individual acted as a prudent merchant, processor, or speculator, as the case may be. The primary reason that defendants are confined to their own behavior is the limited availability of information about the actions of other market participants. The specifics of the futures and cash positions and trading of all large-scale traders are available to the CFTC, but they are held under rules of confidentiality.

DELIVERABLE SUPPLY

The matter of deliverable supply inevitably enters consideration of alleged manipulations. Exchanges, under the jurisdiction of the CFTC, write delivery terms of contracts. Delivery terms must be sufficiently restrictive that they are known and understood. At the same time they must be broad enough that price on delivery is representative of real commercial value. There is a delicate balance. If delivery locations and qualities are numerous so that delivery terms are broad, the use of futures markets is difficult because definition of that which is traded lacks precision. But if delivery terms are extremely narrow, markets are subject to manipulative distortion. If delivery terms are too narrow, it becomes impossible to arbitrage between the prices of the technically deliverable supply and the total supply of the commodity. When there is good arbitrage, a manipulator must control the whole of the supply of the commodity, a virtually impossible task. Thus, delivery terms became central in alleged manipulations. It is necessary to define and identify the deliverable supply.

The establishment of delivery terms is one of the more delicate tasks that exchanges face. They attempt to set delivery terms so precisely representative of commercial value that there is no advantage to the taker or to the maker of delivery, and as a result relatively little delivery is made or taken. Experience proves that when delivery is extensively made and taken, indicating that the terms of delivery are advantageous to one side or the other, trade decreases and finally ceases. The thing that seems to work best is delivery terms as narrow as feasible, that is, delivery at a single or a limited number of points.

In the interest of keeping delivery terms as narrow as possible, it is necessary to put a broad construction on the deliverable supply when matters of alleged manipulation are under consideration. Interpretations of what the deliverable supply is can and do cover a wide range. There is a technically deliverable supply that is the certificated and registered amount in delivery position during the delivery month. One interpretation of the deliverable supply is that it is the amount of the technically deliverable supply minus the amounts of it that are committed for processing or shipment by commercials and thus not available to the shorts for delivery. Such is the most narrow interpretation possible. The case for subtracting the committed part of the technically deliverable supply is extremely weak. Everything is available at a price. Use can be delayed and shipping commitments shifted to other points. Reservation prices represent real commercial value, and if the futures price is less, it is below economic value.

The first extension of the interpretation of the deliverable supply past the technically deliverable supply is to include all of the commodity in deliverable position that could but has not been certificated for delivery. There are typically substantial quantities at central markets that are not part of the technically deliverable supply but that can be readily made a part by the simple process of grading and making out warehouse receipts. Still further amounts can be made a part of the technically deliverable supply by sorting, screening, and blending. The amount of the total supply at the market that is or can be made eligible for delivery is variable. There have been occasions when the average quality at delivery points is low, so that little can be added to the technically deliverable supply, but such occasions are rare. Traders, both commercial and speculative, pay but little attention to the technically deliverable supply but, rather, watch the total supply at the delivery point during the delivery month.

The first extension of the interpretation of the deliverable supply is totally reasonable. Shorts should be expected to see that the available supply is certificated if they cannot otherwise fulfill their contracts. If they elect to bid up the futures price rather than see that available stocks are certificated, the consequences are quite their own fault, and if accusations of causing price distortion are made, they should be directed at the shorts.

The second extension of the interpretation of the technically deliverable supply is to include stocks that are in normal tributary position that can be put into delivery position without incurring more than normal marketing costs. Delivery points are established at locations of normal market flow, stocks, and use. For example, there is a flow of grains and soybeans to Chicago, stocks are held in store at Chicago, grains and soybeans are processed in Chicago, and there is a regular outflow from Chicago. Supplies in tributary position that can be readily brought in and certificated are reasonably interpreted as being a part of the deliverable supply.

The Congress recognized the need for a broad interpretation of the deliverable supply when, in the Commodity Exchange Act of 1936, it required a grace period of seven business days after the end of trading in a given contract for delivery to be completed.

There is a wide range of interpretations of what constitutes deliverable supply when we add the amounts tributary to the delivery point to the technically deliverable supply. The Congressional mandate seems to be the amount that can be put in deliverable position within seven business days (ten to twelve calendar days). This, in itself, is narrow. Shorts don't just go into the last day of trading short, particularly commercials. They go into the delivery month short and, hence, have a full calendar month to put stocks in delivery position if their short positions cannot be covered at a price less than the price in the tributary area plus normal marketing costs.

Interpretations and measurement of the deliverable supply play a central role in most long-side manipulation cases, and the decision is apt to go the direction of the interpretation. What it goes to is the extent to which shorts are responsible for seeing that they are capable of fulfilling their commitments.

LIMITATIONS OF STANDARD DOCTRINE

The usual treatment of alleged manipulations is much too simplistic for the real world. Markets are competitive and competition is among people. A futures contract is an agreement to later buy and sell a commodity. Trading is in contracts for later consummation. For every commitment to later buy, there is a commitment to later sell; for every long, there is a short. Trades are exercises in futurity, and the future is uncertain.

An investigation of an alleged manipulation requires an inquiry into the cause of the suspect price change; and if the price is judged to have been distorted, an assessment of the responsibility. An adequate inquiry requires a thorough look at all of the market forces that made the price behave as it did. The matter in question must be put into the context of the total market and the actions of all of the people concerned. Such is the case because futures prices are formed in a crucible of competitive forces. They are not learned seminars in which men meet to discuss and arrive at what is judged to be a proper price. They are, in a sense, arenas in which buyers and sellers meet and compete for gains and losses. Prices are competitively determined in contrast to administratively determined.

An inquiry into the cause of a price change and the assessment of responsibility is a complex process because factors affecting prices of a commodity are numerous and complex. The futures market is a central registration point at which all market forces are brought into focus. It is but the tip of an iceberg. To understand a given futures price, it is necessary to look into the total commercial base of the commodity: existing supplies, prospective supplies, rate of use, prospective rate of use.

The economic forces underlying prices are transmitted through the actions of market participants, through people. The behavior of futures prices is the result of the position-taking activity of all traders in futures. The actions of the numerous traders are affected by cash positions and commitments that have been made and by their expectations about price relationships that will exist in the future. All of this is done in a context of uncertainty. Experienced traders are never certain about that which will happen in the future.

At a given time, the futures price of a commodity reflects a balance of forces. The longs are a force toward higher prices, and the shorts are a force toward lower prices. These are countervailing competitive forces. The balance changes as events that affect market actions change.

The objective is fully competitive markets, and under conditions of pure or perfect competition no one market force can have an appreciable impact on price. Such atomistic competition is a laudable goal but does not exist in the real world. There are large-scale operators in markets. The really large entities in markets are the commercials who, backed by cash positions, can be powerful forces with disruptive capabilities. There are large-scale speculators in markets. Their disruptive capabilities are less than the commercials because (1) the size of the positions that they may take is limited by both governmental and exchange regulation; and (2) except as they take delivery, they lack a cash base with which to back their futures operation. For example, a commercial who is short three million bushels of corn is much more of a market factor than a speculator who is short a like amount because he is much more apt to move corn into a deliverable position than is the speculator.

INHERENT CONFLICT

All of this leads to a matter of basic conflict in the administration of markets. Markets are competitive contests among people whose judgments are backed with money and where gains and losses are at stake. Competition markets are inherently conflictive. The formulation of prices is a process of conflict between buyers and sellers. Each uses the power, however small, at his command. Every participant in the market has some power, and the large traders have more power, individually, than do the small traders. Each has an impact on price that is proportional to the size of his position. The basic principle in the establishment of competitive prices is the use of conflict to discover value—to tell people to use their beginning power to establish price.

Market regulation by government and by exchanges is an administrative limitation of market power. It is a limitation of the conflict that is inherent in competitive price formation. It is a regulating of the principle of competitive price formulation. Market regulation is directed toward the prevention of the establishment of prices that reflect something other than real commercial value. At the same time, market regulation prevents the establishment of fully competitive prices. Hence, a conflict in principles and objectives exists.

Exchanges and government are sensitive to the contests that sometimes occur near the expiration of contracts. When they note congested situations—those in which there is a large open interest and a small deliverable supply or in which a large proportion of the open interest is held by one or a few interests—they sometimes take steps to assume an orderly liquidation. Orderly is usually construed as without much price variation. Their powers of moral suasion are great. Some exchanges have rules under which they can direct liquidation or fix settlement prices. This process reduces the extent to which the full forces of competition are allowed to work themselves out in price formulation. Any directed settlement reduces the strength of one side or the other and is thus in itself a manipulation.

On the one hand, we seek situations in which economic forces are expressed through traders, each of whom has no perceptible influence on price—that is, the absence of the use of power. On the other hand, we recognize the need for power to be met with countervailing power. It boils down to a matter of degree of conflict that should be tolerated. To what extent should parents let their quarrelling children settle their own differences? When should the neighbors call the police when there is a husband-wife conflict, and at what stage of mayhem should the police haul the combatants off to separate points of incarceration? These are delicate questions. The very notion that parents or police will intercede is conducive to further conflict, and the notion that parents or police will let them fight it out is conducive to settlement. If government and exchanges intercede, the integrity of the market is weakened and intercession is conducive to further conflict.

HOW MUCH TOLERANCE?

How much conflict, hence how much distortion, to tolerate in the interest of market integrity? Perhaps the game of basketball is a good example. It is a non-contact sport in which there is a lot of contact. The guiding principle is "no harm, no foul." The comparable principle in futures markets would be "no cash price and movement distortion, no punishable distortion." What the principle says is that traders in futures markets should be put on notice that they are expected to honor their contract commitments to buy and sell and that there will be no intercession until the commerce in the commodity is affected.

Under such a principle, the judgment of whether a price was or was not distorted would go to the cash price of the commodity and to the flow of the commodity to and from the delivery point. A long-side manipulation would be judged to have existed if the cash price of the commodity at the delivery point was higher than it would have been under ordinary forces of supply and demand so that a more than economically necessary amount of the commodity was moved in to delivery position. A short-side manipulation would be judged to have existed if the cash price of the commodity at the delivery point was lower than it would have been under the ordinary forces of supply and demand and the stocks that were moved into delivery position were returned to the deliverers and had to be moved out at losses. The principle would tolerate the free interplay of forces in futures with their accompanying gains and losses so long as the cash price was not disturbed.

A strong case can be made for the application of such a principle. First, it would strongly reaffirm the integrity of contracts and thus reduce the likelihood of distorted futures prices. If the shorts knew that no one would lean on the longs in the interest of "assuring an orderly liquidation," they would be more apt to look further forward in deciding on actions to take in liquidating positions and/or preparing to make delivery. If the longs knew that it would be incumbent on them to accept delivery and use it or merchandise it to users, they would be more prudent about persisting in long positions. The way that market regulation has marked out in the past is that most of the leaning has been on the longs so that shorts have been somewhat confident of protection. The longs have recognized the need to be prepared to take delivery and dispose of it. There have been a lot more accusations of long manipulation than there have been of short manipulation. But markets sometimes expire weak and sometimes strong.

Second, it would lead to the improvement of delivery terms of contracts. When there is full arbitrage between the futures price and all of the supply of the cash commodity, manipulation is virtually impossible. The manipulator would have to control a significant share of the total supply and extract a monopoly price from the users. Thus, distorted futures prices would call attention to the lack of sufficient arbitrage, hence to weaknesses in contract terms.

Third, it would avoid the necessity for judging how much exploitation of an advantageous position is permissible and how much is too much, how much distortion of futures prices to tolerate. Suppose the price of a commodity is $2.00 per bushel and that a large long finds the shorts in a disadvantageous position. It is doubtful that anyone would argue that he was manipulating if he liquidated at $2.00 ¼. It is probable that he would be accused if he were able to and did force the price to $3.00 on the last day. The point is that there is a line drawn somewhere if futures prices are not allowed to seek their own competitive level. Should it be at $2.05 ¼ but not at $2.05? It should be kept in mind that a trader is a competitive, profit-oriented person. In such a circumstance, we are really asking the question: At what price is the long obligated to take his hands out of his pockets? It is the short who is bidding the price up. It is an unnatural act to cut off his profit. It is a heavy burden on the long to require that he act against his own best financial interest.

The problem of saying this much but no more tolerance of a futures price out of line with the cash also involves the uncertainty always present in markets. Suppose that in the above circumstance the long puts a price of $2.10 ¼ on his contracts because he honestly believes that he can accept delivery and merchandise the commodity at such a price, that $2.10 ¼ represents real commercial value. Suppose further that the price goes to $2.10 ¼, he liquidates, and the cash prices subsequently fail to go to above $2.01. Should he be held accountable for his bad judgment? Suppose that the price subsequently goes to $2.20; should he be held accountable for his bad judgment in liquidating too soon? How much tolerance is a thorny question.

The problem also involves who to blame; the long stands with his hands in his pockets or goes out for coffee. It is the short who has put himself in an untenable position and who must put the futures price above real commercial value. Who is the more responsible for the distortion? It is the shorts who have acted irresponsibly toward their contractual obligations. But they too must be allowed to make honest mistakes.

The judgment of how much tolerance to allow is also a heavy burden to put on regulatory bodies, whether they are business conduct committees of exchanges or the CFTC. The trader has to know in advance what he can and cannot do. It is not sufficient to remind him that he has a responsibility to see that there is an orderly expiration. He must be told (although in practice he never is) what is disorderly. When the regulator draws the line, either before the event or after, as in the case of manipulation trials before exchanges or the CFTC, he is forming and enforcing a judgment about what a proper price is or was and is thus becoming a manipulator.

CONCLUSION

The application of the principle of judging market—hence people—behavior on the cash rather than futures prices goes beyond generally accepted doctrine about manipulation. But generally accepted doctrine does not define manipulation. The definition ebbs and flows as cases are tried. No clear line that traders can identify and be guided by has been drawn. Each new case has required the drawing of a new line because the circumstances surrounding each case are peculiar to it.

The judgment of guilt or innocence in alleged manipulations is not a simple matter. It is the more difficult as the definition of manipulation is the more narrowly drawn and as it relates to futures prices. Markets are immensely complex because the forces going into the formation of prices are multitudinous and because the forces are implemented by people who act in a context of uncertainty. The judgment of manipulation is first a matter of identifying a distorted price which, in itself, can never be done with precision and certainty. Second, it is a matter of evaluating the behavior of people who act in a context of competitiveness and uncertainty for reasonableness. The central question in judging manipulation is whether the market participants—merchants, warehousemen, processors, speculators—acted with prudence and reasonableness in their various roles and with proper regard for the orderliness and integrity of the market.

All of this argues for a broad definition of manipulation and a high level of tolerance for the competition that is the essence of futures markets. Such a definition would free the market to police itself, and unfettered the market is a powerful policeman. Manipulation is its own worst enemy because to manipulate a price is to put it where it does not belong. The overpriced inventory or the underpriced commitment is a target for the rest of the market to shoot at, and shoot it will. A limited amount of regulation is conducive to prudence and reasonableness, hence to orderly markets.

Chapter Thirty-Nine

People with Orderly Minds Should Not Trade Commodities

1978

AUTHOR'S NOTE: In 1978, I received the Paul A. Funk award. The purpose of the program is "to recognize outstanding performance and high achievement among the faculty of the College of Agriculture." It carried a stipend of $1,500, a free dinner, and recognition at the dinner. But there was a hook. It required that each recipient write an essay that, as I recall, described the knowledge and programs that resulted in his achievement. I decided to construe this to mean an essay describing the core wisdom about agricultural markets and marketing that I had accumulated from more than thirty years of research, teaching, and extension. The essay got somewhat long and tedious, but thirty years of study, it seemed to me, should result in substantial wisdom, and $1,500 was not an inconsequential sum in 1978.

The commodity world is a rough-and-tumble one of competition, with its gains and losses.[1] It is a world of price variation where the unexpected is to be expected and where unusual is normal. It is a world in which Murphy's Law is alive and well—that which can go wrong inevitably will. And when the trader has mastered this bit of wisdom and learned to cope, the converse is true and things go according to plan. The commodity world is a vast and complicated system that

---

1. T. A. Hieronymus is professor of agricultural economics, University of Illinois.

defies attempts to bring order out of chaos. At the same time, it has some things going for it. It rewards generously those people who contribute to reduction of the chaos. It somehow functions and takes on its most favorable cast when compared to its alternatives. The people who trade commodities, misguided though they may be, like their lifestyles.

This essay is an inquiry into the nature and role of markets in the establishment of prices, with particular emphasis on commodity futures trading. It is an attempt to combine consideration of three essential elements of an effectively functioning economy: markets, competition, and speculation. It is a strange anomaly that price determination is treated in economic literature as a free gift rather than as the complex activity it is. Prices are made in markets, and the efficiency of price determination is of major importance in the efficiency of an economic system. Competition is described as a laudable goal, and conditions of pure competition are established. Speculation is an "evil" word and an activity engaged in by "mysterious and unscrupulous" people for "unproductive" gain. But almost all economic activity has its roots in expectations about the future, and the future is uncertain, hence speculative.

The subject of competitive, speculative markets has not received the attention that it deserves. Why? The subject inevitably draws one into the quicksand of considering the behavior of people operating in a climate of uncertainty about the nature of events to come. The future is infinitely complex, and the myriad forces that go into its determination are interactive. It defies orderly anticipation. But the more orderly the anticipation brought to bear, the greater the chances that events to come will be foreseen. It is possible that the future could be foreseen if its anticipation were left to a small group of trained specialists. Such is not the case; everyone gets into the act. Almost every action taken by individual entrepreneurs, government officials, workers, and consumers is taken not only in response to current stimuli but also in anticipation of events to come. Skill and training are highly variable, so that both actions and results are variable and uncertain.

All of this is repugnant to the orderly mind that is offended when results do not turn out as planned. The world of commodity trading is infinitely complex and participated in by people with a broad range of knowledge and skill. This results in highly variable behavior or prices. We shall look in turn at each of these three elements of the markets in hopes of describing the whole.

PRICES

Prices surround us. They are of concern to everyone. The prices of things we need determine how much money we have left over for the things we would like. The wages and salaries that we receive are themselves prices. Costs of inputs of productive activities are important determinants of profit and loss, and costs are measured by prices. The price of com and soybean meal are important to the profitability of hog production, and the profitability of hog production is related to the price of broilers.

Money has a price, called interest. It is the amount paid to the owner of money for its use for a time. And monies themselves have prices that are expressed in terms of other monies. The price of the U.S. dollar is expressed in units of German marks, Japanese yen, etc. Everything has its price.

There is not just individual interest in prices but public interest as well. Prices are never right in an approval-disapproval context. They are always too high to the buyer and too low to the seller. Salaries and wages are too low, and the cost of living is always too high. Farmers are always caught in a cost-price squeeze, sometimes more severe and sometimes less. The cost of land is so high that it is impossible for young people to get started in farming, yet returns to land are so low that retired farmers have difficulty living comfortably. When there is an excess of imports over exports, the dollar declines in value, which is of public concern. When the general level of prices rises, there is said to be inflation.

Throughout all history, measures have been taken to correct the inequities of prices. Modern-day manifestations of these measures take a variety of forms. National wage and price controls were implemented during World War II, the Korean War, and from 1971 to 1974. The whole complex of labor legislation and organization is a set of measures designed to establish equity in the pricing of labor. There have been only very short periods during the past fifty years when agricultural prices have not been subject to major governmental intervention. Prices charged for public utilities such as electricity, gas, water, and telephone services are regulated by public bodies. The same is true of the transportation system. There are or have been international price regulatory agreements for wheat, rubber, coffee, and tin, and many more have been proposed. For more than twenty-five years, the relative values of the various major currencies were regulated under the Bretton Woods Agreement.

The assortment of public measures affecting prices is and always has been in a state of flux. There are always pressures for more regulation in the interest of equity. And there are always market pressures for the deregulation of prices. The orderly world of known, stable, and fair prices is offensive to the rough-and-tumble, dynamic inclination of the market. To the market there is but one price that is of consequence. It is the totally pragmatic one of a price that will make the economic system function.

The central focus of the market is on an equilibrium price and an equilibrium set of price relationships. Prices have functions to perform in every economic system, and no system will function without prices. There are various lists of functions of prices. These vary more in inclusiveness and detail than in substance. They generally include (1) allocation of productive resources, (2) determination of the amount and kind of product, (3) direction of inventory accumulation and liquidation, (4) distribution of products among people and places, and (5) distribution of the rewards for production among productive resources. Individual prices combine into a set of price relationships that guide and direct production and distribution.

The first of these functions is readily illustrated with land. Shall a given piece of land be used for agricultural production, recreation, housing, or strip mining? If the public bands together and bids enough for land to make a park, it goes to recreation; or if a developer can sell enough houses for enough money, it goes to urban sprawl; or if the price of coal is high enough, it may go under shovel of the strip miner.

The second function of price is illustrated with choice of crops. Corn competes with soybeans, soybeans with cotton, and cotton with rice. Grain sorghums compete with wheat and wheat with rangeland for cattle. These all interrelate, and there is one optimal balance of use. Some of the products such as corn and grain sorghums are substitutes in use, which further ties the whole together.

Third, different kinds of products are produced seasonally, and the yearly production varies because of vagaries of weather. Inventories must be held from time of abundance to time of scarcity. This introduces a temporal dimension to prices. When the price of current consumption is low and the price for consumption later is high, inventories are accumulated and held for later consumption.

Fourth, in a complex industrial society, individual products are produced at many places and consumed at a multitude of places. Economic goods are, by definition, scarce goods. Always more people wish to consume a given product than there is a product available. If this were not so, all things would be free, and production (work) would not be necessary. The task of deciding how much of what to move where for whom is tremendously complex. Goods move to the place of the highest prices and go to the highest bidder.

Finally, decisions must be made about how much of economic output goes to whom. This is the place of greatest conflict between a market system and the perceived public interest. The market is simplistic. The Little Red Hen planted and harvested the wheat, baked the bread, and therefore should eat the bread. Equity of distribution of income is of major concern, and it is clear that there is a compromise between the ruthlessness of the market and the concept of "Each shall produce according to his ability and consume according to his needs." The point at this juncture is that the determination must be made by some method.

COMPETITION

In most twentieth-century industrial nations, there has been a trend for three centuries or so toward less direct governmental control of economic activity. Feudal and preindustrial conditions were replaced by what is generally characterized as "free private enterprise" or "competitive capitalism." But it has been observed that the system is neither free, private, nor enterprising and that the owners of capital are often not competitive. A better term might be "competitive price ordered system." This not only more accurately describes the system as it has evolved but also characterizes one widely accepted concept of an optimum system. But for more than a century the downtrend has reversed, and governments of the industrial nations have played an increasing role in economic activity. They own and operate productive resources, redistribute income, and establish the rules within which private enterprise functions. Some enterprises are better operated by government, as the highway and educational systems. Governments have widely accepted regulatory functions relating to health, safety, and violations of competition. These several things touch on the pricing system and affect its operation. The generally accepted proposition is that where the competitive system works to provide essential services, protect the well being of individuals from incursion of others, and equitably distribute the fruits of production, it should be allowed to operate freely. The superior productivity of a freely operating private enterprise system is recognized. The right to compete, to be more productive, and to receive greater rewards is almost universally recognized as an essential part of liberty. Thus, a competitive economic system is an optimum.

Perhaps the most articulate statement of the way a competitive system works was made by Adam Smith in the *The Wealth of Nations* in 1776: "Every individual endeavors to employ his capital so that its produce may be of the greatest value. He generally neither intends to promote the public interest, nor knows how he is promoting it. He intends only his own security, his own gain. And he is led in this by an INVISIBLE HAND to promote an end which was no part of his intention. By pursuing his own interest he frequently promotes that of society more effectively than when he really intends to promote it." As each of us does his own thing in pursuit of his own selfish ends, he unwittingly and inevitably maximizes productivity and, hence, social welfare. As each of us chooses the job that pays the best, we choose the ones that contribute to the satisfaction of the wants of others. To choose a lesser paying job in the interest of doing good in the world is to waste human resources.

The statement assumes that every individual endeavors to employ his capital so that its produce may be of greatest value. It is generally true in the employment of inanimate resources such as land, factories, and machinery, but is not so true in the employment of human resources. People elect to work and consume at varying proportions of capacity. Somewhat less than a maximum effort is not only tolerated by society but also approved; however, indolence is not. There is still a strong work ethic that rests on a concept of obligation to further the general welfare by being productive.

To make the system work at full tilt requires greed. It is the greedy people who are the great producers. A college placement officer submitted three students to an employer for interviews, and the employer chose the one that seemed least likely to the placement officer. When asked why, the employer answered, "I asked each how much money he wanted to make in a lifetime, and the winner replied, 'They haven't printed that much yet—I want it all'—well motivated."

The corollary motivating characteristic is fear—fear of not getting rewarded and not having anything to consume or of having too little. If the system pays off on the basis of productivity, fear of loss of income is an important contributor to total output, hence, to the general welfare. The cowards, as well as the greedy, are the nobility of a competitive economic system.

We almost universally approve of competition in economic activity as a general proposition. We extol a competitive system as an intricate mechanism of great beauty. But at the same time we seek to avoid competition for ourselves. We form conglomerates that will give us dominating market positions from which we can reap monopoly revenues. We seek to enact fair price laws that will protect us from competition. We form teacher and labor unions to negate the full impact of competitive forces. We seek licenses that will give us exclusive rights to operate television stations, bus lines, and electric utilities in restricted geographic areas. College professors and civil servants work out tenurial arrangements so that they cannot be fired except for the worst of performances. These arrangements are worked out under the most laudable banners of the public interest, but one must wonder about the roles played by greed, fear, and indolence. One must wonder, too, about how valuable these protective backwashes are. Could it be that they stifle productivity and prevent individuals from rising to the top and force the more productive to share with the less?

The point of this is that it is a mistake to talk about the beauties of competition. It both rewards and punishes. It is a hard taskmaster, mean and ruthless. It has only two things going for it. First, it is inordinately productive. No other system yet devised has resulted in such rapid increases in productivity. It is often criticized for producing the wrong things, but it produces the things that people want as measured by how they spend money. The automobile companies either produce automobiles that people want or go broke. Henry Ford once thought that consumers should have only black automobiles and so lost sales leadership to Chevrolet.

Second, it offers the reward of succeeding, the exhilarance of winning. It affords an opportunity for individuals to climb from one economic level to another, to be more productive and to be rewarded for it. Perhaps more important, it offers an opportunity to compete. The proposition is that winning is better than losing, but losing beats not playing.

The key to a competitive economic system is the pricing mechanism. In this system no individual or organization is charged with the responsibility of what, how, or for whom to produce; yet the things that satisfy consumer demand get produced in the right amounts and get to the right places at the right time. A competitive system is coordinated by an elaborate mechanism of prices and markets.

There are sometimes discussions of planned versus unplanned economies. This is the purest of nonsenses; all that is at issue is how planned. There is no such thing as nonplanning. A competitive system is said to be without a central intelligence, but this is not so. Fluctuating prices, reflecting the ebbs and flows of supplies, factors of production, wants and purchasing power, form into a market that is the central intelligence that orders the processes. In this context, market is an elusive concept, being many transactions in many places at a multitude of prices. The market is the omniscient invisible hand of Adam Smith.

The system works perfectly in a situation of pure competition. But pure competition is an economic ideal that never exists in the real world. The conditions of perfect competition may be listed as (1) a large number of buyers and sellers so that no one individual has an influence on price; (2) a homogeneous product, the characteristics of which can be objectively measured and described; (3) free entry and exit; (4) full information about production, stocks, price, and distribution; and (5) independence and impersonality of decisions and operations.

As we have noted, nearly everyone tries to prevent the existence of perfect competition in his own area. In addition, industrial development into an efficient market structure requires large-scale operations that violate the conditions of perfect competition. It is impossible to have an efficient steel industry that even remotely meets the conditions. Perfect competition in the railroads or public utilities would result in duplication and waste; perfect competition in radio and television would result in chaos.

Thus, the model of perfect competition is more honored in the breach than the observance. It nevertheless remains the design ideal of the private-enterprise system, particularly in the United States. As the model is breached, rules are devised to establish a simulation of competition in which no one is allowed to achieve a position of market dominance. Outstanding among these are the antitrust laws. A second kind of rule making is exemplified by labor legislation, to maintain equality of bargaining power. Both kinds of rules are designed to make the pricing system work as though perfect competition existed.

SPECULATION

There is another dimension of operation of an economic system that needs to be included in our scheme. It is that of speculation.

As we noted above, there is only one set of prices and price relationships that will result in a balanced production and use; that will equate supplies and demand. This is the equilibrium price or set of prices. In a dynamic economy, equilibrium is never achieved-something is always out of balance. The underlying conditions affecting supplies and requirements are in a constant state of flux, resulting in constantly changing prices and price relationships.

There is a major element of futurity in prices. Investments made today affect production tomorrow and throughout the life of the investment. Inventories are accumulated or liquidated today in anticipation of tomorrow's requirements. Consumers spend all or more than their incomes or forgo consumption until a later time, depending on their expectations about the future. The implementation of expectations results in the establishment of prices that apply not only to the present but to the future as well. Today's prices are a function of expectations about the future as well as today's spot market situation. Forward prices are established on the basis of expectations about the situation and prices that will exist in the future.

The future is unknown and uncertain. To speculate is to contemplate the future, to reach conclusions about the shape of things to come, and to act on the basis of such expectations—in short, to buy now in anticipation of higher prices or to sell now in anticipation of lower prices.

This definition of speculation is more interesting when it is put in the context of common usage of the words speculate and invest. These words are often used in a contrasting manner, but viewed in a context of the impact of the future on today's values and the uncertainty about the future, speculation becomes investment in the purest sense. Whether one trades in commodity futures, puts money in securities, deposits money in a savings account, explores for minerals, buys farmland, or feeds cattle, he is allocating resources at a current cost that will result in production at a future time. The same is true of investment of time and effort, such as the pursuit of further education or work in building a business.

From these things it follows that speculation is of major importance. Speculation does make a difference. As the quality of speculation is higher, the economic system is better guided and directed.

MARKETS

The efficiency of an economic system is significantly dependent upon the efficiency of the performance of prices in their allocating and distributive functions. Prices are central to effectiveness of competition. Prices are made in markets. Markets and market forms are of major importance in the effectiveness of prices. The market itself must be properly organized if prices are to be efficient and competition effective.

During the past half century, markets have been severely criticized and many changes have been made that are restrictive of market operation. An earlier focus of criticism that extends to the present time is that of distributive effects. The distributive justice of markets has been brought into question. This has resulted in a wide range of governmental intervention designed to modify rewards as these are transmitted through the system. Chief among these are taxation systems that transfer incomes from sector to sector and from individual to individual. The game is played, the marbles collected by the government and then redistributed. But such is not the end of it. Restrictions are placed on what the recipient is permitted to do with marbles. Income transfers are designated for specific purposes such as food stamps, housing for the elderly, etc. Transfer payments are a significant fraction of the gross national product of the United States. The fraction is higher in other countries, particularly the Third World.

It is difficult to criticize attempts to remedy distributive injustices that can be traced to market sources. However, it is important to question the outcome of the attempts. Many are demonstratively costly in terms of the total product to be divided; effects on the size of the pie to be divided should be considered. Moreover, the impact of redistributive measures on real income distribution is uncertain and questionable. Many appear to result in a less equal distribution rather than more. Poverty relief may do more to perpetrate poverty than to relieve it.

More recently, markets have been criticized for distortion of allocative efficiency in social terms. This focuses on environmental impacts of unfettered market operation. It is difficult to evaluate the social cost of smoke emissions, a thing that is outside of the purview of calculus of factory management. At the forefront of this is the question of land utilization. The case for central planning and determination is easy to make. But the long-range impacts are difficult to appraise. What is the trade-off between the use of agricultural chemicals that have greatly enhanced food supplies and the environmental impacts of those chemicals? The history of mankind has been one of conquering his environment, and that great progress has been made is unquestionable. The central device for guiding this progress has been the market.

The market is a powerful institution. It has the power that can convert acquisitive behavior of economic men into socially useful contributors. Put in this context, the form of market organization and operation becomes of great importance and should be examined carefully.

Market forms have had a long history of development and regulation. This can be readily brought into focus in the world of commodity trading and commodity exchanges. The history of organized commodity exchanges extends as far back as western civilization. Extensive reference to trade and commerce, its ethics, manner of operation, and place in society are found in the Old Testament. The early empires of the Middle East—the Persians, Egyptians, and Assyrians—developed extensive commercial activities and with them rules and practices for trading. The Greeks and Romans drew upon these early experiences for their own laws and customs of trading. The foundation of modern, intricate commercial systems can be found in the legal-economic writings of the Greeks and Romans.

The basic form of modern competitive markets is found in the medieval fairs and markets. The medieval marketing system reached a peak of development in England about 1400. English law and practice of the period 900-1400 carefully prescribed the locations of marketplaces, allowed only one central market within a market area, established the days and hours for trading, and required that transactions be made before witnesses and that sellers cry out in public their wares and prices.

The customs and practices developed during the course of several centuries by the fairs and markets became a part of the "Law Merchant." In addition to the establishment of the nature of the market, they prescribed rules for weights and measures, grading of merchandise, and settlement of contracts.

The early American colonists brought with them the English market concepts and laws. The general pattern of the first American markets was copied from English counterparts. In 1566 Governor Stuyvesant of New York established a public market in "the neighborhood of Master Haus Kierstede's house." The High Street Market was established in Philadelphia in 1693. The Faneuil Market in Boston was established in 1742.

As the United States developed, the huge traffic in grains gave rise to a need for central markets. Merchants in the various cities in the grain areas established exchanges and boards of trade for organized market trading. The first of these was the Chicago Board of Trade, organized in 1848. Its organization was followed by that of the Merchants Exchange in St. Louis in 1854 and the Kansas City Board of Trade in 1869.

The charters of these exchanges stated their general purposes as follows: (1) to provide an organized marketplace, (2) to collect and disseminate market information, (3) to provide uniform rules and standards for trading, and (4) to adjust controversies among members.

From these early developments there followed commodity futures markets. The form was a codification of existing market practices. They were formed out of a crucible of need for developing market forms to cope with existing commercial conditions. Futures markets are a product of their long history, and the story of futures markets is closely related to that of trade in cash commodities.

The basic impetus for futures trading related to inventory risks, and to financing and pricing problems. As commerce developed and required the accumulation of inventories, merchants and processors found themselves with problems that were best managed by forward contracting. This forward contracting developed into standard procedures that were eventually codified and formalized into futures trading.

Forward contracting quickly moved away from commercial interests into the hands of speculators. Relatively little was gained by passing risks from people who did not want them and could not carry them to people who did not want them or could not afford them either. Forward contracts could be made with other commercial people only by the payments of substantial risk premiums, which partly compensated the buyers for risk but in addition reduced prices enough to eliminate a high proportion of the risk. Thus, early in the development, speculators became an essential part of the process. They were better able to assume the risks of price changes than were the commercial interests.

During the nineteenth century markets were beset with problems of rigging, manipulation, power plays, financial failures, and technical problems of delivery. All of these things led to changes in trading rules that greatly reduced or eliminated the problem.

The first federal regulation of futures trading was established in 1922. The law and public regulation have been continually changed during the past one half century.

Both kinds of regulatory action—exchanges and the federal government—have had as an objective regulation to conform with conditions of pure competition as nearly as such conformation is possible. The guiding slogan of the markets is "open outcry." These markets are the closest approximation to the conditions of pure competition in any economic system in the world.

Futures markets are extraordinarily successful and are growing at a rapid rate. The volume of trading doubled during the 1960s. Volume nearly tripled between 1969 and 1975. New records have been established each year since. Trading in the old established markets, primarily grains and soybeans, has increased. Livestock and product markets were established in the 1960s and have grown rapidly. New markets have been established over a wide range of commodities during the 1970s. These include futures markets in foreign currencies and various financial instruments such as home mortgages and government obligations (money is a commodity).

In considering market form, there is an interesting anomaly. There is on the one hand increasing public intervention in markets for the purpose of correcting inequities in distributive justice and misallocation of resources and, on the other, rapid growth in markets that give unbridled freedom of expression to competitive forces. Futures market put their trust in the wisdom of people whose self-serving actions form the prices that direct and order the operation of the economic system. This is in sharp contrast to central planning that results in prices designed to maximize distributive justice and efficiency of resource use. The anomaly raises a question about the market form that can best advance social welfare.

CONCLUSIONS

These several parts of prices, competition, speculation, and markets lead to some general observations. First, there is an inevitability about prices. The forces that go into the determination of price can be suppressed and distorted for a time, but they will eventually surface. This has been the history of every price-controlling scheme. We develop coupons that give us purchasing rights to gasoline, or meat, or shoes, and they take on market value in exchange for money, other purchasing rights, or gifts. There is a hierarchy of rewards in state-controlled economies.

Second, competition is inordinately efficient in getting the economic system operated consistently with the wishes of people. If people want a product, it gets made, and if a product is made that people do not want, it will not sell for enough to cover cost—which is conducive to discounting production.

Third, speculation should be viewed positively. The speculators are the innovators. They are the savers who forgo rewards today in an attempt to achieve greater rewards tomorrow. They are the risk takers who hazard what they have in an attempt to get more. Without them there would be little, if any, economic advance.

Fourth, market forms are important determiners of pricing efficiency and degrees of competition. When market forms are regulated to the competitive model, prices are established that enable free expression of competition. Careful attention needs to be paid to market form.

In all of this, there is an overtone of human values. The pattern of competition, competitively established prices, and speculation has in it elements of individual liberty that are an important part of our value system. Not only is such a system highly productive of goods and services, but it also contributes much to liberty and the excitement of a lifestyle. Without economic freedom there cannot be individual freedom.

This now gets back to the title "People with Orderly Minds Should Not Trade Commodities." The thrust of this essay is that, however disorderly competitive markets may be, the economic system should not be directed in an orderly fashion. For nearly a half century there have been increasing inroads on markets by government, and government has assumed more and more of the directive responsibility. Through taxation, increasing national debt, inflation, regulation, and income transfer, government has moved deeper and deeper into the system. These things are done in the name of an orderly economic system and social justice. In the Good Society (1937), Walter Lippman wrote, "The predominate teachings of this age are that there are no limits to man's capacity to govern others, therefore, no limitations ought to be imposed on government. The older faith, born of long ages of suffering under man's dominion over man, was that the exercise of unlimited power by men with limited minds and self-regarding prejudices is soon oppressive, reactionary and corrupt." These teachings, which Lippman opposed, have persisted, so that the underlying philosophy of government is that the state, under a strong leader, has both the moral obligation and competence to run the economy and guarantee security and prosperity to its citizens.

Such is an impossible task. No one can run an economic system. To translate the whole of the processes into mathematical terms would take trillions of equations. The system is fantastically complex and perverse. This is so because people are fantastically complex and perverse. To tamper with one part of the system requires one patch on another until the system is patch upon patch. To "run" the system in an orderly fashion is to defeat the purpose of "running" the system.

But such is not the great weakness of a directed economic system or the great strength of a competitive market system. The great issues are in human values. John Locke, a British philosopher of pre-revolutionary times, wrote, "A man ... having, in the state of nature, no arbitrary power over life, liberty or possession of another, but only so much as the law of nature gave him for the preservation of himself and the rest of mankind, this is all he doth or can give up to the commonwealth, and by it to the legislative power, so that the legislative can have no more than this." Thus Locke said that the power of the government was limited to the protection of liberty and property. This was written into the *Declaration of Independence* and the *Constitution* of the United States.

The disorderly world of commodity trading is a microcosm of an efficient economic system and a showplace of assertion of liberty and dignity. The two are inextricably mixed. Without economic liberty there cannot be personal liberty, and without personal liberty there cannot be economic liberty. There can be neither personal liberty nor economic liberty without respect for liberty and dignity of other men. Let he who is without humility trade oats, and he will learn. Let he who is without self-respect, be long soybeans in a bull market, and he will learn. People with orderly minds should not trade commodities, but everyone should, for his own good and that of the order, be long or short.

Chapter Forty

Survival and Change: Post World War II at The Chicago Board of Trade

1982

AUTHOR'S NOTE: In 1982, the Chicago Board of Trade held a seminar on the history of futures. I was asked to chronicle the history of trading during the first twenty-five years following World War II. I protested that I was not historian and thus not qualified. The response was that they did not want me to write a proper history but, rather, to reminisce. It was a little startling to be told that I was old enough to remember history. The paper was an attempt to describe the tenuousness of competitive markets in a climate of governmental intervention in markets, the shining light of market prices for soybeans in the survival and growth of the Chicago Board of Trade, and the role of the cooperation of the exchange and academia in the growth and development of futures markets.

The twenty-five years following World War II formed a period in which the institution of futures trading in general and the Chicago Board of Trade in particular were threatened with extinction.[1] They were casting about for new directions and modifications of old procedures that would enable them to survive and possibly expand. It was a period in which the foundation was laid for the

---

1. T. A. Hieronymus is professor emeritus of agricultural economics, University of Illinois. Remarks at the Chicago Board of Trade, History of Futures Seminar, September 21, 1982.

dramatic growth that took place during the 1970s. This paper is not a chronicle of the events of the period but rather an attempt to describe the mood and temper of the times and some of the steps that eventually led to rapid expansion. From this it is hoped that we can identify some of the underlying forces that determine the nature of markets and that affect their size and influence on the course of economic events.

The ending of wartime controls that had essentially put a stop to futures trading, both in the United States and abroad, serves as a point of departure. At this time, futures trading, its form, and the exchanges reflected their long past. The table below shows the volume of futures trading in grains, which made up a high proportion of all futures trading prior to World War II.

Volume of Futures Trading in Cereal Grains, Wheat, Corn, Oats, Barley, and Rye on U.S. Markets, Five-Year Averages, Millions of Bushels.

1884-88	23,600	1931-35	13,489
1889-93	18,000	1936-40	10,491
1894-98	21,600	1941-45	6,481
1899-03	19,400	1946-50	9,640
1904-08	18,900	1951-55	8,898
1909-13	16,000	1956-60	7,764
1914-18	19,400	1961-65	10,430
1921-25	21,753	1966-70	16,202
1926-30	20,336		

Source: Federal Trade Commission and Commodity Exchange Authority, U.S. Department of Agriculture.

The table is a reasonable description of volume change prior to the war. It is not a good measure for the postwar period because of the introduction of new commodities (soybeans, soybean oil, soybean meal, live cattle, live hogs, and frozen pork bellies, in particular). The first point of particular interest is that the all-time trading peak in grain probably occurred in the 1880s. The general level of activity was fairly constant through the 1920s. The great depression of the 1930s, the introduction of various farm price-support and inventory schemes, and the fixed prices of World War II pulled the volume down to about one-third of the earlier level. The Depression, wartime, and immediate postwar volume looks even smaller in comparison to earlier periods when we note that the production and trade in grain was increasing rapidly throughout most of the 65-year period. At the end of the war, futures trading and the Chicago Board of Trade were shrinking vestiges of their former selves, and a disinterested observer would have to put the matter of survival high on his list of questions about the future.

VOLUME OF TRADING

The following table shows the volume of trading on the Chicago Board of Trade for the years 1946 through 1968. Wheat trading was suspended during the war and was resumed in 1946. Wheat volume was the largest reached until 1962. The carryover of wheat on July 1, 1946, was 100 million bushels, approximately a minimum pipeline requirement. The 1946 crop was in excess of 1.1 billion bushels, a record. The federal government exported large quantities for food relief in Europe. The shipments were large enough to create an acute shortage in domestic markets, resulting in a major price increase. The price of the May 1947 futures contract rose from an average of $1.91 ¼ in August 1946 to an average of $2.67 ½ in May 1947. With a large crop in 1948, prices decreased, as did volume of trade. The volume of trading in wheat was of the same general magnitude throughout the period 1948 through 1965. But that volume was of the same general magnitude does not mean that there was stability in year-to-year volume. Note that volume in 1962 was 2.2 times as great as in 1960 and that volume in 1965 was only 78 percent of 1962.

The 1947 corn crop was small (2.4 billion bushels vs. 3.2 billion in 1946), which got futures trading off to a banner start in 1947. The 1948 crop was 3.7 billion bushels, and the volume of trade decreased. Volume of trading in corn followed much the same pattern as that of wheat from 1948 through 1961. Throughout the period 1948-1965, there were chronic and growing surpluses of corn, and the price of corn was dominated by governmental price-support and inventory management programs.

Volume of Futures Trading by Commodities, 1946-68

YEAR	WHEAT	CORN	OATS	RYE	SOYBEANS	COTTON	SOYBEAN OIL	SOYBEAN MEAL	LARD
	MILLION BUSHELS					000 CONTRACTS			
1946	278	661	2,878	584	—	125	—	—	0.2
1947	4,294	3,839	2,781	—	19	63.3	—	—	30.2
1948	3,208	3,740	1,648	35	523	49.6	—	—	99.7
1949	3,618	2,526	776	279	2,545	21.4	—	—	53.4
1950	2,887	1,901	1,220	527	3,907	15.6	18.8	—	57.3
1951	3,519	2,496	1,715	495	2,397	9.6	28.7	2.8	33
1952	2,588	2,710	2,350	492	3,089	16	44.9	3.9	38.7
1953	3,648	2,808	1,874	880	3,553	9.6	46.7	12.1	42.9
1954	3,172	2,028	810	683	6,084	3	82.4	37.9	77.9
1955	3,401	2,455	659	655	4,247	2.4	66.1	36.1	33.9
1956	3,641	2,485	647	709	5,722	1	204.8	54.9	62.8
1957	4,117	2,003	474	935	4,331	0.4	173.5	50.5	54
1958	3,971	2,108	476	864	3,041	1.1	156.1	114.1	21.6
1959	2,871	1,846	501	816	4,338	0.6	141.1	211.5	11
1960	1,971	1,584	727	481	5,827	0	212.1	149.2	14.1
1961	2,585	1,316	1,121	962	12,048	0	348.6	322.8	16
1962	4,384	4,828	1,362	1,112	4,731	0	319.8	335.3	2.9
1963	4,121	4,123	700	640	14,231	0	507.7	262.7	0
1964	3,719	3,422	505	456	12,940	0	398.5	290.7	0
1965	3,418	3,971	450	227	17,827	0	594	324.6	0
1966	5,913	10,231	558	415	15,763	0	574.6	465.8	0
1967	9,671	9,728	3000	229	5,525	0	284.5	353.6	0
1968	6,532	7,837	616	141	4,718	0	300.9	367.3	0

Source: Annual Reports of the Chicago Board of Trade.

There was a dramatic increase in both wheat and corn volume in 1966. This was associated with weather-reduced crops in the United States and throughout much of the world. There was widespread discussion in the media about world food shortages and the need to increase U.S. agricultural production to "feed a hungry world." Prices rose sharply in the summer of 1966 and so did volume of grain futures trading on the Chicago Board of Trade. The euphoria of agricultural prosperity was quickly dispelled by a 4.8 billion bushel corn crop in the United States in 1967, up from 4.1 billion-bushels in 1966. The volume of trading in corn, as in wheat, remained large in 1967 and 1968. There were changes in government farm programs that reduced government dominance of prices.

In spite of being a much smaller and economically less important crop, the volume of trading in oats during the 1946-53 period was large in comparison to wheat and corn. Prices were relatively free of governmental influence. The volume of trading in oats decreased significantly and regularly from the mid-1950s, with the exception of a brief flurry in 1961 and 1962. Production of oats in the United States decreased throughout the period, and the areas of concentrated production moved to the north and west so that fewer oats were tributary to Chicago. Receipts at and shipments from Chicago decreased so that prices at Chicago became increasingly less representative of oats' value on a national scale. The market became increasingly vulnerable to tight delivery situations. Even so, Chicago remained the delivery point for oats, and futures trading volume decreased.

Trading in soybeans and soybean products was the focal point of futures trading during the first twenty-five years following World War II and may well have been the basis of survival of the exchange. It most certainly was a source of viability that contributed to the eventual growth of the exchange. Futures trading in soybeans began October 5, 1936, but volume was at quite low levels through mid-1940. Volume in fiscal 1940-41 was 860 million bushels but decreased to 399 million during fiscal 1941-42. Trading was suspended on February 19, 1943, and resumed July 7, 1947. The 1947 crop of soybeans was damaged by drought so that only 186 million bushels were produced (compared to 203 million in 1946). Prices rose rapidly and became volatile. Soybeans became the leading performer in futures markets with the trading increase in 1948. The volume of trading in soybeans is even more notable when relative crop sizes are taken into account. For example, trading in soybeans in 1954 was nearly as large as that in the four grains combined, but the 1954 soybean crop was only 341 million bushels compared to a combined total production of the four grains of 5,473 million. Three characteristics of soybean accounted for the rapid growth and large size of the market. First, almost the entire crop is sold by farmers, whereas a substantial proportion of grains are consumed on farms. Farmers carry most of their own price risks, but merchants, warehousemen, processors, and exporters must hedge in futures. Second, soybeans are processed into oil and meal. These distinctly different products move into different markets, and the prices of both are highly inelastic, hence, volatile. Price volatility makes two contributions to volume of trading. It increases risk and uncertainty, hence, hedging, and it presents profit opportunities, hence, attracts speculators. Third, throughout the history of the industry, soybean prices have been free to move to competitively determined market levels. There have been government price-support programs that have occasionally resulted in government controlled stocks, but these have been quickly corrected to market levels.

Trading in soybean oil started in 1950 and in soybean meal in 1951. Both markets grew rapidly and in parallel with the increase in soybean trading. Trading in soybeans greatly exceeded trading in oil and meal. For example, the volume of soybean trading in 1960 was equal to 1.070 million contracts of oil, but only .212 million contracts were traded. Soybean trading was equal to 1.384 million contracts of soybean meal, but only .149 million contracts were traded. Trading in soybean oil and meal is complementary to soybean trading. Prices of soybeans are functionally related to oil and meal prices, but the difference between oil and meal values and soybean prices is variable. It therefore attracts speculative trading.

Trading in rye futures was of substantial size prior to World War II. Trading was suspended on June 13, 1946, and resumed on July 12, 1948. The two-year suspension was on account of a corner of the market by the noted speculator Daniel F. Rice. In 1945 the price of rye was forced to the ceiling established by the federal Office of Price Administration and held there by concerted actions of large traders, Rice in particular. The exchange fixed prices on the outstanding contracts and suspended trading in new contracts. There was litigation related to the corner, and questions of suitability of rye for trading were raised. The resumption of trading was delayed long past the end of federal price ceilings. As shown in the second table, volume recovered quickly and increased through 1962. A downtrend in volume then followed until the demise of the market in 1970.

Rye futures trading held a unique position in markets. The rye crop is small in relation to other crops. In 1959 the total rye crop was 21 million bushels compared to a wheat crop of 1,184 million; corn, 4,361 million; oats, 1,074 million; and soybeans, 538 million. Comparison of crop size and volume of trading show that volume was large. The open interest in rye futures during the 1950s was about one-half as great in relation to volume of trading as was open interest in relation to volume for the other grains. There was a rapid turnover of rye contracts. Short hedges in relation to open interest are a measure of commercial versus speculator use of markets. The percentage of the open interest in rye futures held by short hedgers was about one-third as great as for other grains. The share of the open interest held by reporting speculators and members of the trading public was large. The demand for rye is highly inelastic, and prices are volatile. Rye futures were an attractive speculative vehicle and were highly speculated.

The rye market was notorious during the 1950s and early 1960s. The number of traders in the pit was small and generally thought to be clubby with traders showing favoritism. It was said that one had to be of the right religion to trade rye. There were constant rumors of dominant positions held by one name trader or another, most often Dan Rice. The movement of rye into delivery position was small, and deliverable supply was small in relation to open interest in expiring contracts. The market was typically vulnerable to squeezes. Rye trading was often on the agenda of the Business Conduct Committee. It is unknown whether rye trading died a natural death because of the decreasing importance of the crop (and hence, decreasing economic need for futures trading because of the retirement and demise of the leading local traders) or because speculative enthusiasm in rye was superseded by speculative enthusiasm in soybeans. The fact is that rye trading was a highly speculative market that is no more.

The Chicago Board of Trade had an active futures market in cotton in 1946. It was small in relation to the other markets, New York and New Orleans. Trading gradually dwindled and finally stopped in 1959. Of particular note is that it was a long and tedious death that took fourteen years.

The lard futures market was of importance from the time trading was resumed after the war until about 1957. There then followed five years of desultory activity until all trading ended in 1962. There were probably four major factors in the decline and demise of the market. First, lard production in the United States decreased as hogs were bred to produce more lean and less fat. As edible fats and oils production and use in the United States expanded, lard's market share went from major to minor. Lard was of less economic importance, and therefore there was less economic need for a futures market. Second, soybean oil increased in importance in domestic fats and oils markets to the extent of assuming a dominant market and price position. Lard and soybean oil are interchangeable in major uses, particularly shortening, and their prices are functionally related. Lard could be effectively hedged in soybean oil futures. There is probably an inverse relationship between the growth of soybean oil and end of lard trading. Third, the terms of the lard contract were not kept abreast of changing trade practices. The contract specified delivery in drums. Prior to World War II, a substantial proportion of lard moved in drums in commercial channels, but this was changed to movement of loose lard in tank cars. It was sometimes necessary to specially drum lard to meet delivery needs on the futures market. Trading in a loose lard contract was initiated in 1958, but trading in the drummed contract was retained, and the new contract failed after a three-year experiment. The new contract was much too late in development and was hindered by retention of the old contract. Fourth, as trading decreased there were fewer locals in the lard pit. They tended to be older traders who had been there for a long time, and they gradually disappeared. Lard futures trading probably continued as long as it did because of the influence of local members who specialized in lard. In the end, they were trading among themselves.

OTHER EXCHANGES AND COMMODITIES

The long period of limited trading and growth in futures markets was not unique to the Chicago Board of Trade. In the first edition (1971) of his book *Economics of Futures Trading*, Hieronymus included a table showing the detail of trading volume by exchanges and commodities from 1955 through 1969 and said,

> There are several points of interest.
>
> 1. Total volume of trade in all commodities was about constant during the late 1950s and increased rapidly during the 1960s, more than doubling.
>
> 2. Some exchanges declined in importance and disappeared from the list and others were fading throughout most of the period. Memphis, Milwaukee, New Orleans, and Seattle declined and disappeared. St. Louis came in and left promptly. This is an old market that had a large volume of trading at an early time and remained an important cash grain market at the end of the period. The New York Produce Exchange, after a rally in the early 1960s, declined to almost nothing. The number of commodities traded and the volume of trading decreased at Minneapolis.
>
> 3. The number of commodities traded increased. There were 37 different commodities traded in 1955 and 44 in 1969. There was a tendency to add rapidly near the end of the period. Note particularly silver, palladium, apples, lumber, plywood, cattle, hogs, and propane. Some exchanges, note particularly the Chicago Mercantile Exchange, were venturesome in trying new commodities.
>
> 4. Trading in some commodities declined and stopped or nearly stopped (rubber, onions, butter, cottonseed oil, cottonseed meal, millfeeds, shrimp, feeder cattle, rice, burlap, pepper, and fishmeal). Volume in others declined gradually and then recovered sharply, such as eggs on the Chicago Mercantile Exchange. Some commodities were introduced and flopped.

The Chicago Board of Trade fared well in comparison to most other exchanges. In 1955, it had 59 percent of the total 4.1 million contracts traded; in 1962, 16 percent of 5.2 million contracts; and in 1969, 44 percent of 11.2 million. The lower percentage in 1969 represented a 24 percent increase in the actual number of contracts, the result of a major increase in trading at the Chicago Mercantile Exchange, which went from 8 percent in 1962 to 34 percent in 1969. The increase was mainly the result of initiation and growth of trading in pork bellies, live cattle, and live hogs.

NEW COMMODITIES AT THE CHICAGO BOARD OF TRADE

The Chicago Board of Trade was not without innovation in the development of new commodities during the postwar period. A grain sorghum contract was introduced and failed during the 1955 to 1965 period. The shift to a loose lard contract that failed was mentioned earlier. A steer carcass-beef contract was traded in very small volume in 1965 and 1966. This was followed by a live contract that was traded from 1966 through 1971. Trading in iced broilers was started in 1968, and trading in plywood and silver in 1969. The growth of trading in grains, soybeans, and soybean products that took place during the second half of the 1960s appears to have stimulated development of new commodities and changed the mood and tenor of the exchange from one of survival to one of expansion and growth.

POLITICAL CLIMATE

The political climate within which futures markets operated during the period prior to World War II was largely negative. There was a long history of attempts to prohibit and control futures trading. In the 60th Congress, following the panic of 1907, no less than twenty-five such bills were introduced, and more than forty in the 62nd Congress. The first federal regulation was the Futures Trading Act of 1921, which was found unconstitutional. It was followed by the Grain Futures Act of 1922, which was extensively revised and renamed the Commodity Exchange Act in 1936. The various bills introduced and the hearings before enactment of the laws and amendments had a common theme. It was grudgingly recognized that futures trading served useful economic purposes of risk transfer through hedging but that there were growing abuses of price manipulation, market corners, sudden and unreasonable price fluctuations, market control by large-scale inside traders, and speculative excesses caused by uninformed and exuberant trading of the public. The attitude was expressed in a typical fashion by Representative Rich in hearings of the Joint Committee on the Economic

Report in December 1947: "I am not interested in trying in any way to stop legitimate business; I want that to proceed. But I thought if there was anything you could suggest to our committee whereby we might, from your experience, stop speculation, pure and simple, and let legitimate trade go on, I wish you would make that recommendation." Speculative excesses, manipulation, and large-scale trading were blamed when producers' prices fell and when consumers' prices rose. When the federal government oversold the existing wheat supply immediately following World War II, President Truman blamed "gamblers in human misery" for the subsequent price increase. Futures markets were frequently the whipping boys of political demagoguery.

New laws were written and regulation increased. However, most of the more onerous proposals were defeated so that the exchanges and the institution of futures trading survived. To some extent, knowledge and wisdom imparted to the Congress by representatives of the grain trade and the exchanges prevailed. However, much of the control of legislation was accomplished by the crudest of political processes: bagmen went into home districts and to Washington.

Legislative proposals and amendments to existing laws along the same old lines of speculative control continued throughout the postwar period, but understanding of the economic validity of futures trading, including speculation, gradually increased. Hearings in 1973 and 1974 preceding the Commodity Futures Trading Act of 1974 generally were held in a climate of limited demagoguery and an appreciation of the importance of developing legislation favorable to the growth and expansion of futures markets. Whether or not the act has been favorable is not the issue. It was passed in a relatively favorable climate of understanding.

THE 1948 BENCHMARK YEAR

The centennial of the formation of the Chicago Board of Trade was celebrated in 1948—a significant benchmark year. There was a special edition of the *Chicago Journal of Commerce* reporting the occasion, reviewing some of the history of the exchange and of commerce in Chicago, and describing the status and functions of the exchange. Richard F. Uhlmann was elected president. J. O. McClintock, who had been president in 1947, was appointed executive vice president and thereby became the first paid executive officer of the exchange.

At that time, the exchange was a great democratic organization, run by a board of directors and committee members. In addition to the president, there were first and second vice presidents and fifteen directors elected from the membership. The three lead committees were Nominating, Appeals, and Arbitration. Much of the day-to-day business was run by committees of three to eleven members. There were twenty-five committees with a total membership of 139. Some of the diversity of functions of the Board of Trade is revealed by committee names: Business Conduct, Claims and Insolvencies, Clearinghouse, Cotton, Cottonseed Oil, Executive, Finance, Floor, Floor Practices, Grain, Law, Market Report, Membership, Personnel, Provisions, Public Relations, Real Estate, Rules, Securities and Stock List, Soybeans, To-Arrive Grain, Transportation, Warehouse, and Weighing and Custodian.

The annual reports of the committees show a wide diversity of functions not directly related to futures trading. The Chicago Board of Trade was directly involved in freight rate establishment and change. There was active trading in the Securities Department. There was a major cash grain market where trade by sample took place on the floor of the exchange. Receipts of grain at Chicago were sampled by the Grain Sampling and Seed Inspection Department. Grain was weighed into and out of Chicago elevators, and warehouse operations were supervised. Meat and various other packing-house products were sampled, weighed, and inspected. These activities facilitated trade and commerce in commodities at Chicago. The Chicago Board of Trade was a board of trade as well as a futures market.

The financial operation of the Chicago Board of Trade was small. Operating income in 1948 was $348,000, of which $155,000 was building rental; $110,000 quotations, private line, and floor rental; and $64,000 was from the switchboard. Operating expenses were $642,000, scattered over a long list of expenses, a few of the larger of which were market department, $94,000; transportation, $20,000; public relations, $77,000; telephone switchboard, $78,000; legal expenses, $54,000; weighing and custodian, $36,000; executive office, $89,000; and cloakroom, washroom and towel service, $10,000. The deficit of $294,000 was nearly covered by a membership assessment of $248,850 ($175 per member). The organization operated at a loss and had to rely on membership assessments. In general, members were less than enthusiastic about assessments, and the size of assessments was regularly an issue in elections. There was great pressure to hold operating expenses at a minimum. This limited financing and pressure to restrict expenses was characteristic of the Chicago Board of Trade throughout the 25-year period under review.

EARLY EDUCATIONAL EFFORTS

In his presidential address in 1948, Richard Uhlmann said,

> During the past year we celebrated our 100th anniversary, which was an outstanding event in the history of our country and our city, and it was a great testimonial to free markets everywhere. People came from all parts of this country and from Canada to pay tribute to a marketing system which had served many millions of people so faithfully since its inception. A symposium was also inaugurated so that professors from thirty-three colleges and universities could come here to learn at first-hand the functions and accomplishments of the Chicago Board of Trade. It has been felt for some time that education was the only method to better acquaint the public that an exchange was not an individual to be loved, hated, feared, laughed at, or wept about. It is an inanimate thing, an institution, an apparatus, an auction establishment, a device or arena, or a scoreboard.

The statement reflected a sensitivity to the constant attacks on the exchange by politicians, farm organizations, and the media. The members of the exchange truly believed in the economic usefulness and fairness of futures trading and the desirability of its expansion. They thought that they were wrongfully maligned and were hindered by regulation. In effect, Uhlmann said, "We are tired of sending bag men to Washington. We are a great and good institution and we should proceed to make this known." As a part of the centennial celebration and his presidency, Uhlmann contributed $3,000 for an awards contest that was designed to generate papers from academia and the trade evaluating the institution of futures trade. The awards contest was continued for eight years until it was changed to a scholarship award.

The report of the Public Relations Committee in 1948 listed the following activities:

> 1. Under the direction of the J. W. Hicks organization, our public relations counsel, several public opinion surveys were initiated and completed.
>
> 2. More than 150 news, feature, pictures and radio releases were made, relating to general or specific news and functions of the exchange.
>
> 3. An educational radio program was developed consisting of twelve five-minute transcribed programs.
>
> 4. A mimeographed bulletin in clip sheet form is being sent periodically to newspapers.
>
> 5. The Board of Trade published a 26-page booklet entitled "Hedging An Insurance Medium in Marketing Agricultural Commodities," which it is hoped will be the first of a series dealing with organized commodity markets.
>
> 6. A symposium attended by 37 educators, representing 33 colleges and universities, was held in Chicago on September 9 and 10. Out of this meeting an Advisory Educational Committee to the Chicago Board of Trade was appointed to counsel with members of the Exchange for future plans with reference to teaching aids such as textbooks, pamphlets, etc.
>
> 7. A recommendation that the Board of Trade make a colored motion picture to tell "The Board of Trade Story" was approved by the directors.

The first symposium featured papers by J. O. McClintock on "History, Development, and Functions of the Chicago Board of Trade" and Professor O. G.

Saxon and Julius Baer on "Commodity Exchanges and Futures Trading." There were extensive freewheeling discussions by the professors on the feasibility and methods of developing literature about futures trading and the introduction of the subject matter of futures trading into college curricula. One result of the symposium was the appointment of an Educational Advisory Committee, which has continued in existence.

A second symposium was held on September 8 and 9, 1948, and featured papers by Holbrook Working of Stanford on "The Purposes and Functions of Futures Markets," Roy Godfrey of Faroll and Company on "Cash and Futures Market Relationships," J. O. McClintock of the Chicago Board of Trade on "Relation of Margins to Speculation," and Homer Hargrave of Merrill Lynch on "Brokerage House Procedures." There was extensive give-and-take discussion among trade and academic participants. In addition to the seminar sessions, there were tours of the trading floor and grain-processing facilities in Chicago.

The symposia were continued on an annual basis through the 1950s and on a less regular basis during the 1960s. They generated an extensive amount of literature written primarily by active members of the trade who described their own activities. Some of this literature was combined into *Readings in Futures Markets*, Book III, *Views from the Trade*, A. E. Peck, ed., Chicago Board of Trade, 1978.

The eleventh symposium, held in 1958, was expanded to include agricultural writers and members of the banking industry. Subsequent symposia continued to mix members of the trade and academic communities as well as commodity related people such as members of the media, bank, trade associations, and agricultural organizations.

The symposia and other educational efforts produced a quantity of literature, at least some of which was introduced into college curricula and adult education programs. In addition, they increased the awareness, knowledge, and appreciation of the subject matter of futures trading by college-level instructors. The papers and formal discussions were recorded in proceedings. Perhaps a greater usefulness of the symposia is not on record. These were the informal discussions held, often late at night, in the Men's Bar at the Union League Club. In the course of the symposia, members of the trade and academia got to know and appreciate each other. The process probably influenced not only teaching and research in academia but also the operation of firms and of the exchange. Learning occurred on a two-way street.

GENERAL COMMENT

What are the lessons to be learned from the 1947-60 period? First, markets go the way of competitive pricing. At the end of World War II, most futures trading was in agricultural products, grain in particular. The decline in the importance of futures trading was primarily the result of governmental price programs that reduced the need for hedging and reduced the price variability that attracted speculation. The extent to which commodities were affected varied by program from the near extinction of cotton trading to the rapid growth of soybean trading. The growth in the late 1960s was associated with relaxing of price-inhibiting government programs and the initiation of trading in commodities where such programs were nonexistent. The continued success of futures trading is dependent upon the existence of free, open, competitive markets; and the extent of the success of futures trading is a measure of free markets, hence, personal liberty.

Second, organized regulation of markets inhibits growth and development. There are three levels of market regulation. In order of ascending importance, they are federal government, exchange government, and market competition. The first two are organized and inhibiting. The third is the ultimate and inevitable regulator and the circumstance under which exchanges most prosper.

Third, educational efforts have paid dividends in (1) developing a market structure conducive to expansion, (2) generating commercial and speculative business, and (3) including an appreciation of competitive markets in the education of college students and furnishing better employees to the commodity industries.

Fourth, great democratic institutions change slowly and tend to be slow in grasping and exploiting their opportunities. A part of the slow growth of the Chicago Board of Trade was the reluctance to change contract terms and trading rules, niggardly financing, and slowness in initiating trading in new commodities. However, slow change is more apt to be solid, enduring, and successful than is rapid change. As in market price establishment, there is a compromise.

Chapter Forty-One

Improving The Efficiency of Commodity Futures Markets

1984

AUTHOR'S NOTE: There was a major drought in 1983 which, as was to be expected, was accompanied by a high level of volatility in futures prices and subsequent complaints about futures markets. The Congress was sensitive to complaints, and the Joint Economic Committee held hearings. Senator Jepson posed a list of questions to be answered by the people invited to testify before the committee. My paper was an attempt to appraise the quality of speculation and to make a case for research into the nature and quality of speculation. At the hearing, the questions from the committee were moderate and showed a much better appreciation of the role of markets than I had experienced at earlier hearings. No legislative proposals came forth. That was downright encouraging.

Grain and soybean prices have been unusually volatile during the past year.[1] This has led to criticism of and questions about the pricing performance of futures markets. The central question should go to the quality of speculation in futures markets because these are indeed speculative markets. Has the quality of speculation measured up to the standard of performance that we have come to

1. T. A. Hieronymus is professor emeritus of agricultural economics, University of Illinois. Testimony before the Joint Economic Committee of Congress, April 25, 1984.

expect? How can speculative performance be improved? These are the questions on which we should focus.

The past year has been an unusually difficult challenge to the market because of the combined effects of government programs and adverse weather on the supply of grain and soybeans. Evaluating the quality of the job that markets have done is very difficult because these are not established standards of excellence—such as par on a golf course—by which we can measure performance. We can establish an ideal and then observe that it was not met, but how close we should reasonably expect the market to come to the ideal has not been established. Ideally, the markets should have quickly appraised the impact of programs on acreage and adjusted prices. Then, as the adverse growing season developed, they should have moved up to a level that would have pulled carryovers down to minimum pipeline levels and held stable until the next harvest. Some modification of the ideal is necessary. In actuality, it is necessary to put prices above the equilibrium levels to get users' attention and get them to make adjustments. Thus, historically we have had price patterns of early seasonal peaks during short crop years. And such peaks have been essential to effective market performance. Lacking performance standards, we can only look at what has happened and make some qualitative judgments. We can take a cursory look at wheat, corn, and soybean price performance.

May 1984 wheat futures started trading at about $4.15 in April 1983 and decreased to $3.75 in July. Early on, the market overestimated the impact of government programs on production and corrected its mistake. The mistake was not large. With the drought, the price rose rapidly from $3.75 in July to a $4.20 to $4.30 range in late August through early September. These then followed a decline to $3.30 in February and a recovery to $3.75 in early April. I should judge this as a poor price performance. The market should have recognized that there would be a large carryover and gone no higher than necessary to pull wheat out of the reserve and then gone no lower than necessary to hold substantial quantities in the reserve. The basic mistake that the wheat market made was to follow the lead of corn and soybeans, which were in real shortage.

May 1984 corn futures decreased from $3.20 in May 1983 to $2.90 in late June. The decrease was the result of overestimating the effect of government programs on production. The planted acreage was larger than expected. Beginning in early

July, the price rose to more than $3.80 in late August as the drought continued, and its effects became apparent. The price stayed in a $3.65 to $3.85 range for several weeks before falling to $3.40 by the third week of October. There followed an increase to $3.60 by the third week of November, a subsequent decrease to about $3.22 in February, and a rise to $3.60 in early April.

How good was this performance? First, it is too early to tell because I don't know where this thing is going to wind up. Is the current price just right to make the existing supply last until the new crop is available, or is it so high as to result in an excessive carryover, or is it so low that an increase will be necessary to make supplies last until harvest? I don't know. One reason is that I don't know how large existing supplies are. This comment is necessarily written before April 23, and on the afternoon of April 23 the USDA estimate of stocks of corn on April 1 will be released. At that time I will have a more accurate measure of the rationing problem. I do know that there will have to be a major reduction, on the order of 32 percent, in feed use from the average of the past three years. Even when I know the size of the estimate of existing stocks, I will not have the price that will be required to just run out at the end of the year. We have not had enough experience with an adjustment of this magnitude to make a reliable estimate.

When the crop year has ended, we can look back and form some judgments about the market's performance. At this time, the rapid rise from $2.90 to $3.80 does not appear excessive because of the magnitude of the short fall in supply. The volatility of prices during the August-September period with limit-up days followed by limit-down days does appear large. The length of time that the price stayed high does appear to be briefer than we should think necessary to get users of corn to make adjustments. The rally in late October and early November was the result of an unexpectedly small carryover from last crop year. It was not evidence of poor market performance. At this time the decline from November to February appears to have been excessive and a speculative error. But I can only say that since the price has gone back up to its November level. The market may have to go back up to a level that will pull CCC corn out of inventory. It may not. I don't know.

May soybean futures decreased from $7.25 in April 1983 to $6.35 at the end of June. The impending shortage took over and put the price above $9.50 by the end of August. There was a quick, vigorous, and fully justified response to supply conditions. The market traded in a $9.00 to $9.70 range for six weeks. Prices were quite volatile during the period. Much of the criticism of market performance during the past year is focused on this volatility, and it did seem excessive. However, the range was only 7.5 percent of the median for the period. This is not large when we recall that estimates of the equilibrium ranged from $8.00 to $12.00 and higher. It is quite small when compared to volatility in securities markets thus far in 1984.

The May futures price decreased from $9.00 in late September to $7.10 in mid-February and has since recovered to the $8.00 area. The future is uncertain. The April 1 stock report is uncertain and of critical importance. At this time and with the benefit of hindsight it appears that the decrease from September to February was greater than justified by the supply-demand conditions. But we cannot evaluate the pricing performance of the soybean market until the season has ended.

How good has the pricing performance of grain and soybean futures markets been since last summer? Compared to what? Compared to optimum, it has moved excessive amounts and been too volatile. But these markets have operated in situations of unprecedented uncertainty. The supply-demand-price situation is much less uncertain today than it was last fall, but great uncertainty remains. What will be the average price of corn and soybeans between now and harvest? I have some thoughts about it, but I would not be so pretentious as to think that I could come within 10 percent. What I am saying is that we may expect and demand too much from speculative markets. It has been a frustrating year for us fundamental-type market analysts. We have had a lot of surprises. There may be a lot of "sour grapes" in some of the current criticism of markets.

I would now turn my attention to the specific questions that Senator Jepsen posed.

HAS THE MARKET MOVED AWAY FROM "FUNDAMENTALS?"

No. First, there is no way that a market can move away from fundamental forces. There is one inevitable equilibrium, market-clearing price. The market makes errors in anticipating the equilibrium price and moving to it, but the errors are always corrected. Some of the lines of causation run from speculation in futures markets to their influence on cash prices. To the extent that speculators control inventory, they influence interim prices. However, the primary lines of causation in interim price behavior are between producers and consumers. Producers almost always hold a high proportion of the existing inventory and the rate at which they feed it on the market is the dominant factor in interim prices. Processors and end users take a lot or a little forward cover and thereby influence interim prices. The decisions that these people make are speculative. They form judgments on the basis of their perception of market fundamentals. Second, the USDA supply-demand releases get widespread attention and reaction and, I sometimes think, too much credence. Commission houses spend a lot of money on fundamental analysis, and most of their releases treat with fundamentals. The statistical releases of the USDA are anticipated and responded to. It is my impression that there has been an ever-increasing amount of information about supplies, rates of use, and prices during the past thirty-five years.

HAS THE QUALITY OF TRADING BEHAVIOR CHANGED?

I don't know. I have the general impression that is held by many people that much position taking is based on past price patterns and "technical" considerations. If this impression is correct, the quality of trading has deteriorated. These are speculative markets; and the essence of speculation is foresight, the anticipation and discounting of futures events into current prices. However, to the best of my knowledge no one knows who takes and holds positions or the basis on which judgments are made. There need to be studies made of market composition similar to the old Commodity Exchange Authority cross-section surveys.

WHAT ROLE AND INFLUENCE DOES "SYSTEM-TYPE" TRADING HAVE IN TODAY'S FUTURES MARKETS?

Again, I don't know. Judging from the proliferation of commodity funds and the amount of money involved, I should judge that it is a growing role and influence. It is my impression that a high proportion of these use "system-type" trading. The funds are a significant source of new speculative capital, but I doubt that they are of major influence on price behavior. I think that in the aggregate the funds break even gross and lose net by the cost of commission and management fees. I suspect that they largely offset each other in a given market. But again, the answers are not known. There needs to be more information developed and studies made.

IS THERE A NEED TO IMPROVE THE ACCESSIBILITY, QUALITY, AND TIMELINESS OF MARKET INFORMATION?

The amount of supply, use, and price information has increased rapidly and is instantly available. The communication revolution is alive and well. Volume of trading and open interest are available. However, information about the composition of open interest is collected by the CFTC, but only a little is made available and it is quite late. More and timely information would be useful.

HOW CAN THE LIQUIDITY OF THE MARKET BE IMPROVED?

Major markets are adequately liquid. Volume of trading is quite large in relation to changes in open interest. In some markets in some contract months, a reasonable amount of prudence is required in placing orders. The patience required is not an undue burden on out-of-pit traders. It should be kept in mind that there is a cost of liquidity.

ARE SELF-POLICING METHODS AND CFTC RULES AND REGULATIONS ADEQUATE TO PROMOTE MARKET ACTIVITY YET ENSURE THE PROTECTION OF THE PUBLIC INTEREST?

There are three levels of futures market regulation: CFTC, exchanges, and markets. The self-policing by exchanges is of greater importance than regulation by the CFTC. But the great regulator is the competition of the market itself. Futures markets are the closest approximation to pure competition in existence. Competition regulates itself into efficiency and equity.

We should look for places to deregulate rather than regulate. One first point of deregulation should be daily trading limits. Position limits may be desirable, but trading limits are not. I think that regulation of position limits should be removed from the CFTC and made a responsibility of exchanges. Problems of balance have arisen because of control of managed accounts. The exchanges are in a more flexible and thus a better position to maintain competitive balance than is the CFTC.

TO WHAT EXTENT HAS SPECULATIVE TRADING AFFECTED TRADING FOR HEDGING PURPOSES?

It has enabled it. On the other side of a hedged position is a speculative position. Speculators have accommodated hedgers very well during the past year. Open interest in wheat, corn, soybeans, soybean oil, and soybean meal has been much larger than during the preceding two years. The same is true of both long and short reported hedges. The markets have fulfilled their risk-shifting function very well.

We should note in passing that the unusually large short hedges in corn and soybeans last fall had a lot of forward selling by farmers behind them. Open interest increased rapidly during July and August. Farmers were taking advantage of rising prices.

WHAT ARE YOUR VIEWS ON THE FUTURE PROSPECTS AND POTENTIAL BENEFITS OF COMPUTERIZED TRADING VERSUS PIT TRADING?

As everyone knows, electronic communication and data processing are increasing rapidly. Potential is limitless, thus some system may be devised that will supplant direct person-to-person trading. But the state of the art is not so advanced at this time. I think such a system will gradually evolve in bits and pieces.

WHY HAVE THE FUTURES MARKETS FAILED TO ATTRACT GREATER FARMER PARTICIPATION?

They do not fail to attract farmer participation, and the amount of farmer participation has been increasing, especially during the past decade. Surveys indicate that farmers make relatively little direct use of futures markets in marketing their crops and livestock. I think that the primary reason is that they prefer to use forward contracts and delayed pricing arrangements. Thus, the use of futures markets by farmers is indirect. They make forward contracts with elevators, and the elevators hedge in futures.

Over time farmers have shown a great deal of interest in improving their marketing skills. This interest expanded rapidly during the price turbulence of the 1970s. I have worked closely with farmers in this connection. It is my observation that farmers are increasingly knowledgeable about factors affecting prices, increasingly skilled in price forecasting, and are doing an improved job of distributing sales over time so that they balance risks and aim toward high average prices.

I think that when the year is over, we will find that farmers have done a respectable job of marketing their 1983 crops. Reported short hedges in soybeans last September 30 were 399 million bushels compared to 211 the year before. Short hedges in corn were 532 million, up from 380 million the year before. Farmers sold more than a usual amount into what turned out to be high prices. Farmers are pretty respectable speculators and are improving.

HOW USEFUL WILL OPTIONS TRADING BE FOR FARMERS?

It remains to be seen. Buying puts is a conceptually useful insurance system. It will be actually useful if it is cheap enough. Usefulness of options will depend on options prices, and that remains to be seen.

I would make a summary comment. The past year has been one of unusually great speculative stress in grains and soybeans. The futures markets have performed well in their basic risk-shifting functions. Their speculative pricing performance has been less than optimum, but given the extreme uncertainty of the supply-demand situation it is difficult to fault them, at least until we know at the end of the year what they should have done. My first point is that markets work well and that a basic principle should be observed: If it ain't broke, don't fix it.

We need to recognize, however, that improvement in the quality of speculation that would lead to greater price stability is desirable. How to achieve it? In my foregoing comments I have alluded to three things. First, some of the volatility of prices may have been the result of one set of thinking directing managed accounts that aggregate more than speculative limits. Resulting imbalance of power and countervailing power may have been responsible for some of the large and erratic price variations. If so, a first step is to remove CFTC speculative limits and add the maintenance of power balance to the responsibility of the exchanges.

Second, we do not know the relative importance of commodity fund trading or its influence on price behavior. The basic data are available to the CFTC, and I think that the CFTC should be responsible for making and encouraging others to make studies appraising the importance of the growth in fund trading.

Third, more and timely information about the composition of open interest in markets would be useful to market analysts, as would cross-section surveys of market composition. The CFTC has unique access to information, and more use should be made of it.

Finally, the central lesson to me from my own observations and deliberation is that we need to have faith in competitive markets. Exchanges succeed or fail (and more have failed than succeeded) on the basis of their ability to maintain competitive markets that serve the public interest. Futures trading is a zero-sum game. The better speculators gain and grow in importance, and the poorer speculators lose and go away. Markets are a continuous spelldown. They are very hard to beat, which is convincing evidence that they are quite good.

Chapter Forty-Two

Letter to The Editor of Choices

1991

AUTHOR'S NOTE: In the second quarter 1991 issue of Choices, the magazine of food, farm and resource issues published by the American Agricultural Economics Association, a commentary by Harold Breimyer related to, and deplored, one word in discussions of economic policy, including that for agriculture: intervention. He called it a "snarl word" intended to tum people sour as it seems to call for just pulling out rather than facing up to problems and trying to solve them. It struck me as a call for politically correct terminology in advancing governmental actions in addressing social problems. Word games are fun. So I wrote a letter to the editor. The pot can call the kettle black.

June 17, 1991
Mr. Lyle Schertz, Editor
Choices
12708 Oak Farms Road
Herndon, Virginia 22071

Dear Mr. Schertz:

Breimyer's commentary in the second quarter issue of *Choices* is provocative and cries out for response. Insofar as intervention is a "snarl word" that carries negative connotations toward governmental activities in the economic sphere, it is a very good word that should be drilled into the regular usage of every student of Economics 101 and Political Science 101.

Intervention is a word to be avoided by self-perpetuating politicians. They much prefer "facing up to problems and trying to solve them." By delicate selection of words, they can circumvent the need to confront the most basic tenet of American society: property rights. The omission of accurately descriptive words and the substitution of delicate nonsense words is of great and severe consequence. Among our most sacred documents is the *Declaration of Independence* stating that all men are created equal with certain inalienable rights-life, liberty, and the pursuit of happiness. An earlier version by the followers of John Locke was life, liberty, and property. Happiness was substituted for property (probably by Thomas Jefferson) for reasons of political delicacy. Property rights were the central thrust of the American Revolution and have been the driving force of western economic development and growth.

Governments have essential functions. "In the economic sphere, its most essential and pervasive role is to enforce contracts." The enforcement of contracts is the protection of property rights. So is the defense of the nation from foreign intrusion. And so is the enforcement of criminal laws, traffic regulation, etc.

But government goes past the protection of life, liberty, and property and intervenes in economic activity. "Government provides schools, a postal service, roads." The current status of our schools, the price of stamps, and the condition of roads raise doubts about the efficiency of governmental intervention. As one looks further, say into agricultural commodity price and income programs, the record of negative impacts on economic productivity becomes increasingly pronounced.

Governmental intervention into economic affairs involves property rights. Governments confiscate property through systems of taxation. What is at issue in the current social order is the effects of governmental confiscation of property and intervention in economic activity on productivity and equity of product distribution. The issue is glaringly apparent in Eastern Europe and the USSR. It will become increasingly apparent in the United States as taxes confiscate ever increasing shares of production and pervert them to "facing up to problems and trying to solve them."

Intervention is a good word. It is gratingly descriptive. Confiscation is another good word. It is gratingly descriptive of taxation. It should find its way into our literature.

T.A. Hieronymus

Sincerely,
T. A. Hieronymus
Professor Emeritus

Chapter Forty-Three

The Role of Futures Markets and Opportunities for OFOR

1993

AUTHOR'S NOTE: In September 1993, the Office for Futures and Options Research of the University of Illinois at Urbana-Champaign held a symposium (at the Chicago Board of Trade) in recognition of Thomas A. Hieronymus. My assigned topic was "The Role of Futures Markets and Opportunities for OFOR." I had something of a feeling of being Tom Sawyer at his own funeral and that what I said would be subtitled "The Voice from the Tomb." The symposium provided one (probably) last opportunity to call the attention of my academic colleagues to the basics about futures trading and suggest that some of them move away from standard inquiring deeper into the same things and into currently topical problems and serious study of the nature of speculation. My comments were politely received, indicating once again, that there is deference to antiquity. It remains to be seen whether there is also attention.

BASIC CHARACTERISTICS OF FUTURES MARKETS

Futures markets are a microcosm of the way that a competitive, price-driven economic system should function. As such, they can and should serve as a model for changes in economic systems that will increase their productivity.

First, futures markets come remarkably close to meeting the conditions of pure competition. There are a large number of participants in active futures markets, and margin requirements are held at low enough levels to permit ease of entry. The rules requiring that all trading occur in one pit or ring assures the maximization of the number trading in a given market, preventing fragmentation into separate monopolistic markets. The face-to-face trading, open entry, specified hours of trading, and equal access to all bids and offers contribute to the prevention of significant individual influence. There is full information about prices, trading, and the commodities traded. Independence and impersonality of operations is forced on the participants by the organization and regulation of markets.

Second, futures markets provide a mechanism for shifting commodity ownership risks from firms and individuals who acquire price risks incidental to their business operations to others better qualified and financed to assume them. Futures trading rests on needs to shift risks.

Third, futures markets are equity financing institutions. Through speculative processes, they provide capital needed for the development of production, storage, processing, and distribution facilities for commodities. This is risk capital that can be had at minimal interest rates because risk of price changes are assumed by speculative interests.

Fourth, futures markets are institutions for the establishment of speculative prices. Prices have essential functions to perform in a competitive economic system. Lists of functions generally include (1) the allocation of productive measures, (2) determination of the amount and kind of product, (3) direction of inventory accumulation and liquidation, (4) distribution of products among people and places, (5) distribution of the rewards for production among productive resources. Individual prices combine into a set of price relationships that determine production and distribution. There is a major element of futurity in prices. Investments made today affect production tomorrow and throughout the life of the investment. Inventories are accumulated or liquidated today in anticipation of tomorrow's requirements. The implementation of expectations results in the establishment of prices that apply not only to the present but to the future as well. Today's prices are a function of expectations about the future as well as today's spot market situation. Forward prices are established on the basis of these expectations about the situation and prices that will exist in the future. The future is unknown and uncertain. To speculate is to contemplate the future, reach conclusions about the shape of things to come, and to act on the basis of these expectations. By the processes of shifting risks through forward pricing in futures, speculators become entrepreneurs guiding and directing the production and distribution processes. To a substantial extent, the quality of planning of the production and distribution of commodities depends on the quality of speculation in futures markets.

Fifth, futures markets arise as there is a need for speculative, forward prices and risk shifting, and they fail and go out of existence as the need is no longer present. The grain markets decreased and nearly failed as government price programs dominated markets in the 1950s. The New Orleans Cotton Exchange ceased to function as the government dominated prices. Currency markets developed when the Bretton Woods agreement ended. Gold futures trading started when private ownership of gold was legalized. Financial futures developed when the government allowed interest rates to respond to market forces. Futures markets expand and prosper as the economy is freed from government influence and fail as the government usurps the role of markets.

OPPORTUNITIES FOR OFOR

The Office for Futures and Options Research (OFOR) is in an excellent position to be of service to the futures industry. It is a collection of scholars who have expertise in both futures and options themselves and the economics of the underlying commodities and financial instruments that are traded. They know the context out of which futures and options trading evolves. They are thus able to evaluate questions concerning futures and options with full knowledge of the relationship of cash and futures trading and with awareness that futures and options are an extension of cash commodity and financial operations.

The office is a part of a major teaching, research, and public service institution. There is opportunity for independence of research and public service that does not depend on financing, inspiration, or guidance from political interests, exchanges, or regulatory bodies. Thus, the work of OFOR can be directed with a broad view of current and potential problems and potential development of futures and options trading. Results of work have added credibility because of independence of stature.

The existence of opportunities for research and teaching are obvious. The importance of public service should be recognized. The growth and development of futures markets has been closely associated with the amount of knowledge about them. As firms in an assortment of industries have learned more about markets, the commercial use of markets has increased. Perceptions of markets by politicians have changed as public perceptions have changed. Regulatory legislation has changed as knowledge about markets has grown. Regulation of markets changes as knowledge develops. Exchanges make changes as knowledge about relationships between commerce and futures markets increases. Much is unknown about futures markets, but much more is known than has been taught to commercial interests, exchanges, regulatory agencies, the public, and politicians. More needs to be taught. Much of teaching is general in nature, but much of the most effective teaching has been in the context of specific problem solving. There is an opportunity for OFOR to develop research results having to do with specific aspects of such things as delivery terms, margin requirements, commission house performance, dual trading, trade tracing, impact of commodity funds, position limits, impacts of trading on price volatility, risk management methods, etc. And there is the opportunity to push the results through to application by commercial interests, the public, exchanges, and regulatory bodies. Public service is a major role for OFOR.

This emphasis on public service does not preclude inquiry into some more general and obscure aspects of futures markets. Three things come to mind:

FLOW OF FUNDS

There have been studies of results of speculation by commission house customers, the cost of hedging, etc. But there are no comprehensive studies of the redistribution of money that flows into the clearinghouses of exchange by kinds of clearing members or the redistribution of money that flows into the clearing members as margin deposits. Such a study would go far in answering questions about the costs of market operation and who pays the costs. The large markets are large business operations. They require and consume a lot of facilities and equipment. A lot of people are employed or otherwise gain a livelihood from markets. The productive services of providing price establishment, risk management, and entrepreneurial capital is not without substantial cost. It would be interesting, indeed, to know what those costs are and who pays them.

INFLUENCE OF COMMODITY FUNDS

It is widely thought that commodity funds have largely taken the place of individual members of the speculating public. It is also thought that most of the funds are directed by various computer-driven price behavior models. Questions are raised about the influence of funds on price volatility and adjustment of changing market conditions. It would be interesting to know how the funds make out vis-a-vis put and take to the clearinghouses. It would also be interesting to know the extent fund trading methods are based on past price behavior and how much on changing market forces. Answers would make an evaluation of the usefulness of funds possible.

QUALITY OF SPECULATION

The speculative pricing mission of markets is to discount existing and forthcoming events affecting current and subsequent prices into current prices; that is, optimally markets would be omniscient and discount their omniscience into current prices. But markets are less than perfect; nor should we expect perfection. Many events such as droughts, floods, hurricanes, revolutions, and the fickle behavior of consumers and politicians are random and not forecastable. But markets should react quickly, adjust to the appropriate level, and stabilize until the next unforeseeable random event occurs. The greater the accuracy with which markets discount future events into current prices, the greater their contribution to economic productivity. The question raised is: How well do futures markets perform as devices for planning economic processes? The problem is to establish a reasonable standard of optimum performance and measure actual market performance against the standard. This sounds unreasonable and impractical, but quality speculation is what futures markets are really about.

Other Titles by Ceres Books

Economics of Futures Trading: For Commercial and Personal Profit

In *Economics of Futures Trading*, the renowned scholar Dr. Thomas A. Hieronymus takes you on a deep dive into the world of commodity futures trading, from its historical beginnings to its modern intricacies. Readers learn about the mechanics, regulations, and economic impacts of futures markets. The book provides an unparalleled foundation in trading terms and processes, making complex concepts accessible.

Written in a witty and engaging style, *Economics of Futures Trading* is suitable for both novices and experts in the field.

- ***Economics of Futures Trading*** **is available in ebook, paperback, and hardcover versions.**
- **Visit this webpage to find links to purchase *Economics of Futures Trading* from your favorite retailer: https://scotthirwin.com/books/economics-of-futures-trading.**
- **Don't miss this rare opportunity to learn about commodity futures markets from a legendary expert!**

Back to the Futures: Crashing Dirt Bikes, Chasing Cows, and Unraveling the Mystery of Commodity Futures Markets

Back to the Futures provides a unique and educational perspective on the world of commodity futures markets, shaped by the personal experiences and professional insights of Dr. Scott Irwin, a leading expert in the field. Readers will learn about the role of speculators, price discovery, the evolution of trading practices, the impact of regulatory measures, the transition from open outcry to electronic trading, commodity investments, and much more. This wildly entertaining book uses a storytelling format to keep you laughing from start to finish.

Dr. Scott Irwin has been studying, teaching, and participating in the world of commodity futures since growing up on his family farm in Iowa. His expertise and captivating storytelling abilities make him the ideal guide for this unforgettable journey through the world of commodity trading.

- ***Back to the Futures* is available in ebook, audio, paperback, and hardcover versions.**
- **Visit this webpage to find links to purchase *Back to the Futures* from your favorite retailer: https://scotthirwin.com/books/back-to-the-futures/.**
- **Reviews of the *Back to the Futures* at sites like Amazon are deeply appreciated!**

"Rousing introduction to and defense of future trading, with stunts."

—BookLife Reviews by Publishers Weekly